We Were Not the Savages

A Mi'kmaq Perspective
on the Collision between European
and Native American Civilizations

New Twenty-First-Century Edition

Daniel N. Paul

Fernwood Publishing • Halifax

Editing: Douglas Beall
Illustrations: Vernon Gloade
Design and production: Beverley Rach
Printed and bound in Canada by: Hignell Printing Limited

A publication of:
Fernwood Publishing
Box 9409, Station A
Halifax, Nova Scotia
B3K 5S3

Fernwood Publishing Company Limited gratefully acknowledges the financial support of the Department of Canadian Heritage and the Canada Council for the Arts for our publishing program.

Canadian Cataloguing in Publication Data

Paul. Daniel N.

    We were not the savages

    Includes bibliographical references and index.
    ISBN 1-55266-039-7

1. Micmac Indians -- Government relations. 2. Micmac Indians -- History.
3. Micmac Indians -- First contact with Europeans. 4. Indians, Treatment of --
Maritime Provinces -- History. I. Title.

E99.M6P38 2000   971.5'004973   C00-950167-3

Contents

List of Illustrations

Dedication

To the memory of my ancestors, who managed to ensure the survival of the Mi'kmaq people by their awe-inspiring tenacity and valour in the face of insurmountable odds! For more than four centuries these courageous, dignified and heroic people displayed a determination to survive the various hells on earth created for them by Europeans with a tenacity that equals any displayed in the history of mankind. May their brave accomplishment inspire the Mi'kmaq and others to meet the challenges of today and tomorrow!

Acknowledgements

Thanks goes to my wife Patricia, who gave her love and support during the four years it took to rewrite the new edition of this book. The assistance she provided when needed was invaluable.

Donald M. Julien was a key source and deserves a special thank you. Without Don's support and assistance, the manuscript would have taken twice as long to complete. His knowledge and the research material he collected over the years were invaluable in crafting this history.

Vernon Gloade provided the drawings for this book, which aptly describe situations the Mi'kmaq faced in their struggle for survival. Thanks Vernon!

Douglas Beall, my copy editor, is another friend who deserves credit and thanks for the extra mile he travelled to help identify sources for the original edition. Also a hearty thank you to the many others who provided their support and encouragement!

For the French translation I owe a special thanks to a very nice lady who originally hails from France but is now a resident of New Brunswick, Nicole Jones. Her generous contribution of time and expertise made the French version possible.

Finally, during the extensive revision of *Savages,* Geoffrey Plank of the University of Cincinnati provided valuable data, and his assistance was greatly appreciated.

I give thanks to the Great Spirit for sending such good friends my way!

Foreword

When I wrote this book, I knew the contents would cause great pain for many Canadians of English descent. It must be discomforting to come to grips with the fact that many of your ancestors were not always the kind, gentle folks that some historians have depicted but were in fact barbaric in the way they treated other humans. However, the destruction of every civilization that thrived in the Americas and the annihilation of 70-100 million indigenous souls during the European invasion speaks for itself.

Because of these assaults, committed against innocent people in the name of greed, each modern nation in the Americas was founded with the spilling of much Native American blood. Consequently, there can be no real peace in the Americas until each European-founded nation assumes responsibility for its past crimes against humanity and makes atonement to Native Americans for the indescribable horrors they subjected them to.

This book recalls the trials and tribulations of one of the First Nations, the Mi'kmaq. Canada has kept the horrors committed against the First Nations resident within its borders under wraps for centuries. The physical and psychological torment the Mi'kmaq suffered started shortly after significant European intrusions began in northeastern North America in the late 1490s and has continued to some degree right up to the present time.

Prior to 1492, Native North Americans had had innumerable encounters with Whites who had come mainly from what is today Scandinavia. Apparently, these Whites were well received, because early reports indicate that blue-eyed and light-skinned Native Americans were not rare. In fact, because some Mi'kmaq were able to dress up in French or English uniforms and mingle with European soldiers while gathering information for war councils, some of the French and English wondered whether the Mi'kmaq were not possibly a White race. Therefore the term *pre-European contact* will not be used in this history. In its place the term *pre-Columbian* will be found, because in my opinion no one can say with certainty when the first contact took place.

Any sensibilities the Europeans may have had based on their racist views about Mi'kmaq ancestry were soon obscured by their drive to satisfy one of the European societies' worst traits: greed. The plundering of the Americas for gold and other riches became the top priority. To justify the horrors that would soon commence, the invaders branded the Mi'kmaq and other Native Americans "heathen savages," so no consciences would need to be disturbed when the slaughter of the People and the theft of their property began.

The atrocities recounted in this book have not been placed here to engender pity. They have been retold to persuade people of the majority society to use whatever power they have to see that Canada makes meaningful amends for the horrifying wrongs of the past. The Mi'kmaq were, and are, a great people. To be a descendent of this noble race, who displayed an indomitable will to survive in spite of the incredible odds against them, fills me with pride. I am in awe whenever I think of their tremendous courage in overcoming the daunting obstacles placed in their path!

Daniel N. Paul

Civilization, Democracy and Government

The Need for a Native American Historical Perspective

To begin this chronicle, I would like to explain the need for a Native American historical perspective, and also my use of certain historical references. The subjugation of the Northeastern North American Native American Nations by the English Crown was accomplished with the use of much barbarity. Not surprisingly, these actions have been studiously ignored or downplayed by most White male historians. However, their reluctance to enter into honest discussion and critically comment on the matter does not obscure the facts that the documents and journals left behind by colonial English and French scribes irrefutably prove: the blood of the citizens of the Mi'kmaq, Maliseet and their smaller sister Nations, located in what is today eastern Canada and the New England States of the United States of America, was spilled by the English to the point where many were left on the verge of extinction or had passed into it.

The same historical documents also prove beyond a reasonable doubt that supposedly "civilized" colonial English politicians and military personnel used means of terror against First Nations peoples which would repel truly civilized people. Thus, the reluctance of most White male scribes to discuss and put to paper the details of such behaviour is understandable. To do so is to question the very civility of those who perpetrated the atrocities. As a person who has no such reluctance to expose the crimes against humanity committed by the English, I wrote this book. It details a chronicle of man's inhumanity to man which has few, if any, equals in human history.

When amassing the information that was needed to write about the English invasion of the territory of the Mi'kmaq, reams of information about the Tribe's Amerindian allies also had to be digested. For data on the early stages of the invasion, I relied heavily upon doctorial dissertations by White male scholars and on documents, books and articles prepared by White male historians, politicians etc. From these I retrieved praise of the Mi'kmaq and other Amerindians, and also minute descriptions of the shocking racist behaviour of English colonial authorities. To assure as much accuracy as possible I compared their conclusions against one another and with many other original sources, and then formed my own conclusions from a Mi'kmaq perspective.

I used the research of these men as sources for two reasons. First and foremost, because of my ancestry, White society would tend to discount, as biased and exaggerated, research on the subject presented by an "Indian." But, I reasoned, how can they argue with the documents and findings of their own? Second, why do work that has already been done?

In later chapters I have also quoted heavily from well-researched papers about the Mi'kmaq struggle for survival prepared by two White women. In distinct contrast to the whitewashing of the subject by most White male writers, these women condemn the monstrous mistreatment of the Mi'kmaq and their allies.

However, I want to emphasize that the information contained herein about treaties, the Indian Act, Colonial Council meetings, court cases, centralization etc. was gleaned from Nova Scotia and Indian Affairs archival records and other sources by Don Julien and myself.

National Identity

The term "Mi'kmaq" rather than "Micmac" will be used in telling this story because it is now the preferred choice of our People. However, the word "Micmac" has been around for at least 350 years and is cherished by many. Its historical root was included in a book penned by historical author Marion Robertson:

> The Micmacs were known by the early French settlers as the Souriquois, "the salt water men," according to Roth in "Acadia and the Acadians," to distinguish them from the Iroquois, who inhabited the fresh water country. The name "Micmac" was first recorded in a memoir by de La Chesnaye in 1676. Professor Ganong in a footnote to the word "megamingo," earth, as used by Marc Lescarbot, remarked "that it is altogether probable that in this word lies the origin of the name Micmac." As suggested in this paper on the customs and beliefs of the Micmacs, it would seem that *megumaagee* the name used by the Micmacs, or the *Megumawaach*, as they called themselves, for their land, is from the words *megwaak*, "red," and *makumegek*, "on the earth," or as Rand recorded, "red on the earth," *megakumegek*, "red ground," "red earth."
>
> The Micmacs, then, must have thought of themselves as the Red Earth People, or the People of the Red Earth. Others seeking a meaning for the word Micmac have suggested that it is from *nigumaach*, my brother, my friend, a word that was also used as a term of endearment by a husband for his wife....
>
> Still another explanation for the word Micmac suggested by Stansbury Hagar in "Micmac Magic and Medicine" is that the word *megumawaach* is from *megumoowesoo*, the name of the Micmacs' legendary master magicians, from whom the earliest Micmac wizards are said to have received their power.[1]

The Horrors to Come

The Prophecy, a short story written by a Native North American, Basil H. Johnston, relates a fictional visionary's dream about the post-Columbian horrors that awaited the First Nations of the Americas. The visionary Daebaudjimoot begins by saying:

> "Tonight I'm going to tell you a very different kind of story. It's not really a story because it has not yet taken place; but it will take place just as the events in the past have occurred.... And even though what I'm about to tell you has not yet come to pass, it is as true as if it has already happened, because the Auttissookaunuk told me in a dream."

Daebaudjimoot tells of a strange people who are white and hairy and wear strange clothes they practically never take off. He describes them as having round eyes that are black, brown, blue or green, and having fine hair that is black, brown, blond or red.

He says they will arrive from the East in canoes five times the length of regular canoes. These big canoes will have sailed using blankets to catch the wind to propel them from a land across a great body of salt water. His words are greeted by his audience with laughter and disbelief. He continues:

> "You laugh because you cannot picture men and women with white skins or hair upon their faces; and you think it funny that a canoe would be moved by the wind across great open seas. But it won't be funny to our grandchildren and their great-grandchildren....
>
> "The first few to arrive will appear to be weak by virtue of their numbers, and they will look as if they are no more than harmless passers-by, on their way to visit another people in another land, who need a little rest and direction before resuming their journey. But in reality they will be spies for those in quest for lands. After them will come countless others like flocks of geese.... There will be no turning them back.
>
> "Some of our grandchildren will stand up to these strangers, but when they do, it will have been too late and their bows and arrows, war-clubs and medicines will be as nothing against the weapons of these white people, whose warriors will be armed with sticks that burst like thunderclaps. A warrior has to do no more than point a fire stick at another warrior and that man will fall dead the instant the bolt strikes him.
>
> "It is with weapons such as these that the white people will drive our people from their homes and hunting grounds to desolate territories where game can scarce find food for their own needs and where corn can bare take root. The white people will take possession of all the rest, and they will build immense villages upon them. Over the years the white people will prosper, and though the Anishinaubaeg may forsake their own traditions to adopt the ways of the white people, it will do them little good. It will not be until our grandchildren and their grandchildren return to the ways of their ancestors that they will regain strength of spirit and heart.
>
> "There! I have told you my dream in its entirety. I have nothing more to say."
>
> "Daebaudjimoot! Are these white people manitous or are they Beings like us?"
>
> "I don't know."[2]

This fictional prophecy seems almost civilized in comparison to what the Mi'kmaq actually suffered after the European invasion of their territory began in the early sixteenth century. Over the course of history they were spared few indignities.

Mi'kmaq and European Civilizations

Exaggerated reports about the facial features, clothing and customs of the Amerindians by early Norse and Viking travellers were probably the reasons pre-Columbian contacts promoted stories in Europe about a strange people—non-humans, hairy monsters, subhumans—inhabiting a far-off land. Probably not much thought was given to the prospect that they could be intelligent and civilized human beings, an existence well documented by early European colonial scribes.

Prior to European settlement the Mi'kmaq lived in countries that had developed a culture founded upon three principles: the supremacy of the Great Spirit, respect for Mother Earth, and people power. This instilled in them a deep respect for the laws of the Creator, the powers of Mother Earth and the democratic principles of their society. As a result they enjoyed the benefits of living in a harmonious, healthy, prosperous and peaceful social environment.

The nature of their society, which included sharing and free expression, was so advanced in the establishment of equitable human rights principles that greed and intolerance were all but unknown. Thus, the European concepts which separated people into a distinct hierarchy based upon birth, colour, race, lineage, religion, profession, wealth, politics and other criteria would have seemed to them unbelievable. This absence of biases about the differences of others found among the majority of Amerindians is one of the best indicators of how far advanced their cultures were in the development of human relations. The lofty plateau they had reached, where all people were accepted as equals, is an ideal that modern society is still working towards. In retrospect, if the Native Americans had not reached this stage by 1492, European colonization could not have occurred. Instead, because of their skin colour and strange religions, Whites would have been either enslaved, repulsed, or exterminated upon arrival.

In a discourse about Amerindian tolerance for the differences of others, Ronald Wright relates a Seneca Chief's response to the efforts of a White preacher to convert his people to Christianity:

To welcome a stranger

In a scene reminiscent of the debate between Franciscans and Aztec priests nearly 300 hundred years before, the formidable Red Jacket rose to reply. His answer is one of the best ever given to Christianity's claims. Which mentality, he makes one wonder, is the more primitive: that which believes itself to have a patent on truth or that which pleads for cultural diversity, for tolerance, for mutual respect?[3]

Chief Red Jacket's words:

Brother ... listen to what we say. There was a time when our forefathers owned this great island. Their seats extended from the rising to the setting sun. The Great Spirit had made it for the use of Indians. He had created the buffalo, the deer, and other animals for food. He had made the bear and the beaver. Their skins served us for clothing. He had scattered them over the country, and taught us how to take them. He had caused the earth to produce corn for bread.... If we had some disputes about our hunting ground, they were generally settled without the shedding of much blood. But an evil day came upon us. Your forefathers crossed the great water and landed on this island. Their numbers were small. They found friends and not enemies. They told us they had fled from their own country for fear of wicked men, and had come here to enjoy their religion. They asked for a small seat. We took pity on them, granted their request; and they sat down amongst us. We gave them corn and meat; they gave us poison in return.

The white people, Brother, had now found our country. Tidings were carried back, and more came amongst us. Yet we did not fear them. We took them to be friends. They called us brothers. We believed them, and gave them a larger seat. At length their numbers had greatly increased. They wanted more land; they wanted our country. Our eyes were opened, and our minds became uneasy. Wars took place. Indians were hired to fight against Indians, and many of our people were destroyed. They also brought liquor amongst us. It was strong and powerful, and has slain thousands.

Brother, our seats were once large and yours were small. You have now become a great people, and we have scarcely a place left to spread our blankets. You have got our country, but are not satisfied; you want to force your religion upon us.

Brother, continue to listen. You say that you are sent to instruct us how to worship the Great Spirit agreeably to his mind, and, if we do not take hold of the religion which you white people teach, we shall be unhappy hereafter. You say that you are right and we are lost. How do we know this to be true? We ... only know what you tell us about it. How shall we know when to believe, being so often deceived by the white people?

Brother, you say there is but one way to worship and serve the Great Spirit. If there is but one religion, why do you white people differ so much about it?...

Brother, we do not understand these things. We are told that your religion was given to your forefathers, and has been handed down from father to son. We also have a religion, which was given to our forefathers, and has been handed down to us, their children. We worship in that way. It teaches us to be thankful for all the favours we receive; to love each other, and to be united. We never quarrel about religion.

Brother, the Great Spirit has made us all, but he has made a great difference between his white and red children. He has given us different complexions and different customs.... Since he has made so great a difference between us in other things, why may we not conclude that he has given us a different religion?...

Brother, we do not wish to destroy your religion, or take it from you. We only want to enjoy our own.[4]

The tolerance shown by Chief Red Jacket for different views was also a trait deeply imbedded in Mi'kmaq society. It was well reflected in the method the Nation had devised to resolve disputes, whereby disputing parties were brought together for mediation and reconciliation by community members, who would then assist them to reach an agreement based on justice and fairness. When struck, the final agreement would address all major concerns of the individuals, groups or governments involved. After the opposing parties accepted an agreement, it was understood, and supported by the will of the people, that they would live by its provisions.

In contrast to the First Nations' democratic approach to the adjudication of problems, European civilizations of the day, with a few notable exceptions (e.g., the Swiss), used a totalitarian approach. This was a direct result of the fact that they were governed by a titled elite who considered themselves to have a divine right to rule. Therefore, democratic principles were not permitted to interfere to any great extent in matters they adjudicated. Because of this elitism, average citizens within these domains were routinely denied basic human rights and freedoms. Many were treated as property and held in bondage from cradle to grave. Disputes that arose among them more often than not had settlements devised and imposed by the aristocrats. Justice was often denied.

It is easy to conclude that the Mi'kmaq approach was more civilized. Of course, this reality would have been difficult to reconcile with the European definition of what being civilized was. At that time their intelligentsia equated civilization with Christianity. They declared that if the people of a land were not Christian, then they were not civilized. This ignoble declaration was the root cause of the living hell that the Natives of the Americas would have to endure. Unfortunately, the rest of the world was also not left untouched by it. Superiority attitudes led Europeans to attempt to Christianize the Middle East, Africa, and Asia by force. They failed monumentally, primarily because these regions had their own self-perceived superior religions, which in some cases predated Christianity by thousands of years.

When reviewing the history of this era, it is difficult to conclude which European nation was the most arrogant in insisting that the Amerindian blindly accept the superiority of its cultural conventions and doctrines. In hindsight, when making an honest attempt to rate the period's major powers according to their presumptuous picture of themselves as superior, the nod must go to the English, followed closely by the Spanish and Portuguese, with the French a distant fourth.

These European superiority complexes hampered the efforts of their early scribes to make fair judgments about the human values of American cultures. Because of their belief that European civilizations were superior, and therefore all others were inferior or savage, these writers reported the superior human rights practices of Amerindian civilization as if they were abnormal. Later, using these biased records as gospel, many White authors have written works about Mi'kmaq civilization that do not present a true picture. Their efforts were probably undertaken with sincerity and honesty, but many, if not all, are lacking in two respects: they ignore the Mi'kmaq perspective on civilization and fail to appreciate that the values of the two cultures were in most cases completely opposite.

An excellent example of how Amerindian and European perceptions of being civilized conflicted is a statement contained in a progress report about the "civilizing" of the Cherokees made by Colonel Thomas L. McKenney to his superiors in the United States federal government in the early 1800s. He proudly noted that, under White influence, the Cherokees had progressed to the point where many were becoming involved in selling and buying Blacks as slaves. The majority of Cherokees, uncomfortable with this term, referred to these Blacks as servants, not slaves. After Emancipation these servants formed their own Tribe and are known today as the Black Cherokees.

More contemporary authors who have written about Amerindian civilizations have also used European standards to evaluate the relative merits of these cultures. Thus their efforts are flawed.

When writing on the subject of civilization, one must understand that the ability to read or write a European language does not create a superior civilization. Nor does the ability to point exploding sticks that cause instantaneous death or injury, or to launch missiles that could blow the world apart, provide a moral basis to declare one's culture more civilized than another. The question to ask when judging the values and merits of a civilization must always be: "How does the civilization respond to the human needs of its population?" By this standard, because they created social and political systems that ensured personal liberty, justice and social responsibility, most Amerindian civilizations must be given very high marks.

When making an unbiased assessment, and comparing the values of early American civilizations with those of European civilizations, one cannot but find that the suppression and wanton destruction of American civilizations by European civilizations was in many ways a case of inferior civilizations overcoming superior ones. This is especially true in the area of respect for human rights. Although they were not as technologically advanced as the Europeans were by 1492, many Amerindian Nations possessed democratic political practices that were light years ahead.

Mi'kmaq Government

The Mi'kmaq have been occupants of a large section of northeastern North America for approximately 5,000 to 10,000 years. The Nation's original territory covers most of what is today Canada's Maritime Provinces and a good part of eastern Quebec. There is evidence that the boundary line may have included northern

Maine. The approximate boundary of the vast territory is shown on page 17.

The territory was divided into seven distinct "Districts." Their names were: Kespukwitk, Sipekne'katik, Eskikewa'kik, Unama'kik, Epekwitk Aqq Piktuk, Siknikt, and Kespek. The English translations are shown on the map and are as close as one can come to conveying their true meaning in that language.

Citizens lived in small villages which were populated by fifty to five hundred people. The number of villages and total population within each District is subject to conjecture.

District governments comprised a District Chief and Council. The Council included Elders, Band or Village Chiefs, and other distinguished members of the community. Among these leaders the Elders, both men and women, were the most appreciated. The Mi'kmaq held them in the highest regard and accorded them the utmost respect. Their advice and guidance was considered to be essential to the decision-making process, and thus no major decision was made without their full participation. A District government had conditional power to make war or peace, settle disputes, apportion hunting and fishing areas to families, etc. Thus a District may be likened to what we call a "country" today.

At an unknown point in the distant past a Grand Council was established by the Districts to coordinate the resolution of mutual problems, promote solidarity and act as a dispute mediator of last resort. District Chiefs elected one of their number as Grand Chief. The Grand Council's influence was derived from the esteem in which the District Chiefs were held. The Council did not have, beyond friendly persuasion, any special powers other than those assigned to it by the Districts. At sittings of these Councils, all men and women who wanted to speak were heard, and their opinions were given respectful consideration in the decision-making process. In modern terms, the Grand Council may be compared to the British Commonwealth of Nations, which also has no real powers other than persuasion.

Mi'kmaq Districts also belonged to a larger association known as the "Wabanaki Confederacy," which had been formed by the northeastern First Nations for the purpose of providing mutual protection from aggression by Iroquoian and other hostile Nations. The Confederacy continued to function until the early 1700s, at which time the decimation of its member Nations by disease and wars with the English caused its demise. The Confederacy may be compared to the modern North Atlantic Treaty Organization (NATO) in function.

The offices of Grand, District and local Chiefs were filled by men who were well-respected members of their communities. The myth created by certain European accounts of Mi'kmaq history that an ambition to become Chief was helped by being a member of a large family was based on misperception. In fact, the customs of the Nation were such that all members of the community considered themselves to be an extended family. Because of this they used family salutations to greet one another, which could have led an outsider to believe they were all blood-related. This custom survived into the 1960s. For example, in the 1940s, when I was young, we were required to call all the Elders of our community "Aunt" or "Uncle." It was a good tradition—the community was much closer because of it.

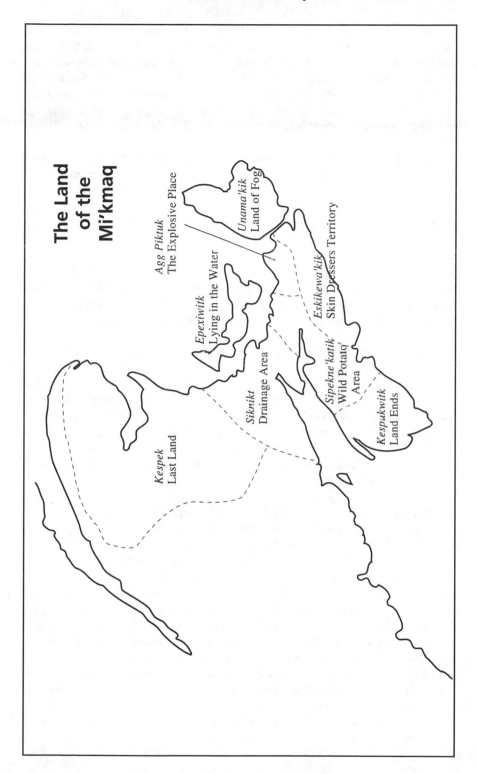

**The Land
of the
Mi'kmaq**

Agg Piktuk
The Explosive Place

Unama'kik
Land of Fog

Epexiwitk
Lying in the Water

Eskikewa'kik
Skin Dressers Territory

Siknikt
Drainage Area

Sipekne'katik
Wild Potato
Area

Kespukwitk
Land Ends

Kespek
Last Land

In contrast to most of the cultures of Europe, where the divine right to rule was the province of the aristocrat, Mi'kmaq culture held that a leader had to earn the right to lead. The standards were rigid for men who aspired to leadership. Aspirants had to be compassionate, honourable, intelligent, brave and wise. The term of office was indeterminate, and if a leader conducted himself well, his leadership could continue until death. Grand Chief Membertou, the greatest Mi'kmaq chief in living memory, remained in office until his death at an age said to be well over one hundred.

A Mi'kmaq leader's social status was also sharply different from that of his European counterpart, who was paid handsomely, perked indiscriminately and feared. Chiefs and other office holders were not accorded special perks and privileges because of their positions. Those they did receive were freely given by the people as rewards for services rendered and as tokens of esteem.

Because of the nature of Mi'kmaq culture, political corruption was unknown. The European practice of using one's leadership to enhance personal and family fortunes by extracting favours from the community or its citizens would not have been tolerated. Any leader who engaged in such dishonourable practices would have soon found himself deposed and disgraced. The early Mi'kmaq had no taste for corruption and, given the principle of community ownership, there was no need for it.

Sieur de Dièreville wrote about leadership within Mi'kmaq society:

> The cherished hope of leadership inspires resolve to be adept in the chase. For it is by such aptitude a man obtains the highest place; here there is no inherited position due to birth or lineage, merit alone uplifts. He who has won exalted rank, which each himself hopes to attain, will never be deposed, except for some abhorrent crime. No wise noteworthy are the honours paid his high estate, for he is merely first among a hundred..., more, or less, according to the size of his domain.[5]

In contrast to the respect accorded the Mi'kmaq leader because of honourable performance, English and other European leaders mostly garnered their reputations through brutal force. Even the most minor offense committed against a European official met with swift retribution. The severity of punishment inflicted is illustrated in the minutes of a Council meeting held at Annapolis Royal on September 22, 1726. Robert Nichols was tried by Council for insulting the Governor of the province. After a very short trial, Mr. Nichols was found guilty and sentenced to brutal punishment "in order to terrify the other Citizens." For three days, he was to sit upon a gallows for a half hour each day with a rope around his neck and a paper upon his breast with the words "audacious villain." Afterwards, he was to be whipped with a cat-o-nine-tails at the rate of five stripes upon his bare back every one hundred paces, starting from the prison to the uppermost house of the Cape and back again. Finally, he was to be turned over to the army to be made a soldier.[6]

The contributions made by the Mi'kmaq and other North American Nations towards establishing democracy in the world was acknowledged for the first time by a White jurisdiction in 1988. In November of that year the Congress of the

United States passed a resolution recognizing that the U.S. Constitution and Bill of Rights were modelled to a large extent upon the tenets of the constitutions and bills of rights of the Iroquoian Nations and other Amerindian groups.

Religion

The Great Spirit's directives were the Mi'kmaq Nation's eternal light. The People believed that His dominion was all-inclusive, and that He encompassed all positive attributes—love, kindness, compassion, knowledge, wisdom etc., and that He was responsible for all existence and was personified in all things—rivers, trees, spouses, children, friends etc. No initiatives were undertaken without first requesting His guidance. His creations, "Mother Earth" and the Universe, were accorded the highest respect. Religion was blended into daily life—it was lived. Nature, as was the case with most American civilizations, supported Mi'kmaq religious beliefs.

In comparison, Europeans followed religions, collectively called Christianity, which are based upon blind belief. They too promote a belief in a Supreme Being who possesses all good qualities, but until recent times they also promoted a belief that God condoned the use of several bad qualities, e.g., vengefulness to spread and protect the word. Horrendous events such as the Crusades and Inquisitions were initiated under the dogma of Christianity. Innocent people who could not defend themselves against charges of heresy were found guilty and thrown into prison or burned at the stake. Non-believers were branded pagans and heathen savages. The Mi'kmaq, as non-Christians, were also thus branded.

In most European minds, the vision of Mi'kmaq savagery was solidified by the fact that the Mi'kmaq offered tobacco and other tokens to the Great Spirit as a mark of respect and humility. Yet "Christian" and "civilized" Whites saw no contradiction in their own offerings of bread, wine, incense and so on to their God. Most Europeans, especially religious leaders, also found it strange that the Amerindians viewed the Great Spirit as a likeness of themselves, but these same Europeans did not find it strange that they saw their own God as a White man.

The Mi'kmaq, like most other Amerindians, had a place similar to what the Christians called "Heaven" for the repose of their dead, called the "Land of Souls." It was a place of eternal rest, peace and happiness where the dead were welcomed by the Great Spirit and their ancestors.

"Evil spirits" were also part of Mi'kmaq belief. The People believed that these were the cause of disease, famine, natural catastrophes and all other evils which can afflict mankind. To limit the damage these spirits begot, the Mi'kmaq beseeched the Great Spirit for assistance. There is little evidence that they used these spirits to terrorize and intimidate one another. In contrast, Christianity's "demons," especially the "Devil," were used by priests and ministers to strike the fear of God into their congregations.

European Christians also believed that their God was to be feared because, if they erred, He would damn them to eternal pain and suffering. This kind of vengeful action by God was incompatible with the Mi'kmaq belief that the Great Spirit was goodness incarnate and there was thus no need to be terrified of Him.

Nevertheless, many people remark on the seeming ease with which the Mi'kmaq and many other Amerindians adopted Christianity. The simple explanation for this is the civility of the People. They believed that a host should make every effort to please a guest. If it required them to worship the Great Spirit in another fashion, then so be it. After all, they reasoned, if the same God is worshipped by all men, the mode of worship is incidental.

Morality and Customs

The modesty and chastity of the Mi'kmaq, especially the women, were virtues well remarked upon by those who wrote about the ideals of the culture. The fact that a woman took pride in her honour and would not willingly compromise herself was seen as incredible by many European writers. From their racist points of view it was inconceivable that a people they considered heathen savages would act in a more civilized manner than they.

From their moral outlook, the Mi'kmaq developed laws governing relationships between the sexes. Thus marriage rites were celebrated with great pomp, ceremony and feasting, and included present exchanges between the families of the bride and groom. The preliminaries leading up to a marriage provide an excellent example of the individual freedoms the People enjoyed.

If a boy wished to court a girl, he had to ask the permission of her father before he began. This was more a courtesy than an obstacle. The father would normally, after much teasing, give the young man permission to approach his daughter to ascertain if she was willing to involve herself romantically with him. Chrestien Le Clercq describes the process:

> If the father finds that the suitor who presents himself is acceptable for his daughter ... he tells him to speak to his sweetheart in order to learn her wish about an affair which concerns herself alone. For they do not wish, say these barbarians, to force the inclinations of their children in the matter of marriage, or to induce them, whether by use of force, obedience, or affection, to marry men whom they cannot bring themselves to like. Hence it is that the fathers and mothers of our Gaspesians [Mi'kmaq from Gaspé] leave to their children the entire liberty of choosing the persons whom they think most adaptable to their dispositions, and most conformable to their affectations.[7]

Under the Nation's laws marriages between blood relations, up to second cousins, were strictly forbidden. However, there were no taboos against marrying in-laws.

The culture also permitted polygamous marriage, but the record indicates that it was rarely practised. Marc Lescarbot expressed amazement that "although one husband may have many wives ... there is no jealousy among them."[8] Pierre Biard wrote:

> According to the custom of the country, they can have several wives, but the greater number of them that I have seen have only one; some of the Sagamores pretend that they cannot do without this plurality, not because of lust, for this nation is not very unchaste, but for two other reasons. One is in order to retain their authority and power by having a number of children; for in that lies the strength of the house; the second reason is their entertainment and service,

which is great and laborious, since they have large families and a great number of followers, and therefore require a number of housewives to (serve).[9]

The head wife in a polygamous household was usually the one who had borne the first boy. The extent to which polygamy was practised, like the misunderstanding about extended family, was no doubt exaggerated by the Jesuits and others. For example, Grand Chief Membertou had only one wife.

Love was the prime factor in creating marital bonds between Mi'kmaq couples. For European couples, especially among the elite, marriages were often entered into to enhance personal fortunes and stations in life rather than for love. As a result, children were sometimes "promised" at birth to individuals who were deemed by their families to be the best prospect for the child's future. To the Mi'kmaq this practice would have been considered uncivilized. However, in later years, up until the early 1900s, many Mi'kmaq parents followed this European custom. My maternal grandmother was victimized by the practice and lived in a loveless marriage until she was widowed, after which she met and married a man she loved.

Although not much mention of divorce is found in European records of the pre-Columbian Mi'kmaq, that it was practised is another example of their respect for human rights. However, because harmony in relationships and respect for each other's needs were paramount, one can conclude that instances of divorce were rare.

Funerals also called for ceremony and feasting. The Chief would be the first to speak at "the feast of the dead" and, as related by Le Clercq, he would talk about

the good qualities and the most notable deeds of the deceased. He even impresses upon all the assembly, by words as touching as they are forceful, the uncertainty of human life, and the necessity they are under of dying, in order to join in the Land of Souls with their friends and relatives, whom they are now recalling to memory.[10]

Others spoke after the Chief. Nicholas Denys relates:

Each one spoke, one after another, for they never spoke two at a time, neither men or women. In this respect these barbarians give a fine lesson to those people who consider themselves more polished and wiser than they.

A recital was made of all the genealogy of the dead man, of that which he had done fine and good, of the stories that he had heard told of his ancestors, of the great feasts and acknowledgements he had made in large number, of the animals he had killed in the hunt, and of all the other matters they considered it fitting to tell in praise of his predecessors. After this they came to the dead man; then the loud cries and weeping redoubled. This made the orator strike a pose, to which the men and women responded from time to time by a general groaning, all at one time and in the same tone. And often he who was speaking struck postures, and set himself to cry and weep with the others.

Having said all he wished to say, another began and said yet other things not said by the first. Then one after another, each after his fashion, made his praise on the dead man. This lasted three or four days before the funeral oration was finished.[11]

Denys, although impressed with many aspects of Mi'kmaq culture, was among those with little ability to appreciate the values of a non-Christian culture possessed by a people of colour. Instead, as his writings indicate, he had a blind belief in the superiority of his own. As a demonstration of how long bad habits can linger, in the year 2000 there is still a reluctance among many Whites to accept the fact that Amerindian cultures were well defined and that the values they possessed are among those that modern humanity is still reaching for!

One can safely conclude that the social structures and democratic forms of government found in the Americas were deemed by the European ruling classes as a serious threat to their own exercise of absolute power and unchallenged authority. The determination the European aristocracy displayed in their efforts to destroy the Amerindians speaks for itself.

Mi'kmaq Social Values and Economy

The pre-Columbian Mi'kmaq were a nomadic people who moved from place to place in harmony with the seasonal migrations of fish, game and fowl. These provided the principal components of their diets, supplemented by some farming. Their food supply was bountiful, dependable and extremely healthy, and materials needed to construct snug wigwams and make clothing suited to the changing seasons were readily available. They were not wanting.

Because of the communal nature of the society and the abundance of food, poverty among the people was virtually unknown. Material things, other than clothing and household goods, were shared equally. Thus the old, sick, infirm and otherwise disadvantaged were protected from destitution. Endowed with a high level of personal security, the People had a relatively low level of stress in their lives. This, combined with a healthy diet, blessed them with unusually long life spans, and centenarians were not rare. Comparing their comfortable and serene lifestyles with the hardships then being endured by much of the world's other peoples, one must conclude that the Mi'kmaq were very well off.

Denys, who wrote after the Mi'kmaq population had undergone a substantial decline, describes their dietary habits:

> There were formerly a much larger number of Indians than at present. They lived without care, and never ate either salt or spice. They drank only good soup, very fat. It was this that made them live long and multiply much. They often ate fish, especially seals to obtain the oil, as much for greasing themselves as for drinking; and they ate the Whale which frequently came ashore on the coast, especially the blubber on which they made good cheer. Their greatest liking is for grease; they ate as one does bread, and drink it liquid.[1]

"Cacamo" was their greatest delicacy. In order to make it, the women:

> made the rocks red hot ... collected all the bones of the Moose, pounded them with rocks upon another larger, reducing them to powder; then they placed them in their kettle and made them boil well. This brought out a grease that rose to the top of the water, and they collected it with a wooden spoon. They kept the bones boiling until they yielded nothing more, and with such success that from the bones of one Moose, without counting the marrow, they obtained five to six pounds of grease as white as snow, and as firm as wax. It was this which they used as their entire provision for living when they went hunting. We call it Moose butter; they Cacamo.[2]

The Mi'kmaq civilization was, like most others of the day, patriarchal. A few Mi'kmaq disagree with this assessment and promote the notion that the culture was matriarchal. However, as of January 2000, they have not produced any evidence, which I've requested on several occasions, to support their contention. On the other hand, the patriarchal culture conclusion is well supported. In modern times, Professor Harold McGee Jr. of Saint Mary's University published a paper in support called "The Case for Micmac Demes."[3] He further argues against a matriarchal conclusion in a foreword he wrote for James Wherry's "Eastern Algonquian Relationships to Proto-Algonquian Social Organizations."[4] The patriarchal conclusion is also confirmed by the records left behind by colonial European scribes. When penning their observations about female and male roles in Amerindian societies, for example, amazement was expressed that such robust men as the Iroquoian Warrior permitted their women to dominate them. Although the scribes made many degrading remarks about the permissiveness of Mi'kmaq culture, no similar comments can be found in their musings about the Mi'kmaq male.

However, both genders were involved in setting the agenda and dispersing responsibilities for the orderly conduct of the Nation's livelihood. The men were responsible for providing food for their communities by hunting and fishing and for carrying out chores involving heavy work. The women and older children were responsible for such chores as the limited farming the community indulged in, and for collecting, cleaning and preserving produce, game and fish. No demeaning connotations were associated with the assignment of different community responsibilities to each gender. The division of duties was pragmatically based on which gender was most suitable to the requirements of each job.

The involvement of older children in survival duties was an educational regime that began at an early age at the knees of their parents, grandparents and

Mother Earth provides

Elders. This education was designed to instill in them a desire to grow into caring and honourable adults. The Keepers taught the children the Nation's history and its legends. All adult members of the community participated in teaching the basic skills and knowledge deemed necessary to ensure the Nation's survival. However, as in all civilizations, the maturation of an individual's capabilities and understanding came in adulthood through experience and experimentation.

Force was never used to compel children's participation in the education process, nor would it have been tolerated. Children were raised in an atmosphere of communal devotion. Not only were they loved and cherished by their parents, but also by members of the community in general. This ingrained devotion assured that children were never left homeless; instead such a child would be adopted by a loving family. Adoption procedures were simple. If a child's natural parent or parents could not provide care for any reason or the child had been orphaned, then with the consent of the Chief a couple with or without children would simply take the child into their family. The child was then treated by the community as though it was the family's natural-born.

This ancient practice, which was carried over to relatively modern times, has caused difficulties for quite a few people who were trying to verify their ancestry in order to collect old-age pensions etc. They often had no inkling that they were not the natural-born children of the people they thought of as parents and were trying to acquire data that did not exist.

Several years ago, while a superintendent with Indian Affairs, I was involved in such a case. A man in his mid-seventies, unable to prove his age, asked me to help him prove it so he could collect old-age pension benefits. Although his parents had never told him that he had been born in Cumberland County, it was his belief that he had because he had grown up there. With this clue I had the records of every church denomination in Cumberland, Colchester and Pictou counties searched, but no luck! Then, as luck would have it, while visiting a late friend, a very elderly Mi'kmaq lady who lived in the town of Shelburne, I happened to mention the problem. Her response was: "Why don't you go over to the Catholic Church and ask for a baptismal record for —, because he was born here to — and then immediately adopted by the —s." Problem solved!

Although cross-cultural problems related to ancient Mi'kmaq laws such as those for adoption crop up from time to time, none to date have been insurmountable. However, the same cannot be said for those related to stereotyping. One particularly long-standing and obnoxious problem, that causes immeasurable grief for today's Mi'kmaq and other Amerindians, stems from the fable that has evolved in White society over the years since 1492 to the effect that Amerindians are not competitive. The fact that all living things on Mother Earth compete in one manner or other makes such an assertion a grossly offensive racial insult. Contrary to such an ignorant belief, it can be stated emphatically that competition was not absent because the very existence of the People depended upon it.

Thus the urge to compete was a trait instilled in children at an early age and reinforced throughout adulthood. The competition to be the best hunter, the best leader, the best fisherman and so on kept the larders full and assured that the most qualified graduated to leadership. For most of their lives women also competed intensively to produce the finest clothing, designs and other things needed and valued by the Nation. However, the motivation for competing in Amerindian societies was quite different from the motivation in European societies. In most Amerindian cultures one competed to provide the best service and most wealth to the community. In European societies the competition was to see how much wealth one could accumulate for oneself.

Mi'kmaq territory, blessed with generous endowments by the Great Spirit, permitted Mi'kmaq men to hone their competitive skills in many fields. The annual moose and bear hunts were occasions where individuals went all-out to be the most productive. Of course, the festivities associated with these events were eagerly anticipated community celebrations.

Although land-based competitions were very important, those associated with harvesting food from the bountiful ocean were of no less importance. From working the sea, Mi'kmaq warriors developed exceptional skills in seamanship. In fact their sailing abilities were such that many of their British and French peers recognized them as being among the greatest sailors on Mother Earth. During their wars with the British, they routinely commandeered European war and merchant ships, sailing them up and down the coast of eastern North America with such great skill that it seemed they were born to it.

Father Lallement wrote a letter in 1659 describing Mi'kmaq seamanship with awe: "It is wonderful how these savage mariners navigate so far in little shallops crossing vast seas without compass, and often without sight of the sun, trusting to instinct for their guidance."[5]

The "shallops" referred to by Father Lallemant, and sea canoes, were routinely

Preparing tommorrow's provider

used by the Mi'kmaq to cross the Bay of Fundy, the Northumberland Strait, and the North Atlantic between Nova Scotia and Newfoundland. Their skills probably had more to do with their ability to read tides, currents and other directional information than with instinct. Dan Conlin comments:

> Mi'kmaq were masters of wooden boats … and seafaring. When threatened with aggression … the Mikmaq proved formidable sea raiders, capturing over 80 vessels at sea in the wars (with the British) of the 1700s.… Some scholars have suggested the pirates of the Caribbean may have learned many of their tactics while living among the people of Glooscap.[6]

The recreational and entertainment needs of the culture were met by various social activities and functions. Dancing and feasting to commemorate small and great occasions were very popular. The People also enjoyed games such as Waltes, which is still played. They also participated in canoe racing, archery and physical-contact sports among themselves and in competition with neighbouring Nations.

Besides being keen sportsmen, the Mi'kmaq were also skilled and imaginative storytellers. Tales of the escapades of many real and legendary heroes were told for a dual purpose: education and entertainment. Featured in many stories was Glooscap, who, according to legend, had been endowed by the Great Spirit with supernatural powers. One story relates how in anger he once used his ability to change forms and turned himself into a giant beaver. Then, to vent his anger, he slapped his huge tail five times with such force upon the waters of the Bay of Fundy that enough earth was stirred up to create the five islands that can still be seen off the Nova Scotia coast near Economy Mountain.

Another form of recreation was the production of beautiful works of art. The women in particular were, and still are, highly creative and skilled artisans. Their many talents may be witnessed in their quality carvings, paintings and other masterpieces, such as stunningly beautiful quill and basket products. Contemporary Mi'kmaq artists are actively involved in producing a full range of traditional and modern arts and crafts.

Health care was the responsibility of people trained in the science. Physical and mental health problems were treated with care and compassion by the community. The medicine men had available to them a wide range of potions, poultices etc. to take care of physical problems. Psychology, where practical, was the prime tool used to treat the rare mental-health problem.

The rarity of mental diseases among the Mi'kmaq was a direct result of the secure and stable lifestyles they enjoyed, which were most conducive to keeping them exceptionally well adjusted. When mental illness did occur, it bore no social stigma. By comparison, European civilizations of the period considered mental and even some physical illnesses to be social aberrations that should be concealed. As a result, hellholes called lunatic asylums housed their mentally ill in deplorable and pitiful squalor.

Instead of physically punitive measures, psychology was used by most Amerindians to persuade people to behave according to the laws of their Nation. Because no evidence to the contrary exists, one can conclude that extreme punishments such as shunning and the death penalty were probably only used in extreme and rare cases. The compassionate manner in which erring individuals were persuaded to comply caused many Europeans to write unflattering comments about what they viewed as permissiveness within Amerindian societies. From their perspective, force was the only truly effective method to assure compliance.

Mi'kmaq and European attitudes also differed in most other societal matters. For instance, attitudes towards sex and nudity held by the citizens of the two civilizations were vastly different. Very few, if any, sexual hang-ups were harboured by the Mi'kmaq. Sex was accepted for what it is, a natural act. However, decency required that sex be conducted in private.

Having children out of wedlock was frowned upon by the People but, contrary to the social stigma it begot in European cultures, it had no long-term negative consequences. As a matter of fact, because of their proven fertility, in some cases single women with children were especially prized by men seeking wives. Upon marriage, a child previously born out of wedlock to the bride would be adopted by the new husband as his own. Although the People were of chaste views, virginity was not considered a virtue an unmarried woman had to take to her grave.

Sexual assault was not a problem among the Mi'kmaq. As a matter of fact, the men of the community, like men in most other civilizations, took great exception to sexual advances being made upon their wives and daughters. Biard reports an incident which occurred at Port-Royal when some Frenchmen made unwelcomed advances towards some of their women: "They came and told our Captain that he should look out for his men, informing him that anyone who attempted to do that again would not stand much of a chance, that they would kill him on the spot."[7] This reaction did not mean that a Frenchman, or an individual from any other ethnic group, could not carry on a normal relationship with a Mi'kmaq woman. What it indicated was that the relationship had to be carried on according to civilized customs. The Mi'kmaq and the Acadians came to an understanding in this regard and, later on, as social exchanges developed, a great number of intermarriages took place.

The healthy attitude the Mi'kmaq held towards sex shocked the puritanical Europeans. The historical material left behind by the British and by Christian missionaries certifies that they viewed these attitudes as a further indication of heathen depravity.

In line with their enlightened societal attitudes, most Amerindians had no hang-ups about nudity. From their sophisticated outlook, nudity was, like sex, a natural thing, and no shame was associated with one's body. Clothing was worn for protection against the elements and for fashion display, not for modesty. This healthy attitude about nudity, like their sexual attitudes, tended to reinforce the perception in puritanical European minds that the Amerindians had pagan and animal-like habits.

From the Amerindian perspective, English attitudes towards sex and nudity must have been hilarious. The English reacted to sex as if it were the cousin of the plague, and towards nudity as if it were the work of the Devil himself. One can imagine the jokes and comments made in Amerindian circles about European peculiarities.

Another conviction of Mi'kmaq society which strongly highlights the differ-ences between the two cultures was their belief that it was impossible for a mere mortal to own any part of Mother Earth. The validity of this belief is amply dem-onstrated today by the power of nature. When Mother Earth decides to create a tidal wave, earthquake, volcanic eruption or some other violent movement, a mere mortal's infantile efforts to control Her can be obliterated in the blink of an eye. Human civilization continues with Mother Nature's benevolence, and its end is Her prerogative.

Civility and generosity were so engrained in Mi'kmaq society that to be rude or mean was unthinkable. If pressed to the contrary, they would respond: "How could one refuse to treat all people with kindness and not share with them the bounties of Mother Earth?" A modified version of this trait still survives in many Mi'kmaq homes today. When I was an economic development officer with Indian Affairs I would go to a community and visit several homes. In each a cup of tea would be offered. "Have a cuppa and a snack" was the welcome. On one trip to Eskasoni, I visited ten homes. Not wanting to insult anyone by refusing, I accepted their hospitality. As I left the village feeling bloated, I could actually hear and feel the tea sloshing around in my stomach.

In showing hospitality a Mi'kmaq would, to save face for the other person, agree for the moment to something he or she knew to be untrue. It was considered very rude or disrespectful to pronounce someone else a liar. The philosophy was simple: accept the sincere beliefs of the other individual and then proceed to win the person over to the truth by tactful and diplomatic means. If this approach failed to achieve the desired result, unless the matter was of life-and-death or national importance, it was left alone; for they felt that in the overall scheme of things the right or wrong of an opinion would not make that much difference.

Cornelius J. Jaenen provides an excellent example of how Europeans viewed this behaviour. He reports that, when discussing the Amerindian attitude towards religious conversion, Calvin Martin found that it was sometimes difficult to distin-guish between genuine conversion and a tolerant assent to strange views:

> Such generosity even extended to the abstract realm of ideas, theories, stories, news and teachings. The Native host prided himself on his ability to entertain and give assent to a variety of views, even if they were contrary to his better judgement. In this institutionalized hospitality lies the key to understanding the frustration of the Priest, whose sweet converts one day were the relapsed heathens of the next. Conversion was often more a superficial courtesy, rather than an eternal commitment, something the Jesuits could not fathom.[8]

Martin's observation is supported by Louis Armand Lohontan, who reported that some Amerindians thought Christianity was baseless and illogical. In spite of this conclusion, as an act of civility, they converted anyway:

> But the poor wretches are such obstinate Infidels, that all the Characters of Truth, Sincerity, and Divinity that shine throughout the Scriptures, have no impression on them....

> They plead, that a man must be a Fool who believes that … God created Adam on purpose to have him tempted by an evil Spirit to eat of an Apple, and that he occasion'd all the Misery of his Posterity by the pretended transmission of his Sin. They ridicule the Dialogue between Eve and the Serpent, alleging that we affront God in supposing that he wrought the Miracle of giving this Animal the use of Speech, with intent to destroy all the Human Race....
>
> They argue, "That …. the Christians build a religion without a foundation, which is subject to the Changes and Vicissitudes of Humane Affairs. That this religion being divided and subdivided into so many Sects, as those of the French, the English, etc., it can be no other than a Human Artifice: For had God been the Author of it, his Providence had prevented such diversity of Senti-ments.... That if the Evangelical Law had descended from Heaven … God … would have deliver'd his Precepts in such clear and precise terms as would leave no room for Disputes."[9]

When trying to understand why the Mi'kmaq converted, a logical explanation might be that it was done in the hopes that by being part of Christianity they might be influential in making positive change. However, only the Great Spirit can now provide the true answer, and so far He has not felt compelled to do so.

Mi'kmaq civility mandated that being right was secondary to the need to maintain productive interpersonal relationships with one's relatives, friends and associates, but the need to be right among members of most European societies was almost an obsession. Thousands upon thousands were sacrificed in wars in order to establish that one's own faction held the correct view.

The multitude of other great cultural differences between European and Ameri-can societies left European scribes in various states of perplexity. However, the difference they understood the least was the Amerindian concept of honour. They could not grasp that honour was so sought after and protected by the Amerindian that in the mind of the Warrior death was preferable to dishonour. Bernard Gilbert Hoffman gives this description:

> For a young man to rise in the esteem of his people, it apparently was necessary for him to be superior in hunting, to be among the bravest in warfare, to be generous and hospitable to all the people in his camp and to visitors, stripping himself of all his wealth, and seeking only the affections of his people. It was also absolutely necessary for him to remain unpretentious and humble.[10]

To live up to the standards of maturity set by society was an ongoing struggle for the young male. Le Clercq tells how loss of honour could affect a young man's outlook on life: "The Gaspesians [Mi'kmaq] … are so sensitive to affronts which are offered them that they sometimes abandon themselves to despair, and even make attempts upon their lives, in the belief that the insult which has been done them tarnishes the honour and the reputation which they have acquired."[11] The following incident reported by Le Clercq emphasizes how deeply felt the sense of honour was:

Such were the feelings of a young Indian who, on account of having received by inadvertence a blow from a broom being used by a servant who was sweeping the house, imagined that he ought not to survive this imaginary insult which became greater in his imagination in proportion as he reflected upon it. "What," said he to himself, "to have been turned out in a manner so shameful, and in the presence of so great a number of Indians ... and after that to appear again before their eyes?"

"Ah, I prefer to die! What shall I look like, in the future, when I find myself in the public assemblies of my nation? And what esteem will there be for my courage when there is a question of going to war, after having been beaten and chased in confusion by a maidservant from the establishment of the Captain of the French? It were much better ... that I die."

In fact he entered into the woods singing certain mournful songs which expressed the bitterness of his heart. He took and tied to a tree the strap which served him as a girdle, and began to hang and strangle himself in earnest. He soon lost consciousness, and would have ... lost his life if his own sister had not happened to come by chance ... to the very place where her miserable brother was hanging.

She cut the strap promptly, and after having lamented as dead this man in which she could not see any sign of life, she came to announce this sad news to the Indians who were with Monsieur Denys. They went into the woods and brought to the habitation this unhappy Gaspesian, who was still breathing, though but little. I forced open his teeth, and, having made him swallow some spoonfuls of brandy, he came to himself....

His brother had formerly hung and strangled himself ... in the Bay of Gaspé, because he was refused by a girl whom he loved tenderly, and whom he sought in marriage. For, in fact, although our Gaspesians, as we have said, live joyously and contentedly, and although they ... put off, so far as they can, everything which can trouble them, nevertheless some among them fall occasionally into a melancholy so black and so profound that they become immersed wholly in a cruel despair, and even make attempts upon their own lives.[12]

Honour played such a significant role in the daily lives of the males of Mi'kmaq society, and the lives of the males of most other First Nations, that they jealously guarded it with their lives. The abiding requirement that they conduct their affairs in an honourable manner was reflected in their treatment of enemies. In this regard many European writers have made unflattering remarks about what they viewed as the cruelty of Amerindian Warriors, who almost always killed enemy Warriors taken prisoner. They probably spent many hours trying to reconcile this practice with another Warrior custom that conflicted with the first. This custom dictated that if women and children taken prisoner were not adopted into the community, they were to be set free. That these practices were connected to honour has been rarely understood.

Thus, the European observer could not seem to grasp that death was usually the preferred option for both prisoner and executioner. To understand this one has only to look at honour as the Amerindians perceived it. From their point of view, to take a Warrior prisoner and then turn him over to the community as a person to do chores normally done by women and children would be to demonstrate the utmost disrespect for a valiant enemy. One must also understand that at the time of being taken prisoner, the Warrior himself would be completely disheartened, feeling that his reputation was forever damaged and that he could never again walk among his people with head held high and know their esteem. To be taken prisoner was viewed as one of the worst circumstances that could overtake a man. Therefore, knowing how the prisoner felt, his captor would not deliver the death blow in anger but as an act of mercy. No cruelty was intended.

Of course, cruelty was sometimes found amongst the Mi'kmaq in individual instances. All the peoples of Mother Earth have among them people who are capable of committing abhorrent crimes against other human beings, and we are no exception. However, in most Amerindian societies cruelty was not a practice promoted and organized by governments or private groups.

The same cannot be said for Europe. In Europe today museums house the instruments of death and torture that autocratic rulers deliberately developed to terrorize their populations and others into submission. These barbarous instruments are so cruel in their intent that one can barely look at them without being sickened. No such tools were ever invented or tolerated by the Mi'kmaq.

The tenacity of Amerindians in refusing to accept foreign models of "civilization" and to fight to preserve their own indigenous cultures and lifestyles was probably very frustrating for European leaders. And the belief espoused by some of their own people that certain social values inherent in Amerindian civilizations were superior to their own would have compounded the frustration. In view of the racist attitudes rampant among European leaders of that era, such observations would have been considered akin to heresy.

Jaenen relates an Amerindian Chief's eloquent response to an insistence on the superiority of European culture:

> For all your arguments, and you can bring forward a thousand of them if you wish, are annihilated by this single shaft ... they say. "That is the savage way of doing it. You can have your way and we will have ours; everyone values his own wares."[13]

One of the historical falsities born and nurtured during the European colonization of the Americas, and still promoted to a certain degree today, was that White prisoners held by Amerindian Nations were always anxious to return to their own communities. The truth was that, for many, experiences of living among these peoples exposed them for the first time to a taste of real freedom within a just and caring society. Thus, a good number, when given the opportunity to return to their former lives of oppression and economic slavery, flatly refused and chose instead to stay with their captors. These free decisions to assimilate contrasted starkly with the coercion used to try to assimilate First Nations people into White society.

The democratic practices and freedoms offered by Amerindian societies also enticed many other Europeans to assimilate. French officials in particular feared that large numbers of their citizens would do so. These fears were heightened by the fact that many were already cohabiting with Amerindians and adopting their lifestyles. Jaenen comments:

> The French ... had introduced a multiplicity of elements which would continue to modify and influence the direction Native societies would take in the future. In this process, French colonial society was itself profoundly affected not only by the American environment but also by its contacts with Native cultures. The possibility that many French might become assimilated, rather than the Native people being "reduced to civility," was discussed in the closing years of the French regime. One officer remarked: "There are not wanting here those who defend this strange attachment of some of their countrymen to this savage life ... by a willing conformity to their actions, and by intermarriage with them. They pretend that even this savage life itself is not without its peculiar sweets and pleasures, that it (is) the most adapted and the most natural to man. Liberty, they say, is nowhere more perfectly enjoyed than where no subordination is known, but what is recommended by natural reason, the veneration of old age, or the respect of personal merit."
>
> That such a possibility was not necessarily equated with dangerous degeneration and American barbarism, but defensible adaptation to a new environment and new circumstances, indicated that whatever official policies and objections might be, whatever the thrust of church pronouncements and missionary endeavours, there were pragmatic considerations which operated at a more popular social level in New France.[14]

One cannot help wondering what kind of society we would be living in today if the British had set aside their notions of racial superiority and, instead of trying to force them to assimilate, adopted many of the Amerindians' human rights principles. Such a society would probably be one in which racial discrimination had long ago disappeared. A sad loss for humanity!

Among the worst failings of many early European writers was their failure to properly identify the ranks of Chiefs according to the protocol of the Mi'kmaq political hierarchy. Whether the Chief they refer to in their journals was a District Chief, Grand Chief, local chief etc. is anyone's guess. This has posed problems in trying to sort out Mi'kmaq historical events.

The way Chief Membertou is identified in the following passages provides a good example of the omission of proper titles. Membertou was the District Chief of Kespukwitk and had been appointed by his peers from the six other Mi'kmaq Districts as the Grand Chief. He was a respected and influential man who, as tradition demanded, wielded the powers of his office with humility. Lescarbot described the Grand Chief:

> At Port Royal, the name of the Captain or Sagamore of the place is Membertou. He is at least a hundred years old and may in the course of nature live fifty years longer. He has under him a number of families whom he rules, not with so much authority as does our King over his subjects, but with sufficient powers to harangue, advise, and lead them to war, or to render

justice to one who has a grievance, and like matters.

He does not impose taxes upon the people, but if there are any profits from the chase, he has a share of them, without being obliged to take part in it. It is true that they sometimes make him presents of beaver skins and other things, when he is occupied in curing the sick, or questioning his demon to have news of some future event or of the absent: for, as each village, or company of savages, has an Acutmoin, or Prophet, who performs this office, Membertou is the one who, from time immemorial, has practised this art among his followers. He has done it so well that his reputation is far above that of all the other Sagamores of the country, he has since his youth been a great Chief, and has also exercised the offices of Soothsayer and Medicine Man, which are the three things most officious to the well-being of man, and necessary to human life.

Now this Membertou today, by the grace of God, is a Christian. Together, with all his family, having been baptised ... last Saint John's day, the 24th of June, 1610. I have letters from Sieur de Poutrincourt about it, dated the eleventh day of July following. He said that Membertou was named after our good late King Henri IV, and his eldest son (Membertousoichis) after Monseigneur the Dauphin, today our King Louis XIII, whom may God bless.[15]

Biard wrote that Membertou

was the greatest, most renowned and most formidable savage within the memory of man; of splendid physique, taller and larger-limbed than is usual among them; bearded like a Frenchman, although scarcely any of the others have hair upon the chin; grave and reserved; feeling a proper sense of dignity for his position as commander.[16]

Lescarbot says Membertou was

already a man of great age, and saw Captain Jacques Cartier in that country in 1534, being already at that time a married man and the father of a family, though even now he does not look more than fifty years old.[17]

None of these commentators identified Membertou as the Grand Chief. Grand Chief Membertou died at what is now Saint Mary's Bay, Digby County, on September 18, 1611. No one knows his exact age; that it was well over one hundred years has been widely acknowledged.

In attending to the governance of his domain, the Chief of a District would, at least once a year, call a District Council meeting which brought together all levels of Chiefs, the Elders and other community leaders. The main order of business was readjusting, if necessary, hunting and fishing territories and attending to the administrative and political needs of the District and its communities. Council decisions were made by consensus. The District Chief was the chairman at these meetings and thus the person expected to persuade everyone to come to a meeting of minds.

Reaching consensus was necessary because, in contrast to European leaders, who had the power to impose their own decisions, Mi'kmaq leaders had to lead in accordance with the will of the People. Thus, if a Mi'kmaq leader wanted to undertake a new initiative, he was dependent upon his powers of persuasion to convince fellow citizens of the merit of his proposal. This requirement decreed that the Mi'kmaq leader become an eloquent orator and a master of descriptive language. When thus engaged he incorporated the full wealth of the Nation's legends and stories into his orations.

The following records of a missionary priest abroad in Mi'kmaq country in the 1600s and 1700s attest to the descriptive eloquence and civility of the People:

> The Mi'kmaq is a poetic child. His distances are measured in rainbows. His words sound the sense. His fancy is illimitable. He is a born orator. He loves justice and hates violence and robbery. He is courteous, and Father Biard says: "Never had we to be on our guard against them."[18]

Another priest, impressed with the legends he heard while in the company of the Mi'kmaq, wrote:

> The story of the Mi'kmaq is one of the most fascinating studies that a person can take up. His legends carry you back from the first sight of the big Canoe, as they called the white man's ship, to the dawn of Creation when Glooscap, the master, lay prone on his back, head to the rising Sun, feet to the setting of the Sun, left hand to the South, and the right hand to the North. This wonder worker was not Nisgam, "Father to us all," nor Gisolg, "Our Maker," nor the "Great Chief," but he was par excellence the Mi'kmaq. He was co-existent with Creation.

The legend being described continues, illustrating the rich imagery of the Mi'kmaq storyteller:

> After the seventy times seven nights and the seventy times seven days appointed there came unto him a bent old women born that very noonday Sun. She was Nogami, the Grandmother, and she owed her existence to the dew of the rock. Glooscap thanked the Great Spirit in fulfilling his promise.
>
> On the morrow of the noonday Sun a young man came unto Glooscap and Nogami. He owed his existence to the beautiful foam on the waters, and Glooscap called him Nataoa-nsen, my sister's son.
>
> When another morrow came, and when the sun was highest another person came unto the three who saluted and said, my children. This was the mother of all the Mi'kmaq. She owed her existence to the beautiful plant of the earth. So there we have the "Beresheat Baru," the Birth of the Race.
>
> The Master himself retained the monopoly in stone ware, knowledge of good and evil, pyrotechnics and all other commodities, until the time to apprentice others had arrived. He shaved the stone into axes, spear points and other forms, but the Braves preferred plucking their beard to scraping with one of his razors. He got fire by rubbing two sticks together.... Knowledge of all

The storyteller

sorts was his. He had power over the animals and the elements, and on one occasion, while engaged in bringing all the wild ferocious animals under the control of man, he changed a big monster into the squirrel for refusing subjection.

Another brute who depended on the thickness of his skin and the depth of his flesh to ward off man's weapons came to grief as his pride deserved and his bones to the end of time are to be a sign that "pride will stand only for a moment."

He then cleared rivers and streams for navigation and before leaving for the Happy Hunting Grounds taught his people how to make Canoes.[19]

Early European Descriptions of Mi'kmaq Character

The complex social character of the early Mi'kmaq was described by many Europeans. Perhaps the writers who did the most justice to the subject were Marc Lescarbot, Pierre Biard, Nicholas Denys and Chrestien Le Clercq. These writers possessed European biases and incorporated them into their writings, but their observations are descriptive and help the reader to understand the values of the civilization. Biard and Le Clercq were Roman Catholic priests and missionaries who lived among the Mi'kmaq for many years. Denys was a businessman and adventurer, and Lescarbot a lawyer and historian. All four left behind extensive diaries, journals and letters that provide a good picture of Mi'kmaq culture as it existed in the early 1600s—if interpreted with an unbiased mind. Lescarbot wrote:

Our savages, though naked, are not void of those virtues that are found in civilized men, for every one has in him, even from his birth, the principles and seeds of virtue. Taking then the four virtues in their order, we shall find that they share largely in them.

For first, concerning fortitude and courage. They have thereof as much as, indeed more than, any nation of the savages. I am speaking of our Mi'kmaq and of their allies, in such sort, that ten of them will always adventure themselves against twenty Armouchiquois; not that they are altogether without fear but, with the courage which they have, they deem that wisdom gives them much advantage.

They fear then, but it is that which all wise men fear, death, which is terrible and dreadful, as she that sweeps away all through which she passes. They fear shame and reproach, but this fear is related to virtue.

They are stirred to do good by honour, forasmuch as he amongst them is always honoured and renowned who has done some fair exploit. Having these characteristics they are in the golden mean, which is the very seat of virtue. One point makes their virtue of force and courage imperfect, they are too revengeful....

Temperance is another virtue, involved in moderation in the matters which concern the pleasures of the body ... in the things of the mind a man is not called temperate or intemperate who is driven by ambition, or with desire to learn, or who employs his time in trifles. Our savages have not all the qualities requisite for the perfection of this virtue, for when they have wherewith they eat perpetually, going so far as to rise in the night to banquet.

Liberality is a virtue as worthy of praise as greed and excessiveness, her opposites, are blameworthy. Our savages are praiseworthy in the practice of this virtue, according to their poverty; for as we have said before, when they pay visits to one another, they exchange presents. And when some French Sagamos visits them they do the like with him, casting at his feet a bundle of beaver or other furs, which are all their riches.... This custom of the said savages could not come but from a liberal mind, with much of good in it....

And to show the high-mindedness of our savages, they do not willingly bargain, and content themselves with that which is given them honestly, disdaining and blaming the fashions of our petty merchants, who bargain for an hour to beat down the price of a beaver skin.... In short they have nothing but frankness and liberality in their exchanges.[20]

Biard makes similar statements but also contradicts himself, seeming to be uncomfortable about praising the Mi'kmaq:

In truth, they are by nature fearful and cowardly, although they are always boasting, and do all they can to be renowned and to have the name of "Great Heart." "Great Heart," among them, is the crowning virtue.

If the offenses are not between Nations, but between compatriots and fellow-citizens, then they fight among themselves for slight offenses, and their way of fighting is like that of women here. [This probably means that they showed their emotions when engaged in disagreements with family and friends—only natural in a society based upon free human expression.] The little offenses and quarrels are easily adjusted by the Sagamores and common friends.

And in truth, as far as we know, they are hardly ever offended long. I say, as far as we know, because we have never seen anything except ... great respect and love among them; which was a great grief to us when we turned our eyes upon our own shortcomings.

They are in no wise ungrateful to each other, and share everything. No one would dare to refuse the request of another, nor to eat without giving him a part of what he has. Once when we had gone a long way off to a fishing place, they passed by five or six women or girls, heavily burdened and weary. Our people through courtesy gave them some of our fish, which they immediately put to cook in a kettle that we loaned them.

Scarcely had the kettle begun to boil when a noise was heard, and other savages could be seen coming; then our poor women fled quickly into the woods, with their kettle only half boiled, for they were very hungry. The reason for their flight was that, if they had been seen, they would have been obliged by a rule of politeness to share with the newcomers their food, which was not too abundant.

We had a good laugh then, and were still amused when they, after having eaten, seeing the said savages around the fire, acted as if they had never been near there and were about to pass us all by as if they had not seen us before, telling our people in a whisper where they had left the kettle; and our people, like good fellows ... knew enough to look unconscious, and to better carry out the joke, urged them to stop and taste a little fish. But they did not wish to do anything of the kind, they were in such a hurry, saying, many thanks, many thanks. Our people answered: "Now may God be with you since you are in such a hurry."[21]

Biard's comment that the Mi'kmaq were "cowardly" was related to the "guerrilla" techniques they used when conducting a war. The Europeans felt their own method of sending wave after wave of soldiers out into the open to be slaughtered was the proper one. The Mi'kmaq style of warfare was designed to keep casualties to a minimum. They saw no value in sending their male relatives and friends to war without allowing them as much chance to survive as possible. Their methods of war were not only sensible but smart. As time passed, the American colonists saw the value of the Amerindian method and used it to their advantage to defeat the English during their War of Independence.

Denys wrote of the Mi'kmaq:

The law which they observed in old times was this, to do to another only that which they wished to be done to them. They had no worship, all lived in good friendship and understanding. They refused nothing to one another, if one wigwam or family had not provisions enough, the neighbours supplied them.... And in all other things it was the same. They lived pure lives; the wives were faithful to husbands, and the girls very chaste.[22]

Le Clercq provides the best description and seems to be the least affected by European biases:

They walk with dignity as if they had always some great affair to think upon, and to decide.... They all have naturally sound minds, and common sense beyond which is supposed in France. They conduct their affairs cleverly, and take wise and necessary steps to make them turn out favourably. They are very eloquent and persuasive among those of their own nation, using metaphors and very pleasing circumlocutions in their speeches, which are very eloquent, especially when they are pronounced in councils and public assemblies....

Our Gaspesians can call themselves happy, because they have neither avarice nor ambition, those two cruel executioners which give pain and torture to a multitude of persons.

They have neither police, nor taxes, nor office, nor commandment which is absolute, for they only obey their head men and chiefs in so far as it pleases them. They scarcely give themselves the trouble to amass riches, or to make a fortune more considerable than that which they possess in their woods. They are content enough, provided they have the wherewithal for living, and that they have the reputation of being good warriors and good hunters, in which they reckon their glory and ambition.

They are naturally fond of their repose, putting away, as far as they can, all subjects for annoyance which would trouble them. Hence it comes about that they never contradict anyone, and that they let everyone do as he pleases, even to the extent that the fathers and mothers do not dare correct their children, but permit their misbehaviour for fear of vexing them by chastising them.

They never quarrel and never are angry with one another, not because of any inclination they have to practice virtue, but for their own satisfaction....

Indeed, if any natural antipathy exists between husband and wife, or if they cannot live together in perfect understanding, they separate, in order to seek elsewhere the peace and union which they cannot find together. Consequently, they cannot understand how one can submit to the indissolubility of marriage. "Dost thou not see," they will say to you, "that thou hast no sense? My wife does not get on with me, and I do not get on with her. She will agree well with such a one who does not agree with his own wife. Why dost thou wish that we four be unhappy for the rest of our days?"

In a word, they hold it as a truism that each one is free. They believe that one can do whatever they wish, and that it is not sensible to put constraints upon men. It is necessary, say they, to live without annoyance and disquiet, to be content with what one has, and to endure with constancy the misfortunes of nature, because the sun, or he who has made and governs all, orders it thus.

If someone among them laments, grieves, or is angry, this is the reasoning with which they console him: "Tell me, my brother, wilt thou always weep? Wilt thou always be angry? Wilt thou come nevermore to the dances and the feasts of the Gaspesians? Wilt thou die, in the weeping and in the anger in which thou art at present?" If he who laments and grieves answers him no, and says that after some days he will recover his good humour and his usual amiability, they respond: "Well, my brother ... thou hast no sense; since thou hast no intention to weep nor to be angry always, why dost thou not commence immediately to banish all bitterness from thy heart, and rejoice thyself with thy fellow-countrymen?"

This is enough to restore repose and tranquillity to the most afflicted of our Gaspesians. In a word, they rely upon ... not becoming attached to the goods of the earth, in order not to be grieved or sad when they lose them. They are, as a rule, always joyous, without being uneasy as to who will pay their debts.

They have the fortitude and the resolution to bear bravely the misfortunes which are usual and common to all men. This greatness of spirit shows grandly in the fatigues of war, hunting, and the fishery, in which they endure the roughest labours with an admirable constancy....

It is very rarely that the sick one complains. He is content with that which he is given, and takes without repugnance whatever is presented to him for the purpose of restoring him to his original health.

Also they endure with patience the severest punishments when they are convinced that they deserved them. They even make considerable presents to those who punish them severely for their misbehaviour, in order, they say, to remove from the hearts of the former all the bitterness caused by the crime of which they are guilty. They always allege, as their usual excuse, that they had no sense when they had committed such and such actions.

When they are convinced at length of their fault, one can threaten to break their bones with blows of clubs, to pierce their bodies with swords, or to break their heads with guns, and they will submit to these punishments. "Strike me," say they, "and kill me if thou wilt; thou art right to be angry. I am wrong to have offended thee."

It is not the same, however, when they are ill-treated without cause, for then everything is to be feared from them.... They preserve resentment for the ill-treatment in their hearts until they are entirely avenged for the injury or for the affront which will have been wrongly done them.

They do not know what it is, as a rule, to give up an enterprise which they once have formed, especially if it is public and known to their fellow-countrymen; for they fear to incur the reproach ... that they did not have heart enough to carry out the design.

They are so generous and liberal towards one another that they seem not to have any attachment to the little they possess, for they deprive themselves thereof very willingly and in very good spirit the very moment when they know that their friends have need of it. It is true that this generous disposition is undergoing some alteration since the arrival of the French. The French, through the commerce they have had with them, have gradually accustomed them to trade, and to not give anything for nothing. Prior to the time when European trade came into use among these people, it was as in the Golden Age, and everything was common property among them.

Hospitality is in such great esteem among our Gaspesians that they make almost no distinction between the home-born and the stranger. They give lodging equally to the French and to the Indians who come from a distance, and to both they distribute generously whatever they have obtained in hunting and in the fishery, giving themselves little concern if the strangers remain among them for weeks, months and even entire years. They are always good-natured to their guests, whom, for the time, they consider as belonging to the wigwam, especially if they understand even a little of the Gaspesian tongue.

You will see them supporting their relatives, the children of their friends, the widows, orphans, and old people, without ever expressing reproach for the support or the other aid which they give them. It is surely necessary to admit that this is a true indication of a good heart and a generous soul.

Consequently it is truth to say that the injury most felt among them is the reproach that an Indian is … stingy. This is why, when one refuses them anything, they say scornfully, "Thou art a mean one," or else, "Thou likest that; like it then as thou wishest, but thou wilt always be stingy and a man without a heart."

They are sweet-tempered, peaceable, and tractable, having much charity, affection, and tenderness for one another: good to their friends, but cruel and pitiless to their enemies: wanderers … but industrious nevertheless, and very clever in all that they undertake, even to making the stocks of guns as well as it can be done in France.

I can say with truth that I have specially devoted myself to the mission of the Gaspesia because of the natural inclination the Gaspesians have for virtue. One never hears in their wigwams any impure words, not even any of those words which have a double meaning. Never do they in public take any liberty, I do not say criminal alone, but even the most trifling; no kissing, no banter between young persons of different sexes; in a word, everything is said and is done in their wigwams with much modesty and reserve.

All the Gaspesians must without fail aid the sick; and those who have meat or fish in abundance must give some of it to those who are in need.

It is considered shameful to show anger or impatience for the insults that are offered, or the misfortunes which come, to the Indians. Unless it is to defend the honour and reputation of the dead, who cannot, they say, avenge themselves, nor obtain satisfaction for the insults and affronts done them.[23]

The word "savage" (*sauvage* in French) used by these four scribes and other early historians when describing Amerindians is a reflection of the racial biases that Europeans harboured at that time. The word was not then and is not now a fitting description. According to Webster's *New World Dictionary*, it means:

Adjective: belonging to a wood; wild. 1. wild; uncultivated; rugged; etc. 2. fierce; ferocious; untamed. 3. without civilization; primitive; barbarous. 4. lacking polish; crude; rude. 5. cruel; pitiless. 6. furious; ill-tempered. Noun: 1. A member of a preliterate society having a primitive way of life. 2. A fierce, brutal person. 3. A crude, boorish person.[24]

Because the Amerindian is none of the above, we must assume that the early writers used the term because of their belief in the superiority of their own race. In other words they were racist. Their belief that European civilization was the most superior in the world prevented them from forming unbiased opinions about civilizations that clearly had certain human values superior to their own.

Given their civility, the American peoples would not have used the same degrading terms to describe Europeans. They did think that Europeans were strange dressed in their outlandish clothing and thought they had barbaric habits and customs, but they accepted them as equals, not inferiors.

To be called a "savage" and to be treated like one is the ultimate insult to an Amerindian. The term was never applicable and should never be used unless citing historical quotes. The glimpses of the Mi'kmaq offered by Lescarbot, Biard, Denys and Le Clercq do not reveal an uncultured, uncivilized and barbarous people. Instead, they show a sensitive, generous, caring and progressive people who had not developed their technologies as fast as they had developed the social fabric of their societies. One can even detect hints of envy when these writers describe the loving and caring nature of Mi'kmaq civilization.

Trade and Commerce

Prior to Columbus, the Nations of the Americas had economies linked together by need. Horticultural Nations traded farm produce for the pelts and meat of hunting countries. Salt and other minerals that were scarce in one territory could be acquired in exchange for products or produce in another. In many instances, the Nations traded with were located halfway across the continent. For example, artifacts found in the 1980s at White's Lake, Halifax County, were left behind by Amerindian traders from the Ohio river valley in the United States. The trading patterns of the American Nations were not entirely dissimilar to those found among the nations of Europe.

Shortly after the European invasion began in earnest these time-tested and mutually beneficial trading patterns quickly fell by the wayside. The infusion of new wares and foodstuffs from Europe soon eroded the centuries-old, mutually beneficial relationships that the Mi'kmaq and other Amerindians had established. Amerindian social values were by the end of the seventeenth century profoundly altered for the worse by the new traders. The freedom from greed and dishonesty that had served the People well for countless centuries was slowly replaced by European values concerning acquisition. These transformations took several centuries to come about because the People valued and revered the social systems they and their cherished ancestors had created. In the end, radical changes were reluctantly made based on the need to survive.

In the new system, wealth exchanged hands and came to be viewed as a necessity to purchase European goods. Notions of personal property and obligations to pay debts owed to another were alien to Amerindian thinking and it took the People a long time to accustom themselves to them. Jaenen explains:

> The French often commented on the absence of a sense of exclusive ownership of goods and lands among both nomadic bands and sedentary tribes. The observation of an officer at Louisbourg is typical of such comments: "They are also very uncurious of paying the debt they contract, not from natural dishonesty, but from their having no notion of property, or of owing a debt. They will sooner part with all they have, in the shape of a gift, than with anything in that of payment. Honours and goods being all in common amongst them, all the

numerous vices, which are founded upon those two motives, are not to be found in them."[25]

Eventually, learning the hard way through negative experiences with European traders, the Mi'kmaq and other Amerindians became more adept at using the European barter and monetary systems. They knew the value of their wares and demanded a fair price in exchange. Honourable European traders accepted this state of affairs, but the dishonourable among them, of which there were many, turned to another means to extract wares and real property without paying an honest return—alcohol. (The devastating effect of this poison is examined in Chapter 3.)

In trade and land acquisition, Europeans adopted the gift-giving practices of the Amerindian Nations. For the Mi'kmaq, the exchange of presents was intended to create a brotherly atmosphere, but it had different connotations for most European traders and real-estate procurers. However, French authorities, in particular, appreciated that gifts and trade with the Amerindians were essential for reasons other than financial profit. Le Maire's memo of 1717 expressed their position nicely:

> The trade with the Indians is a necessary commerce, and even if the Colonists could get along without it, the State is, as it were, forced to maintain it, if it wishes to hold onto the country, unless one wished to adopt the cruel decision of destroying all the Natives, which is contrary at once to both nature and Religion. There is no middle course; one must have the Native either as friend or foe; and whoever wants to have him as a friend must furnish him with his necessities at conditions which allow him to procure them. Already one hears only murmuring among our new Allies, and even among our old ones; and one and the other are at the point of slipping away from us.[26]

The French and British profited handsomely from these trade exchanges, as did the Mi'kmaq initially. However, while satisfying the insatiable appetite of the new traders, the Mi'kmaq were participating in the destruction of their own traditional means of livelihood. The animals that provided fur and meat became more scarce and eventually an unreliable commodity to exchange with Europeans for what had become essentials of life. The People soon came to appreciate that they lacked the kind of education and experience needed to participate effectively in the new economic order. Thus the die was cast for the decline and near extinction of their culture.

The disruption and eventual destruction of traditional trading patterns by European intrusion was a major factor in hastening the end of independence for indigenous American Nations.

3

European Greed and
the Mi'kmaq Resolve to Fight

Where today are the Pequot? Where are the Narragansett, the Mohican, the Pokanoket, and many other once powerful tribes of our people? They have vanished before the avarice and the oppression of the white man, as snow before a summer sun.—Tecumseh

On June 24, 1497, John Cabot laid claim on behalf of England's King Henry VII to what thereafter would be called Newfoundland. The fact that the land was then owned and occupied by human beings whose residency stretched back for millennia was not viewed by Cabot or England as a legal impediment to this claim. In addition to appropriating another Nation's land, Cabot's explorations revealed for future European exploitation the region's fabulously endowed fishing grounds. These events soon led to a full-scale European invasion of northeastern North America.

In retrospect, the speed at which the news of the wealth of the Newfoundland fishing grounds spread around Europe in an age without mass communications seems incredible. This news spread so fast and proved so alluring that within a very short period of time European fishermen began arriving en masse. By 1506, only nine years later, the fishery was so large that the Portuguese government was taxing it. This uncontrolled and largely unpoliced foreign fishery would prove to be extremely bad news for the region's Amerindian peoples. In fact, the nature of the bad news was visited upon one Amerindian Nation almost immediately. The intruders launched a murderous assault on Newfoundland's harmless and non-aggressive Beothuk (or Red People) in retaliation for the "crimes" they were committing by removing items, such as nails, from the fishermen's fish-drying stations along the coast. As early as 1506, many of the Beothuk were being sold as slaves in Europe. In time these barbarities led to the extinction of the Tribe.

Mi'kmaq Decline
Not satisfied with the massive wealth being generated by the new fishery, Europeans soon set their sights westward in hopes of finding other means to enrich themselves. Thus French Bretons made the first confirmed European contact with Cape Breton Island and mainland Nova Scotia in 1504. However, European fishermen left these lands mostly untouched until about 1540. During the following decade, because the Newfoundland fishery had become so overcrowded, many began to establish stations along the coasts of what is now Nova Scotia. The invasion had begun.

Thus the Mi'kmaq earned the dubious distinction of being among the first North American Natives to come into major contact with Europeans. Because of the scarcity of reliable information related to events in the area during the early

V.GLOADE

An ocean unsafe

1500s, one can only speculate about what the Mi'kmaq were thinking about the intrusion. Assuming that their fishing and trading activities would have made them aware of the horrors being suffered by the Beothuk, one can conclude that they probably had a strong premonition of bad things to come. It is not much of a stretch to further conclude, given the well-documented and horrific assaults against lightly armed Amerindians by heavily armed Europeans at many locations in the Americas, that bad things were already happening. It doesn't appear that the Mi'kmaq were involved at the time in open hostilities with the fishermen, but they could easily have fallen victim to the slave trade.

Fishermen participating in this repugnant activity would have put unaccompanied individuals and small groups of Mi'kmaq at high risk, because selling Amerindian captives to Europe's slave traders was a very lucrative sideline for some of them. Therefore, one can assume that more than a few Mi'kmaq mysteriously disappeared while out fishing and hunting and, unbeknownst to their fellow citizens, ended up being killed or sold into slavery. Based on this assumption it is probable that Mi'kmaq fishermen were by this time taking pains to avoid being caught on the open water by European fishermen. Fishing in the waters they had fished from time immemorial in canoes that were no match for the speed and firepower of the larger foreign vessels had become a very dangerous enterprise.

Loss of easy access to this large portion of their traditional food resources, coupled with other factors such as alcohol and diseases imported by European fishermen and traders, affected Mi'kmaq survival efforts dramatically and triggered a decline in the Nation's population that continued, aided tremendously by wars with the British, for roughly 347 years before being arrested in 1867.

This poses a timeless question: How can a credible estimate of the pre-Cabot Mi'kmaq population be established in order to measure the extent of the decline? The lack of reliable records for the period makes this task very difficult. Experts have offered estimates ranging from a credible half million to a ridiculous two thousand. My own estimate is 200,000 minimum.

Here is how I arrived at this figure. I considered that there had to be a significant population of Mi'kmaq remaining by 1800, because at that time, even though the People were in dire straits, the English were still wary of them. Then I considered the horrendous genocide the People had endured up to that time. I also took into account these known facts: (1) an abundant and healthy food supply was available, (2) Grand Chief Membertou at an advanced age recalled to the missionaries that in his younger days, during the time of Cartier's mid-1530s explorations, the Mi'kmaq were as plentiful as the hairs on his head, (3) at the time the Grand Chief recalled these memories in the early 1600s, his forces were still large enough within his own District to cause the Europeans to treat him with respect and (4) the People had occupied the area for over five thousand years and had presumably done all the natural things that cause a population to grow.

But perhaps the most important consideration was the vast size of Mi'kmaq territories. In the year 2000, with well over two million people residing in our territory, the land is still largely unoccupied. The size of the territory would have required a large population to produce enough Warriors to defend it from invasion by the Mi'kmaq's historic and numerous enemy, the Iroquois. Without a substantial army of warriors to stop them, such formidable enemies as the Mohawk would have easily overrun the territory. Based on all these facts, even an estimate of 200,000 seems rather low.

Among the many factors involved in causing the population decline, alcohol contributed significantly. It was first introduced into Mi'kmaq communities by traders in the form of brandy in the early part of the sixteenth century, probably as early as 1520. Because the Mi'kmaq had no prior contact with it, and thus no tolerance for its effects, the substance caused the People to react in a very uncharacteristic manner, doing severe damage to themselves and their loved ones. There are reports that some traders actually sold brandy with the hope of witnessing the spectacle that might ensue. Le Clercq, in outrage, describes the situation:

> Injuries, quarrels, homicides, murders, parricides, to this day the sad consequences of the trade in brandy.... One sees with grief Indians dying in their drunkenness, strangling themselves, the brother cutting the throat of the sister, the husband breaking the head of his wife, a mother throwing her child into the fire or the river, and fathers cruelly choking little innocent children whom they cherish and love as much as and more than themselves when they are not deprived of their reason.
>
> They consider it sport to break and shatter everything in the wigwams, and to bawl for hours together, repeating always the same word. They beat themselves and tear themselves to pieces, something which never happens ... r at least very rarely ... when they are sober. The French themselves are not exempt from the drunken fury of these barbarians ... who, through a manifestation of the anger of God, justly irritated against a conduct so little Christian, sometimes rob, ravage, and burn the French houses and stores, and very often descend to the saddest extremes.[1]

The suffering that alcohol initially caused in Mi'kmaq communities is beyond comprehension. The number who died from alcohol poisoning alone must have been in the thousands.

This unfavourable initial reaction to alcohol experienced by the northern North American Natives created for the Europeans a stereotyped mental image about Amerindians and alcohol that has lasted to this day. This image was reinforced for future generations by unprincipled European traders who preceded White settlers across the Americas and traded alcohol to other uninitiated Amerindian peoples, eliciting identical reactions. This stereotype became so strong in White Canadian minds that Canada refused until 1985 to remove from the Indian Act those sections that made it illegal for "Registered Indians" to purchase, possess or use alcohol. I can attest from personal experience that these alcohol-related provisions were strictly enforced. Thousands were charged.

Today, many White Canadians find it hard to believe that countless numbers of irresponsible Registered Indian Canadians of legal age were once prosecuted for possessing or consuming liquor, even as little as a pint of beer. However, many thousands of living Registered Indians, including myself, were incarcerated at one time or another for committing this "heinous crime." Up until the mid-1970s, it was common practice for the RCMP and other police forces to arrest us for liquor offenses stipulated under the Act, and for judges to enter convictions almost automatically. Because of poverty and lack of funds among the People to pay fines it was not rare for individuals to be locked up for stretches of ten to thirty days.

These arrests often involved many people at once. On one occasion, several dozen men from Indian Brook and Millbrook were locked up for Indian Act liquor offenses at the same time. One Mi'kmaq, who had already been in custody for the same offense for several days prior to the mass arrest had been designated by the jailor to burn trash that day. The next day the jailor told him: "I'll not be permitting you to burn trash again, because you used the smoke to invite half the Mi'kmaq to join you!"

The pea-sized mentality that created the apartheid provisions of the Indian Act and begot such behaviour against a race of people sometimes elicited a chuckle even among us. However, putting aside the mirth, the White supremacist thinking behind the Act degraded and humiliated all who were forced to suffer from it. I was deeply offended by the fact that we suffered such gross humiliation because we were not White, and I took pains to speak up constantly against it, a practice that identified me as an "uppity Indian" and an "Indian troublemaker."

Many of our women were also picked up for Indian Act liquor violations and suffered the same degrading treatment. In addition, many of them suffered the further humiliation of being brutally, and singularly or plurally, raped by those holding them.

With time, Amerindian peoples have developed much the same tolerance for alcohol that other racial groups have. However, the incidence of alcoholism is still far above average in our communities when compared to other groups. This is caused primarily by the loss of self-respect related to the negative impact of the European invasion and is not the result of racial origin. Nevertheless the stereotype lingers.

Although the population was stabilized by 1867, the Registered Indian population in Nova Scotia did not start increasing until the late 1940s.

European Greed

The *New World Dictionary* gives the following definition of "greed" and "greedy":

> Greed 1. excessive desire for getting or having, especially wealth; desire for more than one needs or deserves.... Greedy 1. wanting or taking all that one can get, with no thought of others' needs; desiring more than one deserves or needs.... 2. having too strong a desire for food or drink.... 3. intensely eager ... implies an insatiable desire to possess or acquire something to an amount inordinately beyond what one needs.

Throughout history, whenever the mentality of a people has been corrupted by selfish greed, unimaginable horrors have occurred for humankind. The unquenchable desire to accumulate wealth and the power it begets can grow so strong, if left unchecked, that it kills the conscience of a country. This was the case among European countries during colonial times in the Americas. All were included because none ever protested or made any effort to stop the carnage unleashed on the Americans; guilt by silence is condemnable. Greed created in the ruling class of the empire-building countries of Europe an insatiable need to dominate, gather power, and accumulate wealth. The invasion of the Americas was driven by greed. This is the only credible conclusion that can be made.

This conclusion is strongly supported by the fact that the Europe of the late 1490s was underpopulated and had resources enough to comfortably support tens of millions of additional people. Therefore, no additional land and wealth were required to improve the standard of living of the continent's impoverished masses. All that was needed was a better distribution of existing wealth. However, such was not possible under the political systems then prevalent in Europe without revolution, because the self-serving European aristocracy would not permit it. To ensure that their privileged stations in life were not compromised or threatened by notions of democracy, they had developed a system that guaranteed that dissenters met with quick and often fatal retribution. This autocratic political system they cherished and protected allowed them to amass wealth at the expense of the lower classes without fear of retribution. (Of course, they had to watch their backs when it came to dealing among themselves.) Wages were so low that most workers were effectively held in bondage from cradle to grave.

Unfortunately for the well-being of Europe's poor and middle classes human rights protections were almost nonexistent under the dictatorial political system imposed. Edicts proclaimed by the ruling class were brutally enforced, and horrific tortures were used to force an accused to see the "truth" as the accusor saw it. Altogether, it was not an environment that fostered humane treatment of others. For the initiated, living and being victimized in such a way was probably next to hell; for the uninitiated, the experience would have been indescribable.

Thus, greed twinned with racism caused Europeans to create an indescribable hell for First Nations peoples that had no limitations. Greed also pitted European against European in efforts to hold onto ill-gotten gains. The perpetuators were blind to all except wealth and land acquisition.

To enhance the prospects of satisfying their insatiable appetites for acquisitions, Europeans began to build forts and trading posts in North America by the mid-1500s. Contrary to a popular belief, forts were not initially built to protect White settlements from Amerindians, but rather to reinforce and protect claims to Amerindian territory from overlapping claims by fellow Europeans; and trading posts were built to carry on trade with Amerindian Nations and to establish a presence to support future claims.

At this time, Europeans did not consider Amerindians a serious threat to safety, and a similar perception was held by many Amerindians towards their new guests. This mistaken Amerindian perception quickly changed as news of European barbarities spread. But full realization would come too late to allow the First Nations to unite and take common remedial action.

If in the mid-1500s the American Nations had fully appreciated the threat, organized, and mounted an all-out effort to expel the Europeans, they could have succeeded and European colonization would have been halted. But the lack of coordinated action among them permitted the European incursion to become, for all intents and purposes, irreversible by the late 1600s. Cultural inhibitions set the stage for this disastrous outcome for Amerindians. Their beliefs that most people were honourable and generous and that honourable treatment would elicit an honourable response held them back from responding with violence until it was too late. The early Mi'kmaq were true adherents to this belief. Bernard Gilbert Hoffman portrays them as a people with pacifist tendencies who welcomed strangers with the utmost courtesy:

> The behaviour pattern requisite of any Micmac was such as to virtually eliminate any overt and direct forms of aggression. The ideal man was one who was restrained and dignified in all his actions, who maintained a stolid exterior under all circumstances, who deprived himself of his possessions to take care of the poor, aged, or sick, or the less fortunate, who was generous and hospitable to strangers but implacable and cruel to his enemies, and brave in war.
>   In such a situation, with their "emotions strongly weighed on the side of restraint," not only in enduring the fortuitous circumstances of life, but in all the daily face-to-face relations with others that inevitably must have aroused emotions of annoyance, anger, or a desire to criticize or correct, all of which had to be suppressed for fear of arousing resentment in others, [we see] that individuals must have developed an extreme sensitivity to overtones of anger, or the overt expression of it.... As a result of this psychological pattern, the Micmac developed a stoicism that would have rendered credit to the Stoics.[2]

This stoicism and other values their ancient culture had instilled in them were invaluable in helping the Mi'kmaq survive the initial European intrusion. But it did not prevent the ideals of their society from being severely damaged over time by European trade and settlement. Perhaps the damage could have been contained if the Mi'kmaq had been fortunate enough to be dealing with people who had some humility, but they were not. The two European powers that irreversibly disrupted Mi'kmaq lifestyles each applied their self-perceived cultural superiority when appropriating Mi'kmaq lands, though using drastically different styles.

The English had an ironclad conviction that their own culture was the ultimate. Thus they were blindly determined not to learn about or accept as equal the cultures of the Americas. They sought only the suppression, by assimilation or more forceful means, of the citizens of these cultures. Their ignorance and contempt for the complexities of indigenous civilizations involved the English in centuries of wars with many Amerindian Nations, causing indescribable sufferings on both sides. Because of their attitudes of superiority and contempt, English efforts to settle in Mi'kmaq and other Amerindian territories were strenuously opposed.

By comparison the Mi'kmaq were willing partners of the French. The French respected them as human beings, ate their food and were quite willing to learn about Mi'kmaq culture and adapt to their ways while enjoying the People's hospitality. Most importantly, although they also thought their own culture to be superior, the French did not exhibit an overwhelming desire to make the People conform to French cultural values. And they extended them many courtesies. For example, if a Mi'kmaq family or individual moved to France, they were accorded all the benefits of citizenship, and full French citizenship if they desired. No genocidal actions were taken. Consequently, French settlement in Nova Scotia did not encounter organized Mi'kmaq resistance.

However, the fact remains that both England and France were in North America to acquire wealth and power. Neither, as some would have us believe, were here to spread noble ideals, and the same applies to other European intrusions into the Americas. And, without a doubt, it was their blind desire to appropriate land and other wealth that was the cause of the barbarism they perpetrated against the peoples of the Americas. Thus, European countries had no moral justification to mount military offensives against Amerindians whom they were dispossessing of everything, including their lives, simply because these people chose to fight back. There are no excuses for committing murderous theft!

Unfortunately, the lust for acquisitions and power possessed by Europeans were not traits instilled in most Amerindian peoples. I say "unfortunately" because this lack, although commendable in a moral sense, reduced the Natives' survival chances tremendously. If they had known what greed was and how to deal with it, this knowledge would have limited and prevented a great deal of the carnage. However, because they were unable to conceptualize how greed might twist minds so that a country and its citizens could visit unthinkable evil on other peoples, they were sitting ducks for the Europeans whose familiarity with greed was expert.

It was this inability to conceptualize societal greed and the notion of personal ownership of Mother Earth that prevented the Mi'kmaq from appreciating the motives behind French and English hostilities in Acadia. Evidence shows that well into the nineteenth century many Mi'kmaq still believed that land could not be owned or sold by human beings.

Thus, in the late 1500s, when the British and the French began a struggle that would last for more than a century and a half over ownership of their territories, the Mi'kmaq would have been astounded if they had known it was all about acquisition. And they would have been more than a little peeved had they known that the Europeans were struggling to claim land that the Great Spirit had reserved for their own use. What the Mi'kmaq were witnessing for the first time was the spectacle of two nations drawing each other's blood solely motivated by greed.

The European passion for acquisition caused incomprehensible damage in the Americas. In fact one can state without fear of contradiction by any but White supremacists that the carnage and destruction wrought upon the Americas in the European pursuit of wealth remains unmatched in human history. Four centuries after the European invasion began, all the civilizations of two continents lay in ruins and the remaining people were dispossessed and impoverished. The uncontested victors were greed and racism.

When comparing the destruction caused in the Americas to other atrocities perpetuated by mankind elsewhere, not even the carnage caused by Adolph Hitler's mad thirst for power during the Second World War comes close. Although Hitler badly damaged many civilizations, they have all recovered; in the Americas none have!

The following is possibly the first official account of an assault upon the Mi'kmaq related to acquisition. It happened in Cape Breton in 1593:

Here diverse of our men went on land upon the very cape, where ... they found the spits of oak of the savages which had roasted meat a little before. And as they viewed the country they saw diverse beasts and fowls, as black foxes, deer, otters, great fowls with red legs [probably wild turkeys], penguins [possibly puffins or murres], and certain others.

But having found no people here at this our first landing, we went again on shipboard and sailed a farther four leagues to the west of Cape Breton, where we saw many seals. And here having need of fresh water, we went again on shore. And passing somewhat more into the land, *we found certain round ponds, artificially made by the savages to keep fish in*, with certain weirs in them made to take fish.

To these ponds we deployed to fill our casks with water. We had not been long here, but there came one savage with black long hair hanging about his shoulders, who called unto us, waving his hands downward towards his belly, voicing these words, *calitogh, calitogh*: as we drew towards him one of our men's musket unawares shot off, whereupon he fell down, and rising up suddenly again, he cried, thrice with a loud voice, *chiogh, chiogh, chiogh*.

Thereupon nine or ten of his fellows running right up over the bushes with great agility and swiftness came toward us with white stakes in their hands, like half pikes, and their dogs of colour black, not so big as Greyhounds, followed them at the heel, but we retired unto our boat without any hurt at all received.

Now be it one of them broke an hogshead [cask] which we had filled with fresh water, with a great branch of a tree which lay on the ground. Upon which occasion we bestowed a half a dozen musket shots upon them, which they avoided by falling flat to the earth, and afterwards retired themselves to the woods.

One of the savages, which seemed to be their captain, wore a long mantle of animal skins hanging on one of his shoulders. The rest were all naked except for their privates, which were covered with a skin tied behind. After they had escaped our shot, they made a great fire on shore, belike to give their fellows warning of us.[3]

The first shot fired was probably not an accidental discharge; for when the English had retired safely to their boat and were in no immediate danger, they fired other shots, not over but at the Mi'kmaq. The mention that the Mi'kmaq were engaged in fish farming at this time in history is most interesting. It appears that modern Mi'kmaq fish farmers are following a long-established tradition. And, in view of this, the White man's belief that he himself was the first to start fish farming in North America needs revisiting!

In the pursuit of accumulating wealth many underhanded practices were used by European traders to extract goods from Amerindians, and alcohol was high among them. Brandy trading, besides being a significant factor in population decline, was heavily used for the purpose. Once the Amerindians had become intoxicated, traders could acquire their goods at little or no cost and realize enormous profits.

This immoral method of making profits was made even more effective by the fact that the Amerindian, having virtually no experience with alcohol, was very vulnerable to addiction. Unscrupulous traders even provided liquor free to encourage addiction, because they knew that with addiction came the need to acquire money to purchase the product and that the addict would sell off goods that belonged to the entire community to acquire it.

The same reprehensible strategy was used to acquire lands. To induce individual Mi'kmaq to sign papers that purported to transfer title to lands, men without honour would entice a few of them to participate in an alcoholic binge. Even with the knowledge that these land deals had been made fraudulently, European colonial governments simply closed their eyes to the thefts and afterwards sought means to legitimize them. The illegal appropriation became so prevalent that in 1763 the British Crown issued a Royal Proclamation declaring that such deals were of no value. But the proclamation was virtually ignored and no European was ever prosecuted for violating its provisions.

Perhaps, in hindsight, nothing could have stopped the theft, because profiteering by any means possible by governments, individuals and institutions at the expense of others was and still is, to an unacceptable degree, a trait well ingrained in Europeans. Over the centuries, this trait has led to the plundering and destruction of entire civilizations worldwide. Conflicts caused by the pursuit of wealth can be traced to the dim beginnings of European history. In modern times it has ignited wars that have killed tens of millions of people and led to the production of weapons so deadly that life on Mother Earth could be extinguished if they were used. This was the mentality that begot the early traders who came to the Americas with agendas of mayhem and plunder.

In contrast, there is no evidence to indicate that the Mi'kmaq ever maliciously organized an assault upon any human population with cruel plunder in mind. This kind of conduct would have been morally unacceptable to them. Thus they were ill-prepared for commercial exchanges with the experienced Europeans. They were ripe for greedy people to pick, and picked they were.

European Settlement

The first unofficial European settlement may have been established in Cape Breton as early as 1525. It was recorded that a group of settlers left Europe for Newfoundland around that time but found the climate too cold and sailed westward until they came to a coast that seemed more hospitable. There they found the soil fertile and the natives friendly; however, after some time one finds no further record of them. One logical explanation is that these settlers were among the first Europeans to be converted to the indigenous way of life.

No further attempts at settlement were made by the Europeans until 1604. At that time, under the stewardship of De Monts and Samuel de Champlain, the French made their first official attempt to establish a settlement in Nova Scotia they christened Port-Royal. The attempt lasted two years and several months. Marc Lescarbot, who recorded the event in detail, came to the colony with relief ships sent from France in 1606, remaining until the settlement was abandoned in 1607.

The harsh climatic conditions the ill-prepared French found in northeastern North America in the early stages of their colonization efforts seemed to present them with an insurmountable barrier. Those who first tried to settle in Mi'kmaq territory suffered terribly from the cold temperatures and disease and died off in large numbers. Eventually, in a display of compassion, but to the People's long-term detriment, the Mi'kmaq would provide the French with the knowledge and skills they needed to survive in the new environment.

After an absence of three years, the French, showing determination under the leadership of Jean de Poutrincourt, re-established their settlement at Port-Royal in 1610. The colony again experienced difficulty with scurvy but, with Mi'kmaq help, persevered. In the fall, Poutrincourt sent his son Biencourt back to France with a load of furs. During his stay in France, Biencourt went to the French court to deliver his condolences to the Queen over the death of the King. There he was greeted with a request to transport two Jesuit priests to the Americas, Fathers Pierre Biard and Ennemond Massé. Thus began the Jesuit influence among the first Americans.

From this point onward a continual game of brinkmanship was played between the French and the English in North America. In 1613 the British Governor decided to remove the French colonies from the fur trade by pillaging and burning the settlements at Port-Royal and St. Croix, in what became Maine. This was accomplished with the assistance of a warship from the Jamestown colony of Virginia, commanded by Samuel Argall. The attack was initiated in full knowledge that France and England were officially at peace.

After Argall's raid and the subsequent departure of French forces, a good many of the original Acadian settlers remained in the colony without formal protection from anyone except the Mi'kmaq. An explanation of sorts of the Acadian situation was given in the report of an English commissioner:

> The remainder of this French colony after 1613, not having occasion to be transported to France, stayed in the country. Yet, they were neglected by France not owning them.... They were ... supplied in that which was necessary for them by voluntary adventurers, who came to trade, in hopes of acquiring their

commodities in exchange for what they brought.

After ... the Scottish colony was planted at Port Royal, they and the French who dwelt there ... met with the Commanders of the Mi'kmaq, called by them Sagamoes.... One of the Chiefs of them, called Sagamo Segipt ... came in the name of the rest, to His Majesty's Subjects, craving only to be protected by His Majesty, who did promise to protect them.

Monsieur La Tour, who was Chief Commander of the few French then in that Country, being neglected, as was said, by his own Countrymen, and finding His English Majesty's title not so much ... questioned ... did along with the same Sagamo, come requiring and demanding the like protection in the name of the French who live here.

So that His Majesty ... by possession of His Majesty's Subjects, by the removal of the French, who had seated themselves at Port Royal, and by Monsieur La Tour, commander of them there his turning tenant, and by the voluntary giving tenants of the rest to His Majesty ... willingly offering their obedience unto His Majesty; so that His Majesty is now bound in honour to protect them.[4]

The unfortunate part of this event is that the Mi'kmaq, probably in hopes of accommodating their guests the Acadians, mistakenly gave the English the impression that they were willing to submit to English rule. However, the Mi'kmaq located around Port-Royal at that time were only a small fraction of the District's total population and would not have had the authority to commit the other Districts or, for that matter, their own to any long-term arrangement.

As a result of the English raids, the French government abandoned its settlements in Acadia and no further attempts were made to settle the area between 1613 and 1621. England then stepped into the picture and made a grant to Sir William Alexander of what is today Nova Scotia, New Brunswick, Prince Edward Island, part of the State of Maine, and eastern Quebec south of the St. Lawrence River. The area covered by this grant was called New Scotland.

During this period, between 1621 and 1630, the English made several half-hearted attempts to settle in the Port-Royal area. Then, in 1632, England and France signed the Treaty of Saint-Germain-en-Laye, which returned Port-Royal and Quebec to France. With the evacuation of most of England's settlers, France was free to make another attempt to colonize the province.

The Mi'kmaq of this period seem to have taken a neutral position and continued to maintain cordial relations with both parties. Several theories are advanced about this state of affairs: some hold that they were simply being diplomatic, and others assert they were waiting to see who would win the war. Perhaps there is truth in both theories, but neither completely stands up to scrutiny. Probably the best explanation is that the Mi'kmaq, having a relatively large population to draw upon, presented an imposing force of Warriors who had to be reckoned with. This simple fact would have motivated the English and French to court Mi'kmaq neutrality or alliance.

Although they were cautious about the way they treated the Mi'kmaq, the English saw no need to use restraint with the New England First Nations. The means they used to force these people into submission, including bounties for scalps, was brutally inhuman. This violence and a great plague contracted from European fishermen in 1617 completely depopulated some sections of the eastern coast of New England. A report submitted to authorities concerning that sickness stated:

> The hand of God fell heavily upon them with such mortal strokes that they died on heaps as they lay in their houses, and the living that were able to shift for themselves would run away and let them die, and let their carcases lie above the ground without burial.
>
> For in a place where many inhabited, there has been but one left alive, to tell what became of the rest; the living being not able to bury the dead, they were left for crows, kites, and vermin to prey upon. And the bones and skulls upon the several places of their habitations made such a spectacle that as I travelled in that forest ... [of] Massachusetts, it seemed to me a new found Golgotha.[5]

Whether this epidemic spilled over into Mi'kmaq territory is unknown. The Mi'kmaq so revered their dead that they would, even in times of battle, take extraordinary risks to retrieve bodies for proper burial. This practice in later times deprived many of the King's bounty hunters of their payments for human scalps.

After reacquiring control over Nova Scotia in 1632, the French appointed Isaac de Razilly as Governor. Governor de Razilly, Charles de La Tour and Nicholas Denys all received large grants of lands within the province from the French King. The English fort at La Have was taken over and roughly two hundred settlers were sent to the area by French authorities.

Then an episode began that would have, given their values, struck the Mi'kmaq as strange—two Frenchmen fighting between themselves for control of the colony. When Governor de Razilly died in 1636, his position was taken over by Charles D'Aulnay. This appointment precipitated a power struggle with La Tour that lasted until the demise of D'Aulnay in a canoeing accident on the Riviere du Moulin near Port-Royal on May 24, 1650. Following this death, La Tour wrapped up the feud quickly. In 1651 he secured an appointment as Governor and Lieutenant-General in Acadia, and then ended the squabble in 1653 by marrying D'Aulnay's widow.

Now began a bizarre episode. A French gentleman by the name of Emmanuel le Borgne, a creditor of D'Aulnay, obtained a decree in France that allowed him to take over his deceased debtor's grant. The Mi'kmaq must have been astounded by what happened next: a Frenchman arrived with an armed force and destroyed the French settlements at Chedabuctou and La Have.

The fratricidal conflict ended in 1654 when an English force, sailing under orders from Cromwell and the Commonwealth, attacked and took La Tour's forts at Saint John and Port-Royal. From this point onward, the Acadians were pawns in a chess game for power and money played from London and Paris. Control of the colony was under constant review by power brokers in both capitals. This continued until the English and French signed the Treaty of Whitehall in 1686.

Not much information is available about how the Acadian settlements fared during this period. Some researchers indicate that the community's population in

1670 may have been as low as five hundred. This figure is questionable, for by 1755, when the British moved to expel them, their estimated population was twelve thousand.

The population of the Mi'kmaq in the late 1600s, although still declining, was probably fifty thousand or more. In view of what they would endure over the next 150 years, this figure may be on the conservative side, for if it had been any less the Nation could not have survived the holocaust yet to come.

The British-French war over the ownership and the right to settle Acadia began to heat up again in the early 1690s. By this time the Colony of Massachusetts Bay was fast becoming a power of its own in North American political and military affairs and had begun to make independent military decisions. It decided to renew attacks upon Acadia and dispatched a force under the command of Sir William Phips. New Englanders arrived in Acadia from Boston in 1690, destroying settlements and Port-Royal. This raid was probably *the* incident that ensured that New Englanders would henceforth be considered mortal enemies by the Mi'kmaq. In addition to destroying Acadian settlements, the New Englanders pillaged Mi'kmaq villages near Port-Royal, burnt their mission church and seized the missionaries, imprisoning them at Boston.

The Mi'kmaq were involved in fighting between the French and English in Saint John Harbour in 1691. Sixty Mi'kmaq Warriors were part of the crew of a French warship joined in the battle. This increased involvement in European military confrontations by the Mi'kmaq signified a deepening concern for cultural survival. That particular French-English war came to an end in 1696, when the two parties signed the Treaty of Ryswick. As in the past, this was simply a chance for both parties to rearm and regroup, and they took up arms against one another almost immediately thereafter. However, the Acadian settlements in Nova Scotia continued to flourish despite the hostilities. European settlements were now firmly entrenched.

European Disrespect for Mother Earth

One particularly unwelcome aspect of European civilizations that English and French settlers brought to Mi'kmaq territory was a well-developed expertise in how to pollute and destroy Mother Nature. Their uncontrolled industrial development would eventually turn whole parts of the Americas into wastelands. The People who welcomed the Europeans would today be extremely dismayed to see the damage that has been done to Mother Earth. Two examples: In the year 2000, the Sydney tar ponds site had the unenviable distinction of being the most polluted site in Canada, and Halifax Harbour was an open sewer.

In 1854, President Franklin Pierce offered to buy Amerindian lands in what is today Washington State. A letter reputed to be Chief Seattle's response to his offer is a profound and eloquent description of how the Amerindian viewed the human relationship with nature:

> How can you buy or sell the sky, the warmth of the land? The idea is strange to us. If we do not own the freshness of the air, and the sparkle of the water, how can you buy them?

Every part of this earth is sacred to my people. Every shining pine needle, every sandy shore, every mist in the dark woods, every clearing, and every humming insect is holy in the memory and experience of my people. The sap that courses through the trees carries the memories of the red man.

The white man's dead forget the country of their birth when they go to walk among the stars. Our dead never forget this beautiful earth, for it is the mother of the red man. We are part of the earth, and it is part of us. The perfumed flowers are our sisters; the deer, the horse, the great eagle, these are our brothers. The rocky crests, the juices in the meadows, the body heat of the pony, and man—all belong to the same family.

So when the Great Chief of Washington sends word that he wishes to buy our land, he asks much of us. The Great Chief sends word he will reserve us a place so that we can live comfortably to ourselves. He will be our father and we will be his children. So we will consider your offer to our land. But it will not be easy. For this land is sacred to us.

This shining water that moves in the streams and the rivers is not just water but the blood of our ancestors. If we sell you land, you must remember that it is sacred, and you must teach your children that it is sacred, and that each ghostly reflection in the clear water of the lake tells of events and memories in the life of my people. The water's murmur is the voice of my father's father.

The rivers are our brothers, they quench our thirst. The rivers carry our canoes and feed our children. If we sell you our land, you must remember and teach your children that the rivers are our brothers, and yours, and you must henceforth give the rivers the kindness you would give any brother.

We know the white man does not understand our ways. One portion of land is the same to him as the next, for he is a stranger who comes in the night and takes from the land whatever he needs. The earth is not his brother but his enemy, and when he has conquered it, he moves on. He leaves his fathers' graves, and his children's birthrights are forgotten. He treats his mother the earth, and his brother the sky, as things to be bought, plundered, sold like sheep or bright beads. His appetite will devour the earth and leave behind only a desert.

I do not know. Our ways are different from your ways. The sight of your cities pains the eye of the red man. But perhaps it is because the red man is a savage and does not understand.

There is no quiet place in the white man's cities, no place to hear the unfurling of leaves in the spring or the rustle of an insect's wings. But perhaps it is because I am a savage and do not understand. The clatter only seems to insult the ears. And what is there to life if a man cannot hear the lonely cry of the whippoorwill or the arguments of the frogs around a pond at night? I am a red man and do not understand. The Indians prefers the soft sound of the wind darting over the face of the pond, and the smell of the wind itself, cleaned by rain or scented with the pine cone.

The air is precious to the red man, for all things share the same breath: the beast, the tree, the man, they all share the same breath. The white man does not seem to notice the air he breathes. Like a man dying for many days, he is numb to the stench. But, if we sell you our land, you must remember that the air is precious to us, that the air shares its spirit with all the life it supports. The wind that gave our grandfather his first breath also received his last sigh. And if we sell you our land, you must keep it apart and sacred, as a place where even the white man can go to taste the wind that is sweetened by the meadow flowers.

So we will consider your offer to buy our land. If we decide to accept, I will make one condition. The white man must treat the beasts of this land as his brothers.

I am a savage and I do not understand any other way. I have seen a thousand rotting buffalos on the prairie, left by the white man who shot them from a passing train. I am a savage and I do not understand how the smoking iron horse can be more important than the buffalo that we will kill only to stay alive.

What is man without the beasts? If all the beasts were gone, man would die from a great loneliness of spirit. For whatever happens to the beasts soon happens to man. All things are connected.

You must teach your children that the ground beneath their feet is the ashes of our grandfathers. So that they will respect the land, tell your children that the earth is rich with the lives of our kin. Teach your children what we have taught our children, that the earth is our mother. Whatever befalls the earth befalls the sons of the earth. Man did not weave the web of life, he is merely a strand in it. Whatever he does to the web, he does to himself.

Even the white man, whose God walks and talks to him as a friend to a friend, cannot be exempt from the common destiny. We may be brothers after all. We shall see. One thing we know, which the white man may one day discover— our God is the same God. You may think that you own Him, as you wish to own our land, but you cannot. He is the God of man, and His compassion is equal for the red man and the white man. This earth is precious to Him, and to harm the earth is to heap contempt upon its Creator. The Whites, too, shall pass; perhaps sooner than all other tribes. Contaminate your bed and you will one night suffocate in your waste.

But in perishing, you will shine brightly, fired by the strength of the God who brought you to this land and for some special purpose gave you dominion over this land and over the red man. That destiny is a mystery to us, for we do not understand when the buffalo are all slaughtered, the wild horses are tamed, the secret corners of the forest heavy with the scent of many men, and the view of the ripe hills blotted out by talking wires. Where is the thicket? Gone. Where is the eagle? Gone.[6]

The prophetic wisdom contained within Chief Seattle's letter gives cause for reflection. The Whites have, to their peril and to the peril of the world's other Tribes, polluted Mother Earth, perhaps to the point of no return. Forests are perishing, lakes are dying, many are already dead, and the land is so poisonous in some locations that life cannot exist.

The atmosphere is under attack. Mindless exploitation of resources has despoiled the air. Acid rain destroys the habitat of the beasts and many scientists warn of the "greenhouse warming trend." The decade of the 1990s was the warmest since

The boy and the beast

the recording of such information began, and 1998 and 1999, in that order, were the two warmest years recorded. The United States weather service has attributed this to global warming. Yet the businessmen pursue almighty profit without pause and disregard environmental damage. Humankind, in the name of greed and profit, has fouled its own bed.

The damage probably can be reversed if we change course and adopt a carefully planned and environmentally sound approach towards realizing our economic expectations. With the preservation of an inhabitable Mother Earth as a global goal we should survive. If we do not meet the needs of nature for renewal, we shall surely perish.

To have come uninvited and then dispossessed the original inhabitants without respect for their rights and freedoms, exchanging grief and destruction for their human kindnesses, may be unforgivable in the eyes of the Great Spirit. However, to despoil Mother Earth to the point where She is unfit to sustain life will be beyond forgiveness because life itself will have been extinguished by our own hands!

The Mi'kmaq Resolve to Fight

The contempt the English displayed towards the Mi'kmaq is an example of human arrogance of immense proportions. This attitude was naturally an affront to the sensibilities of an intelligent people and thus engendered determined opposition. Human beings do not normally sit idly by and watch a foreign power treat them as subhumans and dispossess them of their lives and property without resorting to violence, and the Mi'kmaq were no exception.

In the face of English aggression, the Mi'kmaq and their allies decided to fight for their liberty. As a result, British settlement of the Maritimes, New England and eastern Quebec was realized only with the spilling of much Amerindian blood, creating an atmosphere of animosity and mistrust that to a certain degree still survives.

4

Persecution, War, Alliance
and Terrorism

In a critique of the mistreatment of Amerindians by Europeans, nineteenth-century historian Francis Parkman described how it varied at their hands: "Spanish civilization crushed the Indian; English civilization scorned and neglected him; French civilization embraced and cherished him."[1] Parkman's observation about the English is true, but they also, like the Spanish, crushed the Indian.

Persecution

The barbarism employed by Great Britain, Spain, Portugal and other European Nations to subjugate Amerindian peoples during colonial times, and by the countries they begot in the Americas as a result of colonization, probably exceeds, or at the very minimum equals, the barbaric performances of the twentieth-century regimes of Nazi Germany and the Stalinist Soviet Union combined. Like the people who suffered horribly under those regimes, Amerindians at various times and places over the past five hundred years were imprisoned and executed without trial or recourse, enslaved, tortured, relocated without consent, treated as inferior human beings, subjected to deliberate genocide, and demonized by monstrous lies; children were removed from families, properties were confiscated by the state without compensation, cultures were destroyed and so on.

These inhumanities were carried out and condoned by a White supremacist population under the guise of helping the Christian Church spread its version of enlightenment. To disavow that most of the White population were involved rings hollow, because the evil was known by everyone and largely unopposed—a fact verified by the historical record.

From the before-mentioned it can easily be deduced that the majority's mentality was warped by a combination of religious zealotry, greed and White supremacist beliefs. This combination raised hate levels in Europeans towards Amerindians to the point where conscience died and no wrong was seen in crushing them. This example, along with hundreds of others, prove that there is an evil in most populations just waiting for the right circumstances to erupt. In modern times the horrors committed during the conflicts associated with the breakup of the Yugoslav federation in the 1990s provided an excellent example of this mentality in action.

The event that led European Nations to destroy many of the civilizations of two continents and drastically diminish the remainder resulted from what was an almost impossible accident of fate. If it had not already occurred, it would be virtually impossible to envision.

In 1492, Christopher Columbus, on a sea voyage to chart a shortcut to the Indies, funded by Queen Isabella of Spain, set the stage for the rape of American civilizations by going astray at sea. By chance he eventually landed on a small island in the Caribbean sea populated by a defenseless and friendly pacifist race of people, the Taino. These people were ripe for picking by unscrupulous men, and Columbus and his crew pillaged with impunity. The blind luck that led him to land on this small defenseless island instead of somewhere else along the thousands of miles of North and South American coastline—where people wouldn't have been so complacent—is akin to finding a needle in a haystack.

In retrospect, if he had instead landed in a non-pacifist country, such as that of the Iroquois or Maya, history would have turned out differently. Their Warriors would have fought back ferociously, very probably ending his voyage on the American side of the Atlantic. If this had happened, and no Europeans had appeared for another century, population growth and technology development would have reduced the possibility of European colonization considerably. However, history turned out the way it did and no amount of fantasizing can change that.

Columbus, thinking he was in the Indies, did not waste time paying lip service to the pretence that he was importing "shining" European ideals to the people he mistakenly labelled Indians. Instead he wrote in his journal: "We can send from here, in the name of the Holy Trinity, all the slaves and Brazil wood which could be sold." True to the intent of these words, he initiated the Amerindian slave harvest on his first voyage. When he embarked from the Americas for Spain, it was with a cargo of five hundred Native Americans to be sold on the continental slave markets. Upon landing at Seville, only about three hundred of these unfortunate souls were still alive. These and booty were turned over to Queen Isabella.

The news of the riches offered by Hispaniola and surrounding islands soon spread across Europe. The notion of fabulous wealth for the picking was like a magnet for other European Nations. Within a few years, harvesters from Spain and other European countries were travelling from island to island seeking artifacts, precious metals, spices, and human beings for enslavement. The cruel assault mounted by these people against the defenseless and non-aggressive Taino, who had numbered in the millions in 1492, was so effective that forty years later they were virtually extinct.

In 1493, possibly based on reports of the cruelty inflicted upon the Taino by Columbus and crew during their first trip to the area, the Roman Catholic Church intervened in the plans for the conquest of the Americas by issuing a "Bull," or edict, designed to prevent the enslavement and slaughter of Amerindians. By its issuance the Church acknowledged the capacity of many of its members to commit barbaric acts. In the Bull, Pope Alexander VI stated that the Church condoned conquest if it was designed to bring the people of the Americas into Christian subjugation. However, the Church's own example of inflicting cruel punishment set broad limits and, as the fate of the Taino attests, the Bull did not have the desired effect.

The old saying, "If at first you don't succeed, try, try again," applies to the Church's future efforts. In 1537, in acknowledgement that the slave trade and slaughter were out of control, Pope Paul III issued a Bull entitled "Sublimus Deus," which declared that the Amerindians were "truly men capable of understanding the Catholic faith" and should not be destroyed as opponents of Christianity or enslaved as supposedly inferior and "dumb brutes created for our service." Although the horrors continued unabated, for some reason the Roman Church waited another 102 years before restating its stance in 1639.

To its credit, the Roman Catholic Church, as witnessed by these edicts, at least made some effort to stem the cruelty. The same cannot be said for the Church of England and its associated Churches, or the other Churches created by the Protestant Reformation. These remained virtually mute throughout the centuries of agony for the Amerindian peoples, and only in recent times have several finally apologized. On behalf of the Roman Catholic Church, Pope John Paul II, on March 12, 2000, issued a blanket apology for the sins of Roman Catholics throughout the ages, including the wrongs inflicted on Jews, women and minorities.

The Amerindian slaughter initiated by Columbus's arrival continued unabated in several White jurisdictions of the Americas well into the late twentieth century. And racial oppression, in one form or other, was still running rampant across the Americas in the year 2000. In modern times, in spite of reams of historical material attesting to the contrary, there are still among the White population many apologists for the evils committed by the colonists. Many try to justify what occurred by saying that Europeans had a moral duty to God to use whatever means necessary to convert the Americans to Christianity. In response, I firmly believe that a caring God would disapprove of and be repulsed by the reprehensible methods used by European political and religious leaders in their zeal to instill Christianity in the souls of Native Americans. I know with certainty that the Great Spirit I believe in would not bless such monstrous behaviour.

However, one has to remember that European Christians, deeming themselves "soldiers of God," also used at times some very barbaric methods to instill Christianity in their own people. History clearly details times when Christian religious leaders condoned and participated in the use of the rack, drawing and quartering, burning at the stake and other methods of torture to persuade people to see the light as they themselves saw it.

Other apologists will offer, with conscienceless sincerity, the excuse that Europeans had a moral duty to bring to the Americas the then modern wonders of European technology in order to improve the lives of the Natives. The facts that uncountable millions of Amerindians died as a result of European colonization and that the survivors were reduced to a degrading poverty that prevails to this day contradict such a stupid argument. Try as one might, no valid excuse can be made for the inexcusable.

The notion that the use of any method was permissible to force people to accept Christianity was first used in Europe against non-Christians. Queen Isabella of Spain, for example, subscribed to the belief that non-Christians should not hold property, and financed the voyages of Columbus with monies she had acquired by stripping tens of thousands of Muslims and Jews of their citizenship, deporting them and seizing their assets. It was these warped beliefs about property ownership that set the stage in the Americas for the greatest grand larceny of all time, the theft of two continents.

Christianity's cruel treatment of non-believers unwittingly instilled in believers a conviction that to be racist and intolerant of the differences of others was acceptable. As most of the world's population at the time were non-Christian and non-White, people of colour became synonymous in White minds with heathens.

Raising the level of intolerance for differences were the feuds that racked and split Christianity in the 1500s and onwards. These feuds, caused by Martin Luther's Protestant Reformation and Henry VIII's break from the Roman Catholic Church in the early sixteenth century, encouraged hatred based on Christian affiliation to blossom and grow vigorously, leading to religious wars in Europe. These conflicts laid the groundwork for the religious persecution of Amerindians based on their conversion to a particular Christian sect. Such was especially true for peoples like the Mi'kmaq, who were converted to the Roman Catholic faith by one European power and then ended up under the "jurisdiction" of another that despised Catholics. Even White English Roman Catholics residing in such jurisdictions suffered persecution. However, in the case of the Mi'kmaq, persecution based on affiliation combined with persecution based on colour made life almost intolerable.

The animosity between the Church of England and the Vatican was so deep that White English citizens affiliated with the Roman Catholic Church were disenfranchised in most parts of the British empire. Catholics were not permitted to vote, hold public office or freely practice their religion. This was finally changed in Nova Scotia in 1783 when five Catholic men, led by William Meany, convinced the legislature to repeal the restrictive laws that enforced religious persecution and segregation, thus creating a precedent for the repeal of similar laws throughout the empire. However, separate hospitals, schools and so on for the two faiths existed in the Halifax Metro area and many other areas of Nova Scotia until the 1960s.

Intolerance stemming from these practices is still bearing fruit. One instance, observed at a local department store by my daughter Cerena, is typical. On January 17, 1996, she was within earshot of an Easter display of chocolate Pocahontas dolls, when two women, probably mother and daughter, paused to look at them. The younger woman talked about buying one for her child. The older woman replied, "I wouldn't buy something heathen like that for anybody, let alone ..." as they walked off. Once instilled, unreasonable hatred is hard to expunge. The poverty and general exclusion still suffered by Amerindians today bear witness to its durability.

The unreasonable hatred behind the genocide following the arrival of Columbus in the Americas was very effective, because only one hundred years later a great many Amerindian Nations had already disappeared into extinction. The carnage was massive and brought about without mercy. As Europeans moved into other parts of the Americas, the same pattern was repeated. Thus, four hundred years after the arrival of Columbus the population of the Amerindian Nations had been reduced by more than 95 percent. A possible toll of more than 100 million Amerindian lives had been taken. When you add to this figure the millions of Black people who were killed or had their lives inhumanly disrupted by being forcibly brought to the Americas from Africa—to replace the severely depleted Amerindian source for slaves—the immensity of the cruelty and horror is awesome. The Mi'kmaq population decline during this period probably came close to 99 percent.

The cruelty and lack of compassion Europeans demonstrated in the Americas had been learned in their own countries through ages of indigenous application.

The following is an example of how deeply rooted it was in the mentality of English officials:

> Philipps to Armstrong: Dated, Annapolis, Oct. 24th, 1720.
> Lieut. Jephson, long confined in the garrison, starving with a family of small children, pay being garnisheed for debt, is delivered to A. at the latter's request as prisoner, to go with him to Canso, as easier to live there. Jephson must be forthcoming when wanted.[2]

The cavalier reference in the memo to the fact that small White children are starving within the fort, because their father has defaulted on a debt, reflects the callous attitudes of English officialdom that would severely challenge the Mi'kmaq's very survival.

War: Amerindian versus Amerindian

Prior to the European intrusion, the Nations of the Americas had been at times involved in wars among themselves, and the animosities between some national groups were of long duration. The Mi'kmaq were involved in such an entanglement with the Iroquois. The animosity between the two Nations was some time in the making. Two versions of the same legend, found in Silas T. Rand's *The Legends of the Micmac*, tell how this animosity began and provide insight into the way the North Americans made war:

> 1. In ancient times the Kwedeches [Iroquois] and the Micmacs inhabited the same country on terms of friendship and amity. But in time a quarrel arose; two boys, sons of the respective chieftains, quarrelled, and one killed the other. This was the beginning of a long series of conflicts, in which the Micmacs, being the more *numerous*, were usually victorious.
>
> During those wars a celebrated chief arose among the Micmacs, whose name was Ulgimoo, of whom many strange things are related. He drove the Kwedeches out of the region on the South side of the Bay of Fundy, they having been compelled to cross the Bay in their flight from the enemy; and he urged them on farther and farther towards the North, finally driving them up to Montreal.
>
> The Kwedeches having retired to Goesomaligeg (Fort Cumberland or Fort Beausejour), and from there to Tantama' or Tatamalg (Sackville at the northern tip of Cumberland Basin), before their enemies, and thence on beyond Petgotgoiag or Petitcodiac River. Ulgimoo built a mound and fortification at the place now called Salisbury, New Brunswick, on the Petitcodiac River. The mound still remains.
>
> Ulgimoo lived to be a hundred and three years old; having died twice, and having come to life after having been dead all winter. He was a great magician, and shortly before he died for the last time defeated singlehanded a Kwedech war party of several hundred men.[3]

The salmon harvest

2. On the two opposite banks of the Restigouche, near its mouth, were two towns, one inhabited by Micmacs, and the other by the Kwedeches. They were at peace with each other, and frequently attended each other's festivals.

On one occasion the Micmacs had attended a festival of the Kwedeches; and while the children were engaged in some sort of game, a child of the Micmac party was killed. Nothing, however, was said about it at the time, and it was passed over as an accident. Not long afterwards, the Kwedeches were invited to a feast by the Micmacs, and while they were playing a game the Micmac boys took the occasion to kill two boys of the other side. Nothing was said of the matter, however, and it was passed over as an accident: but the young folks laid it up in their hearts, and awaited an opportunity for revenge.

Spring came, and it was time for the annual salmon run. This year it was the turn of the Micmacs to exploit the first and best fishing ground, which was a considerable distance up the river. Fifty of the younger men therefore left, and prepared for their task. After they had gone the son of the Kwedech chief determined to exact vengeance on them. Collecting a band of warriors without the knowledge of his father or of the old men, he went upstream by land to ambush the fishing party.

At this time the Micmacs were spearing salmon by torchlight. Afterwards they came ashore and began preparing the fish for their suppers, to the accompaniment of much joking and laughing. Suddenly a shower of arrows come at them from all sides, and all of them were killed, except one old man named Tunel, who was a powwow or shaman. Although he had great supernatural power he had been surprised; otherwise he would not have been hurt.

As it was, he was struck in the side by an arrow, and just managed to run to the river and plunge in. There he hid among the boulders on the river bottom, and since his magic power had returned, could stay there as long as he wanted. The Kwedeches hunted for him a long time, and eventually found where he was hiding, but they could not reach him with their spears. The next day he managed to elude them, and passed down the river to his village.

When the Micmacs learned of the massacre a meeting was held with the Kwedeches, and the demand was made that they retire from the place within three days or try the fortunes of war. Since the Micmacs were much the stronger, the Kwedeches decided to withdraw, and immediately began preparations.

. Before they left, the chief of the Micmac made a farewell visit to the chief of the other tribe. "We will continue to be friends," he said. "You will once in awhile think of the place you have left; and when there comes over me a lonely longing to see your face again, I will make you a visit; and when you wish it, you can come down and see us" [this is a declaration of war in ironic, polite speech].

The whole village now departed, and went up by easy stages to Canada, travelling onward till winter, though with long intervals of rest, they halted on the borders of a large lake. There a Micmac war party caught up with them, and in the ensuing battle most of the Kwedech warriors were killed.

Thirty or forty years later, when the children of the Kwedeches had grown up into men and warriors, an attempt was made to avenge their defeat. A war party therefore left for the Micmac country in the winter, but at the Restigouche river it encountered a very old and powerful Micmac magician, who killed so many of them before surrendering that they decided to return home. The Kwedeches tried to torture their prisoner, but his power was too much for them and they finally had to release him.

About a year later the Micmac magician or shaman decided to lead a war party against the Kwedeches. He therefore went to the chief and told him that he was filled with a great longing to visit his friends who had treated him so kindly during his captivity among them. The council was immediately summoned, and the modest request of the shaman stated and debated.

"Our comrade," said the chief, "hankers for a visit to his friends." They decided to gratify him. "How many men do you wish to accompany you?" they asked. "About thirty or forty," he replied. The request was soon filled, and the war party began its journey to the Kwedech country. They took their canoes, and moved on at leisure, going round by the open sea, and entering the St. Lawrence and thus proceeding up into Canada.

The party stopped occasionally on their way to supply themselves with food by hunting. As they approached the enemy's country, they moved cautiously, and encamped for the last night on a high hill that overlooked the Kwedech village, which was located on a stream bottom just around a sudden bend in the river.

From the noise in the village they ascertained that a war party had just returned from a successful attack on their tribe. Overcome with rage, the old shaman rushed into the ceremony, seized the scalps that were being danced over, and escaped. Recovering from their surprise, the Kwedeches seized their arms and prepared for battle. The following morning the battle was joined and the Kwedeches were defeated, but the Micmac returned home sadly diminished in numbers.

A long time later, the Kwedech again attempted to avenge their losses. One of their great war chiefs, known to the Micmacs as Wohooneh, gathered together a party of some fifty warriors, who travelled by canoe to attack the inhabitants of the Miramichi region. Near Tabusintac, however, they were surprised by the Micmac chief Mejelabegadasich, who invited them to a formal trial of arms with his warriors, an invitation which they could not refuse.

A duel between the two chiefs was arranged with the end result being that chief Wohooneh was killed. The remaining Kwedech warriors fought bravely for awhile against great odds, but finally surrendered and made the peace which brought the Micmac-Kwedech war to an end.[4]

A reminder of the animosity, a Mohawk burial ground, is located on an island off Caribou in Pictou County, Nova Scotia. The Warriors interred there drowned during an attempt to make a surprise attack on the local Mi'kmaq.

Wars were not a usual occurrence among North American Nations because community consensus was required. For example, in Mi'kmaq society a District Chief had no authority to make war on his own or in combination with other leaders of his District; instead he had to hold a council among the People to seek permission first. During the council he had to use his oratory skills to try to convince them that the cause was worth the sacrifices. If authorization was denied, that ended it.

However, when warfare was decided upon, elaborate rituals were part of the preparations. Great feasts took place at which Warriors were praised and given presents. To give the warring parties a chance to find an honourable and peaceful solution to their disagreements, feasting also often took place between the adversaries. If a consensus was not found, war commenced.

During the war, if the death toll became unacceptable, a truce was declared and the parties chose an alternative solution. One of the preferred alternatives, if no other solution could be found, was for the leaders of the warring factions to enter into one-on-one combat, with the winner awarded victory. Needless to say, these rules of war put a heavy burden upon leaders to act responsibly. The prospect that they themselves might pay the ultimate price for a reckless or foolhardy adventure provided them with a strong incentive to display wisdom and diplomacy in their exchanges with other Nations.

These wars were rarely fought over material things. The Mi'kmaq mostly fought wars for honour or vengeance. Lescarbot wrote:

Our savages do not found their wars upon the possession of the land. We do not see that they encroach one upon the other in that respect. They have land enough to live on and to walk abroad. Their ambition is limited by their bounds. They make war as did Alexander the Great, that they may say, "I have beaten you"; or else for revenge, in remembrance for some injury received.[5]

Amerindian war-making differed sharply from the practices of the Nations of Europe. Under European political systems, powers to make war were usually concentrated in a few hands. Public consultations, up until recent times, were not even remotely considered.

However, as democracy began to take root among European nations and their colonial offshoots, the war-making prerogatives of the White elite have faded. With more power being placed in the hands of the people, the leaders of these cultures have had to adopt war-making policies similar to those of Amerindian Nations. A modern example was when U.S. President George Bush sought and received almost universal approval in 1991 to conduct a war in the Middle East in order to expel the Iraqis from Kuwait.

War: England versus the Mi'kmaq

From before recorded history until the end of World War II, war and the suffering it creates were an almost constant companion for most Europeans. For the most warlike among them, organized violence was a way of life. From almost continuous conflict, a war mentality was instilled that has caused, and is still causing, many European countries, especially Britain and France, to expend vast resources to produce ever more efficient tools of death and destruction.

This ageless drive among Whites to produce better arms borders on fanaticism. It has been so much a part of Europ and of its former American colonies' history that the White man has earned the dubious distinction of being the father of the overwhelming majority of modern weapons. Considering the countless millions who have died, been maimed or suffered otherwise, the civilizations destroyed and the trillions of dollars of property lost, this is not an accomplishment on which to base one's pride.

As a legacy from the war-making mentality that made them the two most powerful and best-armed Nations on Mother Earth during colonial times, England and France are still at the forefront of munitions production. In spite of being reduced to the second rank in military status, they are two of Europe's three nuclear-armed Nations. This fascination with weapon invention and production that Whites have displayed over the centuries was apparent in a speech made by Great Britain's Queen Elizabeth II at the opening of a war museum in Leeds, England, on March 15, 1996:

> We must not forget the horrors of war. But, at the same time, we must recognize that those horrors have given rise to great deeds, great poetry, great music and great art. The weapons of war, which can be as beautiful as they are terrible, are often products of the very finest design and craftsmanship.[6]

Her comments reflect the White man's desire for excellence and supremacy in this horrific field. Only a person insensitive towards human suffering can see beauty in instruments of death. If one contemplates their intended function such inventions are grotesque.

In comparison to the killing power held by European nations, the Amerindian Nations, armed mostly with bows, arrows and lances, were virtually unarmed.

Thus, when the Europeans turned their lethal modern weapons against them, it was a classic case of bullies battering the weak. Because of this imbalance, the Amerindian desire to defend life and liberty was severely disadvantaged from the beginning. Soon after England and France entered Mi'kmaq territory nursing their mutual hatred, the weapons imbalance preordained that the Mi'kmaq would have to ally themselves with one or the other to assure survival. France got the nod. The factors that made France the easy choice were English White supremacist attitudes and their genocidal mistreatment of Wabanaki allies in New England. The exact date when the Mi'kmaq-French alliance was born is not precisely known, but based on the records, it was around 1652 or shortly thereafter.

With their choice of allies made, the Mi'kmaq were plunged into what was, because of English attitudes, an inevitable life and death struggle with Great Britain that would last for more than a century. The Mi'kmaq would have been astonished if they had known the war would last so long, because their culture demanded that wars be kept short. However, the opposite would be true about the duration of their alliance with the French. In comparison to the length of the alliances they had maintained with the Maliseet and other Amerindian allies, their century-long alliance with the French would have been considered relatively short. But in the context of Amerindian-European alliances, it was long lasting. In fact such alliances were rare, and the Mi'kmaq-French relationship may hold the record.

During this period the kinship between the Acadians and the Mi'kmaq was so pronounced that each side began to take exceptional risks to protect the other from English vengeance. Besides being motivated by the need for mutual protection, the Acadian-Mi'kmaq alliance was based on mutual admiration and respect for each other's culture and friendship. According to Bernie Francis, Mi'kmaq linguist and translator, the word *Acadie* (Acadia) itself is derived from a Mi'kmaq word *E' kati*, meaning place of, or land of; *Cajun* is also derived from the same word.

The evolution of a strong alliance between the French and the Mi'kmaq can be credited to the more enlightened policies of the French government. Although France claimed Nova Scotia without informing the Mi'kmaq, it did not presume to exclude them from enjoying the bounties and freedom of their land. Nor did French officials display demeaning racist attitudes or exclude the Mi'kmaq from participating in French councils. This policy extended to social affairs as well and intermarriages were fairly common among them. For example, Charles de La Tour, in charge of provincial affairs in the 1630s, was married to a Mi'kmaq woman.

The fact that both groups were members of the Roman Catholic Church was a factor; however, although religion was used later to help convince the Mi'kmaq to fight against the English, it was not a major factor in fostering the alliance. Neither was alcohol, but the French were not above using the substance to encourage belligerence towards the English. It was even used on occasion to persuade the addicted to commit barbaric acts. The record shows that some Mi'kmaq were induced to commit atrocities in Newfoundland, but only after the French Governor threatened to cut off their brandy supply if they did not fight in the "French fashion," whatever that meant.

The vast majority of the Mi'kmaq were France's willing partners because of their past experiences with the English. They had correctly deduced from their experiences that a victory by the English and the New Englanders over the French in Acadia would be extremely bad news for the survival of their own culture. Therefore, one can conclude that the most influential factor in cementing the French and Mi'kmaq alliance was English racism; mercenary considerations, if any, were secondary.

In contrast, English-Amerindian alliances were mostly mercenary. The English allied themselves with many warlike Amerindian Nations, whose loyalty they bought with wares and presents. Because they were mercenary, these alliances lasted only as long as both sides saw them as mutually beneficial, and they sometimes ended in bloody battles. Later on, in the late 1700s, the English would switch to condescending paternalism in pursuing relationships with Amerindian allies.

Among England's Amerindian allies were the Mi'kmaq's traditional enemies, the Iroquois. Raids into Acadia by English and New England soldiers, assisted by the Iroquois, resulted in many atrocities being committed against Acadian, Mi'kmaq and Maliseet civilian populations. This added more fuel to the already deep-seated animosity held within these communities towards the English.

While this was transpiring, the inhumanities being inflicted upon Amerindians occupying the eastern coast of what is today the United States continued. English determination to subdue or exterminate these people was so pronounced that scalp bounties were offered for them many times throughout the 1600s. For instance, in 1694 the Governor of the Massachusetts Bay Colony issued a barbarous proclamation offering rewards for the scalps of the area's Amerindian men, women and children. The Mi'kmaq were not included, but there is some evidence that this did not stop bounty hunters from journeying into Nova Scotia to collect a few Mi'kmaq and Acadian scalps.

To counter any twinges of conscience these atrocities might engender among their colonists for the Eastern Amerindians, English colonial officialdom turned to propaganda to keep them suitably aroused. In so doing they blamed the Amerindian for most of the outrages committed throughout the region. Thus, the Mi'kmaq were blamed by colonial officials for all the outrages that occurred in Acadia. Most of these accusations were blatant lies. Many of the crimes were in fact committed by rogue Englishmen and their Amerindian allies.

Engendering hate towards opponents by lying is a practice that has been used by humans from time immemorial. An excellent example is the false allegation made by the English that the Mi'kmaq were responsible for the demise of Newfoundland's Beothuk, a lie so well concocted that it endured for centuries. The gist of this falsehood was that the French were paying the Mi'kmaq bounties for the scalps of the Beothuk in order to effect their extinction. There has never been one shred of evidence to support such a gross allegation. In fact, some experts now believe that the Beothuk were part of the Mi'kmaq family. Further and very pertinent, what possible interest could the French have had in the Beothuk? What added credibility to this false rumour was the fact that the Mi'kmaq often travelled to Newfoundland to hunt and fish, an ancient practice predating the arrival of Cabot. In fact, some families may have lived there year-round. However, the main motivation behind the propaganda was that during their wars with the English, the Mi'kmaq often used Newfoundland as a base to attack English shipping and trading posts. To this end they moved a large number of Warriors to the Island in 1705 where they conducted guerrilla warfare against the English on the southern coast. This continued until peace was once again at hand.

Peace arrived on July 13, 1713, when France and Great Britain signed the Treaty of Utrecht, which would in time, like all previous peace deals between them, prove to be no more than a respite from war. The war just ended, like most previous European wars, had been caused by family squabbles among the pampered royal houses of Europe, in this case mainly over religion, which is prominently mentioned in the preamble and in several sections. The treaty also encompassed other matters. In what was to prove to be extremely bad news for the Mi'kmaq, Maliseets and Acadians, Section XII transferred to the British Crown the self-presumed French ownership of Acadia. This event marked the beginning of the end of French power in the Americas.

The clear winners of the peace were the British. They received a renunciation of all claims by the Crowns of France and Spain to each other's Thrones. Thus they forestalled the possibility that the two Catholic Crowns would ever be worn by one person. The French and Spanish Crowns also agreed to recognize that thereafter Great Britain's Crown was restricted to Protestant royalty only. The Spanish, like the French, had to give up several of their prized possessions, including the strategic Rock of Gibraltar.

The main victims of this peace were the Amerindian Nations of the Americas and the Black people of Africa. The tragic destinies of these people were decided by the European Crowns, without an iota of thought being given to their interests. Their rights as free and independent peoples were being abrogated and Amerindian lands were also being taken. The Treaty of Utrecht also gave European nations license to forcibly remove Black people from Africa and bring them to the Americas as slaves.

Section XIV of the treaty deals with the rights of French subjects to stay within the ceded colonies and to practise their religion freely, subject to the discriminatory religious laws of Great Britain. It also placed the Eastern Amerindian Nations under British dominion. However, another section makes this presumption confusing. Section XV of the Treaty of Utrecht reads:

> The Subjects of France inhabiting Canada, and others, shall hereafter give no Hinderance or Molestation to the five Nations, or Cantons, of Indians, subject to the Dominion of Great Britain, nor to the other Natives of America, who are Friends to the same. In like manner, the Subjects of Great Britain shall behave themselves peaceably towards the Americans, who are Subjects or Friends to France. And on both sides, they shall enjoy full Liberty of going and coming on account of Trade. Also the Natives of those Countrys shall, with the same Liberty, resort as they please to the British and French Colonys, for promoting Trade on one side and the other, without any Molestation or Hinderance, either on the part of the British Subjects, or of the French. But it is to be exactly and distinctly settled by Commissarys, who are, and who ought to be accounted the Subjects and Friends of Britain, or of France.[7]

Interpretations of this section have ranged from saying that it gives dominion over the Eastern Amerindian Nations and their lands to Great Britain, to saying that it identifies some of them as French subjects, to saying that it acknowledges them as independent Nations. If this section was meant to place these Nations under British rule, that intention is not clearly stated. In fact, just the opposite may be inferred, given that the British sought a separate treaty with the Eastern Amerindian Nations. If they had thought otherwise, they would have demanded that all Amerindian Nations ratify Section XIV of the Treaty of Utrecht, rather than entering into separate agreements with them.

In view of the White supremacist attitudes prevailing at the time, the fact that Amerindian Nations, including the Mi'kmaq, were left out of the treaty negotiations and not even made aware of its signing should come as no surprise. A letter from Governor T. Caulfield to Vaudreuil, dated May 7, 1714, attests to the fact that the Mi'kmaq had been left in the dark:

> Breach of the treaty of peace and commerce committed by Indians under French government upon a British trading vessel at Beaubassin. Enclosed letter from Pere Felix, giving the Indians' excuse, i.e., *that they did not know that the treaty was concluded between the two crowns, or that they were included in it*. The Indians come from Richibucto. Enclosed John Adams' account of the goods taken from him. Hopes that satisfaction will be given, and promises to prevent similar *outrages* on his side.[8]

Finally, in 1715 the Mi'kmaq were enlightened. At a meeting with the Nation's Chiefs, two English officers informed them that France had transferred them and the ownership of their land to Great Britain via the Treaty of Utrecht and that King George I was now their sovereign. The Mi'kmaq responded in no uncertain terms that they did not come under the Treaty of Utrecht, would not recognize a foreign king in their country and would not recognize him as having dominion over their land.

At the same meeting the English had the audacity to place before the Chiefs the proposal that they permit British settlement in their villages for the purpose of creating one people. The Mi'kmaq, of course, immediately rejected this monstrous request to submit to extinction by assimilation. The Chiefs then clarified for the English that they had never given over ownership of their land to the French King or considered themselves to be his subjects, and therefore he had had nothing to transfer. With no agreement, open hostilities between the Mi'kmaq and the English resumed. Thus the die was cast for close to fifty more years of conflict, with occasional periods of uneasy truce.

After they learned the French had claimed their land and, unbeknownst to them, attempted to transfer their territories to Great Britain by treaty two years earlier, the Mi'kmaq directed protests to St. Ovide de Brouillant, Louisbourg's military commander in 1715 and Governor after September 1717. He responded:

> He [the French King] knew full well that the lands on which he tread, you possess them for all time. The King of France, your Father, never had the

intention of taking them from you, but had ceded only his own rights to the British Crown.[9]

The rights he mentions are derived from when France had claimed Acadia more than a century earlier according to the European law that non-Christians could not own land. Marc Lescarbot, a French lawyer, articulated this warped Christian law in his explanation of France's right to Acadia in 1618:

> The earth pertaining, then, by divine right to the children of God [Christians], there is here no question of applying the law and policy of Nations, by which it would not be permissible to claim the territory of another. This being so, we must possess it and preserve its natural inhabitants, and plant therein with determination the name of Jesus Christ, and of France.[10]

If this warped law were ever to be accorded recognition by modern legalists they would have to take into consideration that, after Grand Chief Membertou and his family converted to Christianity in 1610, the land of the Mi'kmaq had become exempt from being seized because the People were Christians. However, it's hard to imagine that a modern government would fall back and try to use such uncivilized garbage as justification for non-recognition of aboriginal title.

The French Governor, knowing full well that his King had transferred France's self-presumed ownership of Mi'kmaq territory and the Mi'kmaq themselves to England via treaty, deliberately lied in order to maintain an alliance with the People. France's honour was not enhanced by this affair. Excluding the Mi'kmaq from treaty negotiations that grievously affected their lives was unforgivable.

This exclusion of the prime stakeholder in Acadia from the negotiations of the terms of the treaty poses this question. Did the Treaty of Utrecht bind the Mi'kmaq to the provisions agreed to by several royal houses of Europe? The answer is obviously no. The Mi'kmaq, as a free and independent people, had not given their consent to the transfer of their territory or to the extinguishment of their independence and freedoms. The hour the French abandoned their loyal allies to the revenge of the English without consultation, and placed the Mi'kmaq's territorial rights into dispute, is one of the darkest moments of French colonial involvement in the Americas.

This betrayal also had serious implications for others. Besides trying to persuade the Mi'kmaq to meekly accept their rule and submit to assimilation, the English were also giving thought to long-range plans to assimilate the Acadians. These intentions were reflected in a memo from Lieutenant-Governor Caulfield to the Lords of Trade dated November 1715:

> I am now to lay before your Lords my opinion in relation to the French inhabitants of this colony, which if they continue in this country, will be of great consequence for the better improvement thereof; for as you will observe their numbers are considerable and in case they quit us will strengthen our enemies when occasion serves, by so much; and although we may not much benefit from them, yet their children in the process of time may be brought to our

constitution.... But in case the French quit us we shall never be able to maintain or protect our English families from the insults of the Indians, the worst of enemies, which the French by their staying will in a great measure ward off for their own sakes.[11]

The beneficiaries of this English dilemma were the Acadians. The English were forced to suffer the continued presence of these people they despised, because of the situation with the Mi'kmaq. In the words of British Governor Philipps, spoken in 1718, "The French should not be treated as they deserve, until such time as British settlers could be brought to Nova Scotia, and the Indian problem had been dealt with satisfactorily."[12] In the meantime they devoted their full energies towards trying to realize the despicable goals they had articulated to the Mi'kmaq Chiefs.

One can only speculate on the outcome if the French had been victorious in their wars with the English for control of Nova Scotia. Considering the good relationship they had with the Mi'kmaq, it may be reasonably assumed that some kind of union of the two cultures might have occurred. Almost certainly the Mi'kmaq would have prospered and been accorded equality.

The cause and extent of the hatred the Mi'kmaq held towards the English at the beginning of the eighteenth century because of the abuse they and their allies had suffered at British hands is well expressed in the following two quotes. The cause is described by historian John Stewart McLennan:

> The punishments of the Indians for wrongdoing by the English were, as all punishments of that epoch, harsh, and in addition they were humiliating and irritated the Indians. The scalp bounties of the colonies included rewards for the killing of women and children.... [This leads to] the strange conditions, in which we find a benign and devout clergyman praying that the young men who have joined the Mohawks in a scalping expedition against the French and Indians may go in fear of the Lord, and regard the bringing in of French scalps as a good omen.[13]

Its notable that the author did not mention that the clergyman also regarded the bringing in of Amerindian scalps, including those of women and children, as a good omen.

The extent of the hatred is described in a letter written on September 9, 1715, by Isle Royale (Cape Breton) Governor Philippe Pasteur de Costebelle to the French government: "The savages of the French mission on the shores of Acadia are such irreconcilable enemies of the English people that we cannot, with our most peaceable speeches, impress them not to trouble their trade."[14]

Terrorism
After the ratification of the Treaty of Utrecht, the plunder of the resources of Acadia and the adjacent sea increased dramatically. British authorities permitted fleets of English and New England fishermen to fish off the Maritime coast without restraint. By 1715 more than one thousand vessels were involved. Wildlife was

harvested without any sense of conservation, and the forests were cut down before the advance of the White man's version of civilization.

These aggressive acts, which threatened their very survival, combined with the demands made of them at their 1715 meeting with English officers, prompted military responses from the Mi'kmaq. These responses bared one of the strangest quirks that English officialdom exhibited during the colonial period. They felt affronted because the Mi'kmaq took reprisals for the crimes the English were committing against them. Bemoaning Mi'kmaq ungratefulness for the kindnesses they had extended, the English branded the Mi'kmaq responses "depredations" and "outrages." The hypocrisy of the English in labelling the Mi'kmaq as murderers and robbers because they were fighting back to preserve their own country and prevent their own extinction is incredulous. Such arrogance can only be derived from egotistical madness.

In the midst of all this, the increasing instances of squabbling and complaints among settlers from both the French and English communities over unpaid bills and their so-called land entitlements finally moved the British Colonial Council to act. At a meeting held at Annapolis Royal on April 19, 1721, the Governor and Council were named the first British court of judicature for the province. This court's ability to dispense justice would soon be put to the test. The issue would be related to the practice of the British to blame crimes against civilians on the Mi'kmaq, who had no knowledge of these events, as justification for terrorist tactics against the entire People. The practice of blaming the Amerindian for everything has a long history and it survives to a certain degree to this day.

In a rare admission that the Mi'kmaq did not participate in crimes against civilians and were basically non-belligerent, a letter from the English Governor's Council to the Acadian people of Minas said:

Annapolis, March 4th, 1720.
Committee of the Council could not accept the old frivolous excuse for outrage at Minas [fear of Indians]. Because ... their letter of excuse could not be considered as satisfaction, *as the Indians rarely, if ever, commit depredations, except at French instigation.*[15]

In addition to attacks on their food supply and persecution for outrages they did not commit, many Mi'kmaq were forcibly taken prisoner and held in fort stockades in an attempt to secure the Nation's allegiance to the British Crown. Hostage-taking to win compliance with imperial dictates was also a standard British military practice elsewhere in the Americas, even during times of peace. British seizure of Mi'kmaq men, women and children as hostages started in Acadia around 1715, and by the 1720s it had become a common procedure.

The mistreatment of prisoners of war has long been considered a barbarous act by civilized peoples. In the Americas colonial British military authorities proved by their cruelty to Amerindian prisoners in their custody that they were not above such barbarism. That their barbarism towards Natives was related to racism is supported by the fact that I could find no historical evidence to indicate that during the seventeenth, eighteenth and nineteenth centuries the killing, maiming or rob-

The death of an innocent

bing of a Mi'kmaq or any other Amerindian by a White person was considered a crime by the English.

At a Council meeting held at the house of Lt.-Governor John Doucett, in His Majesty's garrison at Annapolis Royal on July 8, 1724, a motion was passed to execute at random one of their hostages in order to try to terrify the rest of the Mi'kmaq into submission to the British Crown:

> Whereas, the savages of this His Majesty's Province of Nova Scotia committed several robberies and murders against His Majesty's subjects in the year 1722, and since have committed in open enmity and rebellion;
>
> And Whereas, to defend against such barbarities, several of their people were seized and detained as prisoners which induced several of the savages of this river to submit to the government, and promise to demean themselves peaceably and to inform the government of any insult that should be intended against it (as appears by the Instrument signed by them), upon which promise the Indian prisoners here were treated with all humanity and kindness, till by some articles of peace with the savages in general they might with security be released, being made to understand at the same time that if any of his Majesty's subjects were murdered near this garrison, or any shot fired against it, without giving timely notice of it, reprisals should be made upon the prisoners in our keeping;
>
> And Whereas, notwithstanding the promises made by them, and the threats made here of reprisals, some of the very Indians who had signed the instrument above mentioned were guides and actors amongst those who, on the 14th of this month, barbarously murdered a sergeant of this garrison and then openly attacked our partys, and the garrison itself, and were the means of another man being killed, and an officer and three private men being dangerously wounded, and of the firing of two English houses, and the taking of two men of this

garrison, with a woman and two children, who have since been released out of their hands by the French inhabitants;

It, is our opinion, that since all the *kind usages* this barbarous people have received seems rather to render them more inhuman and treacherous, it will be for His Majesty's service, the security of this garrison, and the English subjects inhabiting about it, to make reprisals *by the death of one of the savage prisoners in custody*, to deter them from any further outrage, when they will lay under the fear of loosing nine more still left in our possession.[16]

Shortly thereafter, a young Mi'kmaq Chief who stood neither accused nor convicted of any crime was unceremoniously hung. This act of barbarity by what was touted to be a civilized government is indefensible. What makes it even more reprehensible is that the Council was also a court of justice. But the most condemning fact is that no one was ever held accountable for this crime. And since no one was ever held accountable, one can conclude that it was condoned by the highest levels of the British government.

The English were sadly mistaken in their hope that this act of terrorism would deter the Mi'kmaq. Instead it generated a concerted and bloody response from the Mi'kmaq that continued until the signing of the Treaty of 1725 and even then the pause would be only temporary.

Most indigenous American civilizations were to a certain degree pacifist at the onset of the European invasion. This philosophy served individuals such as Mahatma Gandhi well in later times, but in the cruel years following the Middle Ages it was a clear recipe for disaster.

The Mi'kmaq fought with valour against the English to preserve their civilization. By 1725, faced with overwhelming odds, they opted to sign treaties that they hoped would bring an honourable and just conclusion to a ruinous war.

5

The Treaty of 1725
and Proclamations

After 1713 the British had begun consolidating their hold over Acadia by strength-ening military placements, planning the subjugation of the Mi'kmaq and initiating a drive to recruit reliable Protestant settlers. The latter were needed to counterbalance what they considered the unreliability of the hated Catholic Acadian settlements. But to assure that the colony was as peaceful as possible during the exercise they temporarily took pains to accommodate the Acadians.

However, the British plan for a short honeymoon with the Acadians changed quickly after they failed in 1715 to convince the Mi'kmaq Chiefs to meekly sur-render to their rule. As mentioned, the Mi'kmaq, riled by the demands made at that meeting, began taking some military actions. For the English this development mandated that the courtship of the Acadians should continue for a few more years, because having both Acadians and Mi'kmaq in a state of agitation at the same time would not have been conducive to the consolidation of control. However, as they despised the Acadians almost as much as the Mi'kmaq, accommodating them for a little longer must have been a galling experience. They probably took comfort from knowing that their humilation at performing self-serving acts of kindness would one day be avenged.

That day was not long in coming. Once the British military had stabilized the situation, English officials very quickly reverted back to their arrogant attitudes of trying to force people to love them by abusing them. In hindsight, it seems incred-ible that they would expect improvement in relationships with the two communi-ties while remaining unyielding toward their needs. However, their belief that abuse and intimidation were the proper ways to achieve good relations with people was unbending.

Motivated by this belief, they did something in 1722 that speaks volumes about the lack of rights and justice under British rule. On August 1, the British Governor of Acadia, Richard Philipp, issued a proclamation that not only bespoke a disdain for democracy but also reflected how deeply rooted was their paranoia about the close relationship between the Acadians and the Mi'kmaq. Philipp's edict made it illegal for Acadians to entertain a Mi'kmaq in any manner. How strictly this proclamation was enforced is reflected in the minutes of a Council meeting held on May 22, 1725:

> The Honourable Lt. Governor, John Doucett, acquainted the board that Prudane Robichau, senior inhabitant in the Cape, had entertained an Indian in his house, contrary to His Excellency's proclamation, dated August 1, 1722. That he had therefore put him in irons and in prison amongst the Indians for such heinous misdemeanour. This was to terrify the other inhabitants from clandes-tine practices of betraying the English subjects, into Indian hands. A petition

by Robichau for release was then presented to Council for approval: The said petition being read. It is the opinion of the board, upon account of his age, and having been so long in irons, that upon the offers and promises he made in his petition of putting up as security goods and other chattels for his future good behaviour, he be set free.[1]

Given the context of more than a century of friendly relations between Acadians and the Mi'kmaq, Robichau's hospitality was a reasonable action. However, the English were not reasonable when it came to activities involving Amerindians.

By 1725 the non-conciliatory policies the English had adopted to govern Acadia after taking it over twelve years earlier had increased the hatred the Acadians and the Mi'kmaq held towards them. This was not an ideal environment for treaty negotiations.

Treaties

In hindsight, it's fair to say that the majority of British military men and colonists who died in conflicts with Amerindians during England's colonizing days were victims of the pompous attitudes of their leadership. These attitudes caused much pain for their own and others, and were also the main stumbling block in their attempts to find peace by treaties with Amerindians. When you believe yourself to be a member of the "superior race," it's difficult to comprehend how your dictates might be offensive to "inferiors."

Their inflated perception of themselves, which in their opinion destined them to dictate the correct mode of civilization to the world, instilled in English colonial leaders, and their London counterparts, superiority complexes that can only be described as awesome. Their giant egos and White supremacist views prevented them from ever considering that the sovereign non-White civilizations they were forcing into the British empire had cultures worth preserving. The goal was simply to destroy and replace them with English values. Most of these Nations fought hard to prevent this. The historical record is full of instances where the English felt affronted when their victims refused to be thankful for the "gift" they were bestowing upon them. It's akin to a mugger expecting the mugged to be thankful.

Further, bordering on the fantastic, their awesome egos permitted them to believe—and this has been used as a defense for the appropriation of land without compensation and accepted by a judge in at least one Amerindian land claim—that British law was paramount in any Amerindian territory where a White British subject travelled. This kind of belief caused indescribable degradation and suffering for uncountable millions of people of colour victimized by British imperial rule around the world.

The English racial superiority complex described stands out in the records kept by the King's officials about the affairs of the American colonies. From John Cabot onward, and in minute detail, they entered into diaries, letters, council minutes etc. their contempt for Amerindians and the abuse they subjected them to. It was not rare for them to record their intentions to use treachery and other dishonourable means to strip the Native people of everything during treaty negotiations. Many English officials wrote that treaties made with the Amerindians were of no consequence because they had been made with "heathen savages." The frank way they recorded their misdeeds leads to the conclusion that they actually believed the Amerindian was not an intelligent human being. However, thanks to these pompous White-supremacist assessments, the records they left behind are invaluable to Amerindians, who use them very intelligently today when pursuing legal claims.

Their contemptuous attitudes enabled the British to regard the treaties they made with Amerindian Nations as only for the moment, to be abandoned or altered at will, without regard to honour. This was not entirely the fault of racism, because for Britain and other European Nations, treaties were entered into as a matter of convenience, lasting only until one side or the other decided it would be to its best advantage to disregard them. This philosophy caused much warfare and misery among the European peoples.

In contrast to the European view, the tenets of Mi'kmaq civilization demanded strict observance of treaties made with others. They believed that agreements worked out between adversaries and friends alike were binding and could only be altered through mutual consent.

In later years, as witnessed by the Royal Instructions of 1761, a difference of opinion developed between the government of Great Britain and the governments of its American colonies over the validity of treaties with the Amerindians. The home government instructed the colonial governments to undertake "a just and faithful observance of those treaties and compacts," but the colonial government of Nova Scotia, except for the Governor of the day, ignored these instructions almost entirely.

These different views of treaties were no small problem for the Mi'kmaq, but they also encountered a language barrier. They were forced to negotiate with two White tribes who spoke different languages, English and French. At this point in time, their communications skills in English were nil; French was their second language, but their ability to communicate in it was very rudimentary. Consequently, the treaties they entered into with the English had to be first translated into French and then interpreted into Mi'kmaq. To make matters even worse, many English and French words have no comparable meaning in the Mi'kmaq tongue or, for that matter, with each other. To muddy the waters further the language used in the treaties, even today, can only be fully understood by those well acquainted with English legal terminology. Practically speaking, statements such as "enter into Articles of Pacification with his Majesty's Governments" contained in the Treaty of 1725 would have been virtually incomprehensible to the Chiefs.

But the most incomprehensible thing for the Mi'kmaq would have been the land-grab section of the Treaty of Utrecht used by the British when drafting the Treaty of 1725: "Whereas, His Majesty King George, by concession of the Most Christian King, made at the Treaty of Utrecht, is become the rightful possessor of the Province of Nova Scotia or Acadia...." Their lack of understanding of how people can "legally" transfer land that was stolen under the guise of religious beliefs is evidenced by the fact that to this day the Mi'kmaq Nation has consistently refused to recognize foreign ownership of their traditional territory.

By making treaties, the Eastern Nations sought to live in peaceful co-existence with those they had once viewed as welcomed guests. I firmly believe that the

Mi'kmaq would never have signed the Treaty of 1725, which portrayed them as servants paying homage to a lord and master, the English King, if they had understood the meaning and implications of the language.

Considering all this, France, by the Treaty of Utrecht, had indeed given the Mi'kmaq and Acadians a near impossible force to come to terms with when it handed them over to the British for exploitation. Hopes for a better tomorrow must have been near zero at this time in both communities. However, it was only a taste of things to come.

The Treaty of 1725

From what ensued afterwards, I've concluded that the British motivation in approaching the Northeastern Amerindian Nations during 1724 and 1725 with a treaty proposal was a desire to lull these Nations into a false sense of security until an opportune time arose when they could dispossess them of all they owned. However, as the British had already thoroughly battered the smaller New England Nations into submission, why they had included them in the process remains a mystery to me. The only credible explanation is that it was done as a ruse to con the Maliseet and Mi'kmaq, who were still major threats, into thinking that they were interested in helping all these Nations preserve their cultures.

Whatever the reason, the feelers they had put out about working out a peace treaty received a favourable response. On December 15, 1725, delegates from several of the Amerindian Nations of northeastern North America gathered at Boston to negotiate a peace and friendship treaty with the English. This treaty was meant to end the war between the parties, but for many of the First Nations it brought no more than a short interlude in hostilities.

Before getting into the meat of the treaty, I'll make a stab at visualizing the mood of the leaders of these Nations at this dark hour in their histories. Using European records, a fairly accurate picture of their mental state can be developed. There can be no doubt that passionate debates were occurring within their councils over whether to make peace with the English, a people they would have by then considered bloodthirsty barbarians. Their confidence in obtaining justice from such a document, given the acrimonious relations they had had to date with the enemy, must have been nil. Thus their mood was probably one of resignation and despair, for only the most optimistic or mentally defective among them would have had more than the slightest confidence that a treaty would improve their long-range chances of survival as a free people.

Gloom would also have been pervasive among their citizens. By this time they had very little going for them. The justice accorded them by the English was nil. Relatives and friends were being held as hostages. Their Warriors, with their primitive weapons supplemented by some modern weaponry and a very limited supply of ammunition, were no match for the fully equipped and supplied British army. Their French allies had signed a separate peace with the English and were no longer officially involved in the conflict.

Why would these Nations enter into a treaty with the British under these circumstances? One can only conclude that it was an act of desperation. They probably saw the process as one of the few avenues open to them to preserve at least a measure of their territory, independence and freedom.

Annapolis Council minutes of November 3, 1724, show how well founded the pessimism held by the Mi'kmaq would have been. The terms desired by Council would divest the Mi'kmaq of everything but their souls:

The Honourable Lt. Governor laid before the board a letter from the Honourable William Dummer Esquire, Lt. Governor of New England, wherein he stated, that towards the later end of October, or the beginning of November, negotiations for a general peace with the Indians would commence, and therefore wanted to know what demands should be made on behalf of this government.

Which being considered, the board agreed that the Honourable Lt. Governor, should in the name and behalf of His Majesty, send the following articles.

(1) That they shall acknowledge that the Province of Nova Scotia belongs to the Crown of Great Britain.

(2) That they shall not hinder or molest any of the King's subjects who are homesteading, or doing any of their other affairs in the province;

(3) That we expect restitution to be made to our traders, whom the savages without cause frequently plundered, which occasioned the war, and that satisfaction shall be made for all the losses His Majesty's subjects have since sustained through these unjust actions;

(4) That Whereas they are all of the Roman Catholic persuasion, they shall, according to His Majesty's directions, enjoy the exercise of their religion, but shall not have any other missionaries amongst them other than those His Majesty's government shall approve of, because we have undeniable proofs that the priests have always been the ones who encouraged the Indians to fight;

(5) That if any of their people shall disregard any of these articles, and behave themselves disrespectfully to this His Majesty's government, and do any thing contrary to law they shall oblige themselves to yield and deliver up such person, or persons, to be punished according to law;

(6) That, Whereas they have behaved themselves, in spite of all manner of kind usages from the Crown of Great Britain with so much treachery, we expect *that hostages shall be given to His Majesty's government as security for their sincerity in honouring and obeying the articles as shall be agreed upon* for the perpetual continuation of peace;

(7) That, upon their true and faithful performance of all and every article, they shall always meet with a friendly usage from His Majesty's government.

Agreed, that the Honourable Lt. Governor send the said articles to Hibbert Newton Esquire, one of the members of our Council, now in Boston, with directions to meet with the Honourable William Dummer Esquire, and to communicate the wishes of our Council.[2]

The fact that Governor Dummer had contacted the Maliseet and Mi'kmaq Nations about commencing peace treaty negotiations without informing the Colonial Council of the British colony where they resided is a strong indication that he was all but in name in charge of both colonies. This and the fact that he waited until just a month before negotiations were to begin before asking for its terms and conditions could be construed as a sign of contempt for the competency of Nova Scotia's military government.

In any event, as the minutes clearly show, the Council's response was to arrogantly demand that the Mi'kmaq agree to an unconditional surrender, including the complete surrender of all territory. As they were still a force to be reckoned with, the Mi'kmaq would not agree to such terms without a fight.

The minutes also reveal that the British still believed that they would need hostages from the Mi'kmaq to hold them to their word. However, throughout the next half century, this practice simply created more determined opposition among the People. It defies logic, but this crazy eighteenth-century English habit of trying to force people to like and obey them by brute force survives to this day in other jurisdictions. For example, up until the 1999 elections, the Israelis were using similar tactics against the Palestinians. They were not, however, holding innocent Elders, children and women hostage, just men. This tactic did not work for the Europeans in the Americas and, quite frankly, it will not work for Israel in the Middle East.

The following is the "Submission and Agreement of the Delegates of the Eastern Indians" signed at Boston on December 15, 1725:

> Whereas, the several Tribes of Eastern Indians, the Penobscot, Naridgwack, Maliseet, Mi'kmaq and other Tribes residing within His Majesty's territories of New England, and Nova Scotia, from whom Loran Arexus, Francois Xavier, and Meganumoe are delegated and fully empowered to enter into Articles of Pacification with His Majesty's governments of the Mass. Bay, New Hampshire and Nova Scotia colonies, *have contrary to the several treaties they have solemnly entered into with the said governments made an open rupture and have continued some years in acts of hostility against the subjects of his Majesty King George* ...
>
> They being now sensible of the miseries and troubles they have involved themselves in, and being desirous to be restored to His Majesty's grace and favour and to live in peace with all His Majesty's subjects of the said three governments, the province of New York and colonys of Connecticutt and Rhode Island and that all former acts of injury be forgotten. Have concluded to make and we *do by these presents, in the name and behalf of the said Tribes, make our submission* unto his most Excellent Majesty, George, by the Grace of God, King of Great Britain, France and Ireland, Defender of the Faith, *in as full and ample manner as any of our predecessors.*
>
> And, we do hereby promise and engage with the Honourable William Dummer Esq; as he is Lieutenant Governor and Commander-in-Chief of His Majesty's Massachusetts Bay and with the [other] Governors [he represents].... We the said delegates for and in behalf of the several Tribes abovesaid, do promise and

engage that at all times forever from and after the date of these presents we and they will erase and forbear all acts of hostility, injuries and discords towards all the subjects of the Crown of Great Britain and not offer the least hurt, violence or molestation to them, or any of them in their persons or estates, but will hence forward hold and maintain a firm and constant amity and friendship with all the English, and will never confederate or combine with any other Nation to their prejudice.

That, all the captives taken in the present war, shall at or before the time of the further ratification of this Treaty, be freed without any ransom, or payment to be made for them, or any of them.

That, His Majesty's Subjects, the English, shall and may peaceably and quietly enter upon and improve and forever enjoy all and singular their Rights of God and former settlements, properties and possessions within the Eastern parts of the province of the Massachusetts Bay, together with all islands, inletts, shores, beaches and fishery within the same without any molestation or claims by us or any other Indian and be in no ways molested, interrupted or disturbed therein.

Saving unto the Penobscot, Naridgwalk and other Tribes within His Majesty's province aforesaid and their natural descendants respectively all their lands, liberties and properties not by them conveyed or sold to or possessed by any of the English subjects as aforesaid. As also the privilege of fishing, hunting, and fowling as formerly.

That all trade and commerce which hereafter may be allowed between the English and Indians shall be under such management and regulations as the government of the Mass. province shall direct.

If any controversy or difference at any time hereafter happen to arise between any of the English and Indians for any real or supposed wrong or injury done on either side no private revenge shall be taken for the same but proper application shall be made to His Majesty's government upon the place for remedy or induce thereof in a due course of justice. We submitting ourselves to be ruled and governed by His Majesty's laws and desiring to have benefit of the same.

We also the said delegates in behalf of the Tribes of Indians inhabiting within the French territories who have assisted us in this war for a term we are fully empowered to act in this present Treaty. Do hereby promise and engage that they and every of them shall henceforth cease and forebear all acts of hostility, force and violence towards all and every the subjects of His Majesty the King of Great Britain.

We do further in behalf of the Tribe of the Penobscot Indians promise and engage that if any of the other Tribes intended to be included in this Treaty that notwithstanding refuse to confirm and ratify this present Treaty entered into on their behalf and continue or renew acts of hostility against the English. In such case the Penobscot Tribe shall join their young men with the English in reducing them to reason.

In the next place we the forenamed delegates: Do promise and engage with the Honourable John Wentworth Esq; as he is Lieutenant Governor and Commander in Chief of His Majesty's province of New Hampshire ... that we and the Tribes we are deputed from henceforth erase and forebear all acts of hostility, injuries and discords towards all the subjects of His Majesty King George within the said province and we do understand and take it that the said government of New Hampshire is also included and excepting that respecting the regulating of trade with us.

And further we the forenamed delegates do promise and engage with the Honourable Lawrence Armstrong, Lieutenant Governor and Commander in Chief of His Majesty's province of Nova Scotia or Acadia, to live in peace with His Majesty's good subjects and their dependents in the government according to the articles agreed on with Major Paul Mascarene commissioned for that purpose and further to be ratified as mentioned in the said articles.[3]

If the views of the colonial government of Nova Scotia had prevailed, harsher terms would have been inserted in the agreement. Its demand that the Mi'kmaq surrender unconditionally, which would have ended the process before it started, was not included. The final draft was watered down to read that the Tribes "do ... make submission ... in as full and ample manner as any of our predecessors." As the Mi'kmaq's predecessors had never submitted to any European power, this provision was meaningless in their case. Also, the allegation in the treaty that the Tribes "have contrary to the several treaties they have solemnly entered into with the said governments made an open rupture and have continued some years in acts of hostility against the subjects of his Majesty King George" was not applicable to the Mi'kmaq either because they had not entered into any treaties with the English, or any other European Nation, prior to 1725.

The following is the formal agreement in principle signed by the Mi'kmaq and other delegates:

Treaty No. 239 [Better known as the Treaty of 1725]

Articles of submission and agreement, made at Boston, in New England by Loran Arexus, Francois Xavier and Meganumbe, Delegates from Penobscott, Naridgwack, Maliseet, Mi'kmaq and other Nations inhabiting within His Majesty's Territories of Nova Scotia and New England.

Whereas, His Majesty King George, by concession of the Most Christian King, made at the Treaty of Utrecht, is become the rightful possessor of the Province of Nova Scotia or Acadia ... do, in the name and behalf of the Nations we represent, acknowledge His said Majesty King George's jurisdiction and dominion over the territories of the said Province of Nova Scotia or Acadia, *and make our submission to His said Majesty in as ample manner as we have formerly done to the King of France.*

And, we further promise, on behalf of the Nations we represent, that the Indians shall not molest any of His Majesty's Subjects or their dependents in their Settlements already made or lawfully to be made, or in their carrying on their traffic and other affairs within the said Provinces.

That, *if there happens any robbery or outrage committed by any of the*

Indians, the Tribe or Tribes they belong to shall cause satisfaction and resti-
tution to be made to the Parties injured.

That the Indians shall not help to escape any Soldiers belonging to His Majesty's forts, but on the contrary shall bring back any Soldier they shall find endeavouring to run away.

That, in case of any misunderstanding, quarrel or injury between the English and the Indians, no private revenge shall be taken, but application shall be made for redress, according to His Majesty's Laws.

That, if the Indians have made any Prisoners belonging to the Government of Nova Scotia or Acadia during the course of the War, they shall be released at, or before, the ratification of this Treaty.

That this Treaty shall be ratified at Annapolis Royal.

Dated at the Council Chamber in Boston, in New England, December 15, 1725.[4]

Instead of providing an honourable peace for the Eastern Nations, these documents contained all the elements needed to humiliate them further. One does not make a lasting peace by debasing and humiliating one's former enemies. Doing so only lays a foundation of resentment and hate that will eventually erupt into hostilities. Prior to its official ratification of the treaty on June 4, 1726, the Governor's Council at Annapolis took some pains to let the Mi'kmaq know of its terms. At a Council held on March 21, 1726, Lt.-Governor John Doucett told the Council that he had received from Major Paul Mascarene attested copies of the agreement. The Council resolved to order the Acadian Deputies who lived along the Annapolis River area to be at the fort the following Wednesday to be acquainted with the terms of the treaty, and to bring the leaders of the Indians who also resided in the area around the river with them.

The Council reconvened on Saturday March 26, 1726, to meet with the Acadian Deputies to whom the terms of the agreement were read. It was resolved that circular letters would be sent to the Mi'kmaq, via the Deputies, to inform them of the peace and ask them to assemble at the fort on May 4th to ratify the treaty. The date was later changed to June 4th.

A journey for hope

At a meeting on April 20, 1726, Lt.-Governor John Doucett informed the Council that he had received a letter from the Deputies of Cobaquit, informing him that they had explained the letter to the Indians present at their settlement, "and that they had used all possible means to communicate the same to those who were absent, in order that they may be here at the time appointed, and that they, the deputies, would come to the fort with them for the treaty signing ceremony."[5]

At a Council meeting held at Annapolis on May 31, 1726, the Lt.-Governor informed the Council that the Chief of the Cape Sable Mi'kmaq, and other Chiefs of the province were coming to ratify the treaty on June 4th. He asked the Board whether the signing ceremony should go ahead in the absence of the Governor of the province, Lawrence Armstrong, who had not returned from Canso. The Council deemed that the Chiefs might not ratify the articles if the signing did not proceed on June 4th, and that it would not be in the province's best interest to hinder the negotiations of the government of New England. They decided that Lt.-Governor Doucett would sign the treaty on the Governor's behalf.[6]

At a Council meeting held on the 4th of June 1726:

The Lt. Governor acquainted the Board that the Indians, with the Deputies of the Inhabitants of this River, were here to confirm and ratify the Articles ratified and agreed upon by their Delegates at Boston. He wanted to know if, because they had come to ratify the treaty as agreed, he should release the Indian Prisoners.

The opinion of the Board is, that *as those in prison are not worthy to be kept as hostages, they being but of little esteem, some old and decrepit*, and that whereas they have already been a very great expense to His Majesty, that they should be released in order to show the Indians sincerity of friendship and that it may persuade them to support His Majesty's interest.

Then the Board moved, that it was customary on such occasions to give them some entertainments and presents as tokens of friendship. To which, the Honourable Lt. Governor, answered that he had no presents. It was again moved, that His Majesty had some years ago sent presents for distribution to the Indians and that it would be less expensive at this juncture to distribute some of these amongst them....

The opinion of the Board is that it is very necessary to give them tokens of friendship. Therefore, the Lt. Governor of Annapolis Royal, in the absence of Lawrence Armstrong, the Lt. Governor of the Province, should acquire proper presents for distribution to the Indians, in order to maintain the honour of this, His Majesty's Province.

Then, His Honour, acquainted the Board, that he had as per the Articles agreed upon by Major Paul Mascarene and the Indian Delegates, prepared documents for him and the Indians to sign and thus ratify, which he laid before the Board.

Which being read and compared with those stipulated at Boston, were approved. And then it was Judged proper to adjourn to the Flag Bastion, to have them ratified, in as public and solemn a manner as possible.

Where the Indians being present, the said Articles were again read before all the Officers, Soldiers, and the Deputies, first in English. Then the Lt. Governor, having administered an Oath to Abram Bourg, a Deputy, and to Prudane Robichau Senior, had them translate the articles into French. Then the terms of the treaty were again distinctly read in French, paragraph by paragraph, to the Indians.

The Indians then gave their assent, and signed, sealed and delivered the same to his Honour, the Lt. Governor of Annapolis Royal.

Then the Lt. Governor, in absence of the Honourable Governor of the Province, signed, sealed and, for and in His Majesty's name, delivered those, in behalf of this Government, to the Chief of said Indians. And they having moreover swore fidelity, the [Lt.] Governor gave then orders that the Indian prisoners should be released. And gave them an entertainment, and several presents as tokens of His Majesty's protection.[7]

The statement concerning the *worth* of the hostages lays bare English ignorance of the customs of the people they were dealing with. The individuals they were holding were said to be "old and decrepit" and therefore "not worthy" as hostages. If the English had taken the time to find out something about Mi'kmaq culture, they would have known that no others in the Nation were more venerated and valued than Elders.

At a Council meeting held on June 8, 1726, the Lt.-Governor advised the members that Governor Armstrong had sent a letter in which he seemed "to be displeased with our proceedings." He wasn't pleased that the treaty had been ratified by some of the Mi'kmaq communities without his attendance. The opinion of the Council was "that which has been transacted cannot be receded from, without a manifest violation of what has been so solemnly promised in his Majesty's name."[8]

On June 23rd the Council convened to be advised that the Mi'kmaq residing in the far reaches of Acadia were indicating their willingness to come to Port-Royal to ratify the treaty. During these and following meetings, Council members went out of their way to lay blame for past Mi'kmaq hostility towards the English King and his subjects upon the shoulders of the Acadians, especially the missionaries. Never once did they acknowledge that some of their own actions, e.g., holding Elders and other Mi'kmaq hostage and taking their lands, had contributed to Mi'kmaq animosity.

With a lull in the war with the Mi'kmaq, the British turned their attention towards solving the "Acadian problem." An ultimatum was presented to the Acadians: either sign an oath of allegiance to the British monarch or leave the province. Most did not sign, and because the British were still dependent on them for sustenance, they were not forced to leave. This subject was the prime topic of Colonial Council minutes over the next several years and provides insight into how the English tried to balance their dealings with the Mi'kmaq and the Acadians.

An enduring burden for the First Nations was initiated by the fourth paragraph of the agreement in principle, which reads: "That, if there happens any robbery or outrage committed by any of the Indians, the Tribe or Tribes they belong to shall cause satisfaction and restitution to be made to the Parties injured." This insidious burden not only penalized the innocent but had the long-term effect of group stereotyping. This evil, which still haunts First Nations people today, was probably unintentional. I suspect its inclusion in the treaty had a far more treacherous purpose at the time: to provide the British with an excuse to take punitive military action against an entire First Nation for any misdeed committed by a member, no matter how minor, which they considered an infraction of the treaty.

Also, to deflect any argument to the contrary, if the English had had honourable intentions in the treaty making process, they would have written this treaty in a manner easily understood by the Mi'kmaq. As is revealed by the documents they prepared, they didn't. It is therefore indefensible for modern White society to interpret the provisions of these treaties in a manner unsympathetic to Natives. A great nation of ethical citizens such as Canada should not attempt, simply because of greed, to continue to profit from the dishonourable actions of its White ancestors while refusing to atone for their excesses.

Proclamations

British authorities frequently used proclamations to announce their decisions and how they would be implemented. They issued proclamations for almost every reason: to declare holidays, the decisions of tribunals, and so on. After the Treaty of Utrecht of 1713, the British chose to inform the Mi'kmaq, via proclamation, of their proposals for managing what they considered British territorial rights to Nova Scotia. The same translation process was used for proclamations as for treaties, with the same disastrous results for the Mi'kmaq.

6

Flawed Peace
and the Treaty of 1749

By the end of 1726, most Mi'kmaq Districts had, without being properly informed about the consequences, ratified the Treaty of 1725. The assertion that they had signed the treaty without first being properly informed is supported by the military actions they took afterwards to protect their territory from British appropriation. Being sensible people, it makes no sense that they would fight so hard to keep something they had given away willingly. It can be further concluded from their military actions that, if the treaty's complex terminology had been interpreted in their own language so they could have realized that it would deprive their proud Nation of its self-respect, dignity and territorial rights, they would not have signed. The fact that the Mi'kmaq were uninformed about the full meaning of the treaty was enough to assure that the peace would not last, but the British made its failure more certain by continuing to treat the Mi'kmaq with insincerity and contempt.

A perfect example of English insincerity is found in the minutes of a Council meeting held at Annapolis on December 9, 1725, which detail the dishonourable way the Council disposed of criminal charges against three French prisoners from Quebec who had been charged with murdering and robbing two Mi'kmaq. Lt.-Governor Doucett relayed the following information about the case to the councillors in their capacity as judges:

> That three French strangers had come from Quebec seeking refuge, and later, safe passage out of the Province. That they were not in possession of a Quebec Governor's Passport. That they had killed and robbed two Indians. The Board did not believe that they had come as refugees, but rather as spies, in order to discover the state of the Town and Garrison, or to entice the desertion of the Troops.
>
> Whereupon, in order to ascertain the truth of their designs and statements, the Board judged it necessary that they should be put into custody and examined separately. The Lt. Governor informed the Board that he had already made them prisoners, it was then agreed that they should be examined.
>
> The three men, Paul Francois Dupont de Veillein, Saint Joyly de Pardeithan and Alexander Poupart de Babour, were then brought separately before the Board to give testimony. The first gentleman testified: that he was a former Officer of the French Army, that he had done time in the Bastille, for he knew not what. And, as further punishment, by order of the authorities, was transported out of France to Quebec. The second Gentleman related that he also was a former Officer in the French Army: that he had been apprehended by the authorities in France for fighting an illegal duel on behalf of a friend: that, as a consequence, he had been exiled to New Spain by the French Authorities. The third Gentleman related that he did not know the cause of his transporta-

tion out of France, suspected that it may have been somehow connected with his former love life.[1]

The following is the testimony of Dupont de Veillein, which was corroborated in separate testimony by the other two:

> He stated that he was well entertained in Quebec. He was asked: seeing as he were so well entertained there, why had he left in so vagabond manner and come without a Governor's Passport? He replied: the Governor would not give him a passport, but told him to go if he pleased, and that he would not stop him.
>
> When asked why they did not go directly to France or to Cape Breton? He made answer that none of the Masters of Vessels would take them on board without a Governor's Passport. Then asked why they ventured to come to Port-Royal or to any of the other Colonial English settlements without one? He answered: that his father was of Blois, and a Chevalier, and that being sent away in such a manner, he was resolved to run all risks to get home to sue for justice.
>
> And finding that none would take him on board, he and the others had arranged with one Eneas, an Indian, to bring them to the River St. Johns. Whom, with his relative, they killed about fifty leagues above Meductuck, because they found, after they had paid him for his pilotage, that he was going to deceive them and not perform the agreement. They felt that he was planning to tarry in the woods where they would have infallibly perished with hunger had they not taken his canoe by force.
>
> And in the scuffle he shot Eneas, as he was going to fire upon him and his comrades, and that Mr. Babour shot the other Indian, as he was going to kill Mr. Joyly with a Lance, and that they then proceeded in the best manner they could on their journey.
>
> He was asked, if they did not meet with other Indians who knew the Canoe? Answered: not till they came to St. Johns, where the Priest lives, to whom they applied for assistance, and directions on how to get to the French Plantations. There being several Indians going from there to Beaubassin, he recommended them to their care, who not knowing the canoe (it being a new one, just finished before they departed from Canada), piloted them to the River of Beaubassin.
>
> And then being informed of a place called Minas, where there were also French Inhabitants, they choose rather to go there than to Beaubassin, lest, during their stay in Beaubassin they should be discovered and fall into the hands of the Indians. And so, taking direction which way to steer along the shore, they found Minas. After staying a few days, and begging the assistance of the Inhabitants, they told them they had robbed and killed two Mi'kmaq. They were ordered to depart immediately, for there was no shelter for them there.
>
> They were told to make their way to the Garrison and to ask for the protection of the Governor, because the Indians would certainly destroy them. And they said to the Board, having but little provisions and no Guide, they had almost perished along the way.

And being asked, what the other two were, and whether they were all De-serters from the Troops? He said that they were both Gentlemen of good family and had met with ill usage and such misfortunes as his own. He said further that he had a greater acquaintance with Mr. Barbour than he had with Mr. Pordeithan, because they had been imprisoned in the Bastille at the same time and had been in Canada together for some time. He only knew Saint Joyly since he had come to Quebec from Mississippi, which was but a few months before they left Quebec. He also stated that none of them were in the Troops.[2]

As is evident from their testimony, these men committed murder for the sake of robbery. Yet at a Council meeting held on May 12, 1726, at Annapolis, the English officers chose to excuse these heinous crimes as follows:

The Honourable Lt. Governor, laid before the Board a letter, which was sent him from Mr William Wimniett, dated at Minas, the 25th of April, 1726,… in relation to the disposition of the three French prisoners, now that the crimes they committed had been *confirmed*. The opinion of the Board is that it would be cruelty, as they had come to this Government for protection and shelter for killing two Indians in time of war, to deliver them up to the Indians for justice. Therefore, to prevent the Mi'kmaq demanding them when they come to ratify the peace, the three prisoners will be sent away by the vessels now bound for Boston in New England.[3]

If the Council had complied with the terms of the treaty they had agreed to abide by in 1725 and were about to ratify with the Mi'kmaq, they would have convicted these men of murder and robbery and sentenced them accordingly. Its decision not to punish the murderers but rather to secure their escape is, in view of their previous mistreatment of Mi'kmaq and Acadian prisoners, the ultimate in hypocrisy. The freeing of these coldblooded murderers vividly demonstrates the contempt the British had for the lives of the Mi'kmaq and the agreements made with them.

A few years after this incident, with the ink barely dry on the treaty, the English were back to using brutal methods to try to secure the loyalty of the Mi'kmaq and Acadians. Some apologists argue that they were justified because they were militarily weak in the province and *had to* resort to harsh measures to maintain their position. This argument is without basis for four reasons: (1) the Mi'kmaq would have been happy to live side by side with them in a mutually respectful and accommodating partnership, (2) they were looking for a fight soon after the treaties were signed, because on July 29, 1727, they issued an order forbidding trade of any nature between the Mi'kmaq and the Acadians (only the naive would have thought such an order would be obeyed), (3) the Acadians would have accommodated them-selves to British rule if they had not had to worry about the Mi'kmaq punishing them for consorting with the enemy and (4) the capacity of France to make war in the region would have been severely curtailed without their Native allies.

In a continuation of their non-conciliatory ways, on September 16, 1727, the British imprisoned three Acadian Deputies for insolence towards His Majesty's government because they had presented a petition to Council on behalf of the

French inhabitants, apparently a "horrific crime." They also imprisoned a missionary who was the pastor at Minas and the priest to Mi'kmaq in the area. These arrogant and ill-considered moves were not the humble actions of a beleaguered colonial government.

Predictably, the Mi'kmaq began to retaliate. Lt.-Governor Armstrong reported to the Council on November 2, 1727, that several hostile incidents involving the Mi'kmaq had occurred. He reported that a number of His Majesty's subjects had been murdered and that robberies and piracy had taken place. He did not, however, report how many Mi'kmaq had been murdered or robbed by His Majesty's subjects.

Related to these incidents, on November 7, 1727, Armstrong and Councillors met with the Chief of the Cape Sables, Paul Secoumart, and his two sons. They informed the Board that they had no knowledge of the incidents, at which time the Board felt compelled to have read to them the "Indian liability provision" found in the fourth paragraph of the Treaty of 1725. Armstrong then informed them that he expected compliance. The Chief and his sons informed the Council that they would do their best to discover the culprits. Then the English gave them presents to encourage them to commit treason against their own.

From this point onward, the Mi'kmaq increasingly used military action to reassert their sovereignty over Nova Scotia. The British, as usual, blamed such behaviour on the French and the missionaries rather than on the desire of the Mi'kmaq to keep their country intact. In hindsight it seems incredible that their White supremacist beliefs could have prevented them from conceiving that an "inferior" was capable of acting in such a manner without White guidance. If someone had pointed out to them that it was their grab of Mi'kmaq territory that had provoked military responses instead of outside interference, they would have reacted in disbelief. This mindset prompted them, particularly the Governor, to lay the groundwork for more Mi'kmaq reprisals by openly appropriating more of the Nation's lands without considering the consequences. At a Council meeting held on January 10, 1732, Mi'kmaq land was the principal item on the agenda. Discussions during the meeting centered around instructions for surveying the province and making further grants.

During these years, clashes provoked by the British with the Mi'kmaq varied in frequency. Matters would settle down, and then the British would make a move, such as the proposed survey, that incited the Mi'kmaq to arms again. The following is an example of their mindless provocation—it's hard to figure out if incidents such as this should be attributed to stupidity or imperial arrogance. On July 25, 1732, the Lieutenant-Governor told the Council that he had employed René LeBlanc to build a small fort at Minas. He further relayed that the endeavour was being strongly opposed by the Mi'kmaq and that several had visited LeBlanc to inform him that they considered him a treasonous dog for consorting with the enemy. In the face of strong Mi'kmaq military opposition, the British Governor backed down and abandoned his plans for the magazine. Strangely, for a change, the blame for the Mi'kmaq action was not put on the French.

However, that habit was not dead. English inability to recognize that their troubles with the Mi'kmaq were largely brought upon themselves by their arrogance is shown in a letter from Lt.-Governor Armstrong to Belcher dated September 11, 1732:

> Our troubles proceed from the influence the French have over the Indians, which will be maintained as long as the English employ the French to sell their goods to the Indians. The French keep us at a distance, make the Indians depend on them, engross the whole management of the fur trade, and run away with the profits. If the French were cut off from these advantages, the profit would go to the Indians, who would thereby be bound to us by the strong ties of self-interest.[4]

Armstrong talks about using profits and self-interest as a lure to entice the "Indians" away from the Acadians. His proposal once again highlights British ignorance—after more than two centuries in the Americas—about the nature of Mi'kmaq society. After all this time, their arrogance had prevented them from understanding that desires for profit and economic self-interest were not compatible with the values of most Amerindian cultures.

Fortified by the ignorant belief that the sins homogeneous with their own culture were embraced by all others, English officials often made unfounded charges against the Mi'kmaq. For example, related to his belief that greed likewise motivated the Mi'kmaq, following an act of piracy involving a British ship, Armstrong made serious criminal accusations against the Cape Sables. The incident also shows how the "Blame it on the Indians" philosophy was used to advantage. It was accepted then, and still is to a certain extent, that when a White person makes an allegation against an Amerindian, he or she is guilty as charged, regardless of the evidence.

The episode began when the brigantine *Baltimore*, en route to Annapolis, Maryland, from Dublin, sailed into Harbour Tiboque on December 15, 1735, to take shelter from a storm and then grounded. From the floundering ship the Mi'kmaq rescued a woman who claimed to be Mrs. Susanna Buckler, the wife of the ship's owner, Andrew Buckler. After her rescue and transport to the fort, Buckler, who was referred to as a gentlewoman by Armstrong, reported that the ship, captained by Richard White, had had eighteen persons aboard when it left Ireland. She then claimed that the Mi'kmaq had robbed her of her jewellery, money, clothes etc. She also claimed that at the time of her rescue two sailors were left alive on-board and were now missing. Armstrong accepted all this as fact.

On this basis, in a memo to Dentremonts at Pobomcoup, dated May 17, 1736, Armstrong requested that he interview the Mi'kmaq Antoine Tedeumart, as there was reason to suspect him of robbery and murder. The Lieutenant-Governor stated: "He had taken away the ship's boat on or about December 24th, last, and is suspected of murdering a woman, and a negro boy, who were in the boat at the time and were afterwards (as she reports) found dead in the woods."[5]

On the same day, Lt.-Governor Armstrong wrote to the Chief of the Cape Sable Mi'kmaq:

Greetings. Armstrong is mightily pleased with the character you bear, and your prudent and wise conduct in being no ways concerned in the alleged murder and robbery connected with the *Baltimore*, in Tibogue, near your village, which was committed by Antoine Tedeumart and others.

Chief and innocent members of the Tribe are assured of Armstrong's protection and friendship. Such actions are not only repugnant to the laws of God and man, but also expressly against the articles of peace signed by the Cape Sable Indians and the Tribes of New England, one article of which stipulates that "no private revenge shall be taken"; but that, on complaint, an Englishman shall be regularly tried for an offence against an Indian, and an Indian offending shall be delivered by his Tribe for trial.

Not necessary to remind the Chief of these things, as latter must abhor all such vile and abominable actions, which bring down the vengeance of God, and the displeasure of men, *particularly of the Subjects of his most Sacred Britannic Majesty, My Master*. Enjoined to recover the missing property and deliver Tedeumart and such others of the Tribe as are concerned in the wrongdoing, that they may be fairly examined according to the Treaty, and that the Chief himself may be freed from all blame.[6]

Armstrong wrote to many people describing the crimes he believed were committed by the Mi'kmaq and, to a lesser extent, by the Acadians. These crimes included murder, piracy and the theft of cargo from the *Baltimore*. But when he later found out that the Mi'kmaq and the Acadians were innocent of any serious wrongdoing, he made no attempt to renounce his false allegations publicly.

On November 22, 1736, Armstrong wrote to the Secretary of State reporting the true story behind the *Baltimore* incident. It turned out that Mrs. Buckler was not whom she claimed to be. The ship had sailed from Dublin with sixty to seventy passengers on board, most of whom were convicts bound for indentured service in the American colonies. He further reports:

It is supposed they rose upon Mr. Buckler, the Master, and Company and committed a most barbarous massacre. And afterwards not having their course, or afraid to venture into any place where they might be known, put into a most unfrequented harbour in the Bay, where they all perished (God knows how) except for the miserable woman, who perhaps was too deeply involved in the guilt to discover the true story of their misfortune.[7]

Many individuals suffered from Armstrong's false accusations. Two Catholic priests were deported from the province. The Cape Sable Mi'kmaq had to journey to the fort and present a defense for something they had no knowledge of, after which they were falsely branded by Armstrong as liars and unrepentant thieves. Yet, after the truth became known, the Lieutenant-Governor made no apologies.

Accusations like these, and others too numerous to mention here, were the fuel that kept the flame of antagonism burning. Because of such accusations, by the late 1730s, the situation in Acadia had not improved appreciably for the British. This is reflected in a letter Council members wrote to Governor Philipps on June 10,

1738, complaining bitterly about the province's problems, including the military government's inability to attract suitable English Protestant settlers. They listed four prime causes of the province's ills:

(1) The French Inhabitants allowed to remain in their possessions, no proper subjects could be found among them to establish a Government in accordance with the laws of England. *They are Roman Catholic and they are unqualified to form a House of Representatives.*

(2) Their possessing the best lands has been a discouragement to possible English settlers, "to offer themselves for settling any new and uncultivated lands."

(3) The penny an acre quit-rent and the possible tax of another penny is a great discouragement to Settlers, especially as very good lands may be had in adjacent Provinces without any such tax. [Mascarene, who tried to get settlers from the neighbouring province, found this penny tax the chief objection.]

(4) Except for these discouragements, the Province would have made greater progress and civil government established in all its branches; latter not incompatible with Military Occupation, which is an absolute necessity to keep the numerous French to their duty; and [to] protect [British] settlers from Indians, force should be greater....

We understand that some opposition has been made to some proposals of a new scheme offered by you for the settlement of this Province.... [The officers went on to defend their job performance and to deny the problems were caused by them.] We can each of us answer to our consciences that we have acted in our said capacities with a due regard to the liberty and property of the Subjects and the peace and well being of His Majesty's Province.[8]

When the Councillors listed the reasons why English Protestant settlers were not attracted to the province, they failed to cite the most obvious one: civil and military instability. It was not the kind of environment a sensible person would willingly walk into.

While this squabbling among members of Council was taking place, France and Great Britain were once again moving towards military conflict. This prospect instilled hope among the Acadians and Mi'kmaq that the future might rid them of the hated English. Thus, both communities increased their resistance to British rule dramatically.

At the same time, to help prepare for the expected war, the French garrison at Louisbourg was supplying intelligence concerning British military preparedness in the colony to their superiors in France. The source of the garrison's information was the Mi'kmaq "Captains network." This network had been set up by the French military establishment after 1713 to keep track of what was occurring in Acadia. These Warriors were in the employ of the French, who had dubbed them "Captains." As employees of the French, they did not take orders from the Mi'kmaq governments. The Captains were also used by the French to promote their economic and religious interests within Mi'kmaq communities. Louisbourg's Governor occasionally brought them together for meetings and information exchanges, and by 1738 these emissaries were reporting from every important bay in the province. Thus, the French were kept well informed about the comings and goings of the British.

However, use of the Captains network for other than military purposes began to undermine the authority of the elected Councils, generating resentment toward the French. This situation was partially corrected after Mi'kmaq Chiefs and Councillors protested to the French. Following the decline of French influence in the province, the Captains network continued to function but solely to promote the Catholic faith. It still functions to this day, and a "Captain" is still located in every Mi'kmaq community.

The Council's letter of June 10, 1738, had made clear that acrimony among members over land grants and settlement was widespread. On August 4, 1739, Lt.-Governor Armstrong wrote to Shirreff, informing him that Edward Amhurst could not comply with land registration and survey orders: "This is therefore to acquaint you that for the future you are not to make out a Patent, or any other survey or estimation then made by the Surveyor General, Col. Dunbar or one of his Deputies, and that you do in every grant specify his name, or the name of such Deputy of his as shall survey the lands to be laid out."[9]

Ignoring the fact that the Mi'kmaq were stringently opposed to such endeavours, colonial authorities continued to grant land. Entire townships were granted to individuals, and many received grants of up to a thousand acres. This appropriation of Mi'kmaq land without their consent was like driving a thorn into the side of an angry bullmoose and expecting it to calm him down.

However, in spite of the Mi'kmaq response, land grants increased. On August 6, 1738, for example, Edward How Esquire and Company applied to the Council for a patent to build a township at "Chickabucto by the Gut of Canso." Armstrong wrote to Shirreff on August 4, 1739, informing him that he had a report that there was no timber within the proposed township worth reserving for the King's service, and therefore he should issue a patent to How. Shirreff replied on August 6, 1739:

> Acknowledges having received Armstrong's directions "last Saturday" in regard to Amhurst, Deputy Surveyor, and the orders to draw a patent "for a Township at Chickabucto by the Gut of Canso in favour of Edward How and Company, the same being now laid out and surveyed by Amhurst. Shirreff considers it his duty to point out that ... "the Officers in Garrison at Canso and several others there, being thereby alarmed, have remonstrated to your Honour and the Council what a prejudice such a Grant will be to His Majesty's said Garrison, and His other Subjects of that place, and advises that the matter may be reconsidered by the Council."[10]

The officers, enlisted men and civilians at Canso were "alarmed" about the possible negative reaction the Mi'kmaq might have to this intrusion upon their territory. They feared, correctly, that the Mi'kmaq would take military action to stop it.

Armstrong sent back this message to Shirreff on August 8, 1739:

Has received Shirreff's letter of August 6th. Points out that there is no precedent for re-assembling Council to reconsider a matter once assented to....

Points out how such reconsideration will discourage Settlers, especially after a survey, which can only be made in this Country by fitting out a Vessel, and hiring Hands to protect the Surveyor against the Indians, a matter of great expense....

As to the remonstrance from the Officers at Canso, Armstrong should expect it to be addressed to himself and to come from the Commanding Officer. Has heard recently from him, and he makes no mention of the matter. Therefore cannot imagine that the founding of a Township of His Majesty's Protestant Subjects up the Bay can affect the Garrison injuriously.

It is the King's desire to have the Province settled; and this is all the more necessary in view of the great increase of the French population. Renews his instructions.[11]

Shirreff responded to Armstrong on August 9, 1739:

Has received Armstrong's letter of August 9th.... Still thinks that all matters of such importance should be weighed by the Council, especially if attended with disputes. [Commanding officer at Canso] Captain Mitford's silence does not, in Shirreff's opinion, cancel the Officers' complaint: it may be urged on either side of the case. In accordance with His Majesty's instructions, the complaint should be considered by the Council.

Does not see how he can draw up a Patent, "by and with the advice and consent of the Council" until the Council agrees. Is still of the opinion that the Minutes of August 8th, 1738, is not sufficient authority. Further reasons.

(1) The Royal Instructions require a certain proportion of unprofitable land to be granted with the profitable, and no tracts be granted running along the sea coast, or rivers....

(2) All such Townships are to be divided into Town Lots, and granted according to the capacities of the Settlers, no one of which is to have more than one thousand acres....

Shirreff needs the Council's help, if he is to avoid errors. Wishes from his heart there were five hundred Townships for one, settled in accordance with the King's Instructions. Would do all in his power to help not hinder.[12]

Except for mentioning the objections of the officers at Canso, Shirreff does not refer to the fact that Mi'kmaq title might be a hindrance in granting such properties. It's amazing how a people who claimed to be from a society governed by the rule of law could so religiously have ignored the property rights of an entire race of people.

Even today many people defend this expropriation without compensation. Ignoring the warped Christian law that mandated that non-Christians could not own land, which the French had used to lay claim to Mi'kmaq territory, they try to make a case that the taking of Mi'kmaq lands by the British was by "right of conquest." This is a ridiculous assertion for many reasons, the foremost being that the Mi'kmaq had never formally surrendered. Even if the Mi'kmaq had surrendered to the invading English, this in itself would not have extinguished the private property rights of the individual Mi'kmaq. If this had been the case, then the allies who won the Second World War would have acquired ownership over all private property in Germany, Italy, Japan and other Axis-allied countries.

Others try to make a case that the Mi'kmaq lost their right to hold Nova Scotia because they resorted to arms to attempt to prevent foreign seizure. This contention is ridiculous because individual and national rights to protect private and national property from invasion with force has long been a cornerstone of Western civilization. Therefore, by using force to stop the theft of their land by a foreign government, the Mi'kmaq were only doing what was reasonable. It must be recognized that the Nation's right to its lands was not extinguished because it tried to stop criminal acts committed by European governments.

In a bizarre turn of events, on December 6, 1739, Lt.-Governor Armstrong committed suicide. The president of the Council, John Adams, became acting Governor. To satisfy the requirements of law, the Lieutenant-Governor of the Garrison, Major Cosby, ordered his officers to sit as a coroner's jury. Their verdict was that Armstrong's suicide was as a result of "lunacy." No medical examination took place, but they based their verdict on the fact that Armstrong had been afflicted with "melancholy fits."[13]

By the spring of 1740, war in Europe had again broken out. Governor Paul Mascarene sent a notice dated May 12, 1740, to the Mi'kmaq and the Acadians, advising them that the King of Great Britain had declared war with the King of Spain and that at that time the British had no war with any other nation. On May 13, 1740, he further advised that the King had instructed that all governments in America were also to declare war upon Spain. This news created a high degree of apprehension and tension among colonial officials stationed in the province. It was an open secret that the sympathies of the Acadians and the French government were with the Spanish. The colonial government also felt that if hostilities broke out between the French and British, the Mi'kmaq would without a moment's hesitation support the French because, it believed, the "French held complete sway over them."

Over the next two years, both the Mi'kmaq and Acadians were constantly pressured to obey and declare allegiance to the British King. Tension increased dramatically in the Acadian communities as more and more controls were placed over their everyday affairs and the English demanded more taxes and the first right to purchase their wares.

On March 24, 1744, France declared war on Great Britain and, on April 9th, Great Britain declared war on France. The long-anticipated conflict had begun. During this war, known as the "War of Austrian Succession," the Mi'kmaq immediately joined forces with the French in an assault on Canso. The Canso fort was captured on May 24, 1744, and British prisoners were taken to Louisbourg. In joining with the French in this war, the Mi'kmaq and Maliseet—contrary to the British belief that they were not intelligent enough to make decisions on their own—were enthusiastic participants. This conflict was probably viewed by these Nations as a last chance to regain freedom and independence and rid themselves of a brutal oppressor.

The Mi'kmaq expressed their enthusiasm to rid their land of the invader by sending a force of about three hundred of their Warriors, accompanied by their priest, Jean-Louis Le Loutre, to lay siege to the fort at Annapolis on July 1, 1744. The force was supposed to link up with a French regular force, which did not arrive at the appointed time. Because of this, the siege was lifted temporarily and they retired to Minas. Desperate to save the fort from further siege and possible capture, Governor Mascarene appealed to Massachusetts for aid. In response, the Bay Colony sent what troops, supplies and armaments it could spare to shore up British defense efforts. This proved to be a Godsend for the garrison because renewed attacks were not long in coming.

After regrouping, the Mi'kmaq, Maliseet and French, with a combined force of some 250 men, again laid siege to the Annapolis garrison in September 1744. Although the French could have easily retaken the fort at this time—eliminating the last toehold of the British in the province and reasserting their control over Nova Scotia—for some reason they did not act. With the failure of promised French naval support to arrive, the army lifted the seige and retired to Minas in early October. This permitted the British and their New England subjects to regroup and strengthen the garrison's defense.

Part of the troops sent to assist in the garrison's defense by the Bay Colony were Warriors from many of the former Wabanaki allies of the Mi'kmaq and Maliseet Nations. This turn of events had been brought about by the careful cultivation of these Tribes by Massachusetts Governor William Shirley, who, in contrast to his Nova Scotia counterparts, had taken pains to engender Native friendship and loyalty after the peace of 1725.

The racist views of Nova Scotia's British colonial authorities that prevented them from working out a similar relationship with the Mi'kmaq and Maliseet were evident in an address to the Lords of Trade of London by Governor Mascarene, where he offered belittling comments about the value of the volunteers from the New England First Nations who had come to help defend Annapolis:

> This shows how much the preservation of this place is owing to the reinforcements we have received from the Province of the Massachusetts Bay; and how necessary it is to set Indians against Indians; for although *our men outdo them in bravery*, yet being unacquainted with *their skulking way of fighting*, and scorning to fight undercover, expose themselves too much to the Enemy's shot.[14]

It seems Mascarene did not appreciate the irony of his statement about pitting "Indians against Indians," for a good many Amerindian Nations at the time were becoming adept at pitting Europeans against Europeans.

With the fort under siege once again, Mascarene sent another appeal to Governor Shirley for help. Shirley, who was all but in name the true governor of Nova Scotia, responded by declaring war upon the Mi'kmaq and Maliseet. But before he issued his declaration of war, the Governor used the carrot and stick approach with the Maliseet in an attempt to keep them neutral. He promised them presents if they behaved, and threatened them with violence at the hands of the Mohawks if they

The slaughter of innocents

didn't. His threat was a tactical error, for if anything would spur on the Maliseet to fight alongside the Mi'kmaq and the French, it was the knowledge that the hated Mohawks were allies of their enemies. Thus the proclamation was finally extended to include the Maliseet as well. The declaration of war was issued on November 2, 1744:

> By His Excellency Wm. Shirley, Captain General and Commander in Chief in and over His Majesty's Province of the Massachusetts Bay in New England. A Proclamation for encouragement of volunteers to prosecute War against the St. John's and Cape Sable Indians.
>
> Whereas, the Indians of the Cape Sables & St. John's Tribes have by their violation of their solemn Treaties with His Majesty's Governors, & their open hostilities committed against His Majesty's Subjects of this Province & the Province of Nova Scotia, *obliged me with the unanimous advice of His Majesty's Council to declare war against them*,
>
> In consequence of which the General Assembly of this Province have voted, that there be granted to be paid out of the Public Treasury to any Company, Party or Person belonging to and residing within this Province who shall voluntarily & at their own proper cost and charge go out and *kill a male Indian of the age of twelve years or upwards, of the Tribe of St. John or Cape Sables* after the 26th day of October last past, & before the last day of June 1745, or for such part of that term as the War shall continue, ... *the sum of one hundred pounds* in bills of credit of this Province of New England, and *the sum of one hundred and five pounds for any male of the like age who shall be taken captive.*

And *the sum of fifty pounds in said bills for women, and for children under the age of twelve years killed in fight, and fifty-five pounds for such of them as shall be taken prisoners* together with the plunder. No payment shall be made for killing or taking captive any of the said Indians, until proof thereof be made to the acceptance of the Government and Council....

I have with the advice of His Majesty's Council determined that the line ... to the Eastward of which the said Indians may be slain and taken prisoners, shall begin on the sea shore at three leagues distance from the Easternmost part of the Passamaquoddy River, and from thence to run North into the Country through the Province of Nova Scotia to the River St. Lawrence.

I have therefore thought fit ... also to give notice to the said Tribes of Eastern Indians who are still in Amity with us, of the Boundary Line aforesaid, assuring them that this Government have determined to treat as Enemies all such Indians as live beyond the said Line....[15]

By no measure can such a horrendous document be called a product of a civilized people. Its intent was horrible and reprehensible. Only sick and barbaric minds could conceive of and implement such unspeakable crimes against humanity as the document demands. Hitler would have admired the genius of the men who introduced this horrible method of bringing a people they considered inferior to extinction.

After issuing the edict, Shirley wasted no time in taking steps to see that the gruesome harvest got under way. In this regard he immediately dispatched Captain John Gorham and fifty of his bloodthirsty "Rangers" to Nova Scotia. These bounty hunters were mostly Mohawk Warriors, historic enemies of the Mi'kmaq, with a sprinkling of Whites and half breeds. In later years, Whites would make up the majority. Because of their murderous reputations, the civilian and military populations of the garrison did not welcome these barbarians with open arms. As a matter of fact, some say with good cause that many loyal British subjects were terrified of them.

George T. Bates, in a paper read before the Nova Scotia Historical Society in 1951, said: "Not long after their arrival, Mascarene tells us, they fell upon a family of Indians lurking in the woods nearby. The rangers seized this opportunity to establish a reputation for themselves by killing some and scattering the rest."[16] Gorham's murderous initiatives soon satisfied Mascarene that the bounty hunter was well suited for his post. Father Maillard, a Catholic missionary, reports that among the first victims of these monsters—possibly during the incident Bates mentions—were three pregnant women and two small children. The Father also recorded many other barbaric atrocities committed by the English and their allies, including the desecration of Mi'kmaq burial grounds and the use of germ warfare against the Nations. He charged that the English and their New England subjects were deliberately spreading disease among the Mi'kmaq and Maliseet by passing out infected clothing and blankets. The French command speculated that this may have been the source of an epidemic that cost the lives of hundreds of Mi'kmaq and French fighters.

By 1745 the British and their allies had begun to take the offensive against

civilian and military targets in Nova Scotia. Governor Shirley was the key organ-
izer and persuaded the imperial and colonial governments to mount an all-out
attack upon Fortress Louisbourg. With the participation of British regulars, New
England militia, Amerindian allies and a Royal Navy squadron, a siege of Louisbourg
commenced in April 1745. At the same time a force of some seven hundred Mi'kmaq
and French troops commanded by Lt.-Col. Michel Marin laid siege to Annapolis
for a third time.

However, with Louisbourg under attack and in danger of falling, the siege of
Annapolis was dropped and Marin was ordered to Cape Breton to assist in its
defense. But he and his troops arrived too late, after the Fortress had capitulated on
June 26, 1745. With its fall the French position in the Americas became precarious.
To try to rectify this, in the summer of 1746, with their remaining positions in
Canada and elsewhere vulnerable to attack from the British or their New England
subjects almost at will, the French decided to mount an all-out offensive to recap-
ture Louisbourg and take Annapolis. In anticipation of the effort they assembled
in France a considerable invasion force. In expectation of the arrival of this fleet,
a force of some three hundred Mi'kmaq and French troops laid siege to Annapolis
for a fourth time. However, unbeknownst to them, the French invasion force was
struck by two natural disasters: a large part of the fleet was scattered by storms in
the Atlantic, and its troops were decimated by an outbreak of smallpox. When it
became apparent that the promised invasion fleet would not arrive, the siege of
Annapolis was lifted and the Mi'kmaq and French once again retired to Minas.

In late 1746, tiring of the use of Minas as a haven for Mi'kmaq and French
troops, Governor Mascarene sent in a force of New Englanders to secure and
occupy the place. This action initially met with little resistance because the allied
forces had retired to winter quarters at Chignecto. However, on February 11, 1747,
a combined force of three hundred Mi'kmaq Warriors and French troops attacked
the New Englanders, inflicting heavy casualties. By the time the New Englanders
surrendered they had lost more than seventy men. A short time later the survivors
were released and allowed to return to Annapolis.

The Treaty of Aix-La-Chappelle of 1748 once again restored peace between
France and Great Britain. The territories claimed by both powers, including Fortress Louisbourg, were returned to the status quo that had existed before the war.
The peace was bad news for the Acadians and the Mi'kmaq, who were now left at
the complete mercy of the English. This would prove to be a devastating blow to
the Mi'kmaq's hope to reclaim their independence, because this hope had been
intimately entwined with the French cause. In desperation, they sporadically bat-
tled on alone against the British invader for several more years. In hindsight, the
Treaty of Aix-La-Chappelle had been the death knell for Mi'kmaq liberty, but their
final subjugation was yet to come, at great cost to the British.

With the departure of the French from Nova Scotia, the Acadians and Mi'kmaq
came under increasing pressure to declare allegiance to the British King. Because
of their inability to protect their communities from English aggression after the
treaty was signed, the French in Quebec pondered the future of the two communities in Nova Scotia with apprehension. Both the Governor General and the Intendent
at Quebec felt the lives of both groups were at great risk. Serious consideration was

given to the possibility of relocating to Quebec any Mi'kmaq or Acadian who wished to make such a move. They viewed this course for the Mi'kmaq with more urgency in light of the possibility that the government of Nova Scotia might decide to emulate other British colonies that had chosen to exterminate Amerindian Nations or relocate them to other parts of the continent. These concerns of the French authorities were well grounded, because from this time onward the Mi'kmaq, as well as the Acadians, would be subjected to the most barbaric and degrading experiences at the hands of the English. Yet both communities continued to resist.

However, the writing was on the wall, because a mechanism designed to put a permanent end to their resistance had already been decided upon in London. To commence the final solution, in 1749, under the direction of the newly appointed Commissioner of Trade and Plantations, Lord Halifax, a plan was implemented to settle a large number of Protestant settlers in Nova Scotia. It was hoped that the plan would provide a buffer zone between New England and the French positions and secure the economic assets of the British colonies.

To this end, Edward Cornwallis was appointed Governor of Nova Scotia and commissioned to found a military base in the province to rival the threat posed by French-held Louisbourg. He set sail in May 1749 with a large group of settlers and military personnel. Upon arrival at Chebucto Harbour on June 21, 1749, they set about building fortifications and a new town, which was christened Halifax, in honour of the English Lord.

Cornwallis wasted no time in trying to establish his authority over the province. One of his first moves was to send Captain Edward How to the River Saint John to appraise the situation there and provide intelligence about the activities of the Maliseet and French. How contacted several Maliseet Chiefs and asked whether they would be willing to return to Halifax with him to renew the Treaty of 1725. After a short deliberation, the Chiefs agreed to do so, and thus on August 15, 1749, they entered into a new treaty in principle with the British. Now the Mi'kmaq were left as the sole opposition to the occupation of Nova Scotia by the English invaders. Abandonment by their allies must have caused the Mi'kmaq great apprehension; they probably realized that their situation was fast becoming hopeless.

The Treaty of 1749 reveals the single-minded resolve of the British to dispossess the Mi'kmaq and other Eastern Nations of their freedom and lands:

Renewal of the Treaty of 1725
(Chibucto—1749)

[The body of the treaty and provisions are the same as the Treaty of 1725.]

I, Joannes Pedousaghtigh, Chief of the Tribe of Chinecto Indians, for myself and in behalf of my Tribe, my Heirs and Their Heirs forever, and we, Francois Aurodowish, Simon Sactawino and Jean Battiste Maddouanhook, Deputies from the Chiefs of St. Johns Indians, and invested by them with full power for that purpose, do in the most solemn manner renew the above articles of Agreement and Submission, and every article thereof, with His Excellency, Edward Cornwallis, Esquire, Cap. General and Governor in Chief in and over His Majesty's Province of Nova Scotia or Acadia. In witness whereof, I, the said Joannes Pedousaghtigh, have subscribed this Treaty and affixed my seal, and we, the said Francois Aurodowish, Simon Sactawino and Jean Battiste Maddouanhook, in behalf of the Chiefs of the Indian Tribes we represent, have subscribed and affixed our seals to the same, and engage that the said Chiefs shall ratify this Treaty at St. Johns. Done in Chibucto Harbour, this fifteenth day of August, One Thousand, Seven Hundred and Forty Nine, in presence of: L.E. Hopson, Benj. Green, P. Mascarene, John Salusbury, Robert Ellison, Hugh Davidson, James T. Meriner, Wm. Steele, Chas. Lawrence, Ed. How, *John Gorham: Members of the Council for Nova Scotia.*

Joannes Pedousaghtigh (totem) (L.S.), Francois Aurodowish (totem) (L.S.), Simon Sactawino (totem) (L.S.), Jean Battiste Maddouanhook (totem) (L.S),. Maliseet Delegates.[17]

The Maliseet Chiefs ratified this treaty in the presence of Captain How on September 4, 1749, at the River Saint John. The Mi'kmaq continued in a state of war with the English, with some support from a few of the smaller Bands of Maliseet. However, from this point onward the Mi'kmaq were for the most part on their own.

More Bounties for Human Scalps
and the Treaty of 1752

W hen Governor Edward Cornwallis and his entourage founded Halifax in 1749, it was during a lull in the war with the Mi'kmaq. In fact, the Mi'kmaq greeted them with hospitality. One settler wrote home: "When we first came here, the Indians, in a friendly manner, brought us lobsters and other fish in plenty, being satisfied for them by a bit of bread and some meat."[1]

However, at British instigation, this would soon change. At an early September 1749 meeting with the Mi'kmaq Chiefs, a British emissary restated the dictum given to their predecessors in 1715. He also confirmed their fears about the Colonial Council's new settlement plans for the province. This gravely alarmed the Chiefs and they reacted as could be expected. On September 23, 1749, the Mi'kmaq renewed their declaration of war against the British and began attacking military, shipping and trade targets.

Geoffrey Plank lays bare what Cornwallis had planned if such occurred:

> If the Micmac chose to resist his expropriation of land, the governor intended to conduct a war unlike any that had been fought in Nova Scotia before. He outlined his thinking in an unambiguous letter to the Board of Trade. If there was to be a war, he did not want the war to end with a peace agreement. "It would be better to root the Micmac out of the peninsula decisively and forever." The war began soon after the governor made this statement.[2]

Scalping Proclamation of 1749

After he had read the first edition of *We Were Not the Savages,* published in 1993, Charles Saunders, a columnist with the Halifax *Daily News*, sent me a congratulatory note dated February 2, 1994:

> Several years ago, I watched a panel discussion that had several minority members, including a Black and a Micmac. The Micmac representative said that Blacks were slaves in the early days of European colonization, but his people were lower than slaves. At that time, I didn't understand what he meant. What, I wondered, is lower than being a piece of property to be bought and sold like a horse or cow? Then, in the chapter of your book titled "The Edge of Extinction," I read about how your people were systematically starved to death. At least a slave gets fed, simply because the owner has a vested interest in keeping him or her alive to maintain the slave's value as property. So, thanks to you, I know what it is to be "lower than a slave"—to not even have value as human chattel or property.[3]

At the beginning of 1749, in line with the statement contained in this letter, as far as British colonial society was concerned, the life of a Mi'kmaq had no value. Thus they were accorded no civil or human rights. Even the blatant murder or robbery of one or many Mi'kmaq by a White man was not considered a crime and went unpunished. Such was par for the course across the Americas. At that time, the mass murder of the Red People of the Americas, which was often successful in exterminating entire races, was still common and done without fear of recrimination. In keeping with this well-entrenched European practice, in 1749 Nova Scotia's colonial government undertook an attempt to exterminate the Mi'kmaq.

Related to this and other abuses cited in this chronicle, the term *"genocide"* will be used, because it aptly describes the barbaric behaviour of the British in colonial Nova Scotia. Its use in this case is appropriate because the mayhem the British subjected the Mi'kmaq to meets every single definition listed in the United Nations Genocide Convention. Canada's conduct after 1867 also fits into several of its definitions.

The term "genocide" was first used to describe the extermination of most of Europe's Jews by Nazi Germany. It was later used by the United Nations in 1948 in the Genocide Convention to mean crimes against humanity. The "Convention on the Prevention and Punishment of the Crime of Genocide" was adopted by the United Nations on December 9, 1948. Article 2 of the Convention defines the word:

Genocide means any of the following acts committed with intent to destroy, in whole or in part, a national, ethnical, racial or religious group, as such:

(A) Killing members of the group;

(B) Causing serious bodily or mental harm to members of the group;

(C) Deliberately inflicting on the group conditions of life calculated to bring about its physical destruction in whole or in part;

(D) Imposing measures intended to prevent births within the group;

(E) Forcefully transferring children of the group to another group.[4]

When musing over what you have already read and what you will read, please keep these definitions of the Genocide Convention in mind.

During my youth, I had often heard, in offhand or incredulous remarks, about the bounties which purportedly had been put on the heads of the Mi'kmaq in Nova Scotia by the British during the mid-1700s. Although I knew that bounties were put on certain animals, such as porcupines, from time to time by governments I never really took these statements about bounties on the Mi'kmaq seriously because I couldn't imagine that a people who claimed to be civilized could propose such an evil plan. When young, it takes time to shed your innocence.

Then, around 1965, when attending upgrading courses at the old sugar refinery in Dartmouth with my brother Lawrence and the late Norman Brooks, a friend from Indian Brook Reserve, the truth began to dawn. And it dawned in a most unusual way. Getting out of school early one day, we decided to go to the old Picadilly Tavern in Halifax for a few beer. After arriving, we bought our brews with the few bucks we could raise between us and then wondered where we could find a few dollars for a couple more. Norman and I looked at my brother, who was setting across from us with his back to the wall, and told him we didn't know where he was getting his money from, but we knew where we were getting ours. This was because Lawrence was setting directly under a reproduction of a proclamation for Mi'kmaq scalps signed by Governor Cornwallis.

After the joking was finished, I read the document and began to feel sick as I realized it was probably a replica of the original. However, at that time, I was still carving out a niche in life for myself and thus set the matter aside for the time being. Then, after going to work for the Department of Indian Affairs in 1971, I began to study up on the Indian Act, peace treaties and other historical documents. It was during this time that I verified, to my horror, that on three occasions the British colonial governments of this province had in fact issued bounties for the scalps of Mi'kmaq men, women and children!

Perhaps if I had known then about some of the horrors that had been committed by the English in the British Isles and elsewhere, I wouldn't have been so shocked by my discovery. But in school we had been taught a romanticized version of English history which ignored such horrors as those played out in 1746 at the battle of Culloden in Scotland. It was there that English troops, under the command of the Duke of Cumberland, engaged in atrocities such as locking thirty Scots in a house and burning it down around them; shooting and bayoneting the wounded; and slaughtering the retreating army. As if this wasn't enough, after defeating the Highlanders, the English added to their misery by forbidding them to wear their national dress, deporting many and suppressing their Gaelic language. Knowing about such things as this might have helped to prepare me for the discovery I had made. On the other hand, probably nothing can fully prepare one for the barbarities perpetuated by one group of humans against another.

On October 1, 1749, demonstrating that he was well endowed with a heartless cruelty, Cornwallis convened a meeting of Council aboard H.M.S. *Beaufort*, anchored in Halifax Harbour, and won approval for the following sadistic response to the Mi'kmaq's declaration of war:

> That, in their opinion *to declare war formally against the Micmac Indians would be a manner to own them a free and independent people, whereas they ought to be treated as so many Banditti Ruffians, or Rebels*, to His Majesty's Government.
>
> That, in order to secure the Province from further attempts of the Indians, some effectual methods should be taken to pursue them to their haunts, and show them that because of such actions, they shall not be secure within the Province.
>
> That, a Company of Volunteers not exceeding fifty men, be immediately raised in the Settlement to scour the wood all around the Town.
>
> That, a Company of one hundred men be raised in New England to join with Gorham's during the winter, and go over the whole Province.
>
> That, a further present of 1,000 bushels of corn be sent to the Saint John's Indians, to confirm them in their good disposition towards the English, AND,
>
> *That, a reward of ten Guineas be granted for every Indian Micmac taken, or killed.*[5]

The bounty hunters

The horror contained in these words, because of their blind White supremacist views, probably escaped the English. The next day, without a hint of conscience, the following proclamation was signed by Cornwallis and issued:

> Whereas, notwithstanding the gracious offers of friendship and protection made in His Majesty's Names by us to the Indians inhabiting this Province, the Micmacs have of late in a most treacherous manner taken 20 of His Majesty's Subjects prisoners at Canso, and carried off a sloop belonging to Boston, and a boat from this Settlement and at Chinecto basely and under pretence of friendship and commerce. Attempted to seize two English Sloops and murder their crews and actually killed several, *and on Saturday the 30th of September, a body of these savages fell upon some men cutting wood and without arms near the saw mill and barbarously killed four and carried one away.*
>
> For those cause, we, by and with the advice and consent of His Majesty's Council, do hereby authorize and command all Officers Civil and Military, and all His Majesty's Subjects or others to annoy, distress, take or destroy the Savage commonly called Micmac, wherever they are found, and all as such as aiding and assisting them, give further by and with the consent and advice of His Majesty's Council, *do promise a reward of ten Guineas for every Indian Micmac taken or killed, to be paid upon producing such Savage taken or his scalp* (as in the custom of America) *if killed* to the Officer Commanding at Halifax, Annapolis Royal, or Minas.[6]

Thus, at a cost to his Majesty's colonial government's treasury of ten guineas per head, and at a cost to his servants of their immortal souls, an attempt to exterminate the Mi'kmaq was under way. It was an action no civilized nation would countenance, nor could any nation that undertook it be called civilized. Such barbaric behaviour, under any set of circumstances, is unforgivable. In apportioning the blame for the issuance of this hideous document, it was Cornwallis who proposed it and thus shoulders most of the responsibility, but the Councillors share almost as much guilt because they approved the monstrous dictum.

Such inhuman behaviour was not new to Cornwallis. According to data enshrined in a book entitled *Culloden* by John Prebble, Edward Cornwallis was the Lieutenant-Colonel of Bligh's and was stationed in Scotland during the 1740s. Prebble's book details how Cornwallis and his troops helped put down the Scottish rebellion and fully participated in the barbaric mistreatment of the Scots. These events occurred after the English had looted and burned Achnacarry:

> The black smoke of burning Achnacarry was still coiling down Loch Arkaig when Bligh's went away, swinging toward Moidart with Culcairn's militia, "burning of houses, driving away cattle and shooting those vagrants who were found to be in the Mountains."
>
> Much of what they did was not reported ... but John Cameron, Presbyterian Minister and Chaplain at Fort William, wrote down an account of it in his journal. He said that when the party camped for the night on the braes of Loch Arkaig, they saw what they thought was a boat on the shore. A party went down to examine it, and found it to be a large black stone, "but that they might not return without some gallant action, on meeting a poor old man about sixty, begging, they shot him." They also found an old woman, blind in one eye and not much more than a beggar herself, and when she would not say where Lochiel was hidden (if she knew), she too was shot. "This is certain," said Minister Cameron, "but what is reported to have been done to her before she was dead, I incline not to repeat—things shocking to human nature."
>
> "Culcairn's...," according to Cameron, "were responsible for these shootings, but the men of Bligh's did their share. They saw two men carrying dung to their bitter fields and these were ordered to come before Cornwallis. They came but on their way were foolish or thoughtless enough to look back at their field. The soldiers shot them."[7]

Cornwallis displayed a lack of human conscience while doing his part to help the English army subjugate the Scots. In view of this, it can be concluded that the man had an inborn taste for the crimes against humanity he committed in Nova Scotia. Such an affliction is well reflected in the warped rationale he used to try to justify his monstrous edict. The incidents listed in the first paragraph of his scalping proclamation were acts of war carried out by the Mi'kmaq against military targets. They deserved a military response against Mi'kmaq Warriors, not Mi'kmaq civilians. Trying to use a few incidents such as these to justify condemning to death an entire race of people is reprehensible, even more so when one considers that some of these incidents are suspect and possibly no more than propaganda.

For instance, the wood-cutting incident falls into this category (it's also an incident that I've grown very weary of hearing about). It is alleged that it occurred in what is now Dartmouth, across the harbour from Halifax. The proclamation says: "on Saturday the 30th of September [1749], a body of these savages fell upon some men cutting wood and without arms near the saw mill and barbarously killed four and carried one away." The question this poses is, why was this group of "defenseless" Englishmen sent out into the forest alone to cut wood during a time of war without troop protection and thus left vulnerable to attack? If this was the case then it smacks of gross incompetence on a British officer's part. If the story is true and not propaganda, a more credible reason for them being sent out without troop protection is that they were not defenseless but as well armed as the Mi'kmaq and probably more so. This can be reasonably assumed because, as woodcutters, they had axes to cut wood with, which alone would have made them possessors of weapons as lethally effective, and probably more reliable, than most of the arms the Mi'kmaq had access to. In any event, because the English were assaulting the Mi'kmaq and stealing their territory, Cornwallis and his Council should not have been so affronted and reacted so barbarously when the Mi'kmaq fought back.

In fighting back to preserve their freedom and country, the Mi'kmaq paid a heavy price. The records indicate that the barbarous proclamation was very productive. The slaughter was indiscriminate—pregnant women, the unborn, the old, the infirm—there were no exceptions; even some Whites were harvested. As an indication of how many scalps were taken, Bates wrote:

> It is reported that ... a party of Gorham's rangers one day brought in 25 scalps, claiming the bounty of £10 per scalp. It was strongly suspected that not all of the scalps were those of Indians, but included some Acadians too. The paymaster protested the payment, but was ordered to pay £250 anyway.... The records of Chignecto include several instances of extreme cruelty and barbarism by the rangers.[8]

It was further reported that eleven Rangers disappeared around this time. Some believe that their scalps may have been among those presented to the authorities for payment. These sort of accusations by other Whites against them are an indication of the infamous reputations and low morals of these men. However, whatever they did to one another, they must have found the scalp trade very lucrative in Nova Scotia, because many of the killers sent from the Massachusetts Bay Colony to carry out the intention of Governor Shirley's evil 1744 proclamation found the returns so good that they spent many years in the province. In addition, the practice was so widespread that many non-military Whites used it to supplement their incomes.

In all fairness, it must be stated that during this period the French at Louisbourg were not without dirty hands. In retaliation for Cornwallis's proclamation, they issued their own proclamation for the scalps or capture of *British soldiers*. But, it must be emphasized, *it was not for civilians and especially not women and children*. Some Mi'kmaq took up the challenge and delivered such. However, mostly they brought in live military prisoners and collected a bounty for them.

Factually speaking, most individual Mi'kmaq conducted themselves in a relatively humane and civilized manner during this trying period. The few that were involved in the bounty trade committed some atrocities, usually under the influence of alcohol supplied by Whites. However, many of the atrocities that the Mi'kmaq were blamed for were in fact committed by the "friendly Indians" brought in by the English. The English had such a great relationship with these people that they were often their victims. Perhaps this was simply poetic justice.

The Mi'kmaq Nation, to its everlasting credit, even in the face of such horrific provocations as the 1749 Proclamation, did not respond in kind and adopt a policy to attack White women and children. Although some apologists try to make a case to the contrary, no evidence exists whatsoever to support such a contention. Most of the prisoners they took were turned over unharmed to the French at Louisbourg and later released. The same could not be said for Mi'kmaq prisoners held by the English. Many were held indefinitely, while others were taken to Boston and hung. Cornwallis, in an October 1749 memorandum to the Lords of Trade, requested retroactive approval for actions he had already initiated. The memo provides further proof of his insincerity and treachery towards the Mi'kmaq:

> When I first arrived, I made known to these Micmac His gracious Majesty's intentions of cultivating Amity and Friendship with them, exhorting them to assemble their Tribes, that I would treat with them, and deliver the presents the King my Master had sent them, they seemed well inclined, some keeping amongst us trafficking and well pleased; no sooner was the evacuation of Louisbourg made and De Lutre the French Missionary sent among them, they vanished and have not been with us since.
>
> The Saint John's Indians I made peace with, and am glad to find by your Lordship's letter of the first of August, it is agreeable to your way of thinking their making submission to the King before I would treat with them, as the Articles are word for word the same as the Treaty you sent me, made at Casco Bay, 1725, and confirmed at Annapolis, 1726. I intend if possible to keep up a good correspondence with the Saint John's Indians, a warlike people, *tho' Treaties with Indians are nothing, nothing but force will prevail.*[9]

There are three points in Governor Cornwallis's letter on which I'd like to comment:

1. Cornwallis cites everything but the real reason why the Mi'kmaq ended their brief cordial relations with the settlers. The omitted reason—and perhaps due his biases he was unable to recognize it—was that they had discovered that the British had come to seize more of their land and establish more settlements instead of making a lasting peace. Therefore, their disappearance from the site of Halifax at the same time the British were evacuating Louisbourg was only coincidental. The declaration of war made by the Mi'kmaq Chiefs in response to the seizure of ancestral lands attests to this.

2. The statement Cornwallis makes that "Treaties with Indians are nothing, nothing but force will prevail" provides a clear picture of the morally bankrupt people the Mi'kmaq had to deal with. His pretending to promote honour and good faith in dealings with the Mi'kmaq and other Amerindians while at the same time having no intention to act accordingly clearly reveals his own corrupt ethical standards and those of the system he represented.

3. The unfounded accusation he made against the missionary Le Loutre demonstrates both his religious bigotry and White supremacist beliefs. His contention that "De Lutre [sic] the French Missionary" was the cause of the Mi'kmaq disappearance from Halifax reflects both an abiding hatred for Roman Catholics and a firm White supremacist belief that Amerindians did not have sense enough to value their territory and fight for it without being goaded on by a White man. The truth

is that the missionaries did try to assist the Mi'kmaq in their hour of need, but they were not, as almost unanimously characterized by the English, religious devils who held absolute sway over every decision the Mi'kmaq made.

To refute and place in perspective this opinion widely held by English colonial officials which insults the intelligence of the Mi'kmaq, let's examine the role of the missionary that the British hated the most, the Vicar-General of Acadia and missionary to the Mi'kmaq, Abbé Le Loutre. The following are two evaluations of his character quoted from *Challenge and Survival: The History of Canada*:

(1) ... He fed their traditional dislike of the English, and fanned their fanaticism.... Thus he contrived to use them on one hand to murder the English and on the other hand terrify the Acadians.... Le Loutre was a man of boundless egotism, a violent spirit of domination, an intense hatred of the English, and a fanaticism that stopped at nothing.

Towards the Acadians he was a despot: and *this simple and superstitious people*, extremely susceptible to the influence of their priests, trembled before him. He was scarcely less masterful in his dealings with the Acadian clergy; and, aided by his quality of the Bishop's Vicar General, he dragooned even the unwilling into aiding his schemes. Three successive governors of New France thought him invaluable, yet feared the impetuosity of his zeal, and vainly tried to restrain it within safe bounds.[10]

(2) It is not easy at this distance of time to appraise the character of Abbe Le Loutre. Accounts of his activities have come down to us from a period when national prejudices were intensified by the bitterness of the desperate struggle for the mastery of the North American continent. It was not strange that Cornwallis thought him a scoundrel. Nor was it surprising that the French authorities esteemed him a single-minded patriot. Parkman calls him the evil genius of the Acadians.... That he used his influence over the Micmacs to oppose the power of Great Britain is indisputable; that he incited his Indians to acts of barbarity is probable. But, even when this is established beyond reasonable doubt, it remains true that *he used a weapon which was employed by both British and French without scruple during the several phases of the American conflict. It is noteworthy that when he became a priest he did not cease to be a Frenchman. As a Frenchman he caught a vision of a new Acadia, secure in its allegiance to his king and firm in its fidelity to the church. Had he succeeded ... his claim to eminence would not be unacknowledged.*[11]

Instead of the monster depicted by English colonial authorities and many later chroniclers of history afflicted with racial and religious biases, Le Loutre was a humanitarian. He probably was affronted and appalled, as any decent human being should have been, by the inhumanities being committed against the Mi'kmaq and other Amerindians by the English. This line of thinking is confirmed by the fact that he tried in vain in future years to arrange a peace with the British that would have left the Mi'kmaq with enough land to preserve their status as a free and independent people. This, in my estimation, is probably the only unbiased conclusion one can reach when evaluating his motivations.

When trying to understand the hatred the British had for Le Loutre, another factor must be kept in mind—their unwavering resolve to dispossess the Mi'kmaq of everything and to subjugate them absolutely. Anybody with the unmitigated gall to beg to differ with them was branded everything from bandit to devil. This was Le Loutre's folly.

Contrary to what English officials thought, men such as Le Loutre assisted the Mi'kmaq in trying to deal with the impossible situation given them, but he did not think for them. To think otherwise is a racist insult. *The Mi'kmaq are intelligent human beings who survived quite well for thousands of years without having a White man to think for them,* and I'm sure in this case they did their own thinking.

The other thing I wish to add here is that I believe *the paternalistic and patronizing attitudes adopted by many White historians towards the Amerindian intellect is a defensive measure.* If they can convince themselves that the people their ancestors brutalized, dispossessed and in many cases exterminated were little more than savage animals, then they don't have to face up to the horrors committed by these ancestors. After all, when you simply put down pests and varmints, who should complain?

In a memo dated February 16, 1750, the Lords of Trade responded to Cornwallis's letter. They approved of but were not overly enthusiastic about the course of action chosen, for they cautioned him:

> As to the measures which you have already taken for reducing the Indians, we entirely approve them, and wish you may have success, but as it has been found by experience in other parts of America that *the gentler methods* and offers of peace have more frequently prevailed with Indians than the sword, *if at the same times that the sword is held over their heads, offers of peace and friendship were tendered to them, the one might be the means of inducing them to accept the other*, but as you have had experience of the disposition and sentiments of these Savages you will be better able to judge whether measures of peace will be effectual or not; if you should find that they will not, we do not in the least doubt your vigour and activity in endeavouring to reduce them by force.[12]

Many apologists have claimed that the cruelties inflicted upon the Mi'kmaq and other Amerindian Nations were for the most part local acts of depravity and not acts sanctioned by the European Crowns themselves. However, this reaction by British officialdom towards Cornwallis's proclamation proves that contention wrong. By not rescinding or condemning his inhuman proclamation, the Lords of Trade, policymakers for the British government, showed support, thus implicating the British Crown itself in the crime of genocide.

The Lords also put into writing the paranoid fear the English had of Amerindians. It's embodied in the worry they expressed that the bounty on the Mi'kmaq might, "by filling the minds of bordering Indians with ideas of our cruelty,"[13] somehow unite all the Amerindian Nations of the Americas against them in a continental war. The equivalent of such an impossible feat would have been the uniting of all the countries in Europe against an invader, which, based on their mutual dislike of one another, would have been impossible. However, what the Lords proposed might happen poses an interesting point. If the people of the Americas could have overcome their cultural differences and united, and if they had been heirs to a class-based, barbaric and warlike history similar to that of the Europeans, whom they may have outnumbered, most of the citizens of Europe today might be speaking a language imported from the Americas rather than the other way around.

Back to reality. The scalping bounties also adversely affected the Acadian population, because many of them were part Mi'kmaq or were related to Mi'kmaq families by marriage. Many Acadians were also scalped by the bounty hunters simply because they were handy and hated. On several occasions Acadian Deputies protested to the Governor about the existence of the bounties. In his stint as Governor, Mascarene in one instance pointed out to them that the many Acadian inhabitants living close to the fort were doing so quite peacefully. Such remarks did not alleviate the fear and hatred the Acadians held for the Rangers.

On June 21, 1750, in what must have resulted from dissatisfaction with the number of Mi'kmaq scalps being brought in, Cornwallis and his Councillors raised the monetary incentive by proclamation to fifty pounds sterling per head. It's interesting that Gorham himself was part of the Council which approved the 1749 scalp bounty, and he was also a member of the Council in 1750 when the bounty was raised. One might be excused for concluding that he was in a conflict of interest.

How many Mi'kmaq were killed during the carnage following Cornwallis's proclamations is unknown, although some records mention scalps being brought in by the bagful. The government possibly did not keep a close count on the expenditures or charged it off as a miscellaneous expense, or kept an accurate tally but, after realizing the horror of its actions, destroyed the evidence.

In 1752, three years after the despicable proclamation had been issued, the colonial government ordered a temporary halt to bounty hunting in the province. At a Council meeting held at the Governor's house on Friday, July 17, 1752, it was resolved that a proclamation be issued to forbid hostilities against the Indians:

By His Excellency the Honourable Edward Cornwallis Esquire, Captain General, and Governor in Chief, in and over His Majesty's Province of Nova Scotia, or Acadia in America, and Vice Admiral of the same.

Whereas, by the advise and consent of His Majesty's Council of this Province, two Proclamations were, by me, sometime since applied, authority and commanding (for reasons set forth in the said Proclamations) all Officers, Civic and Military, and all of His Majesty's Subjects within this Province, to annoy, distress, take and destroy the Savages called the Mickmack Indians, and promising a reward for each one of them taken or killed;

And whereas, for sometime past no hostilities have been committed by the said Indians against any of His Majesty's Subjects, and some overtures tending to peace and amity have been made by them, I have thought fit, with the advice and consent of His Majesty's Council to revoke the said Proclamations, and every part thereof, and further do hereby strictly forbid all persons to molest, injure or commit any kind of hostility against any of the aforesaid Indians, or any Indian within this Province, unless the same should be unavoidably necessary in defense against any hostile act of any such Indians towards any of His Majesty's Subjects;

And whereas, since the said cessation of hostilities, and publicly known design of a conference to be had between this Government, in conjunction with the Government of Massachusetts Bay, with the Tribes of Indians residing within, or bordering upon the said Governments, some evil minded persons regardless of the public need, and the good intention of the said Governments in their endeavour to effect a renewal of peace, and amity with the said Indians, and in violation of good faith, have, lately, in a vessel said to belong to Plymouth in New England, *treacherously seized and killed near Cape Sable, two Indian girls, and an Indian lad, who went on board the said vessel, under given truce, and assurances of friendship and protection*;

I do hereby, promise a reward of fifty Pounds Sterling to be paid out of the treasury of this Province, to any person who shall discover the author, or authors of the said act, so that the same may be proved before me and His Majesty's Council, of this Province, within six months from the date hereof.[14]

If by reading this document anyone concludes that Cornwallis had suddenly become a humanitarian they should think again. The government of the powerful Massachusetts Bay Province wanted peace with the Mi'kmaq, and therefore he had no choice but to halt hostilities. In fact, the Massachusetts Bay Governor was probably instrumental in pressuring Cornwallis to later resign.

Even after Cornwallis rescinded his proclamations, many colonials still assumed the bounties were in effect and tried to collect for scalps brought in. None were prosecuted.

The three children referred to in the Governor's proclamation died horrible deaths. They were butchered alive. No serious attempt was ever made by the colonial government to find and prosecute the culprits. In view of Cornwallis's own record, it would have been just short of a miracle if there had been.

Cancelling the bounty was one of the last official acts that Cornwallis performed as Governor. Shortly thereafter, he resigned his commission and was replaced by Peregrine Thomas Hopson, who was sworn into office on August 3, 1752.

Although Cornwallis's barbarity is well documented, much of it by his own hand, up to the year 2000 no White jurisdiction had ever condemned him for it. In fact, only honours have been given by authorities in Nova Scotia and Canada to the memory of the author of the 1749 scalping proclamation. A statue of him is displayed in a park located across from the railway station in Halifax, and schools, streets, ships, a naval base and so on have been named after him. In view of this, I ask, and will continue to ask, how can my country, which claims to be civilized, award such honours to a man who authorized ethnic cleansing? In my estimation the only award such an individual deserves is the gallows. From a civilized point of view, only a person subscribing to the same White supremacist beliefs that

Cornwallis and Hitler subscribed to would believe that killing "inferiors" is incidental.

By 1752, through the horrendous death toll taken by genocide, disease, starvation and war, the Mi'kmaq population had been reduced to approximately 20,000 destitute people. However, the English considered even this drastically reduced and impoverished population a threat to their security and sought ways to neutralize it, while at the same time affording the Mi'kmaq no chance to retain their land or their dignity.

Almost two and a half centuries later, in 1998, the Mi'kmaq reacted with outrage to an invitation from the City of Halifax to participate in its 250th birthday celebrations. The city wanted them to provide a canoe filled with Mi'kmaq Warriors to greet an actor portraying Cornwallis entering Halifax Harbour. Reacting to the People's outrage, Mayor Walter Fitzgerald issued this apology on February 1, 1999: "While we cannot change history, I sincerely apologise for any atrocities which were committed against the Mi'kmaq after the founding of Halifax in 1749."[15] I thought then, at long last, some official recognition that the founder of Halifax was a far cry from being the hero he has been depicted to be by many politicians and more than a few historians. Alas, it was not to be. On June 21, 1999, Fitzgerald proved that he had spoken with a forked tongue. On stage with him when he cut Halifax's birthday cake was an actor dressed up as Cornwallis, to whom the Mayor served a piece. In response to reporters' questions about this turnabout he replied, "The Mi'kmaq tribes killed a lot of white people, probably more than we did." When reminded by a reporter that Cornwallis had put a bounty on the heads of the Mi'kmaq, including women and children, he responded, "I think he did. I'm not sure about that." Some sincerity!

Thankfully, there is opposition building to such archaic views among the White population. The enlightened view expressed by Art Gallery of Nova Scotia guest curator Mora Dianne O'Neill to a Halifax Herald reporter on June 26, 1999, may well be that of the majority. When planning the 1999 Great Harbour Exhibit, O'Neill felt that the Mi'kmaq presence in Halifax from 1749 to the present had to be a prominent part of the display. To gather support for the Mi'kmaq part of the project she meet with the Chiefs in February 1999. At the meeting she was asked by the Chiefs how she could justify Cornwallis's 1749 scalp bounty. She said she could not. Later, at a June 26, 1999, media tour of the exhibit, after having read about Cornwallis's brutality during the massacre of the Scots at Culloden, O'Neill added, "After that, there was no way I'd see Cornwallis hanging rather than from a rope."

Otherwise intelligent Whites have told me with a straight face that Europeans were on a civilizing mission when they came and stole the Americas. However, the barbarous methods the Europeans used in stealing the two continents leaves me with the impression that they were the uncivilized attacking the civilized. If what they did was civilized behaviour, may we never be civilized again!

The Treaty of 1752

Governor Hopson found an extremely distressing situation awaiting him in Halifax. The British government was sending foreign settlers over by the boatload without adequate provisions and they were starving to death. The fort was in a serious state of decay, the troops were restless and it was feared that the Acadian French might leave the province and dry up the colony's only reliable source of food. On top of all this the Mi'kmaq and the British were at war. Hopson began at once the tasks of renewing the garrison and put out feelers to several Chiefs about peace talks.

Responding to these feelers, Chief Jean Baptiste Cope, Chief of the Shubenacadie Mi'kmaq—whose territory comprised an area that today covers approximately Cumberland, Colchester, Guysborough, Hants, Halifax and parts of Antigonish, Pictou, Kings and Lunenburg counties—approached the British in September 1752 with a proposal that peace be restored with his District. The British agreed to begin discussions and requested his terms.

In order to help dispel stereotypical views of him as a craven barbarian that still persist among the White population, the following is a short personal history of Chief Cope:

Chief Kopit (translates Beaver), christian name "Jean Baptiste," was born to Paul and Cecile Kopit in the Shubenacadie valley in the year 1698. The date of his death is unknown, however the record shows he was still alive in the 1760s, which indicates he may have lived to a ripe old age. He, siblings, and parents were Roman Catholics and he was baptised shortly after birth. Kopit spoke both Mi'kmaq and French and some English.

In later years he added the title Major to his name, possibly in the belief, because Europeans of those days were known to bow and scrape before those who were titled, or in authority, that a fancy title would enhance his negotiating

The treaty signing (1752)

powers with the English. If this were the case, it demonstrates Kopit's ability to use alien cultural values to advance his cause. I say this because in Mi'kmaq society kowtowing to leadership was unheard of.[16]

During the negotiations the Chief informed the English authorities that they should pay for the land they had arbitrarily taken for their settlements and other uses. He probably realized the futility of this request, but with great foresight thought it should become part of the record. However, with the same stubbornness they had previously displayed, the English refused to discuss the issue of land. With terms finally worked out, the treaty was signed on November 22, 1752:

The Treaty of 1752

Treaty articles of peace and friendship renewed
Between His Excellency, Peregrine Thomas Hopson, Esquire, Captain General, and Governor in Chief, in and over His Majesty's Province of Nova Scotia or Acadia, Vice Admiral of the same and Colonel of One of His Majesty's Regiments of Foot, and His Majesty's Council on Behalf of His Majesty, and
     Major Jean Baptiste Cope, Chief Sachem, of the Chibenaccadie Tribe of Mick Mack Indians, Inhabiting the Eastern Coast of the said Province, and Andrew Hadley Martin, Gabriel Martin and Francis Jeremiah, Members and Delegates of the said Tribe, for themselves and their said Tribe, their Heirs and the Heirs of their Heirs forever....
     1. It is agreed, that the Articles of Submission and Agreement, made at Boston, in New England by the Delegates of the Penobscot, Norridgwalk, and St. Johns Indians in the year 1725, Ratified and Confirmed by all of the Nova Scotia Tribes, at Annapolis Royal in the month of June, 1726, and lately Renewed with Governor Cornwallis at Halifax, and Ratified at St. Johns River, now read over, Explained and Interpreted shall be and are, from this time forward, renewed, reiterated and forever confirmed by them and their Tribe....
     2. That, all Transactions during the late War shall on both sides be buried in Oblivion with the Hatchet. And that the said Indians shall have all favour, Friendship and Protection shewn them, from this His Majesty's Government.
     3. That, *the said Tribe shall use their utmost endeavours to bring in the other Indians to Renew and Ratify this Peace*, and shall discover and make known any attempts or designs of any other Indians, or any Enemy whatever, against His Majesty's Subjects within this Province so soon as they shall know thereof and shall also Hinder and Obstruct the same to the utmost of their power, and on the other hand if any of the Indians refusing to ratify this Peace shall make War upon the Tribe who have now confirmed the same, they shall upon application have such aid and assistance from the Government for their Defence, as the case may require.
     4. It is agreed, that *the said Tribe of Indians shall not be hindered from, but have free liberty of Hunting and Fishing as usual* and that if they shall think a Truckhouse needful at the River Chibenaccadie, or any other place of their

resort, they shall have the same built and proper Merchandise lodged therein, to be exchanged for what the Indians shall have to dispose of, and that in the meantime *the said Indians shall have free liberty to bring for Sale to Halifax, or any other Settlement within this Province, Skins, Feathers, Fowl, Fish, or any other thing they shall have to sell, where they shall have liberty to dispose thereof to the best advantage*.

5. That, a Quantity of bread, flour, and such other Provisions as can be procured, necessary for the Familys, and proportionable to the number of the said Indians, shall be given them half yearly for the time to come; and the same regard shall be had to the other Tribes that shall hereafter Agree to Renew and Ratify the Peace upon the Terms and Conditions now Stipulated.

6. That, to Cherish a good harmony and mutual Correspondence between the said Indians and this Government, His Excellency, Peregrine Thomas Hopson, Esqr., Captain General and Governor in Chief in and over His Majesty's Province of Nova Scotia or Accadia, Vice Admiral of the same and Colonel of one of His Majesty's Regiments of Foot, hereby promises, on the part of His Majesty, that *the said Indians shall upon the first day of October Yearly, so long as they shall Continue in Friendship, Receive Presents of Blankets, Tobacco, some Powder and Shott*, and the said Indians promise once every year, upon the said first of October, to come by themselves, or their Delegates and Receive the said Presents and Renew their Friendship and Submissions.

7. That, the Indians shall use their best Endeavours to save the lives and goods of any People Shipwrecked on this Coast where they resort, and shall Conduct the People saved to Halifax with their Goods, and a Reward adequate to the Salvage shall be given them.

8. That, all Disputes whatsoever that may happen to arise between the Indians now at Peace, and others His Majesty's Subjects in this Province, shall be tryed *in His Majesty's Court of Civil Judicature, where the Indians shall have the same Benefit, Advantage and Privileges as any other of His Majesty's Subjects*.

In faith, and Testimony, whereof the Great Seal of the Province is hereunto Appended, and the Partys to these Presents have hereunto interchangeably set their Hands in the Council Chamber at Halifax, this 22nd day of Nov., 1752, in the 26th Year of His Majesty's Reign.[17]

In view of the increasing strength of the English and their unyielding attitudes, it can be safely concluded that Chief Sachem Jean Baptiste Cope signed the Treaty of 1752 in a desperate attempt to prevent the complete annihilation of his people. For a while he succeeded because the British needed time to refurbish Halifax's fortifications and bring in more White Protestant settlers.

The Treaty of 1752, although including the demeaning provisions the British had included in previous treaties, included a radical departure from the policy of the previous administration. The policy Cornwallis had struck was that the Council could not declare war upon the Mi'kmaq, because to do so would have recognized them as a free and independent people. That policy was jettisoned by Section 2 of the 1752 treaty, which declares that this treaty ends the war. The treaty also provided some benefits to the Mi'kmaq, such as recognition of aboriginal fishing, hunting and other rights. These were probably included to convince the Chief to agree to the inclusion of Section 3, which required him to work to bring in other District Chiefs to sign similar treaties.

When word of Cope's peace treaty reached French territory, he was roundly criticized by Louisbourg's Governor. In anger the Governor invited as many Mi'kmaq Chiefs as possible to the fort to make his displeasure known. There he called upon the remaining Chiefs "not to follow the treasonous footsteps of Chief Cope."[18] When making these remonstrations, the Governor, Comte de Raymond, conveniently overlooked the fact that at the conclusion of all the French and English wars in which the Mi'kmaq had assisted them as allies, his country had never included the Mi'kmaq in the peace negotiations, consulted with them in any way, protected their interests or made allowance for them to be a signatory to any of the treaties concluded. Therefore his protests were those of a hypocrite.

As usual in the case of treaties they signed with Amerindians, the English began to ignore their obligations almost immediately upon ratification. Section 4, promising free liberty of hunting and fishing, is a good example of what later became empty promises. However, after well over two centuries of negating the terms of this treaty, the Supreme Court of Canada finally recognized and affirmed its validity in 1985.

On November 24, 1752, the colonial government issued a proclamation advising the citizens of the ratification and signing of the treaty two days earlier:

By His Excellency Peregrine Thomas Hopson Esqr., Captain General and Governor in Chief, in and over His Majesty's Province of Nova Scotia or Accadie, Vice Admiral of the same and Colonel of one of His Majesty's Regiments of foot &c.

Whereas, the Treaty or Articles of Peace and Friendship hath been renewed on the 22nd Inst. between this Government and Major Jean Baptiste Cope, Chief Sachem of the Chibenaccadie Tribe of Mick Mack Indians, Inhabiting the Eastern Coast of this Province, and the delegates of the said Tribe fully empowered for that purpose;

And Whereas, it is provided by the said Treaty that all the transactions of the late War should on both sides be buried in oblivion with the Hatchet, and that the said Indians should have all favour, Friendship and Protection shewn them from this His Majesty's Government and also all the benefits, advantages and privileges in His Majesty's Courts of Civil Judicature, equal with all others of His Majesty's Subjects;

I have therefore thought fit by and with the advice and consent of His Majesty's Council, in His Majesty's Name to publish and make known the same to all His Majesty's Subjects and strictly to Charge and Command all His Majesty's Officers, and all others His Subjects that they do forbear all acts of Hostilities against the aforesaid Major Jean Baptiste Cope, or His Tribe of Chibenaccadie Mick Mack Indians from and after the day and the date of these presents, as they shall answer the contrary at their peril.[19]

Thus a legitimate British colonial government made public that it had signed a treaty with another nation ending a war. Reason and common sense demand that this event be taken for what it was—a peace concluded between two sovereign and independent peoples.

The British, by ratifying the Treaty of 1752, took a small step towards peace with the Mi'kmaq. However, it was not an act of honour by the English, because it was simply another step towards realizing the complete rape of the Mi'kmaq Nation.

8

The Futile Search for a Just Peace, 1752-1761

The probability that the Peace and Friendship Treaty of 1752 would entice other Mi'kmaq Chiefs to seek similar accommodations with the British was behind Louisbourg's fierce opposition to it. The French knew that such an eventuality would forever end their alliance with the Mi'kmaq, dry up a rich source of military intelligence and assistance, and prove extremely detrimental to their future political and military ambitions in the region.

Thus, Governor de Raymond searched for a way to stop the peace movement before it spread. In this regard he had generous but unintentional help from the British. The help resulted from the ungodly scalping proclamations they had issued in the past and their steadfast refusal to prosecute any White person for killing an unarmed, defenseless Mi'kmaq. This knowledge by Whites of freedom from prosecution resulted in the commission of a horrendous crime by two of his Majesty's subjects that proved a Godsend for the French. The preliminary details of the drama that was played out during the winter and spring of 1753 are cited from the introduction to Anthony Casteel's journal.

The surveyor Morris in a letter to Cornwallis in England, dated April 16, 1753, gives what details he had of the crime:

> Yesterday [the 15th of April] arrived from the Eastward two men, in an Indian Canoe, who have brought six scalps of Indians. The account they gave of the affair, upon their examination, was that James Grace, John Conner (a one eyed man, formerly one of your bargemen), with two others, sailed from this port about the middle of February last in a small Schooner, and on the 21st were attacked in a little harbour to the Westward of Torbay by nine Indians, to whom they submitted, and that the same day on which they landed the Indians killed their two companions in cold blood; that Grace and Conner continued with them till the 8th of the month, when some of the Indians separating, they remained with four Indian men, a squaw, and a child: *that the four Indians left them one day in their Wigwam with their arms and ammunition*, upon which hoping to recover their liberty, *they killed the woman and child, and at the return of the men killed them also* [the number of Mi'kmaq murdered was actually seven], and then taking the Canoe made the best of their way to this place.
>
> This is the substance of their story; but as the Indians complained, a little after the sailing of this Schooner, that one exactly answering her description put into Jedore where they had their stores, and robbed them of forty barrels of provision given them by the Government, it is supposed that these men might afterwards have been apprehended by some of this Tribe, whom they

killed as they describe.

If this be the case, it is a very unhappy incident at this juncture, and time only can discover what its consequences will be. *The Chiefs of every Tribe in the Peninsula had sent in messages of friendship, and I believe would have signed Articles of Peace this Spring, if this incident does not prevent them.*[1]

It appears Morris was willing to give the murderers' story credibility. He does so even in the face of the fact that the Mi'kmaq felt so trusting of these individuals that they left them to roam free in the camp with easy access to ammunition and guns, not suspecting that their kindness and trust would be rewarded by death. This is an example of how the "Blame it on the Indians" philosophy prevails even in the face of overwhelming evidence to the contrary.

This account of the matter was also expressed in "Documents Sur L'Acadie":

Thus for Mr. Morris's (account). But the fact was still blacker than he suspected. After having robbed the Indian store houses, the crew of this unfortunate Schooner was obliged to encounter the fury of the deep. They suffered the shipwreck; were found by the Indians drenched with water, and destitute of everything; were taken home, cherished, and kindly entertained. Yet they watched their opportunity, and *to procure the price of scalps murdered their benefactors, and came to Halifax to claim the Wages of their atrocious deed.*

The Indians, as may well be supposed, were exasperated beyond measure at this act of ingratitude and murder. (Revenge boils keenly in their bosoms, and their teeth were set on edge.) To procure immediate retaliation, they sent some of their Warriors to Halifax, to complain of the difficulty they found to keep their provisions safe during the fishing season, and to request that the Government would send a small Vessel to bring their families and stores to Halifax. In compliance with this desire, the Vessel and Crew mentioned in the journal were engaged, although several suspected, from the first, that it was an Indian feint to spill blood. The subsequent incidents are abundantly intelligible of themselves.[2]

After reporting the murders, expecting that the English would honour Section 8 of the Treaty of 1752 which was meant to enforce prosecution of Whites who committed crimes against them, but then not receiving any satisfaction, the Mi'kmaq Chiefs became very disillusioned with the peace process. Thus they permitted the French to take revenge.

How the French went about it is detailed in the following excerpt from Casteel's journal. The journal's contents, which describe his dealings with Chief Cope and experiences while a prisoner of the Mi'kmaq and the French during May and June of 1753, were presented under oath by Casteel to the Governor's Council:

On the 16th day of May 1753, I sailed from this Port (Halifax) at 8 o'clock in the evening in company with Captain Baunerman, Mr. Samuel Cleaveland, and four bargemen to convey these Indians (the complainants) to Jedore, and there transact certain business by order of his Excellency.

The same evening we came to anchor in Rouse's Cove where we spent the night. On the 17th we set sail at 4 o'clock in the morning, and as we passed Musquodoboit, two of the Indians being urgent to go ashore (Joseph Cope and Barnard), their Canoe was launched out, and they immediately put to land.

We kept our course to Jedore, after arriving, which was near 12 o'clock, Francis Jeremy was desirous of going ashore likewise. Accordingly our boat was manned with two hands and he put ashore at the Eastern side of the Harbour. At about 4 o'clock in the afternoon an Indian came down to the waterside and hailed the Sloop.

Upon which I informed Captain Baunerman that it was Major Cope. He replied, then you must go ashore and speak to him. Accordingly two Hands stepped into the boat with me, and as we were going over the side, I told them by no means to step ashore, but to put off the boat, and return on board as soon as I was landed, which they did.

At meeting, Major Cope embraced me in the manner he used to do, and called me his son, and after common compliments passed, *he asked me what we were coming for*. In reply I said, have you not seen any of your people? He answered me no; then I informed him that we were come to fetch the provisions they had.

He desired that after we had the provisions, we would not go immediately away, for he wanted to write to his brother the Governor; that *he was in very great danger, for the Indians threatened to kill him*, wherever they found him, and that if he thought the Governor would provide a Priest for him he would come to Halifax with his family; and after he had done with the Priest, made Confession, and received the Sacrament, he would not care if the Indians did kill him; then he should be prepared.

During this discourse I observed that he often looked towards a point up the Bay, where … I thought I saw somebody move, and asked him whether any person was there. He said yes, there were his daughters Margaret and Anne, who were afraid because it was a vessel they had not seen before.

I desired him to call them, he did, and they came. I saluted them, and conversed with them for some time upon indifferent subjects. We then parted, Major Cope promising to come the next day to have his letter wrote. They having got some distance from me I hailed the boat and was put on board.

On the 18th, about 11 o'clock, there came four Indian men and one woman to the water side, who hailed the vessel, and desired to be put on board. Accordingly the boat was manned, and soon returned with them. They informed us that they came to deliver their provisions. One of the Indians brought two parcels of gunpowder, and wanted me to give him something for it. I told him that I had nothing to give, and had no occasion for it.

Then they asked if we would go (to their storehouse), and take the provisions (on board). Upon which Captain Baunerman called me aside, and asked how far up the harbour their provisions were? I informed him of the place. He replied, the (small) boat could not fetch the provisions in a day or two, and concluded as we had the Indians aboard, to go … (get them) with the vessel. Accordingly we went that day, and upon our arrival I, with two of our men and two Indians, went on shore.

As soon as I landed I went up to the store house, and at first found nothing but pease (peas). I coopered (repaired) the cask as well as I could. I sent 15 barrels, and a half one in three boat loads, together with a barrel of flour that I found. After the pease were out, we returned on board the Sloop, the two Indians being with us with the last load.

After we got on board, I asked the Indians whether they had seen Major Cope, they said they had, but that he was ill and could not come that day. The Indians then left us in a friendly manner. When they were gone, Mr. Baunerman asked me if there were any more pease ashore; I told him there was, but not fit to bring away. He replied, it was a pity that those pease should be lost when he had a pig starving at home.

I told him we had gone beyond our orders in coming up there. He said we had, and ordered the sails to be immediately loosed, and the anchor weighed. We made two or three trips (tacks) but lost ground. Upon which they were about again to go to anchor; but I told them I was not willing, for I did not care to lie there.

I desired to have my way for once, although not a seaman, and advised to get the boat ahead, (they should) … lower the sails, and get the Sloop into the channel, and then she would (go out to sea) with the tide. Mr. Cleaveland said he was afraid the vessel would run upon the flats, and if she was lost, all was gone, for it was all he had to depend upon for himself and family. However, we proceeded in the aforementioned manner, and got down upon dark. We then divided ourselves into two watches, three men in one, and four in the other, and so we passed the night.

On the 19th, some of the people took the boat, and put a little off from the Sloop, where they killed some flat fish, which we dressed and breakfasted upon. Afterwards, Captain Baunerman said he would go ashore. Accordingly he emptied our meat and bread bag, and went in the boat with four hands to get the pease that was left; whether armed or not I cannot say. (For the sake of some half rotten peas, five men would die, the spoils of greed.)

Mr. Cleaveland went to work below to ease the sliding door of the forecastle, while I was lying in the cabin, having watched the night before. As near as I can guess, in an hour after they were gone I heard a very extraordinary noise, notwithstanding the noise Mr. Cleaveland made of sawing and hammering in the hold of the vessel.

I jumped immediately upon deck, and saw several canoes coming toward us. I called to Mr. Cleaveland, and told him I believed our people were taken, for there were a parcel of canoes coming on board. Before I had done speaking, they began to fire at me both from the canoes and shore. I whipped up an axe and cut the cable, and jumped into the hold immediately; where I had not been long before the Indians boarded on each side of the vessel.

They called us to come up and promised to give us good quarter. I went upon deck, and some of the Indians went into the hold and helped Mr. Cleaveland up. By this time our boat came aboard, in which were some men, and some Indians, accompanied with several canoes. They ordered us to come into the boat, and again told us we should all have good quarter.

The Indians had now hoisted the sail of the Sloop and stood up the Harbour. While we were taken on shore on the Western side of the Harbour, where were some huts, and where the Indians had a strong consultation, with many high words. I addressed myself to my Comrades, and told them that I believed we were not long for this world, and that we had best recommend our souls to God, and improve the little time that we had. Immediately they all fell upon their knees, except Captain Baunerman, who lay flat on his face on the ground. He lifted up his hands, turning his face toward me, and said, "this is no more than I expected."

After the consultation, which lasted about half an hour, one of the Chiefs got up, and asked what Country I was of? I told him I was a Frenchman, and desired him to ask those people who had been so often at Chebucto, whom I had told I was a Frenchman when in no danger. He asked them and they confirmed the truth. With that he pulled out a cross from his bosom, and told me by virtue of that cross, I should not die by their hands, and bade me kiss it, which I did.

I had scarcely kissed it before Captain Baunerman's head was split in two, and the rest slain before my eyes. Then Major Cope was ordered to take me away. We walked together upon the beach about 500 yards, when he ordered me to give him my watch, with my boots, cap and greatcoat, and likewise to give him what money I had. I pulled out six dollars and five half pence, he returned me the five half pence again.

Then he travelled me, as nearly as I could guess, three miles through the

The boarding

wood over to Musquodobit, where we came to his Canoe, and where some of his Indians joined us. He put me into the bow of the Canoe, and put from the shore … for an Island in the middle of the Harbour, but before we reached it one of the Indians made seven screeches, the last different from the rest.

Upon going ashore, we went to Major Cope's Wigwam, where he gave me a pair of Bearskin Moccasins, and where I tarried till it was quite dark. Then three Indians took me into the woods with them, where they lighted a fire and tarried half the night. To save me from the others, who had got rum from on board, they made an alarm. The three Indians hauled me violently through the woods to a Canoe belonging to one of the Chiefs. I embarked with Anthony Batard and his brother. We went up into the Bay, into a river called Musquodobit, where we went ashore, lighted a fire and tarried the rest of the night.

Sunday 20th. In the morning they trimmed the scalps, and fixed them into little round hoops, and after drying them with hot stones, painted them red. Here Major Cope put his hands akimbo, and said to the Indians, "You say I am not a good soldier; I took Picket's vessel and went to Chebucto, and I was the occasion of taking this." Then we embarked, and I was put with two strangers. We continued in that river two days, and on Tuesday morning, the 22nd, we got into a lake, which led us into the Shubenacadie River, in which we continued all that day, and at night we arrived at a place called Shubenacadie.

Upon … landing, there came down an Indian Squaw, to whom I pulled off my hat. She spoke to the Indian named La Glasiere, the moment she was answered, she took me by the hair of the head and hauled me up part of the hill. An Indian (came) after her, cleared me from her hands, and gave her two scalps

The transport of Casteel

... with which she and Major Cope's daughter danced until foam came out of their mouths, as big as my fist, which caused tears to gush out of mine eyes. The Indian men perceiving it, sent me with a little boy to the houses where the rest of the Indians were. That night they made me fry them some pancakes.

On Wednesday the 23rd. We left and went down the river, and after we got some distance, we landed on the Eastern side, and then carrying their Canoes by land, we crossed the river twice to shorten our way. When we came near Cobequit, they gave me one of our firelocks and some powder and bid me load to salute the Inhabitants. When we came within hearing of Cobequit, they again gave the seven screeches, as they did before, and then began to fire, and we repeated our fire several times, until we had got to the last house, into which I went with some Indians, one of whom demanded the Articles of Peace that Cope had before lodged there.

The Frenchman of the house went to his chest and produced them. There was neither seal nor case to them when produced. They ordered me to go out of the house with them, and gave the Articles into my hand, desiring me to read them. They formed a Circle. I read the French part about halfway through, when they were snatched out of my hand by the Indian that first demanded them ... led me into the house, where he threw the Articles into the fire, and told me that was the way they made peace.

Then their Chief called the man of the house, and told him that he must find a bullock, and some bread for his Party. The Frenchman asked him for his order ... he pulled a paper out of his pocket and told me to read it. I did. It was addressed to the Inhabitants ... dated May 5th or 6th, and as well as I can recollect the tenor was as follows: "*This is to command all French Inhabitants; wherever this detachment passes, to furnish them with ammunition, and provisions, or any other necessaries, being upon the king's duty going to Chebucto, per me, Delansett.*"

The Frenchman would have excused himself, having done so much already, and having a great family. The Chief told him if he did not comply, they would go and pick out a bullock for themselves. Upon that the man went immediately and brought a bullock, and likewise baked five oven full of bread for the Indians, and gave them some tobacco. Then the Chief, or *Captain, ordered me to make out a (receipt* for) for one bullock, one barrel of flour made into bread, 12 or 14 lb of tobacco, 6 lb of powder and 150 balls (and give it to the Frenchman).

Thursday the 24th. The bread was divided, about half a loaf to each man, and of beef that each one pleased. He that was called my Master made a bundle of his share, and placed it on my back. We then marched through the woods to Tatamagouche, where we arrived that evening and lodged.

Friday 25th. We crossed the Bay and marched to a place called Remsheag. When we came in sight of an Indian Camp ... one of the Indians in company, repeated the screeches of death, and fired two guns. A canoe then came across the Harbour to convey us over to the other side, where was my Master's wife and family.

When we arrived I was ordered into his Wigwam, where I found an old lame man, who was father-in-law to my Master. He told me I was very lucky in being a Frenchman, for if I had not, I would have been killed with the rest. He further said, that he was surprised the English began (killing) first (because) they had done (them) no manner of harm for a long time.

(He then told me) that *they had taken up two men that had been cast away, who were but just alive, and whom they were sorry for, and nourished,* and (that they) told (them) that as soon as they had an opportunity they would send them home. But the season having come on to go into the woods, *they left these two miserable men (who had two of their companions drowned) with two Indian men, three women and two children, one of which was an infant at the breast, who were all slain.*

These Englishmen, taking an opportunity in the night, killed … the Indians (while they) were asleep, (and) … afterward … sunk their bodies in a Canoe. (He said,) "It was a thing they would never forgive or forget. For if they were to get as many scalps as there were hairs on their heads for those people killed, they would not be satisfied. For *they had always spared as many women as ever they could when they took them,* and that now they would not spare even the child in the mother's womb."

The manner of the above mentioned Indians being killed, Joseph Morrice declares as is above related, and if desired, is willing to come to Halifax, and give evidence of what he knows of the affair.

We tarried at Remsheag, where a number of Indians joined us until the 9th of June, when we set out in Canoes for Baye Verte, and arrived there the 10th, which was Sunday. The Indians delivered me to a Lieutenant in the fort, called Caskaron, who told me he was very glad my life was spared and bade me to go into the kitchen and ordered some victuals for me.

About one or two hours after came his Commanding Officer, who called for me and told me he was glad I was saved, and (then) began to rail against the English on account of the Indians being killed by the two men. Saying, *what a terrible thing it is to kill a child that has not been christened,* and that the English might take care of themselves, for the Indians would have their revenge.

He added, that the English Gentlemen of Chignecto began to play some uncivil tricks, as taking their horses from them, and that they may be made to suffer for it. While they were talking with me *an Indian came and demanded me out of the fort. The Officer told me to go with him, I answered that I thought I was under the protection of the French. But I was obliged to go with the Indians,* who were about to carry me to the Town called … Baye Verte to speak with the Priest, but meeting with him in a Canoe we returned with him to the fort.

We went into the fort together, and after the Priest had spoken to the Indians, he came to me and asked what Countryman I was? I told him of Paris. He asked what part of Paris? I told him of Faubourg Saint Germains. He asked me what street? I told him Prince Street. He asked what Parish I belonged to? I told him Saint Supplice. He told me he belonged to that Parish, and came from it. He then said, he was very glad the Indians had saved me, and added they would do me no hurt.

He called the Indians into the Officer's room, telling me he would call me in when he had done with them; which he did not. But when he came out, I asked him whether there was any probability of recovering me watch, which the Indians had taken from me? He answered me no, and said, whatever they took, they never returned again.

On the 11th, the Indians came and demanded me out of the Fort, took me to their Wigwams, and presently returned me again to the Fort. As soon as I arrived, the Officer called for me and asked me whether those Germans were returned, that had been with them there? I answered, that I believed they had got down to Chebucto by this time....

He asked me if there were not armed vessels out of Boston? I told him I could not tell. He said that as I lived at the Governor's, I must know something of it and that I hid the truth. Then I told him that, although I was a Frenchman, I should be a villain if I answered ... any questions prejudicial to the English.

He then grew into a passion, saying I should suffer for it, and ordered me out of the room. Towards the evening he called me in again, and asked whether the Germans had gone to inhabit Maligash? I answered, that I believed they were. He asked what forces they had with them? And I told him, they were very well provided, for anybody that would go against them; that they had taken several blockhouses, ready made to raise upon their arrival.

He asked what troops were going? I told him two complete Companies of Rangers and a great number of Regular Troops. He asked what number? I told him that I could not tell. He asked what Forts there were in Halifax? I told Him there were six with guns, and mortars in all of them, besides Blockhouses all around the Town, where guards were mounted. He asked me what Troops there were in Halifax? I told him three old Regiments, and two more expected by the first Ships. He lifted up his shoulders and made a wonder at it. Upon which he told me I might go.

On the 12th an Indian came for me, with whom the Officer ordered me to go. He carried me to a point opposite Baye Verte, where the Indians had lately shifted their camp. There I found, as near as I can guess, five hundred of them. The Indian who carried me told me to go into his Wigwam, and charged me not to stir out of it, for he was afraid some ... would harm me.

As soon as we went in, the women were ordered out, and there came in a number of men, with whom was my Master and his father-in-law. They bade me pull off my hat and kneel down. They then held a consultation among themselves in Indian, after which they all turned towards me, and my Master's father-in-law accosted me, saying he was going to tell me what they had concluded, and what I had to trust to.

He then informed me I must either pay my ransom, or die. For answer, I said, how is it possible that I can procure the money whilst I am confined where I can see nobody. He said there was a man in Baye Verte who would lend me what money I wanted to pay my ransom, and thirty Pistole was their demand. If I equivocated the least, when that man would let me have the money, I was a dead man.

I told him I was satisfied to pay the money, if the man would let me have it, and if not, if they would take me up to the Fort at Chignecto I could have the money immediately. He answered there was no occasion to go so far. Then I was taken into a Canoe with Major Cope, and five men more, to go to the Town or Village. When I got on shore, I met Francis Jeremy with several other Indians, one of whom was Paul Laurent, to whom Francis … said that I talked very good English.

Then giving a roll of tobacco out of his hand to a boy that stood by, he took me by the hand and asked me if I could talk English? I answered yes. He asked what Countryman I was? I told him a Frenchman. He asked me if I had any regard for my soul? I said yes. When he said, how come you with the English? I told him I was taken in a French Vessel in the wars, and that speaking French, the English found me useful, and would not let me go away.

He asked me if they kept me in a prison? I answered no. Then said he, you could have got away, and had no need to stay so long with them. I told him I could myself, but that I had a son for whom I would lose my life rather than leave him behind. (Then I told him) I was glad of this opportunity … (to live) … with my own Country people and enjoy my religion, and I hoped that the Governor of Louisbourg would be so good as to send for my son.

He said he was sure the Count would. He further said, are you not come here to pay your ransom? I said yes. He asked me what I was to pay? I answered that I had agreed already with my Master for the sum. *He told me* he was my Master and nobody else, and *that he had sent the young men to kill our people, and take me*, and that he would not take less than 3,000 Livres for my ransom.

I told him, that I was but a poor lad, and that it was impossible for me to find 3,000 Livres. Francis said, "Oh Casteel, don't tell lies, for you have houses in Chebucto, and live with the Governor, and have money enough." Upon that the old Indian was in a great passion, and being somewhat warm myself I told him that I must die for I could not procure the money.

Upon which James Morrice came and struck me on the shoulder and desired me not to be in a passion, for I was in danger. He spoke mildly to the Indian, and told him that I was poor and that it was not good for him to keep me. Upon this the Indian asked me if I looked upon three thousand Livres as more than my life? I answered, that if I had 20,000 I would give them all before I would lose my life.

By this time my Master came, I took him by the hand and asked him if we did not agree for 300 Livres, and whether I was not told that if I equivocated I was a dead man? He answered yes, he was a man, and had but one word and that I should pay no more than 300 Livres. Then Paul Laurent started up from his seat and said that he would pay the money and take off my scalp for his father was hanged in Boston.

My Master said, take him then and pay the money immediately. He put his hand into his pocket and pulled out a knife, there was an Officer … who stood at my left hand, and saw the knife and perceiving the Indian was about to stab me gave me such a violent push as caused me to go backwards three or four paces and fall on my back.

The women screamed out, thinking I was stabbed, and the sons of James

Morrice took me up and carried me into a little room where I fainted away. After coming to myself the wife of James Morrice gave me a glass of wine and asked me if I was hurt? I answered no. She went immediately to her Chest and brought a bag of 6 Livre pieces and told out 50 of them which is 300 livres.

James Morrice called in my Master and desired him to count the money, which he did. Mr. Morrice asked him how much money there was? He said 300 Livres. Then said James, "Is it your money, take it up, the man is mine." The Indian swept the money into his hat, then Morrice said to the Indian, "Let me not see one of you come near my house or molest this man for if you do I'll break your bones."

The Indian took me by the hand and told me I was my own Master and that I must satisfy the man that had paid the money for me. I said to him that the man was not uneasy. The Indians then went out of the house and shoved Paul Laurent out before them and used him very ill. At night a Corporal came from the Fort with a Summons to bring me and James Morrice there, but it being too late we tarried until morning when we set off for the Fort and on the way Mr. Morrice told me that they were all a parcel of rascals and that they owed him a spite for doing good to the English.

When we arrived we went into the officer who in a very great passion asked Mr. Morrice, "How he durst buy anybody without his knowledge?" Mr. Morrice said, "Would you have me see innocent blood shed in my house?" The Officer replied there was no danger and that Christians were not to be bought and sold in that manner. Mr. Morrice mentioned the Officer that saved me from being stabbed and likewise said that it was so late and I was in such danger that he could not possibly let him know of it before he had bought me.

The Commandant immediately sent four hands in a boat to bring the Officer who had pushed me out of the way of the Indians, who said that if he had not so done I should have been stabbed. The Officer of the Fort then said that he understood I was to be sent (home) by way of Chignecto but the Count, *the Governor of Louisbourg, (wanted) to see all prisoners and wanted them to be sent there.*

The conversation the Officer of the Fort had with the other I have from Mr. Morrice, being myself sent out of the room before he came. He likewise told me he had not liberty to take me to Louisbourg himself. I replied, that it was very unjust inasmuch as he had paid money for which he had no security. I then asked him if he would take my note of hand? He answered no, that he believed that I was an honest man, but if he was never to receive a Farthing, that should not hinder him saving the English to the utmost of his power, even to the last shirt to his back.

He then said, that if I wanted anything, he would send it to me. I informed him that I should be glad of a shirt, and since he was so good, would make bold to ask the favour of a small toothed comb along with it. We then parted, and the next day he sent me the above articles, with a 6 livre piece.

On Thursday the 14th, I was sent on board a Schooner bound for Louisbourg, where we arrived on the 16th. The Captain of the Schooner went ashore with me, and took me to the Governor, and presented him some letters he had brought from Fort Gasparaux, one of which related to me. The Governor told me that he had not the time to speak to me at present, but ordered me to come again.

Accordingly I went on the next Monday, and as soon as I entered into his house, he sent me into his room, and ordered me to relate the manner of my being taken. He unfolded a map of this coast, where I showed him all the rivers, creeks and places I was in. *He likewise examined me upon the Treaty of Peace made with the Indians, and with whom it was made.* I told him it was by a letter that Cope sent himself to Governor Cornwallis.

He inquired, what man that was that went to Saint Peters after Cope last Summer? I told him it was one Piquet that carried an answer to Cope's letter from the Governor. He asked me what post I was in at Chebucto? I answered, I was linguist for the French, and messenger for the Council. He asked me what messages I did for the Council? I told him it was to acquaint the Members, whenever the Governor thought proper to call a Council.

He asked me who was Governor? I told him Colonel Hopson, the gentleman that was governor of the Island when Louisbourg was resigned. He asked me what Countryman I was? I told him I was an Englishman. He asked me how I could tell him such a lie, when he was informed by letters from Baye Verte that I was a Frenchman? I told him that I did not dispute, but that he was told so. For I found that the Indians commanded Baye Verte, and I was obliged to stand to what I said before to save my life.

He then asked me why I did not bring a Certificate to prove I was an Englishman? I informed him it was not usual among the English. He replied that he was fully satisfied that I was a Frenchman, and a Subject to the King of France. I then told him I would sooner be cut to pieces than stay away from my own Country people and my family.

He then asked me if the Germans were gone to settle Maligash? I said I believed they were. He asked me what forces they had with them? I told him two Companies of Rangers, and many regular Troops, but I could not specify the numbers. He asked me who was the Chief Commander there? I told him Colonel Lawrence.

He asked, was he that was at Chignecto? I said yes. He said he was but a Major. I told him he was a Major then, but a Colonel now. He then dismissed me, and said he would speak to me some other time. I went the next day, but was denied admittance, upon which I went to the Secretary and desired a pass. He told me he would speak to the Count and give me an answer the next day.

When I went at the hour appointed, the Secretary said that the Count would speak to me himself. He went with me and acquainted the Count that I was come. I was then called into his room, and the Count asked me what forces were in Chebucto? I said three old Regiments, and if any vessel had arrived from England, there were two Regiments more. At Which he made a wonder, and asked me if no vessels were arrived before I came away? I told him they were then expected every day. I then begged him to order me my pass. He told me I must first go to Mr. Le Loutre.

I went immediately, was admitted, and told him the Governor had sent me to him. He asked what I would have him say, or do? "Sir," said I, "the Governor ordered me to come to you." I then informed him, I was the unfortunate young man that had been taken by the Indians. He again asked me what I would have do in it? Adding, I know you not. I told him I could not tell the reason why the Governor sent me to him.

He said if I would come the next day in the morning, after Mass, to the Hospital, he would go with me to the Governor. I attended accordingly, and we went to the Governor, and as we were entering into the house he asked me who he should say I was? I told him the Linguist that was taken by the Indians.

He went into the Governor, and when he returned told me that the Governor did not desire to keep me against my will, but that he would if I did not bring a Certificate to prove that I had paid my ransom. I told him it was impossible for me to have brought a Certificate from them, because they could not write, and that I was in such an agony of mind at the time, that I did not think to ask a receipt. I then asked him whether it would not do, if I brought a person, or two, to prove that the money was paid? He said yes, that was the Certificate he desired.

I then went and got the Master of the Schooner I came in, the Master of a Sloop, and a Merchant that lodged at Mr. Morrice's. He that brought me said, that he heard Mr. Morrice say the money was paid, but did not see it. The two other Gentlemen said they saw a sum of money counted out, but they could not tell the sum, that an Indian swept it into his hat, and took the man by the hand, saying now you are free.

They likewise related the manner of my escape in James Morrice's house, and said if it had not been for such an Officer, I should have been killed. Mr. Le Loutre replied it would have been no great matter, and then began to rail at me, and addressing the people said, don't you see he is a Frenchman, and a renegade, one that denies his Country, and abjures his religion. Adding with vehemence, that if he did right, it would be to keep me, until he got the Indian Girl that Colonel Gorham had taken.

I told him that his Excellency had sent her to Chignecto. Upon the word Excellency, he checked me with passion and disdain. He said your Excellency Cornwallis was titled a gentleman of the Chamber, and that *he had seen some of his letters, which were infamous.* I know said he, *he owes a spite to our robes, but he is nothing but the scum of the Earth.*

He added in a lower tone, that if the Governor of Chebucto had a mind to treat with the Indians, he ought to write to him, and not to the tail, or one of the last of the Tribes. Of this you have seen enough to acquaint the Governor. He then desired me to present the Governor with his respects, for he is an honest Gentleman, and if he would write to him, he would come to Halifax himself, for an honest man need not be afraid anywhere.

He then said he would not detain me, seeing I was taken before his return, but the first Englishman, of what quality soever, he would detain until he saw the Indian Girl. He further said, that he had laid out a great deal of money upon Captain Hamilton, and other Officers with him, and had no return made for it.

That the Governor may build Forts, wherever he pleased, and he would take care the Troops should not come out of them, for *he would torment them with his Indians.* He then desired me to acquaint the Governor, to declare war by the sound of the drum, that his Indians might not receive presents one way, and be trepanned another. He again told me he did not keep me, I might go.

The next day I went to the Governor, and the Secretary had orders to make out my pass, for which I waited upon him the next day, and was admitted to the Governor, who delivered me my pass, saying he knew that I was much a Frenchman as he was.

He then desired me to inform my Governor, that he was very desirous to live friendly with him, and that if he would send him any directions concerning the Annapolis Schooner, taken by the Indians, he should be very glad to serve him. Upon which I was dismissed, with a charge to behave myself discreetly. I left Louisbourg the 28th of June, and arrived at Halifax the 2nd of July, after a painful absence of six weeks.[3]

The French Governor, capitalizing on the atrocities committed by two Englishmen against innocent Mi'kmaq people, had masterminded a brilliant military intrigue designed to frustrate the peace initiatives between Chief Cope's Mi'kmaq District and the British. It's ironic how the English unwittingly assisted French efforts to halt the treaty making process. If they had charged and prosecuted, according to the provisions of Section 8 of the 1752 Treaty, instead of freeing the two Englishmen who killed for profit seven members of a Mi'kmaq family—a newborn infant, its mother, a child, two other women and two men (apparently they did not scalp the newborn because they only brought in six scalps)—De Raymond's hopes of killing the treaty process would have died and the English probably would have had all the Mi'kmaq Districts under treaty by the end of 1753. But, as usual, justice was denied the Mi'kmaq and by its denial the die was cast for further bloodshed.

Reviewing Casteel's statement, we can see that Chief Jean Baptiste Cope, because of his 1752 Treaty with the British, was in some peril during this period. When Casteel first arrived at Jedore, Cope met with him and advised him of the personal danger he was in. The Chief said the Indians were out to kill him because of the treaty, and he asked for refuge in Halifax. Had Casteel understood the seriousness of the situation, he would have immediately arranged for the Chief to come on board and then upped anchor for Halifax. But he ignored the Chief's plea and the plot unfolded as planned. Casteel's capture seems to have been a key ingredient, along with the murders of the Mi'kmaq, in creating the political climate that would discourage the Mi'kmaq Chiefs, most of whom were making overtures to the English for peace agreements, from involving themselves further in the treaty making process.

As a source of information, Casteel, with his knowledge of British affairs of state in Halifax and the colony, would have been viewed by the French as invaluable. Moreover, his capture forced the British to take military action against the Mi'kmaq and thus break the peace. The efforts of the leaders to keep Casteel alive while trying to confuse and intimidate him indicates that he was being used as a pawn in the intrigue.

The stamp of French military approval is apparent. The insolence of some of the Mi'kmaq participants towards Chief Cope and other members of his District is a clear indication that traditional Mi'kmaq leaders were not the planners and executors of the plot. There are several clues that indicate it was instead a French affair.

First, Whites have over the years habitually referred to any Amerindian with authority as "Chief," so when Casteel refers to "the Chief, or Captain" he unknowingly is identifying the true perpetrators of the incident to be the "Captains" whom the French had in their pay throughout Mi'kmaq territory. This is verified by the fact that the group had an authorization from the commander of a French fort to supply "this detachment" with food and military supplies because they were "upon the King's duty." Another clear indication of French control over the entire episode is that whenever and wherever the French wanted Casteel, the Mi'kmaq turned him over without a fuss.

In the 1980s, descendants of the British colonials attempted to nullify the Treaty of 1752 in the courts by claiming that Chief Jean Baptiste Cope had violated the terms of the treaty during the Casteel incident. But they conveniently overlooked the facts that the English, by their refusal to prosecute two murderers, were in clear violation of the treaty, and that Chief Cope had had very little involvement in the affair. In fact, as part of his agreement in 1752, he had used his best efforts to convince his colleagues to consider entering into peace treaties with the English and had all but succeeded.

Even after the incident there were Bands, many in dire straits, that were anxious to achieve peace with the English. This is confirmed in the Council minutes of November 16, 1753. The president told the Council that the meeting was called because the Chiefs of a Cape Sable Mi'kmaq community had approached Colonel Sutherland at Lunenburg with a proposal for peace, and the Colonel had arranged for the Chiefs to come to Halifax. The Band's representatives were then called in to acquaint the Council with their business:

> They declared that they were of the Tribe of the Cape Sable Indians, which consisted of about sixty people, with two Chiefs. That Baptiste Thomas, one of the Indians now present, is one of the said Chiefs, and the other Indian named Francois Jean de Perisse was deputed by the other Chief.
>
> That they were come on behalf of themselves and their Tribe to represent that they had never joined with the other Indians in molesting the English, but on the contrary have, upon all occasions, showed all the kindness and friendship in their power towards them, for which reason they had never received any assistance from the French.
>
> That, if any doubt should arise in regard to their conduct, they were willing to be detained until such time as an account might be had of them from New England, where they were well known, by having always given their vessels all the assistance they could when any of them happened to be drove on that part of the coast which they inhabit.
>
> That, as the other Indians have renewed hostilities by killing some of our people, they were deterred from going amongst the English as usual, lest they

should avenge themselves on them, the innocent, for which reason it is five months since they have been at the fort of Annapolis, and as they have never received any assistance, either from the English or the French, they are now reduced to great extremities for want of both provisions and clothing.

Wherefore, as they are still desirous to remain friends to the English, they desire that some authentic instrument may be given them by which they may show, upon occasion, that they are so, and may be looked upon as such by our people. And as to such relief and assistance as should be thought proper to afford them, they left it to the consideration of the Council, with whose determination they should be entirely satisfied.

The Council, having taken the same into mature consideration, were of the opinion that although it was highly proper, as much as possible, to annoy and destroy such of the Indians as continued to make war upon us, yet on the other hand, it might be of great advantage to support and encourage such of them as should come in and be willing to remain friends with us.

And that by acts of friendship and kindness the whole of them might at length be convinced that it would be more for their interest to be our friends, than enemies. And it was therefore resolved, that the under mentioned provisions and dry stores should be given to the said Francois Jean de Perisse and Baptiste Thomas for the use and support of themselves and their families, being as they say, twenty in number during the winter viz. 2,000 lbs. bread, 3 barrels pork, 20 blankets, 30 lbs. powder, 60 lbs. shott, 50 lbs. tobacco, 1 gross pipes, 2 hats, gold laced for the two Chiefs, 1 hat, silver laced for the Deputy.

It was also resolved, that the sum of Ten Pounds should be paid to the master of the Schooner which brought the Indians from Lunenburg, in consideration of his bringing them to Halifax, and carrying them and their provisions and presents back.

Charles Lawrence.[4]

Thus the once proud and independent Band of Cape Sable Mi'kmaq had been reduced to begging provisions from the English to stave off starvation and pestilence. The great pity is that they were also moved to deny their own people in their bid for survival. The English agreement to assist this community was motivated strictly by self-interest. For, as history will show, their pitiful plight was the goal the English had in mind for all Mi'kmaq.

On August 26, 1754, the Councils of the Mi'kmaq and the small Maliseet Nations, which had not joined with the majority of the Maliseet Bands in signing the Treaty of 1749, held a Council at Fort Beauséjour and formulated an offer for a peaceable settlement of their war with the British which was communicated to the Governor at Halifax on their behalf by Abbé Jean-Louis Le Loutre. They made the following proposals:

(1) They have determined to continue in peace, and to commit no act of hostility against the Subjects of Great Britain, until the reply which you, Sir, and Council are to give them on what they propose to you in writing, shall reach them.

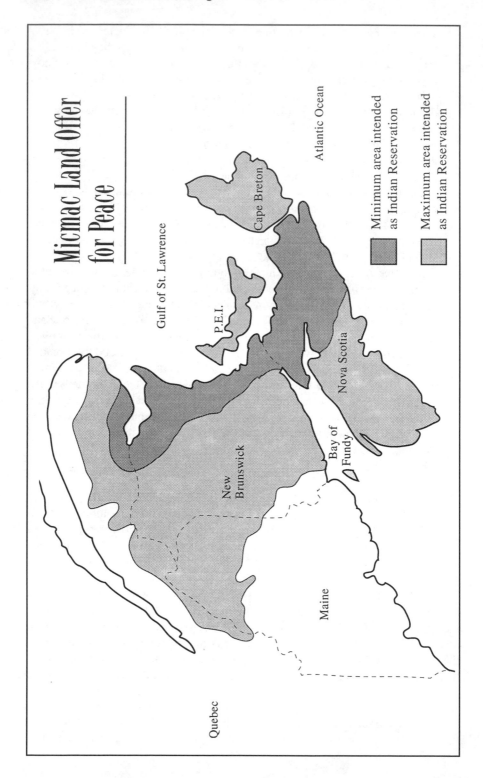

Micmac Land Offer for Peace

Gulf of St. Lawrence

Cape Breton

Atlantic Ocean

P.E.I.

Nova Scotia

New Brunswick

Bay of Fundy

Maine

Quebec

Minimum area intended as Indian Reservation

Maximum area intended as Indian Reservation

(2) They agree to give no insult to those of the English whom they shall meet travelling on the highway; but that those, who shall depart from it, for the purpose of going into the woods, as the Detachment did which came lately to Shubenacadie, which they consider an infraction, shall be treated as enemies.

(3) That in order to arrive at a solid and durable peace, there shall be ceded to them a certain space of territory which they only shall enjoy, suitable for hunting and fishing, and for the establishment of a Village, and a Mission as a Parish.

(4) That this space of territory shall extend from the South of Baye Verte, comprising Fort Lawrence and lands depending on it, to the entrance of Minas, thence ascending into Cobequid as far as and comprising Shubenacadie, and leaving this latter place, formerly my Mission, in ascending and descending afterwards as far as the River Musquodoboit, and from this place which is on the coast of the East, to about eight leagues from Halifax, passing by the Bay of All Islands. Saint Mary's Bay, Mushaboom, as far as Canso, and from Canso by the Passage of Fronsac to the said Baye Verte [the map shows the approximate size of the proposed territory].

(5) That within this space of territory, to which they restrict themselves, and which they consider very moderate, and very limited in view of the *immensity of the land they did possess, and of the amount at present in their possession*, the enjoyment of which they demand for themselves alone, with all possible tranquillity, there shall exist neither Fort nor Fortress belonging to the French or the English.

(6) They most earnestly request, that the replies or decisions concerning the above Articles be given to them between St. Michael and All Saints, that is to say in the course of the month of October next.[5]

The proposals made by the Mi'kmaq and allies were greeted with contempt and derision by Governor Lawrence and his Council. This message belittling the proposals was transmitted back to them through Captain Hussey at Fort Lawrence:

Mr. Le Loutre's letter containing his proposals [Governor Lawrence could not bring himself to acknowledge that the Mi'kmaq and Maliseet Nations were the architects of the proposals] of peace with the Indians has been thoroughly considered by Council.

His Articles are so extravagant, and so much out of our power to comply with, that the Council don't think it consistent to make any answer to, or take the least notice of them. The terms in which they are drawn up shows that he is not serious because he asks what he knows to be both insolent and absurd, but this is no more than a piece with the rest of his conduct.

He will doubtless tell these poor wretches that he has made such overtures of peace for them to us, as we might have well granted, and by that means endeavour to make them believe they can never have peace with us, in order that he may still have them under his influence and dependence, this we can easily see is his drift.[6]

Had the British been truly peace-loving and honourable, this would have been an extraordinary opportunity for them to make a just peace. The Mi'kmaq were willing to exchange most of their territory for a smaller area they could forever call their own, and even to share it with the Maliseet, but the invaders rejected the offer because they wanted it all.

Even after this rejection the Mi'kmaq continued to sue for an honourable peace. Early in 1755 a delegation composed of Chief Algamono and a Paul Laurent was sent to Halifax to again put out feelers for peace with the British government. However, Paul Laurent arrived in Halifax in early February 1755 without the Chief, who had fallen ill at Cobequid.

At a Council meeting held at the Governor's house in Halifax on February 12, 1755, Laurent spelled out the terms the Mi'kmaq sought for a comprehensive peace, including possession of the same land the Council had seen described in the letter written on their behalf by Abbé Le Loutre. Two notable additions had been made to the Mi'kmaq proposal: they were willing, if the English thought their land request too extravagant, to negotiate a more acceptable territory; and, to reinforce their desire to live in peace with their neighbours, they were willing to see their homeland demilitarized.

Governor Lawrence responded on February 13, 1755, in the customarily arrogant fashion of the English gentry:

To the Different Tribes of Micmac Indians:

The Lieutenant Governor in Council has received your Overtures for a Peace between His Majesty's Government and your Tribes. Which Overtures being very general, and the demands you make, in our opinion, are extremely exorbitant, it appears impossible for His Majesty's Council to give any other positive answer thereto, [other] than that they are perfectly disposed to make such terms with you, and an allowance of such a tract of Country for your hunting and fishing, etc., as shall be abundantly sufficient for you.

And what we make no doubt, you yourselves will like and approve, and may be easily adjusted here, if you will send the Chiefs of your Tribes to this place to treat with us. You are sensible that certain Captains of your Tribes (at least persons styling themselves as such) have appeared here and made Peace under promises of bringing in the other Tribes.

That instead of bringing those Tribes, the Treaties have been immediately and perfidiously broken. And that when these things have happened, and we have complained of them, the Tribes in general have disclaimed such proceedings, from whence it is apparent we can have no certain dependence on Overtures made by one, or a few, individuals.

We therefore say if you are really sincere in what you now propose, we conclude you will appear here by your Chiefs, on our promise to receive you kindly, and to allow you such tracts of land, as you have occasion for, and all other such indulgences as you can with reason demand, or we acquiesce in.

This we esteem to be as full an answer as can be given to preliminary proposals, so general as yours are, and is all we can say with any propriety till you appear here, as we have great hopes you will, to enter into further particulars towards establishing a firm and lasting Peace.[7]

The practice of the English to refuse to acknowledge the human dignity and pride of the Mi'kmaq is once again clear in Lawrence's letter. The Mi'kmaq had made an extremely generous offer to share their territory with them for peace. The English had responded by saying, no, we will give you parcels of your own land only as we see fit.

If the Mi'kmaq had any intention to respond to Lawrence's insulting proposals, it was cut short by a resumption of warfare between the British and French. Many raids were conducted by both parties against one another, and although war was not formally declared in Europe again until 1756, in the Americas it had fully resumed during 1754. Commander George Washington lost Fort Necessity to the French in July 1754. Afterward, the war went badly for the British and they lost battle after battle throughout the colonies. The only place they achieved any success was in Nova Scotia. In the midst of all this, members of Nova Scotia's Council were busy setting the stage for the Expulsion of the Acadians.

This cruel decision was not a complete surprise to the French because a report the French Governor and the Intendent at Quebec had submitted in 1745, ten years before the Expulsion, indicates that they then had concerns about such an eventuality: "We cannot imagine that they could entertain the idea of removing those people [the Acadians] in order to substitute Englishmen in their stead, unless desertion of the Indians would embolden them to adopt such a course, inhuman as it may be."[8] Though the Governor and Intendent could not imagine such an inhuman act, the English proved them wrong; the event made famous by the American poet Longfellow in his poem "Evangeline" was soon under way.

In early 1755 the Acadian Deputies were summoned to Halifax by Governor Lawrence and ordered to swear an oath of allegiance to the British Crown. This they refused to do, contending, as they had with Cornwallis in 1749, that if they did so the French would set the Indians against them and they would be massacred. The English lost no time in responding. Colonel Robert Monckton rounded up the Acadians in Chignecto, while Colonel John Winslow ordered those at Minas to assemble at Grand Pré. They were loaded into the holds of ships and scattered to the four corners of the world. Families were separated, never to see one another again, and untold numbers died in transport.

The Mi'kmaq faithfully stuck by their Acadian allies to the bitter end. Some of the Acadians tried to escape and were aided and protected by the Mi'kmaq to the best of their ability. The Mi'kmaq also joined forces with them to drive back the British, as was reported by the French Governor:

> The British burned the Village, including the Church at Chipoudy and was responded to thus. Mr. Boishebert, at the head of 125 Indians and Acadians, overtook them at the River Pelkoudiak, attacked and fought them for three hours, and drove them vigorously back to their vessels. The English had 42 killed and 45 wounded. Mr. Gorham, a very active English Officer, was among the number of the wounded. We lost 1 Indian, and had three others wounded.[9]

Many Acadians went into hiding among the Mi'kmaq and remained with them until the British and French ended their hostilities in 1763. A group of several hundred were hidden by the Mi'kmaq in the area known today as Kejimkujik National Park.

The Expulsion order was almost universal. Even individuals who had sworn allegiance to the British Crown and been promised the right to live peacefully in their ancestral homes were included. To demonstrate how inclusive the Expulsion was, here is what happened to Jacques Maurice (whose real surname has been identified as Vigneau), the man who ransomed Casteel:

Jacques Maurice grew up in a house within sight of the French fort at Port Royal. After England took the fort and renamed it Annapolis Royal, the family stayed in the area until 1720. Records indicate that his father probably was the first Acadian to swear allegiance to the British Crown. They then moved to Beaubassin where by 1732 Jacques had established his own home and was a prominent merchant. He spoke both English and French and probably was fairly fluent in Mi'kmaq. By 1746 Maurice was the owner of a sloop named *Margaret*. He and brother Joseph, with a crew of six, used it to ferry goods and people between the Isthmus of Chignecto and Cape Breton Island. His family, including children and grandchildren, numbered 18 by 1754.

Maurice engaged in trade with all the diverse factions that were competing for power in Nova Scotia. He did business with Acadians, French, New Englanders, British, Micmac and Huron. He was related by blood, marriage, or some less formal connection on the female side, to officers in both the French and British military.

In 1744 the British and French empires went to war. Ransoming captives became a critical part of wartime diplomacy. For Jacques and his brother Joseph, the exchange of prisoners became a business. Maurice became a specialist. Sometimes he arranged the ransom of prisoners, more often he acted as the hired agent of the imperial regimes and returned deserters to their homes and barracks. For twenty-five years he conducted this business.

The part Maurice played in the tale of Anthony Casteel has been related. During these years Jacques often proclaimed himself to be a loyal British subject. He told Casteel: "If he was never to receive a farthing that should not hinder him from saving the English to the utmost of his power, even to the last shirt on his back." However, although the British used him, they didn't believe he was a loyal British subject nor did they trust him. But in reality this was their estimation of all Acadians.

In November 1755, Jacques Maurice, his wife, children and grandchildren were seized, placed on the ship *Prince Frederick* and carried to Georgia.

In Savannah, Maurice argued before the authorities that he should be permitted to return home. He presented himself as a "vigorous British subject." On March 10, 1756, he was given permission to leave Georgia. He, his wife, 16 children and 82 newly adopted dependents removed themselves to South Carolina. From the governor in Charleston the clan was granted permission to move on to North Carolina. After some controversy he was permitted to move on to New York. From thence they travelled to Massachusetts. The Bay colony refused permission for them to return to Nova Scotia. Instead, they were separated and assigned to live in designated towns situated throughout the province.

In 1759 Jacques filed a petition asking the Massachusetts provincial government to reimburse him for the value of his impounded canoes. He received seven pounds, eight shillings and two pence.

The English and French ended their current war with the signing of the Treaty of Paris in 1763. Under the treaty's terms Acadians were granted permission to return to French ruled territory. In anticipation of such an eventuality, sometime after 1759, Vigneau obtained a seaworthy craft—he christened it St.-Jacques. In 1763, free at last to leave his Mass Bay Colony exile, Jacques set sail for Miquelon. He arrived on the island in the company of several other boats, which carried a complement of at least 110 Acadian exiles.

While in Miquelon, Maurice made at least one trip to Nova Scotia to transport a number of Acadians to the French ruled island. Gaudet/Plank report: "Along with him on the journey was a former French Canadien official, a man named Perrault, who planned to assemble as many Acadians as he could on Miquelon in order to transport them to Cayenne, in the Caribbean. Vigneau helped Perrault bring the exiles to Miquelon, but when Perrault asked him to cooperate with the next stage of his plan, Vigneau balked. Jacques, along with his brother Joseph, who had recently joined him on the island, protested the proposed move vehemently—the two men had become informal leaders of the new Acadian community on Miquelon. In a carefully drafted letter to Perrault they assured him that they were faithful servants of France, but argued that the Caribbean would be too warm for them, and that they were acclimatized for life on the coasts of the North Atlantic."

The protests of the Vigneau brothers worked; they and other exiles were granted temporary permission to reside on Miquelon. However, they had difficulty adjusting to its lifestyle, i.e., the fishing methods used by the islanders were quite different from those they were accustomed to and thus, by default, many of them became charges to the Island's French colonial government.

In 1767, Miquelon's governor decided to send them all to France. There is no record that Vigneau protested the move. However, in spite of the Governor's wish to be rid of them, he and Joseph returned to the Island in 1768. Jacques, frustrated in his attempts to return to his beloved Acadia, died on Miquelon in 1772.[10]

Partially because they did their best to assist and protect the Acadians—who were their friends, allies, and, in many cases, relatives—in their terrible ordeal, the Mi'kmaq were subjected to even harsher treatment by the English.

Lawrence's Scalping Proclamation

On May 14, 1756, in retaliation for the many skirmishes that had occurred between Mi'kmaq and British forces between 1753 and 1756, and in line with the "tribal liability" provisions of past treaties, which had branded all Indians guilty for the actions of even one, Governor Lawrence issued the following proclamation:

Whereas, notwithstanding the gracious offers of friendship and protection made by us, in His Majesty's name, to the Indians inhabiting this Province, and the Treaty of Peace concluded with a Tribe of the Mickmacks, bearing date, the 22nd November, 1752, the Indians have of late, in a most treacherous and cruel manner, killed and carried away diverse of His Majesty's Subjects in different parts of the Province;

For these causes, We, by and with the advice and consent of His Majesty's Council, do hereby authorize and command all Officers, Civil and Military, and all His Majesty's Subjects, *to annoy, distress, take and destroy the Indians inhabiting different parts of this Province, wherever they are found; and all such as may be aiding or assisting them*, notwithstanding the Proclamation of the 24th of November, 1752, or any former Proclamation to the contrary.

And, we do hereby promise, by and with the advice and consent of His Majesty's Council, *a reward of thirty Pounds for every male Indian Prisoner, above the age of sixteen years, brought in alive; or for a scalp of such male Indian twenty-five pounds, and twenty-five pounds for every Indian woman or child brought in alive*: Such rewards to be paid by the Officer commanding at any of His Majesty's Forts in this Province, immediately on receiving the Prisoners or Scalps above mentioned, according to the intent and meaning of this Proclamation.[11]

Governor Lawrence's pontifications on the treachery of the Mi'kmaq are the height of hypocrisy. His own treachery during the treaty making process, and the fact that he also signed the scalping proclamation of 1749, prove him to be an uncivilized, sadistic and barbaric monster.

The Governor states that the Mi'kmaq had killed and carried away some of His Majesty's subjects, but he fails to acknowledge that this was done in retaliation for the brutal slaying of many Mi'kmaq families and individuals by British soldiers and civilians. He also overlooks the fact that the peace and friendship treaties previously ratified by both parties demanded that he, in the name of His Majesty, should prosecute Whites who had violated the terms of the treaties, which he failed to do.

The second paragraph of the proclamation, like the 1749 proclamation, authorizes the taking of White scalps. This is reasonably construed from the words "and all such as may be aiding or assisting them." The 1756 proclamation was all-inclusive and didn't exclude the peaceful Cape Sables. One can only wonder what happened to them and members of other small Bands who had already come into Halifax and made peace. They were probably slaughtered like lambs for the money their scalps would bring.

It's ironic that the number thirty was used by the British Governor as a price for Mi'kmaq scalps. "Thirty pieces of silver" was the amount paid to the betrayer of Jesus Christ, the teacher the English professed to follow.

Incredibly, Lawrence's bounty was still on the books in the year 2000. The Chiefs have asked that it be revoked and that an apology be made for its issuance in the first place. The provincial government has decided it is probably a federal matter and has turned it over to them. Lawyers are heavily involved and therefore many, many moons will probably pass before it's attended to. Every time something of this nature arises, governments want to check carefully whether it will put them in legal jeopardy. Justice takes a back seat as usual.

If the reader believes all modern Englishmen would find past scalping proclamations to be reprehensible, think again. This is how Peter Duffy, a transplanted English writer for the Halifax *Chronicle-Herald*, mocked the Mi'kmaq quest for apologies in a column dated January 9, 2000: "Turns out that a bounty for Mi'kmaq scalps is still on our statute books, 200 years after it was issued by the British. Understandably, native people would like to see it removed. And, oh yes, they'd also like an apology. Seems fair. Let's check and see if Lord Cornwallis is still around."

Intermittent fighting continued between the Mi'kmaq and the English until 1758, at which time Fortress Louisbourg fell to the British for the last time and the military influence of France in Nova Scotia ended. With their sources of arms, ammunition and supplies cut off, the Mi'kmaq could not continue the war for long. Their last major battle with the British was at Lunenburg in 1758.

The Mi'kmaq had fought well in defense of their homes and country and had shown unsurpassed bravery and valour on the field of battle. They had been merciful and generous to the enemy, and only rarely had individual members of their community engaged in atrocities. Yet the English were relentless in their determination to destroy them and their culture.

Isaiah W. Wilson's *Geography and History of Digby County* provides a chilling account of one of the horrors visited upon the Mi'kmaq, apparently related to the Proclamation of 1756. However, by the way Wilson writes about it, it seems as if the perpetrators may have still been following the provisions of the 1749 Proclamation, because women and children were also murdered.

> Consequently, the government raised volunteers to hunt down the aborigines, *offering a premium of twenty-five pounds per male above sixteen years of age, and twenty-five pounds for every female prisoner, the same price for a Man's scalp, and ten pounds for a child prisoner*. These volunteer companies were placed under command of Colonel Scott and Major Samuel Rogers.
>
> The following graphic account of an engagement ... was related to the author in 1873 by an old resident, since deceased, who received it from a Mr. Richard Robert Annabury, one of the pursuing party, who subsequently lived and died much respected at Trout Cove, near Centreville.
>
> Intelligence ... reached Annapolis in the Autumn of 1759 that a hostile Micmac settlement existed at Green, now Crowley's Point, on the North side of the Racket. The next morning before day break near the property of the late Sheriff Taylor, Major Rogers surveyed the Indian village and its rude inhabitants, as he put it. Later, Rogers rejoined his company and reported, "I see the Indians are in a great frolic, they will retire at day break." Now, my boys, be prepared to meet them in the morning before they awake.
>
> Those brave defenders of *English Liberty* marched boldly after day break, attacked the aborigines asleep in their camps, killing their Chief on the spot. The savages thus surprised, being destitute of any effective weapons of defense,

fled in disorder before the disciplined pursuers, who followed the skulking tribe along the shore to Rogers Point so called in consequence, near the light house.

Here, most of them were slain, some being shot on the shore, while others plunged into the waters and drowned, a miserable remnant escaped to the woods, and probably resolved to court the friendship of their conquerors, through the praiseworthy influence of their first Catholic missionary, Abbé Antoine-Simon Maillard.

Since, the notable burial of the hatchet in the presence of the Governor and Colonial Parliament took place in Halifax 1761 sealed the Articles of Peace and Amity between Great Britain and the Sons of the forests.[12]

The author seems to take pride in the "accomplishments" of the volunteers against an unarmed and defenseless community. Even after the passage of a century, educated individuals like Mr. Wilson saw no wrong in the slaughter of unarmed and innocent human beings for money.

Cornwallis, Lawrence and other colonial leaders promoted such dishonourable policies in their exchanges with the First Nations that the shame will forever stain the English and Canadian nations unless these actions are condemned in their entirety by modern-day governments. These governments, descended from the colonial era, have failed to acknowledge the horrible injustices done to the Mi'kmaq and other Amerindian Nations during European colonization. Their attempts to absolve themselves of responsibility for the carnage and destruction caused by their predecessors, their efforts to hide behind legal technicalities while continuing to enjoy the fruits of their forefathers' crimes, must be rejected as endorsements of genocide and racism.

What troubles me most about this terrible time for the Mi'kmaq is that not one White male who wrote about it ever expressed any regret, remorse or shock about the horrors that were done. How could they have read about such works of evil and not reacted with revulsion? At times, while reading the mountain of material from which I garnered the information to write this book, I became so repulsed and outraged by the cruel methods used by the colonial English to bring the Mi'kmaq and other First Nations to their knees that I felt physically ill.

However, in modern times there appears to be some movement by White males to take another look at some of the indefensible acts performed by the English back then and make some unflattering comments. For instance, Professor Jeffery Plank states:

Everyone involved understood the conflict to be *a race war*.... During the 1750s the politics of Nova Scotia centered on issues of national identity. At various times during the decade, the British engaged in combat with several different peoples who inhabited, or passed through, Nova Scotia: The Micmac, the French ... and the Acadians.... The British governors of Nova Scotia generally believed that they were surrounded by enemies, that the Acadians, the Micmac and the French would soon find a way to cooperate and overthrow British rule. One of the principle aims of British policy, therefore, was to keep these people separated, to isolate the Micmac, the Acadians, and the French. To achieve this goal of segregation, the colonial authorities adopted two draconian policies. In 1749 the governor began offering bounties for the scalps of Micmac men, women and children. The aim of this program was to eliminate the Micmac population on the peninsula of Nova Scotia, by death or forced emigration. In 1755 the British adopted a different but related strategy: it deported the Acadians, and relocated them in safer colonies to the west. Viewed in the abstract, *these two programs, to pay for the deaths of the Micmac and to relocate and absorb the Acadians, represented very simple thinking. The colonial authorities who endorsed these programs placed the inhabitants of Nova Scotia into two categories, Europeans and savages, and treated them accordingly.*[13]

It's refreshing to know that some Anglo-Saxon men are at long last beginning to recognize, describe and put to paper the barbarities committed by the English! Let's hope that more will adopt the courage of Professor Plank and come forward and talk about the indefensible actions of British colonial authorities in an open and straightforward manner. Plank's statement that there was a period when the British made it a capital crime to be Micmac, and by expelling the Acadians had expressed that it was okay to kill a Mi'kmaq because of his colour, but not a White, is to my knowledge indeed a first.

However, if anyone thinks there isn't an abundance of people who still think White makes right, they should think again. On January 14, 1998, I participated in a CBC radio show called "Maritime Noon." The subject was the naming of a highway after Captain John Gorham by the Nova Scotia Department of Highways. Defending Gorham's scalp hunting was Bob Harvey, Municipal Councillor for Sackville. In a nutshell, his defense of Gorham was that "the end result justifies the means." He could see no wrong, as a means to achieve a goal, in the killing of women and babies by Gorham's Rangers. I did win this battle and the Department of Highways changed the name.

The 1760s Treaties

In their predictably contemptuous manner the English soon forced the Mi'kmaq to enter into treaties that were demeaning and blind to the needs of the People. The Treaty of 1752 had at least left the Mi'kmaq with a small measure of dignity, but this was not the case for the Mi'kmaq Districts after 1760.

The standard format for the 1760s treaties is found in the March 10, 1760, treaty made with the British by the La Have Mi'kmaq:

Treaty of peace and Friendship, concluded by his Excellency Charles Lawrence, Esquire, Governor and Commander in Chief, in and over His Majesty's Province of Nova Scotia, or Accadia, with Paul Laurent, Chief of the La Have Tribe of Indians, at Halifax in the Province of Nova Scotia, or Accadia.

I, Paul Laurent, do for myself, and the Tribe of La Have Indians, of which I am Chief, acknowledge the jurisdiction and dominion of His Majesty, George the Second, over the territories of Nova Scotia, or Accadia, and we do make submission to His Majesty in the most perfect, ample and solemn manner.

And I do promise, for myself and for my Tribe, that I nor they shall not molest any of His Majesty's Subjects, or their dependents, in their Settlements already made, or to be hereafter made, or in carrying out their Commerce, or in anything whatever within the Province of His said Majesty, or elsewhere, and if any insult, robbery or outrage shall happen to be committed by any of my Tribe, satisfaction and restitution shall be made to the person, or persons, injured.

That neither I, nor any of my Tribe, shall in any manner entice any of His Majesty's Troops, or soldiers, to desert, nor in any manner assist in conveying them away, but on the contrary will do our utmost endeavours to bring them back to the Company, Regiment, Fort or Garrison to which they shall belong.

That if any quarrel or misunderstanding shall happen, between myself and the English, or between them and any of my Tribe, neither I, nor they, shall take any private satisfaction, or revenge, but we will apply for redress according to the laws established in His said Majesty's Dominions.

That all English prisoners made by myself, or my Tribe, shall be set at liberty, and that we will use our utmost endeavours to prevail on the other Tribes to do the same, if any prisoners shall happen to be in their hands.

And I do further promise, for myself and my Tribe, that we will not either directly nor indirectly assist any of the enemies of His most Sacred Majesty, King George the Second, His Heirs, or Successors, nor hold any manner of Commerce, Traffic, nor Intercourse with them, but on the contrary, will as much as may be in our power discover and make known to His Majesty's Governor, any ill designs which may be formed, or contrived against His Majesty's Subjects.

And I do further engage, that we will not traffic, barter, or exchange, any commodities in any manner, but with such persons, or managers of such truck houses as shall be appointed, or established, by His Majesty's Governor at Lunenburg, or elsewhere in Nova Scotia, or Accadia.

And for the more effectual security of the due performance of this Treaty, and every part thereof, I do promise and engage that *a certain number of persons of my Tribe, which shall not be less in number than two prisoners, shall, on or before September next, reside as hostages at Lunenburg*, or at such other place or places in this Province of Nova Scotia, or Acadia, as shall be appointed for that purpose by His Majesty's Governor of said Province, which Hostages shall be exchanged for a like number of my Tribe when requested.

And all these foregoing Articles, and every one of them made with His Excellency Charles Lawrence, His Majesty's Governor, I do promise for myself, and on said part, behalf of my Tribe, that we will most strictly keep and observe in the most solemn manner. [Signed with a mark, Paul Laurent.][14]

In what may be considered poetic justice, the Supreme Court of Canada on September 17, 1999, saw more than colonial officials had anticipated in the 1760s treaties and handed down a 5-2 decision that the Mi'kmaq had a right to fish without a licence to earn a living. Justice Ian Binnie stated in the decision: "In my view, the

1760 treaty does affirm the right of the Mi'kmaq people to continue to provide for their own sustenance by taking the products of their hunting, fishing and other gathering activities, and trading for what in 1760 was termed necessaries."

The court's decision limited Native fishing activities to those that would generate for a family or individual a moderate livelihood. It later clarified its decision by stating that the Native fishery was subject to regulation by the federal government. However, the long-term monetary value of the decision for the Mi'kmaq is questionable, as was well expressed in a letter from Linwood Rice to the editor of the Halifax *Chronicle-Herald* entitled, "Does this make sense," published on April 30, 2000:

> The government told the fishermen to get out of the fishery; no fish. Paid TAGS [money] to plant workers and fishermen [to encourage them to get out of the fishery]. Now they want to pay millions to the natives for [them to enjoy] the privilege of fishing, and there are no fish! Then [to get the Natives started] they buy them gear, boats, licences, and train them as well! Go figure!"[15]

Hostilities ceased between the Mi'kmaq and British in the 1760s. Because of their poverty-stricken circumstances and abandonment by their French ally the Mi'kmaq were forced to accept an unjust and demeaning peace.

Burying of the Hatchet Ceremony of 1761, and the Royal Proclamation of 1763

During the early 1760s, destitute and abandoned by their allies, the Mi'kmaq accepted that the departure of the French from the province was permanent. After accepting this, at the urging of their priest Antoine-Simon Maillard, they also faced reality and concluded that their war with the British was hopeless. Thus they opted to lay down their arms permanently and seek peace.

At this time of agony for their Nation, Father Maillard provided much-needed moral and spiritual assistance. He was one of the few Whites left in the province who actually cared about them and their future. Praying that his efforts would help them salvage something from the ruins of their civilization, he helped the Mi'kmaq negotiate the peace of 1761. Father Maillard, known by all as the "Apostle to the Micmac," died in Halifax on August 12, 1762. The Mi'kmaq Nation owes him a great debt. Without his efforts, all of our ancestors may well have perished.

Burying of the Hatchet Ceremony of 1761

On June 25, 1761, a "Burying of the Hatchet Ceremony" was held at the Governor's farm in Halifax. During the ceremony, treaties of peace and friendship were signed between Governor Jonathan Belcher, President of His Majesty's Council and Commander-in-Chief of the province, and the Chiefs from the Mi'kmaq Nations called "Merimichi," "Jediack," "Pogmouch," and Cape Breton, on behalf of themselves and their people:

> The Governor, assisted by His Majesty's Council, also Major General Bastide, the Right Honourable, the Lord Colvill, and Colonel Forester, Commanding Officer of His Majesty's Forces, and the other Officers and Principal Inhabitants of Halifax, proceed to the Governor's Farm where proper tents were erected, and the Chiefs of the Indians being called upon, His Honour spoke to them as follows, the same being interpreted by Father Maillard:
>
> "Brothers, I receive you with the hand of Friendship and protection, in the name of the Great and Mighty Monarch King George the Third, Supreme Lord, and Proprietor of North America.
>
> I assure myself that you submit yourselves to his Allegiance with hearts of Duty and Gratitude, *as to your merciful Conqueror*, and with Faith never to be shaken, and deceived again by delusions and boasting of our Enemies, over the power of the mighty Fleets and Armies of the August King of Great Britain.
>
> You see that this triumphant and Sacred King can chastise the Insolence of the Invader, of the Rights of His Crown and Subjects, and can drive back all his arrows, and trample the power of His Enemies under the footstool of His

sublime and lofty Throne.

As this Mighty King can chastise and punish, *so he has power to protect you and all His Subjects against the rage and cruelties of the Oppressor.*

Protection and Allegiance are fastened together by links, if a link is broken, the chain will be loose. You must preserve this Chain entire on your part, by fidelity and obedience to the Great King George the Third, and then you will have the security of His Royal Arm, to defend you."

Then the Chiefs were conducted to a Pillar where the Treaties with each Chief were to be signed, and there the Commander in Chief went on with his speech:

"I meet you now as his Majesty's graciously honoured Servant in Government, and in His Royal Name to receive at this Pillar, your public Vows of Obedience to build a Covenant of peace with you as upon the immovable rock of Sincerity and Truth, to free you from the Chains of Bondage, and to place you in the wide and fruitful Field of *English Liberty.*

In this field you will reap support for yourselves and your children, all brotherly affection and kindness as fellow Subjects, and the fruits of your Industry, free from the baneful needs of Fraud and Subtility.

Your traffic will be weighed and settled in the scale of Honesty, and secured by severe punishment against any attempts to change the just Balance of that scale.

Your Religion will not be rooted out of this Field. Your Patriarch will still feed and nourish you in this soil as his Spiritual Children.

The Laws will be like a great Hedge about your Rights and Properties, if any break this Hedge to hurt and injure you, the heavy weight of the laws will fall upon them, and punish their disobedience.

In behalf of us, now your fellow Subjects, I must demand that you build a wall to secure our Rights from being trodden down by the feet of your people. That no provocation tempt the hand of Justice against you, and that the great Lenity of His Majesty in receiving you under the cover of His Royal Wings, in this desertion of you by your leader to the Field of Battle against the Rights of His Crown, when He stipulated for himself and His people, without any regard to you, may not be abused by new Injuries.

You see the Christian Spirit of the King's Government, not only in burying the memory of broken faith, by some of your people, but in stretching out the Hand of Love and Assistance to you.

Lenity despised, may not be found any more by your submissions, and like razors set in oil, which cut with the keener edge."

At this point the Presents were delivered to each of the Chiefs, and then the Commander in Chief proceeded:

"In token of our sincerity with you, I give you these pledges of brotherly affection and love. That you may clothe yourselves with truth towards us, as you do with these garments. That you may exercise the Instruments of War to defend us your brethren, against the insults of any Injurious Oppressor. That your cause of War and Peace may be the same as ours under one Mighty Chief, and King, under the same laws, and for the same Rights and Liberties."

The Mi'kmaq were then carried to the place prepared for burying the Hatchet, where he concluded his speech:

"While you blunt the edge of these Arms, and bury them in symbol, that they shall never be used against us by your fellow Subjects, you will resolve and promise to take them up, sharpen and point them against our Common Enemies. In this faith I again greet you with this hand of Friendship, as a sign of *putting you in full possession of English protection and liberty*, and now proceed to conclude this Memorial by these solemn Instruments to be preserved and transmitted by you with Charges to your children's children, never to break the Seals, or Terms of this Covenant."

The Commander in Chief, having finished his speech, proceeded with the Chiefs to the Pillar, where the Treaties were Subscribed and Sealed.[1]

The Governor's speech was a classic expression of English hypocrisy. Statements such as "putting you in full possession of English protection and liberty" would have been considered a sick joke by the assembled Chiefs. Even while the ceremony was in progress, numbers of their relatives were languishing inside British forts as hostages.

For the Governor to call the British King "sacred" borders on the sacrilegious. His reference to English "honesty," "sincerity," "brotherly affection," "love," "truth," "peace," "friendship" and "liberty," considering the brutality and treachery the English subjected the Mi'kmaq to, was the height of contemptuous mockery. Describing the English as "merciful" was also a mockery because they had shown no mercy.

When the Governor told the Chiefs that the Crown would protect them and their people "against the rage and cruelties of the Oppressor," they would have been flabbergasted. Given that the English were the only oppressors they had ever known, they must have wondered with great anticipation how the English would now protect them from the English.

The following is the alleged response given by the Chiefs to the Governor's speeches:

And upon their being delivered and the Hatchets buried, the Chief of the Cape Breton Indians, in the name of the rest, addressing himself as to His Britannic Majesty, spoke as follows, which was likewise interpreted by Father Maillard:

"My Lord and Father, we come here to assure you, in the name of all those of whom we are Chiefs, that the propositions which you have been pleased to cause to be sent to us, in writing, have been very acceptable to me and my Brethren, and that our intentions were to yield ourselves up to you without requiring any terms on our part.

Our not doubting your Sincerity has chiefly been owing to your *Charitable, Merciful, and Bountiful Behaviour to the poor French wandering up and down the sea coasts and woods without any of the necessaries of life. Certain it is that they, as well as we, must have wretchedly perished unless relieved by your humanity, for we were reduced to extremities more intolerable than Death itself.*

You are now Master here, such has been the will of God. He has given you the Dominion of these vast Countries, always crowning your enterprises with success. You were, before these acquisitions, a very great people; but we now acknowledge you to be much more powerful, although less great in the extensiveness of your possessions than in the uprightness of your Heart, whereof you have given us undoubted and repeated proofs, since the reduction of Canada.

You may be confident that the moderation and lenity wherewith we have been treated has deeply imprinted in our hearts a becoming sense of gratitude. Those good and noble sentiments of yours, toward us in our distressed and piteous circumstances, have emboldened us to come out of the woods, our natural shelter, from whence we had previously resolved not to stir, until the establishment of Peace between both Crowns, whatever hardships we may have suffered.

Your generous manner, your good heart, your propensity to clemency, make us hope that no mention will ever be made of any hostilities that have been committed by us against you and yours. The succours so seasonably given us in our greatest wants and necessities have been so often the subject of our thoughts, that they have inspired us with the highest sentiments of gratitude and affection.

We felt ourselves, in consequence, forcibly drawn to Halifax to acquaint the Representatives of the King, not only with the Resolutions we had taken in His favour, arising from His kindness to us, but also to let him understand that the many proofs he has given us of the goodness of His Heart, at a time, and in a conjuncture in which we could not hope for such favourable treatment, have so entirely captivated us, that we no longer have a will of our own. His Will is ours.

You now, Sir, see us in your presence, dispose of us as you please. We account it our greatest misfortune, that we should so long have neglected to embrace the opportunity of knowing you so well, as we now do. You may depend we do not flatter. We speak to you at this time according to the dictates of our Hearts. Since you are so good as to forget what is past, we are happy in its being buried in Oblivion. Receive us into your Arms; into them we cast ourselves, as into a safe and secure Asylum, from whence we are resolved never to withdraw or depart.

I swear for myself, Brethren and People, by the Almighty God who sees all things, hears all things, and who has in his power all things, visible and invisible, that I sincerely comply with all and each of the Articles that you have proposed to be kept inviolably on both sides.

As long as the Sun and Moon shall endure, as long as the Earth on which I dwell shall exist, in the same state, you this day see it, so long will I be your friend and Ally, submitting myself to the laws of your Government, faithful and obedient to the Crown.

Whether things in these Countries be restored to their former state, or not, I again Swear by the Supreme Commander of Heaven and Earth, by the Sovereign Disposer of all things that have life on Earth, or in Heaven, that I will for ever continue in the same disposition of mind, I at present am in.

You confess and believe, as well as I, in Jesus Christ the eternal word of Almighty God. I own, I long doubted whether you were of this faith. I declare moreover, that I did not believe you were Baptised.

I therefore am overwhelmed with great sorrow, and repentance, that I have too long given a deaf ear to my Spiritual Director, touching that matter, for often has he told me to forbear imbruing my hands in the blood of a people who were Christians, as well as myself.

But at present, I know you much better than I did formerly, I therefore renounce all the ill opinions that have been insinuated to me and my Brethren in times past against the Subjects of Great Britain.

To conclude, in the presence of Him to whom the most hidden thoughts of Men's Hearts are laid open; in your presence, Governor, for I conceive, that I see in your person, him who you represent, and from whom you derive your authority, as the moon borrows her light from the rays of the Sun.

And before all this noble Train, who are round about you, I bury this Hatchet as a Dead Body that is only fit to become rotten, looking upon it as unlawful, and impossible for me to make use hereafter of this Instrument of my hostilities against you.

Let Him be happy, and blessed forever, the August Person for the sake of whom I make to Day this Funeral. Great God let him be happy and blessed during his whole reign over His Subjects. May he never have occasion to scruple calling us His Children, and may we always deserve at His Hands the treatments of a Father.

And Sir, we pray you most humbly, as you are instructed by George the Third, our King, that you will be pleased to inform His Majesty, as soon as possible, of what you have this day seen and heard from our people, whose sentiments have now been declared unto the King by my mouth."

The ceremony concluded with dancing and singing, after their manner upon joyful occasions, and drinking His Majesty's Health under three volleys of small arms.[2]

A speech was made that day by the Chief of Cape Breton. However, the language used in the speech quoted above would have required the person who spoke it to be impeccably versed in European customs and languages. The phrasing is not of Mi'kmaq origin and the actual English wording used, because of language barriers, would have been beyond comprehension to the Mi'kmaq. Father Maillard may have translated the Chief's remarks with the intent of appeasing the Governor and his cronies, and the British scribe may have embellished them further. Through his experience in dealing with the English on behalf of the People, Maillard would have known that to pacify the beast was in the Mi'kmaq's best interests at that time in history.

The document also has a very interesting irony. It would be hard to find words with more eloquent sarcasm than these to describe the heartlessness of the people the Mi'kmaq were dealing with: "your Charitable, Merciful, and Bountiful Behaviour to the poor French wandering up and down the sea coasts and woods without any of the necessaries of life. Certain it is that they, as well as we, must have wretchedly perished unless relieved by your humanity, for we were reduced to extremities more intolerable than Death itself."

Following these ceremonies the British continued to treat the Mi'kmaq in a most contemptuous and outrageous manner. The Mi'kmaq reciprocated by harbouring the utmost hatred towards them. Even at this stage, most of them still hoped that the French would return and remove the English from their soil. This hope persisted among the Mi'kmaq for at least another twenty years.

In the latter part of 1761, Royal Instructions were issued which indicate that some feelings of humanity towards the Amerindians may have begun to take root within the hearts of some members of the English ruling class. However, one could also conclude that these instructions were purely designed to safeguard vested interests:

Instructions to Governors, the 9th day of December, 1761

WHEREAS, the peace and security of Our Colonies, and Plantations upon the Continent, of North America, does greatly depend upon the Amity and Alliance of the several Nations, or Tribes, of Indians bordering upon the said Colonies, and upon a just and faithful Observance of those Treaties, and Compacts, which have been heretofore solemnly entered into, with the said Indians, by Our Royal Predecessors, Kings and Queens of this Realm;

AND WHEREAS, notwithstanding the repeated instructions which have been from time to time given by Our Royal Grandfather, to the Governors of Our several Colonies, upon this Head *the said Indians have made and do still continue to make great complaints that settlements have been made, and possession taking of Lands, the property of which they have by Treaties reserved to themselves, by persons claiming the said Lands under pretence of deeds of Sale and Conveyance, illegally, fraudulently and surreptitiously obtained* of the said Indians;

AND WHEREAS, it has likewise been represented unto Us, that the welfare and security of Our Settlements have been put at risk, *because Our Colonies have countenanced such unjust claims and pretensions, by passing Grants of the Lands, so pretended to have been purchased of the Indians*;

We therefore taking this matter into Our Royal Consideration, as also the fatal Efforts which would attend a discontent amongst the Indians, in the present situation of affairs, and *being determined upon all occasions to support and protect the said Indians, in their Rights and Possessions, and to keep inviolable the Treaties, and Compacts, which have been entered*, that neither yourself, nor any Lieutenant Governor, President of the Council, or Commander in Chief of Our Said Colonies, do upon any pretence whatever, *upon pain of Our Highest Displeasure and of being forthwith removed from your Office, pass any Grant or Grants to any persons whatever of any Lands within or adjacent to the Territories possessed, or occupied by the said Indians, or the Property Possession of which has at any time been reserved to, or claimed by them*;

AND, it is Our further Will and Pleasure, that you do publish a Proclamation in Our Name, strictly enjoining and requiring all persons whatever who may either wilfully or inadvertently have seated themselves on any Lands so reserved to, or claimed by said Indians, without any lawful Authority for so doing, forthwith to remove them from the said Lands;

AND, in case you shall find upon strict enquiry, to be made for that purpose, that any person or persons do claim to hold or possess any Lands, within Our said Province, upon pretence of purchases made of the said Indians, without a proper license first had and obtained, either from Us, or any of Our Royal Predecessors, or any person acting under Our Authority, *you are forthwith to cause a prosecution to be carried on against such person, or persons, who shall have made such fraudulent purchases*, to the end that the Land may be recovered by due Course of Law;

AND WHEREAS, the wholesome Laws, that have at different times been passed in several of Our said Colonies, and the instructions which have been given by Our Royal Predecessors for restraining persons from purchasing Lands of the Indians, without a license for that purpose, and for regulating the proceedings upon such purchases have not been duly observed;

It is therefore, Our express Will and Pleasure, that when any application shall be made to you for license to purchase Lands of the Indians, you do forbear to grant such license, until you shall have first transmitted to Us by Our Commissioners for Trade and Plantations, the particulars of such applications, as well as in respect to the situation as the extent of the Lands so proposed to be purchased, and shall have received Our further directions therein.

AND, it is Our further Will and Pleasure, that you do forthwith cause this Our instructions to you to be made Public, *not only within all parts of your said Province, inhabited by Our Subjects, but also amongst the several Tribes of Indians living within the same*, to the end that Our Royal Will and Pleasure in the Premises may be known, and that the Indians may be apprized of *Our determined Resolution to support them in their just Rights, and to inviolably observe Our Engagements with them.*[3]

The King's instructions are clear: they mandate that all treaties the Crown has with First Nations should be honoured and enforced without exception. The Supreme Court of Canada has followed through in this regard, but senior levels of government have their legal beavers busy trying to avoid it.

The last paragraph of the instructions quoted leaves one wondering whether the English deemed the Amerindian to be sovereign without country: "it is Our further Will and Pleasure, that you do forthwith cause this Our instructions to you to be made Public, *not only within all parts of your said Province, inhabited by Our Subjects, but also amongst the several Tribes of Indians living within the same*." This language clearly indicates that the Crown did not view the Amerindians as subjects, but rather as non-subjects, or perhaps members of other nations who had to be consulted. This kind of lack of specificity led to the placement of the First Peoples in a grey area in future years—somewhere between existent and non-existent, having rights on paper but in reality having no rights whatsoever.

On May 4, 1762, Governor Belcher issued a proclamation pursuant to the provisions of the Royal Instructions of 1761:

His Majesty by His Royal Instructions, Given at the Court at St. James, the 9th day of December, 1761, having been pleased to Signify,

THAT the Indians have made, and still do continue to make great Complaint that *settlements have been made, and Possessions taken, of Lands and Property of which they have by Treaties reserved to themselves, by Persons claiming the said Lands, under the Pretence of Sale and Conveyance, illegally, fraudulently, and surreptitiously of said Indians*;

AND THAT, His Majesty had taken this Matter into His Royal Consideration, as also the fatal Effects which would attend a Discontent among the Indians in the present Situation of Affairs;

AND *being determined, upon all Occasions, to support and protect the said Indians in their just Rights and Possessions and to keep inviolable the Treaties and Compacts which have been entered into with them*, was pleased to declare His Majesty's further Royal Will and Pleasure, that His Governor, or Commander-in-Chief, in this Province should publish a Proclamation in His Majesty's Name, for this special purpose;

WHEREFORE, in dutiful Obedience to His Majesty's Royal Orders, I do accordingly publish this Proclamation in His Majesty's Royal Name, *strictly enjoining and requiring all Persons whatever, who may either wilfully or inadvertently have seated themselves upon any Lands so reserved to or claimed by the said Indians, without any lawful Authority for so doing forthwith to remove therefrom.*

AND WHEREAS, claims have been laid before me in behalf of the Indians for Fronsac Passage and from thence to Nartigonneiche and from Nartigonneiche to Piktouk, and from thence to Cape Jeanne, from thence to Tedueck, from thence to Cape Tormentine, from thence to Miramichy, and from thence Bay Des Chaleurs, and the environs of Canso, from thence to Muchkoodabwet, and so along the coast, as the Claims and Possessions of the said Indians, for the more special purpose of Hunting, Fishing and Fowling; *I do hereby strictly enjoin and caution all Persons to avoid all molestations of the said Indians in their said claims*, till His Majesty's pleasure in this behalf shall be signified.

AND, if any person or persons have possessed themselves of any part of the same to the prejudice of the said Indians in their Claims before specified or without lawful Authority, *they are hereby required forthwith to remove, as they will otherwise be Prosecuted with the utmost Rigour of the Law*.[4]

Governor Belcher issued this proclamation without first seeking the advice and consent of the Lords of Trade. The Lords disapproved of his action, feeling the proclamation went too far, and they consequently rescinded it in its entirety.

In defending his actions, Belcher wrote the following letter to the Lords of Trade:

In obedience to this Royal Instruction from His Majesty, I caused a Proclamation to be published in His Majesty's name enjoining all persons against any molestations of the Indians in their claims.

Lest any difficulties might arise it appeared advisable, previous to the Proclamation, to inquire into the nature of the pretensions of the Indians for any part of the lands within the Province. A return was accordingly made to me, for a common-right to the sea coast from Cape Fronsac onwards for fishing without disturbance or opposition by any of His Majesty's Subjects.

This Claim was therefore inserted in the Proclamation, that all persons might be notified of the "reasonableness" of such a permission, whilst the Indians themselves should continue in peace with us, and that this claim should at least be entertained by the Government until His Majesty's pleasure should be signified. After the Proclamation was issued no claims for any other purposes were made.

If the Proclamation had been issued at large, the Indians might have been incited by the disaffected Acadians and others, to have made extravagant and unwarrantable demands to the disquiet and perplexity of the new settlements in the Province.

Your Lordships will permit me humbly to remark that no other claim can be made by the Indians in the Province, either by Treaties, or long possession, *since the French derived their Title from the Indians, and the French ceded their Title to the English.*[5]

The English were so insecure about their claim to title over Nova Scotia that they continually insisted that they derived it from the French, who had derived it from the Mi'kmaq. As the Mi'kmaq had not ceded it to anyone, this is a moot point. I believe that the English knew with certainty that they had no true title and that this was part of the reason they treated the Mi'kmaq so savagely and tried to exterminate or assimilate them. This would have been the easiest and most permanent way for them to clear title.

Belcher's proclamation and his proposal to repeal the Debtor's Act, which had protected debtors within the province from being sued in the courts of Nova Scotia for debts contracted outside the province, sealed his fate. Some of the more influential members of His Majesty's Council themselves had such debts and took great exception to an upstart interfering with an Act that protected their own interests. Like many who came after him, Belcher's efforts to provide some small measure of justice for the Mi'kmaq later led to his being declared incompetent and removed from office.

Many legal questions arise from the cancellation of Belcher's proclamation. Did the Lords of Trade have the legal authority to cancel it? After all, it was issued pursuant to His Majesty's instructions. It would appear that the Lords of Trade acted illegally; because, unless the Governor repealed it himself, its repeal very likely would have required an Act of Parliament.

As could be expected, the Royal Instructions did not impress the King's loyal and most obedient subjects. These directives were ignored and colonists continued to illegally appropriate Amerindian lands. This is probably where the unwritten tradition was founded that laws that were positive for the rights of Amerindians were to be ignored by the public and unenforced by officialdom and that laws enacted that affected them adversely were to be religiously obeyed and enforced.

While all this was occurring on this side of the Atlantic, in Europe two arch-enemies were once again making moves toward peace. Their efforts culminated in the Treaty of Paris signed on February 10, 1763, which effectively ended French involvement in what is today Canada. The signing also officially ended a mutually beneficial 158-year-old relationship between the French and the Mi'kmaq.

That the relationship lasted so long is an indication of French enlightenment. From the time they arrived, the French, instead of trying to debase and beat them into submission, treated the Mi'kmaq as human beings and undertook programs to help the People acquire the skills that were needed to accommodate themselves to the foreign economy being imposed. With this help the Mi'kmaq probably would have gradually created a technologically advanced civilization. This prediction is based on the premise that, until the English takeover in 1713, the French were actively promoting this vision as a future for the Mi'kmaq.

To achieve this vision, shortly after planting their colonies in Nova Scotia, the French focused on providing education opportunities for individual Mi'kmaq. This got under way around 1634 when Cardinal Richelieu sent members of the Capuchin order to New France to engage in missionary work and to set up schools to teach both French and Mi'kmaq children.

By 1635 the Capuchins had opened a college at Port-Royal, probably the first such institution opened by the French in the Americas. It had in attendance about thirty Acadian children and several Mi'kmaq as boarders, and other Mi'kmaq children attended the school on a daily basis. The French also encouraged any Mi'kmaq who aspired to a higher education to travel to France to attend university. While there they would enjoy all the rights and privileges of French citizenship. The mission school functioned until 1654, at which time the English took over the fort and closed it.

In contrast to the French efforts, by 1763, after ruling the province for fifty years, the English had made no attempt to offer even the bare rudiments of education to the Mi'kmaq. In view of this record the prospect that they would do so after the 1763 peace was signed and thus begin to build a positive relationship with the Mi'kmaq was not encouraging.

The Treaty of Paris altered the lifestyles of most indigenous people in the Maritimes but the most adversely affected by it were the Cape Breton Mi'kmaq. Under French rule they had enjoyed freedom from persecution and had been able to practice their culture unmolested. Their experience with the French, compared to the brutality experienced by the mainland Mi'kmaq under English rule, was like the difference between day and night. After the Treaty of Paris was ratified in 1763, Cape Breton and Quebec were placed under British rule and the French were restricted to the islands of St. Pierre and Miquelon. Although ruled by a different British colonial administration, the situation for the Cape Breton Mi'kmaq slowly became more similar to what the mainland Mi'kmaq were being forced to endure. However, because of their relative isolation, they were still better situated to continue practising their culture than most mainlanders.

The Royal Proclamation of 1763

A new King and a new Governor brought a slight change in attitudes in London toward the plight of the Amerindian. On October 7, 1763, in what would prove to be a futile effort to save for the Amerindian Nations their remaining lands, assets and cultures, the King issued a Royal Proclamation giving further strength to the Royal Instructions of 1761. A pertinent excerpt from the proclamation:

> WHEREAS, it is just and reasonable, and essential to our interest, and the security of our Colonies, that the several Nations or Tribes of Indians with whom We are connected, and who live under our protection, should not be molested or disturbed in the Possession of *such Parts of Our Dominions, and Territories, as not having been ceded to or purchased by Us, are reserved to them or any of them, as their Hunting Grounds*; We do therefore, with the Advice of Our Privy Council, declare it to be Our Royal Will and Pleasure, that no Governor or Commander in Chief in any of Our Colonies of Quebec, East Florida, or West Florida, do presume, upon any Pretence whatever, to grant Warrants of Survey, or pass any Patents for Lands beyond the Bounds of their respective Governments, as described in their Commissions; as also that no Governor or Commander in Chief *in any of Our other Colonies or Plantations in America*, do presume for the present, and until Our further Pleasure be Known, to grant Warrants of Survey, or pass Patents for any Lands beyond the Heads or Sources of the Rivers which fall into the Atlantic Ocean from the West and North West, or upon any Lands whatever, which, not having been ceded to or purchased by Us as aforesaid, are reserved to the said Indians, or any of them;
>
> AND, *We do further declare it to be Our Royal Will and Pleasure, for the present as aforesaid, to reserve under our Sovereignty, Protection and Dominion, for the use of the said Indians*, all the Lands and Territories not included within the Limits of Our Said Three New Governments, or within the Limits of the Territory granted to the Hudson's Bay Company, as also all the Lands and Territories lying to the Westward of the Sources of the Rivers which fall into the Sea from the West and North West as aforesaid;
>
> AND, We do hereby strictly forbid, on Pain of Our Displeasure, all Our loving Subjects from making any Purchases or Settlements whatever, or taking Possession of any of the Lands above reserved, without Our special Leave and Licence for the purpose first obtained;
>
> AND, We do further strictly enjoin and require all Persons whatever, who have either wilfully or inadvertently seated themselves upon any Lands within the countries above described, *or upon any other Lands, which not having been ceded to or purchased by Us,* are still reserved to the said Indians as aforesaid, forthwith to remove themselves from such Settlements;
>
> AND WHEREAS, *Great Frauds and Abuses have been committed in purchasing Lands of the Indians*, to the Great Prejudice of Our Interests, and to the Great Dissatisfaction of the said Indians; In order, therefore, to prevent such Irregularities for the future, and to the End that the Indians may be convinced of Our Justice and determined Resolution, to remove all reasonable

Cause of Discontent, We do, with the Advice of Our Privy Council, strictly enjoin and require, that no private Person do presume to make any purchase from the said Indians, of any Lands reserved to the said Indians, within those parts of our Colonies where We have thought proper to allow settlement; *but that, if at any Time any of the said Indians should be inclined to dispose of the said Lands, the same shall be Purchased only for Us, in our Name, at some public Meeting or Assembly of the said Indians, to be held for the Purpose by the Governor or Commander in Chief of our Colony respectively within which they shall lie; and in case they shall lie within the limits of any Proprietary Government, they shall be purchased only for the Use and in the name of such Proprietaries, conformable to such Directions and Instructions as We or they shall think proper to give for the Purpose*; And We do by the Advice of our Privy Council, declare and enjoin, that the Trade with the said Indians shall be free and open to all our Subjects whatever, provided that every Person who may incline to Trade with the said Indians, do take out a Licence for carrying on such Trade from the Governor or Commander in Chief of any of our Colonies respectively where such Person shall reside, and also give Security to observe such Regulations as We shall at any Time think fit, by ourselves or by our Commissaries to be appointed for this Purpose, to direct and appoint for the Benefit of the said Trade;

AND, We do hereby authorize, enjoin, and require, the Governors and Commanders in Chief, of all our Colonies respectively, as well those under Our immediate Government, as those under the Government and Direction of Proprietaries, to grant such Licences without Fee or Regard, taking special care to insert therein a Condition, that such Licence shall be void, and the Security forfeited in case the Person to whom the same is granted shall refuse or neglect to observe such Regulations as We shall think proper to prescribe as aforesaid;

AND, We do further expressly enjoin and require all Officers whatever, as well Military as those Employed in the Management and Direction of Indian Affairs, within the Territories reserved as aforesaid for the Use of the Said Indians, to seize and apprehend all Persons whatever, who standing charged with Treason, Misprisions of Treason, Murders, or other Felonies or Misdemeanours, shall fly from Justice and take refuge in the said Territory, and to send them under a proper Guard to the Colony where the Crime was committed of which they stand accused, in order to take their Trial for the same.[6]

This proclamation reinforces the statements made in Governor Belcher's proclamation. It acknowledges that the treaties reserved lands for the Mi'kmaq, and it repeats a pledge to keep inviolate the treaties and compacts that had been entered into with First Nations. The proclamation also declared that many colonists were guilty of land theft; however, the theft of Amerindian land did not abate, nor did anyone try to stop it.

Canadian governments have tried to say that the Royal Proclamation of 1763 does not apply to Atlantic Canada. This illustrates an unwillingness to act responsibly. Rather than looking for honourable solutions, they have wasted, and are still wasting, time and money in searching for a way out. It seems only logical that the proclamation did apply to Atlantic Canada; otherwise why would the Governor have circulated it throughout the colony?

Another compelling argument for why the proclamation applies throughout Canada is based upon the provisions of the Indian Act. Sections of this Act, first legislated in 1876, which deal specifically with the selling or leasing of Reserve lands and renewable assets are almost an exact duplication of certain provisions of the proclamation. For instance, if a First Nations community wishes to sell or lease any of its land, it first must go through the surrender process, whereby it yields its interests to the federal Crown. The Crown then has the responsibility to ensure that the community's interests are fully protected. This is essentially what the Royal Proclamation of 1763 also prescribes. Fittingly, the Royal Proclamation of 1763 has proven to be an invaluable asset for First Nations in furthering their land claims. The 1760s peace agreements the Mi'kmaq and the British had signed, and the 1763 Treaty of Paris, did not end the Mi'kmaq's tenacious struggle for survival. In many respects the struggle only got harder.

10

Dispossession and the Imposition of Poverty

The cruelty the British used to subjugate and then degrade the Mi'kmaq vividly demonstrates that their policy of ridding the province of them never deviated from 1713 to Canada's founding in 1867. However, their genocidal effort in Nova Scotia wasn't an isolated case; they used the same barbarism in all of their North American colonies. The records show that many high English officials were very imaginative in finding ways to achieve their evil goals.

The following is an excellent example of their racist mentality in action. In July 1763, General Jeffery Amherst, the Commander-in-Chief of British forces in North America, sent a memo to Colonel Bouquet, a Huguenot in the service of England, asking:

"Could it not be contrived to send the Smallpox among the disaffected Tribes of Indians?"

Bouquet replied: "I will try to inoculate the Indians with some blankets that may fall into their hands, and take care not to get the disease myself."

Amherst answered: "You will do well to try to inoculate the Indians by means of blankets."

Amherst's contempt for the Indians is amply reflected in his journals and correspondence, though it may perhaps be doubted whether he was more bigoted than the average official of his Time![1]

An "execrable race" was the General Amherst's favourite description for the Amerindians;[2] Colonel Bouquet's favourite was "the vilest of brutes."[3] This racist language clearly reveals that White supremacist beliefs were prime factors in their desire to commit genocide. Lawrence Shaw Mayo states in his biography of Amherst:

As he sped on his way to the relief of Fort Pitt, the Colonel exchanged interesting suggestions with the General as to the most efficient manner of getting rid of the redskins. His first orders to Bouquet were that he wished "to hear of no prisoners should any of the villains be met with arms." Besides using smallpox the two gentlemen contemplated another method: "As it is a pity to expose good men against them, I wish we could make use of the Spanish method, to hunt them with English dogs." Amherst lamented that "the remoteness of merry England made the canine aid impracticable."[4]

Like Cornwallis, Amherst made no distinction between men, women and children in his genocidal strategy. By indiscriminately using germ warfare and other barbarities, he was responsible for the deaths of thousands of innocent Amerindians.

These Englishmen were typical of the barbarians the Mi'kmaq had to contend with.

An apologist for British barbarity might argue, but not very successfully, that Amherst wrote his letter to Bouquet proposing genocide in the knowledge that Pontiac, "Chief Detroit,"[5] was trying to organize all of the Amerindian Nations from the east coast to the midwest, including the Mi'kmaq, into a unified force to eject the British from North America. Thus, they might venture, Amherst had no choice but to take drastic measures. This type of argument might have some legitimacy if the British had been the defender. But, as they were the aggressor, it has none. Also, when assessing Amherst's actions, one must remember that Great Britain was the top military power in the world at that time.

The Imposition of Degrading Poverty

Many historians, anthropologists, archaeologists and others have argued that the horrendous death toll suffered by Native Americans during colonization was caused primarily by European-originated diseases. This was so, in their opinion, because the original Americans had little or no natural immunity against them.

Let's examine another, more plausible, theory. Amerindians had been in contact with Europeans for at least five or six centuries prior to European colonization. Many had also traded with the Inuit, a people who had been in contact with their Asian relatives for uncountable centuries. When these centuries of contacts with people exposed to the diseases of Europe and Asia are considered it is reasonable to assume that by 1492 the Americans had acquired considerable immunity.

Therefore, it can be assumed that diseases imported from Europe were not solely responsible for the deaths of tens of millions of Native Americans. What did most of the damage, besides cold-blooded murder and genocide, was the destruction and cutting off of traditional food resources by Europeans. With this came

Starvation and death

famine, malnutrition and starvation, which severely lowered resistance to all sicknesses and created ideal conditions for disease to run rampant among them with deadly consequences. These were the major factors which caused the 90-percent decline in the Amerindian population over a short period of time. The European way of life and livelihood, entirely foreign to indigenous American cultures, was also a prime factor.

However, after acclimatizing themselves to residing within a foreign social environment, where racism was paramount, the populations of many Amerindian civilizations began to stabilize around the middle of the nineteenth century, and some began to increase around the middle of the twentieth century; but many others had already become extinct.

After 1763, enjoying the "English Liberty" doled out by "compassionate" and "generous" colonial government officials, the Mi'kmaq were outcasts in their own country. One writer describes them as "living on the fringes of civilization" during this period. A more accurate description would be "living on the fringes of a civilization governed by cold-blooded barbarians"! Under these officials they were denied education and employment and were excluded from enjoying the relative prosperity Anglos enjoyed at the time. The hardship and discrimination they suffered in the midst of plenty, although smaller by scale, does not greatly pale in comparison to that suffered by the Jewish people at the hands of Hitler in the 1930s and 40s. Although they did not face death in gas chambers or suffer other indignities in concentration camps, as did those unfortunate souls, they did suffer the horror and pain of something just as bad: slow starvation. They, like the Jews, were treated as "non-persons" in their own country.

What helped them to eke out an existence during these terrible years was that the White population was still sparse enough to permit them some freedom of movement to gather scarce food. The only other buffer the Mi'kmaq had against complete disaster was that the English still perceived them, even in their dismal state, as a threat and continued to provide some provisions as presents.

With the war behind them, and both the Acadian and Mi'kmaq "problems" under control, the British again put effort into recruiting European Protestant settlers. These efforts were expedited in the 1770s by an event that would deprive the English of some of their most lucrative colonies, the American Revolution. Unrest in these colonies had been mounting towards the end of the 1760s. In 1770, in an attempt by the mother country to tighten its control over the colonies, British troops massacred several citizens in the town of Boston. This and negative policies imposed on the colonies raised the anger level further. The straw that finally broke the camel's back was the British Parliament's decision to impose new taxes which the American subjects felt they could ill afford. In 1773 the famous "Boston Tea Party," organized to protest the imposition of a new "Tea Tax," added fuel to the flame of revolution. In response to these British provocations the American colonial governments set up two "Continental Congresses."

The first was held in 1774 to protest British colonial policy, especially taxation without representation. The second was convened in 1775 to organize the Continental Army as a means to carry the war to the British. On July 4, 1776, the Second Continental Congress of the American colonies reconvened in Philadelphia and adopted the "Declaration of Independence." France, Spain and Holland, all old enemies of Great Britain, declared war and joined in the battle on the side of the Americans.

What probably prevented France from reclaiming its former colonies in North America during the American revolutionary period was its proven unreliability with its allies. It had abandoned the First Nations, the Acadians and the Canadiens to the mercies of the English once too often. It's ironic how this loss of confidence thwarted the last chance of the First Nations and their French Canadien allies to regain independence. Their loss of confidence in French resolve resulted from:

1. France's past lack of will to fight a vigorous war in concert with its First Nation and colonial allies against the English and their allies,
2. the signing of treaties by France with Great Britain that had not attended to the welfare of its allies,
3. distrust of the Americans, who for more than a century had assisted Great Britain in its wars against them and the French, and
4. the suspicion that the Americans would, if they won the war, take over where the English had left off. After all, the Americans had been used as surrogates by the English to mount the Expulsion of the Acadians; and the Rangers who had joined in the hunt for Mi'kmaq scalps had come from New England.

In spite of these factors, the Mi'kmaq and the Maliseet Nations did flirt with the idea of assisting the Americans in their war of independence. Their delegates met with the Governor of the State of Massachusetts Bay and worked out the terms of the "Watertown Treaty," an agreement in principle signed at Watertown, Massachusetts, on July 19, 1776:

> WHEREAS, the United States of America, in general Congress Assembled, have ... declared that these United Colonies are ... free and independent States ... and ... have full power to levy War, conclude Peace, contract Alliances, establish Commerce, and to do all other Acts and things which independent States have the right to do;
>
> WE THE GOVERNORS, of the State of Massachusetts Bay, do ... enter into and conclude the following Treaty of Friendship and Alliance....
>
> 1st, We the Governors of the said State of Massachusetts Bay, in behalf of the said State, and the other United States of America on the one part, and Ambrius Var, Newell Wallis, and Francis, delegates of the St. John's Tribe, Joseph Deneguarra, Charles, Mattahu Antrane, Nicholas, John Battis, Peter Andre and Sebattis Netobcobwit, Delegates of the Micmac Tribe of Indians, inhabiting within the Province of Nova Scotia, for themselves, and in behalf of said Tribes on the other part, do solemnly agree that the people of the said State of Massachusetts Bay, and of the other United states of America, and of the said Tribes of Indians shall henceforth be at peace with each other, and be considered as Friends and Brothers united and allied together for their mutual defence, safety and happiness.
>
> 2nd, That each party to this Treaty shall, and will consider the enemies of

the other as Enemies to themselves, and do hereby solemnly promise and engage to and with each other, that when called upon for that purpose, they shall, and will, to the utmost of their abilities, aid and assist each other against their public Enemies, and particularly, that the people of the said Tribe of Indians shall and will afford, and give to the people of the said State of Massachusetts Bay, and the people of the other United States of America, during their present war with the King of Great Britain, all the aid and assistance in their power.

AND, that they the people of said Tribes of Indians shall not, and will not directly or indirectly give any aid, or assistance to the Troops, or Subjects, of the said King of Great Britain, or others adhering to Him, or hold any correspondence, or carry on any Commerce with them during the present war.

3rd, That if any robbery or outrage happens to be committed by any of the Subjects of the said State of Massachusetts Bay, or any of the United States of America, upon any of the people of said Tribes, the said State shall upon proper application being made, cause satisfaction and restitution speedily to be made to the Party injured.

4th, That if any robbery or outrage happens to be committed by any of the said Tribes of Indians, upon any of the Subjects of the said State, or of any of the other of the United States of America, the Tribe to which the offender, or offenders shall belong, shall, upon proper application being made, cause satisfaction and restitution speedily to be made to the Party injured.

5th, That in case any misunderstanding, quarrel, or injury shall happen between the said State of Massachusetts Bay, or any other United States of America, and said Tribes of Indians, or either of them, no private revenge shall be taken, but a peaceable application shall be made for redress.

6th, That the said Tribes of Indians, shall and will furnish and supply 600 strong men out of said Tribes, or as many as may be, who shall without delay proceed from their several homes up to the Town of Boston within this State, and from thence shall march to join the Army of the United States of America, now at New York, under the immediate command of his Excellency, General George Washington, there to take his orders.

7th, That each of the Indians who shall by their respective Tribes, be appointed to join the Army of the United States of America, shall bring with him a good gun, and shall be allowed One Dollar for the use of it; and in case the Gun shall be lost in the Service, shall be paid the value of it.

AND, the pay of each Man shall begin from the time they sail from Machias for Boston, and they shall be supplied with provisions, and a vessel or vessels for their passage up to Boston. Each private Man shall receive the like pay as is given to our own private Men. The Indians shall be formed into Companies when they arrive in Boston, and shall want them not exceeding the term of three years, unless General Washington and they shall agree for a longer time.

AND, as Joseph Denaquarra, Peter Andre and Sabattis Netobcowit, have manfully and generously offered to enter immediately into the war, they shall be sent as soon as may be, to General Washington to join the Army, and shall be considered as entering into our pay at the time of arrival at New York.

8th, The delegates above named, who may return to their homes, do promise and engage, to use their utmost influence with the Passamaquoddy, and other neighbouring Tribes of Indians to persuade them to furnish, and supply for the said service, as many strong men of their respective Tribes as possible, and that they come along with those of the Tribes of St. John's Micmac.

AND, the said Governor, of the said State of Massachusetts Bay, does hereby engage to give to such of the Passamaquoddy, or other neighbouring Indians, who shall enter into the service of the United States of America, the same pay and encouragement in every particular, as is above agreed to be given to the St. John's, or Micmac Indians, and to consider them as our friends and Brothers.

9th, That the said State of Massachusetts Bay shall, and will furnish their Truckhouses at Machias, as soon as may be with proper Articles for the purpose of supplying the Indians of said Tribes with the necessaries and conveniences of life.

10th, And the said Delegates do hereby annul and make void all former Treaties by them or by others in behalf of their respective Tribes made with any other Power, State, or Person, so far forth as the same shall be repugnant to any of the Articles contained in this Treaty.[6]

The Watertown Treaty was never ratified by the duly constituted governmental authorities of the Mi'kmaq Nation. However, probably to gain personal revenge for past wrongs, many individual Mi'kmaq did go to the States to join the war on the side of the Americans. But the vast majority had been burned once too often by the "White man's wars" and were not overly enthused about joining one side or the other in this one. In retrospect, if the Mi'kmaq and other First Nations had assisted the Americans, the young nation, full of thirst for democratic rule, might have felt morally obliged to come north and liberate them.

To encourage the Mi'kmaq to remain neutral, the British—not aware of the People's aversion to getting involved in another White war—cozied up to them and supplied the Nation with the essentials of life until the war ended. These provisions, the neutrality of the French Canadiens and the opposition of the Catholic Church, which threatened to excommunicate any Mi'kmaq who took up arms against Great Britain, helped solidify the People's determination to remain neutral.

However, the French did try to rally their former First Nations allies to action. Admiral Jean-Baptiste-Charles d'Estaing, commander of a French squadron in the western Atlantic, issued a proclamation calling for a general uprising against the English. He had it distributed to the Mi'kmaq and Maliseet Nations, but it failed to generate the desired response.

In 1779 the British, probably with the intent of keeping them neutral, signed a treaty with several Mi'kmaq communities situated in what is today New Brunswick. During these years, with their southern colonies in rebellion, the British could ill afford to have a full-scale "Indian war" break out within the borders of their loyal colonies. Otherwise this agreement would not have been signed:

Treaty entered into with the Indians of Nova Scotia from Cape Tormentine to the Bay De Chaleurs, September 22nd, 1779

WHEREAS, in May and July last, a number of Indians at the instigation of the King's disaffected subjects, did plunder and rob William John Cort and several other of the English Inhabitants at Mirimichy of the principal part of their effects, in which transaction, we the undersigned Indians had no conscience, but nevertheless do blame ourselves, for not having exerted our abilities more effectually than we did to prevent it. Being now greatly distressed, and at a loss for the necessary supplies to keep us from the inclemency of the approaching Winter, and to enable us to subsist our families;

AND WHEREAS, Captain Augustus Gervey, Commander of His Majesty's Sloop Viper, did in July last, to prevent further mischief, seize upon the Mirimichy River, Sixteen of the said Indians, one of which was killed, three released and twelve of the most atrocious have been carried to Quebec, to be dealt with, as His Majesty's Government of this Province, shall in good future direct, which measures we hope will tend to restore peace and good order in that Neighbourhood;

BE IT KNOWN, to all men, that we John Julien, Chief; Antoine Arueau, Captain, Francis Julien and Thomas Dewagonside, Councillors of Mirimichy, and also Representatives of, and authorized by, the Indians of Pagumske and Restigouche, Michael Chief, Louis Augustine Cobaise, Francis Joseph Aruiph, Captains, Antoines and Guiassance Gabalier, Councillors of Richebouctou, and Thomas Tauros Lose, and representatives of the chief of Jedyac, do for ourselves, and in behalf of the several Tribes of Micmac Indians before mentioned, and all others residing between Cape Tormentine and the Bay De Chaleurs in the Gulf of St. Lawrence inclusive, solemnly promise and engage to and with, Michael Franklin Esq., the King's Superintendent of Indian Affairs in Nova Scotia,

THAT, we will behave quietly and peaceably towards all His Majesty King George's good Subjects, treating these upon every occasion in an honest, friendly and brotherly manner;

THAT, we will at the hazard of our lives defend and protect to the utmost of our power, the Traders and Inhabitants and their merchandise and effects, who are, or may be settled on the Rivers, Bays, and Sea Coasts within the fore mentioned district against all the Enemies of His Majesty King George, whether French, Rebels, or Indians;

THAT, we will wherever it shall be required apprehend and deliver into the hands of the said Mr. M. Franklin, to be dealt with according to his deserts, any Indian, or other person who shall attempt to disturb the peace and tranquillity of the said District;

THAT, we will not hold any correspondence or intercourse with John Allan, or any other Rebel, or enemy of King George, let his Nation or Country be what it will;

THAT, we will use our best endeavours to prevail with all other our Micmac Brethren throughout the other parts of the Province, to come into the like measures with us for their several Districts;

AND, we do also by these presents for ourselves, and in behalf of our several Constituents hereby Review, Ratify and Confirm all former Treaties entered into by us, or any of us, or these heretofore with the late Governor Lawrence, and other of His Majesty King George's Governors who have succeeded him in the Command of this Province.

In consideration of the true performance of the foregoing Articles, on the part of the Indians Affairs doth hereby promise in behalf of Government,

THAT, the said Indians and their Constituents, shall remain in the Districts before mentioned, quiet and free from any molestation of any of His Majesty's Troops, or other his good Subjects in their hunting and fishing;

THAT, immediate measures shall be taken to cause Traders to supply them with ammunition, clothing and other necessary stores in exchange for their furs, and other commodities. In witness whereof, we the above mentioned have interchangeably set our hands and Seals at Windsor, in Nova Scotia, this Twenty second day of September 1779.[7]

This time the Mi'kmaq, already being held hostage by their need for food, and with several of their number being held hostage in Quebec, were not required by the British to supply hostages.

In 1783, after a bitter eight-year struggle with much sacrifice, the Americans were victorious. With the determination of the oppressed, they had escaped British imperialism and begun the process of building a great democracy. Unfortunately, its democratic ideals were applied only to Whites, an evil practice which Canada would mirror in future years. People of colour in both countries suffered second-class citizenship, with virtually no citizenship rights up until relatively recent times.

Although the temptation must have been great, the Mi'kmaq had wisely not permitted themselves to be drawn into a war which would probably have ended for them as the others had—*alone holding the bag*. After defeating the British, the French and Americans did not come north to liberate the French Canadiens and their former First Nations allies. They had gotten what they wanted, and the First Nations were left, as usual, to the "mercy" of the English.

Dispossessed and Landless

The love of possessions is a disease with them. They take tithes from the poor and weak to support the rich who rule. They claim this mother of ours, the Earth, for their own and fence their neighbours away. If America had been twice the size it is, there still would not have been enough; the Indian would still have been dispossessed—Sioux Chief Sitting Bull

After the American War of Independence was lost, the English once again dropped all pretension of honourable treatment for the Mi'kmaq. From this time onward, although scalping proclamations and other overt methods of genocide were no longer practised, they used every other means to rid society of them.

To assist them in this goal, the British colonial government implemented a land policy which completely ignored any individual rights the Mi'kmaq had to their land. It is notable that the British also did this to the Aborigines of Australia. Based on this policy, on September 4, 1783, the English delivered the ultimate blow to Mi'kmaq dignity—they made temporary grants of occupation to them of some of their own land. The lands granted were of poor quality and useless to the First Nation in its efforts to survive. One can think or say whatever one likes about this kind of conduct, defend it with all kinds of nonsensical arguments if one wants, but, to me, only barbarians would subject their former enemies to such crass humiliation. For an invader to come onto an independent nation's territory and appropriate all its possessions unto itself without compensation, while claiming to be a civilized nation motivated by compassion, is unbelievable. Then to stoop to making minuscule temporary grants, using licenses of occupation, of the most useless parcels back to the victims, while still claiming generosity, is an act without moral defense.

The unethical seizure of Amerindian lands by the colonials should be atoned for by Canada by a return to the First Nations of large tracts of their former lands. There are plenty of examples of such actions being taken in the world today. For instance, in Eastern Europe, where the former Communist governments expropriated all the land for the state, there is a move by the new democratic regimes to return expropriated properties to former owners or their descendants, or, if not possible, to make financial restitution. Canada can take a valuable lesson from this.

When considering its moral responsibility to make amends, Canada should note that there was one key difference between the English and Communist practices of expropriating private lands. When these totalitarian regimes expropriated privately held land, they did so for the state, not, as was done by Canada, to give it to another racial group.

The total acreage involved in the "generous" licences of occupation made by the English to the Mi'kmaq of Nova Scotia is abhorrent: they allowed them the use of only 18,105 acres, about one-eight-hundredth of the provincial total of some 13.5 million acres. The following are the licenses of occupation that were issued to the Mi'kmaq in September and December of 1783:

Sheet Harbour	11,520 acres
Shubenacadie	1,100 acres
George's Lake	500 acres
Wallace	500 acres
Mergomish	35 acres
Antigonish	100 acres
River Phillip	1,000 acres
Maccan River	500 acres
Mid-Stewiacke	2,850 acres [8]

As the Mi'kmaq had little understanding of the complexities of the new social order's land management laws and did not appreciate the concept of ownership of land by individuals, they were completely at the mercy of the new state for the protection of these grants from the designs of unscrupulous individuals. With no such protection forthcoming their land grants were soon encroached upon by Whites and in a matter of a few years most were fully occupied by them. The government took no action to remove these trespassers but instead found ways to legitimize the encroachments.

While this was going on, the British Crown took a further step that would in the future tend to further complicate the Mi'kmaq struggle for survival and their efforts to acquire legal redress: they divided Mi'kmaq territory into more provinces. Mi'kmaq territory at the time had already been criss-crossed by artificial borders set up by the White invaders into what are known today as Quebec, Maine, Newfoundland, Nova Scotia and Prince Edward Island. In 1784 the British divided Nova Scotia into two separate provinces. The land lying west of the isthmus which connects peninsular Nova Scotia to the mainland became known as New Brunswick, while the remainder continued to be known as Nova Scotia. All this division into separate provincial groupings has created a nightmare of red tape for lawyers to untangle when settling land and other legal claims for the Mi'kmaq Nation in future years.

During the last part of the eighteenth century, traversing the rocky road of survival laid out by English racism was made more difficult for the Mi'kmaq because the invaders still feared them. Although colonial government officials treated them with disdain, they still believed the Mi'kmaq presented a threat to their security and continued to harbour an almost paranoid anxiety towards them. Today this seems incredible, because by this time the Mi'kmaq Nation was almost without means of sustenance, let alone means to conduct warfare. The invaders eventually came to appreciate this, but not for another twenty years or so, which involved other events affecting the future of the province, including the French Revolution.

Reflecting on how the French-Mi'kmaq relationship still affected the British after the start of the French Revolution in 1789, Jaenen observed:

> The wars of the French Revolution brought new anxieties for the British in North America [the British were fearful that the newly liberated French would form another alliance with their former Amerindian allies and retake the colonies] and new hope to some of the Native people of obtaining some *redress of wrongs committed against them*. In 1793, for example, there were revived fears among settlers and officials in Nova Scotia of a French invasion and a Micmac rising in favour of their former allies.[9]

The paranoia the English held about the former Mi'kmaq-French relationship seems strange today. Common sense should have told them that the best way to prevent this relationship from being re-established was to court the Mi'kmaq. But their racism superseded common sense as always. In future years they would try to copy the approach the French had used to create good relationships with First Nations, but the element of sincerity was always missing. Jaenen states:

> The American alliance [between France and the United States] presented many difficulties for the French, particularly in their relationship with the Native people. The position adopted by the English colonists of the United States was

not substantially altered by the [American] revolution, but the British in Canada found it necessary to adopt many aspects of the traditional French policy towards the Native people.[10]

Adding to English fears were the many American and French attempts to stir up rebellion among the French Canadiens. These efforts failed because the French Canadiens were, like France's former Amerindian allies, unwilling to take up arms on behalf of a country that had already proven itself unreliable as an ally. They also had been abandoned once too often to again risk English retribution:

> Because of Citizen Genet's efforts to arouse the French Canadiens to rebellion, it was feared that his agents might also be at work among the Micmac, exploiting their economic and social conditions to French advantage.... Lieutenant Governor [of Nova Scotia] Wentworth thought it essential to pacify them with gifts of food and clothing so "that the peace of our scattered Inhabitants may not be disturbed by them, and also that they will join us in case of an invasion."[11]

Viewed in the abstract, Wentworth displayed incredible paranoia—fearing a poverty-stricken and helpless People! If the die-hard faithful still believe that the Great Britain of that era was awash in democratic practices, these quotes from Wentworth should set them straight:

> Wentworth thought it necessary to warn all to watch out for "*Democratic French Practices among these Savages.*" The British government also allocated funds for financial relief of the Micmacs, when Wentworth described some unusual activity among them at Windsor, "during the expectation of a Descent."[12]

Perhaps it was their fear of a people they had already reduced to unarmed, landless and penniless beggars that motivated the English Governor of New Brunswick to sign the last treaty between the British and a Mi'kmaq community. It was made between the Mi'kmaq of the Miramichi and a representative of King George III, translated from the original written in Mi'kmaq:

Treaty Made With Micmacs on Mirimichy, 1794

Thus was agreed between the two Kings, the English King George the 3rd, and the Indian King John Julian, in the presence of the Governor, William Milan of New Brunswick, and Francis Julian (Governor) the brother of said John Julian, on board His Majesty's Ship, that henceforth to have no quarrel between them.

And the English King said to the Indian King, Henceforth you will teach your children to maintain peace, and I give you this paper upon which are written many promises, which will never be effaced.

Then the Indian King, John Julian, with his brother Francis Julian, begged

His Majesty to grant them a portion of land for their own use, and for the future generations. His Majesty granted their request. A distance of six miles was granted from Little South West on both sides, and six miles at North West on both sides of the Rivers.

Then His Majesty promised King John Julian, and his brother Francis Julian, "Henceforth I will provide for you, and for the future generations so long as the Sun rises and river flows."[13]

Comparing the French and British relationships with the Native peoples of New France and Acadia, Jaenen wrote:

As late as 1796, there were fears in Upper Canada that the French and Spaniards might attack the inland colony and rally the Native people against British and American rule....

Nothing came of the hope [in the First Nations] of a restoration of French sovereignty over the interior region, but the image of the French as having afforded them a measure of economic security while permitting and encouraging them to continue in their ancestral way of life persisted.

From this tangled skein of military relations with the Native people, the thread of a favourable image of the French emerges throughout the seventeenth and eighteenth centuries. The pattern was not consistently one of friendly relations, as wars with the Iroquois and Fox in particular confirm, but it was never generally one of hostility.

Seen in a comparative framework of Anglo-American relations with the Native people, it was a positive relationship between allies. Of course, *a closer examination of English-Amerindian relations would probably reveal more positive aspects than have been assumed generally to have characterized that relationship.*

The keystone of the French relationship, if one can be identified, would appear to have been the inseparability of the military alliances, the commercial encounters, the religious civilizing mission, and concept of Native nationhood under French sovereignty. In comparison to the British in North America, the French appeared to have had what Thomas Mante called a consistent, unitary and centralized policy.

In the military sphere it meant that Canadien militia units and French regulars, "joined to the numerous Tribes of Indians in the French interest, being conducted by one Chief, formed an infinitely more formidable power than the regular and provincial troops of the English, who could not unite their strength on account of the jarring interests of the different provinces." Yet the British proved superior. Ultimately, the French triumph lay not in military superiority, but in the totality of their relationship with the Native people of New France and Acadia.[14]

I take issue with only one statement in this quote. The assertion that "a closer examination of English-Amerindian relations would probably reveal more positive aspects" has not proven to be true. The truth is the opposite. The more one probes, the more one uncovers the enormity of crimes against humanity the English committed in the Americas. There can be no doubt that the English presence in North America spelled death and disaster for the Amerindian peoples. The poverty-stricken state that Canada's First Nations are still in is a stark testament to this!

Jaenen wonders why the British, although possessing fewer military alliances with the Amerindian Nations, were able to win the fight for the continent. Killer instinct probably was the key. History shows that English leaders have inflicted horrible sufferings upon peoples of colour, White European enemies and, when the situation arose, even their own people, without blinking an eye. In contrast, French respect for the sanctity of human life prevented them from practising genocide and other crimes against humanity in the Americas.

If the Mi'kmaq harboured any hopes that the French Revolution would lead to the return of France to the province and freedom, their hopes were in vain. It took the people of France almost eighty-six years, with many setbacks, e.g., Napoleon's dictatorship, to completely shake off the monarchy and realize their objective of a free and democratic republic.

Probably related to British fears of the First Nations and the French, the Americans and British concluded the Jay Treaty on November 19, 1794. Given the racism that abounded at the time, the treaty surprisingly recognized the right of First Nations peoples to unrestricted passage over the artificial boundaries created. Article III refers to the movement of Amerindians and their goods across the borders:

> It is agreed that it shall at all times be free to His Majesty's Subjects, and to the Citizens of the United States, and *also to the Indians dwelling on either side of the said boundary line, freely to pass and repass by land or inland navigation, into the respective territories and countries of the two parties, on the Continent of America* (the country within the limits of the Hudson's Bay Company only excepted), and to navigate all the lakes, rivers and waters thereof, and freely to carry on trade and commerce with each other.
>
> No duty or entry fee shall ever be levied by either party on peltries brought by land or inland navigation into the said territories respectively, *nor shall the Indians passing or repassing with their own proper goods and effects of whatever nature, pay for the same any import or duty whatever*. But goods in bales, or other large packages, unusual among Indians, shall not be considered as goods belonging bona fide to Indians.[15]

In later years the English claimed the Jay Treaty was cancelled by the War of 1812 and would not honour its provisions. However, the borders between the two countries cut through traditional lands of certain Amerindian Nations, who saw divisions in families take place that they could not understand. The Americans realized the injustice of the division and, continued to recognize the treaty. The British and later the Canadians, would not. One can conclude that, after forming an independent country, the Americans adopted a treaty doctrine more in tune with the code of honour of Amerindian Nations than that of Europeans.

Today, because of American recognition of the Jay Treaty, a member of a

Begging for alms

First Nation in Canada can take up residence in the United States and enjoy all the advantages of American citizenship without needing to follow immigration procedures. As a monument to Canada's determination not to reciprocate, an Amerindian moving from the States to Canada must pass through the immigration process.

Besides allowing unrestricted cross-border travel for Amerindians, the Americans, to their credit, have outdone Canada in their political relationships with their First Nations. They recognized that they had usurped a country belonging to other human beings and attempted to accommodate that reality. After the conclusion of the "Indian Wars," the First Nations in the States were accorded recognition as "Dependent Nations" and more or less permitted to go about their business as such. The mature and rational approach of the United States of America towards Amerindian Nations has not prevented that country from becoming the most powerful nation on Earth. Contrast its approach with Canada's paranoid fear that the world might crumble if it were to permit such status for our peoples.

However, the Americans did not treat their Amerindian peoples in a completely honourable manner. Like their cousins in Canada, the Natives of the United States were left to abide in degrading poverty. But the U.S. did recognize from the start that these Nations had an inherent right to self-government and continued to accept that precept without question. Also, as in Canada, the Amerindian peoples in the U.S. were victimized by racial discrimination and neglect. But the U.S. government did not have an official policy, as the English and then the Canadians did, to promote the extinction of Native culture by assimilation. The Americans have even dared to recognize some of the Amerindians of old as great leaders. For example, Sitting Bull is today recognized as one of the top military strategists in history.

By the turn of the nineteenth century the Mi'kmaq were beggars in their own homeland. With the arrival of hordes of new settlers, their traditional sources of food had all but disappeared. Their former allies the Acadians were in bad shape themselves and could offer little assistance. At the dawn of the nineteenth century the Mi'kmaq of Nova Scotia were by any measure in very dire straits.

During this period, if for no other reason than to get them out of sight so that no one would have to witness their pathetic existence, much attention was given by the colonial legislature to finding suitably isolated and barren pieces of land to give back to the Mi'kmaq. This action was made necessary by the fact that most of the small tracts of land set aside for them in 1783 had been encroached upon by White settlers and were no longer available.

In 1801 the colonial government set aside 8,560 acres of lands on mainland Nova Scotia as "Indian Reserves," located in places the government described as "in such situations as they have been in the habit of frequenting." The first Indian Reserves, set aside in Nova Scotia in 1801 and 1820, were:

Afton and Pomquet	1,000 acres
St. Margaret's Bay	500 acres
Gold River	960 acres
Port Medway	1,000 acres
Bear River	1,000 acres
New Ross	1,000 acres
Shinimcas	1,000 acres
Grand Lake	1,000 acres
Shubenacadie	100 acres
Shubenacadie (1820)	1,000 acres
Total	8,560 acres[16]

In 1821 the British Parliament ended the autonomy of Cape Breton and made the Island part of the colony of Nova Scotia. The lands reserved for the Mi'kmaq of Cape Breton prior to its incorporation were as follows:

Eskasoni	2,800 acres
Whycocomagh	2,074 acres
Wagmatcook	4,500 acres
Chapel Island	1,281 acres
Malagawatch	1,500 acres
River Marguerite	50 acres
Total	12,205 acres [17]

By 1821 the acreage set aside for the Mi'kmaq in the entire colony had reached a "princely" total of 20,765 acres. This great estate of swamps, bogs, clay pits, mountains and rock piles represented a tiny fraction of one percent of Nova Scotia's land base. The arable land in the entire grant was probably less than 200 acres. Once again, encroachments by White squatters upon these lands began, in some cases on the very day the lands were granted. The government made some effort to protect the integrity of the grants, but by no means did it go overboard. In disputes between

Mi'kmaq and Whites involving land, the White party's position almost always prevailed.

Thus, by 1821, robbed of their land, freedom, dignity and means of support, and with no access to human or civil rights, the Mi'kmaq were moving slowly but surely to the brink of extinction.

The policies and practices used by the English to persecute and segregate Amerindian people—especially the use of Indian Reserves to separate the Red People from the White—during their colonization of North America later influenced White South Africa in the drafting of its inhuman apartheid policies. In fact, some authorities state that the English and, later, the Canadians created the mould that the South Africans copied.

11

The Edge of Extinction

U.S. President Martin Van Buren said in 1837, "No state can achieve proper culture, civilization, and progress ... as long as Indians are permitted to remain."[1] This statement clearly reflects the White supremacist mentality that the indigenous peoples of the Americas have had to contend with since Columbus landed in 1492.

No one can estimate with absolute certainty what the Mi'kmaq population was when Great Britain assumed control of Acadia from the French in 1713. However, only a large population could have withstood the genocidal campaigns the English conducted against them during the next 154 years. Such a conclusion is also supported by the fact that the English considered the Mi'kmaq a force to be reckoned with for seventy-five years or so after seizing control of Acadia. Further supporting the argument for a large Mi'kmaq population is the fact that the British did not initially pursue the subjugation of the Mi'kmaq Nation with the same cruelty they used against the smaller Amerindian Nations in New England.

But after 1713 the pressure on the Mi'kmaq population began to escalate as the English single-mindedly pursued their long-term goal of subjugation and extinction. They used every means available from military might to poisoned food and germ warfare.

These quotes bear witness to English barbarism: "The English countered ... serving poisoned food to the Indians at a 1712 gathering,"[2] which resulted in the indiscriminate deaths of innocent men, women and children. In one of many incidents recorded by Father Pierre Maillard, "a detachment of English soldiers came across a small camp of five Mi'kmaq women and three children in a remote area of western Nova Scotia and killed and disembowelled them."[3] The English also

A Nation dying

engaged in germ warfare: they "traded poisoned woollen goods to some Micmac, causing the deaths of more than two hundred Indians."[4]

Two contagious diseases, smallpox and a fever, probably typhus, contracted from both British and French military personnel, also caused enormous casualties among the Mi'kmaq. A smallpox epidemic among French soldiers stationed at Louisbourg spilled over into the Cape Breton Mi'kmaq community during an epidemic in 1732-33, causing many deaths. It "reached such proportions that the Indians refused to come in for their gifts, without which they were reduced to the utmost misery,"[5] suffering hunger and starvation. An unknown contagious fever was brought ashore in Nova Scotia in 1746 by the remnants of a French fleet that had been sent to retake Louisbourg:

> The fever took a heavy toll on the Europeans: more than 1,000 men had died at sea and another died on the shores of Chebucto Harbour. However, it wreaked even greater havoc among the Micmac people, a large number of whom had gathered at the harbour to trade with the Frenchmen. Contracting the fever, the Micmac in the area "died like flies".... The result was that fully "one-third of the Tribe in Nova Scotia ... perished.... The devastation of this epidemic left such an imprint in Micmac memory that even as recently as the 1920s, old Indians could recall seeing mounds in the area near Halifax where great numbers of Indians who had died of fever were buried." [6]

Governor Shirley's scalping proclamation of 1744, along with those of Cornwallis in 1749 and Lawrence in 1756, also led to a substantial reduction in the Mi'kmaq population. Thus, direct genocide was also a major cause of the population decline.

Over the period 1760 to 1867, indirect genocide by starvation took a great toll. The groundwork for it had unintentionally been laid by the French. During their sojourn as the benevolent invader they had completely altered Mi'kmaq trading patterns and made them dependent upon an unsecured food supply. Upon their departure this arrangement proved to be disastrous for the Mi'kmaq. After 1763, with the wild meat supply drastically reduced by overhunting and fur trapping, and with their traditional fishing grounds taken over by hostile European fishermen, few traditional food resources remained, leaving them very vulnerable to famine.

Even in this sorry state the Indian Affairs superintendent cautioned in 1779 "that a war vigorously carried on by the Indians against us would throw the whole colony into the utmost confusion and distress."[7] This can be taken as proof that the Mi'kmaq population was still considerable. It would have taken a population of thousands to raise enough Warriors to accomplish this.

To reduce the Mi'kmaq food supply even further the British used a scorched earth policy. One report states that large tracts of land were deliberately fired, destroying Mi'kmaq villages and the animals the People relied upon for food and trade. The destruction of the forests was so great that a Frenchman who viewed the wasteland commented: "I have myself crossed above thirty leagues together, in which space the forests were so totally consumed by fire that one could hardly at night find a spot wooded enough to afford wherewithal to make a temporary cabin."[8]

Through the combination of all these acts of oppression, by 1838 the Mi'kmaq of Nova Scotia were on the verge of extinction. Their situation was desperate, but colonial authorities displayed no interest in improving it. Thus, health services for them were almost non-existent and social assistance, when given, was meagre and miserly. Starvation had become a constant companion.

However, compassion wasn't totally lacking in the White Anglo community—some settlers and legislature members were people of conscience. As early as the 1750s petitions were being sent to the colonial government on behalf of small groups of destitute Mi'kmaq. In 1775 some White settlers had become aware of the plight of the Mi'kmaq residing in western Nova Scotia who, because of a poor hunting season, "were in great distress."[9] These settlers interceded with the government, but to no avail.

In 1774, "a Bill to prevent the destruction of moose, beaver, and muskrat in the Indian hunting ground was introduced in the legislature, but was defeated."[10] The majority of legislators did not want to provide the Mi'kmaq with even this small measure of comfort. However, White settlers in many instances did supply some relief to the destitute and starving People. While they did so the government disregarded petitions and reports coming in from across the province that depicted the horrifying state of affairs that existed. Even reports of people living in wigwams completely naked and without sustenance in winter brought no relief.

George Monk, Superintendent of Indian Affairs at the time, had forwarded many petitions from settlers that begged the government to help the Mi'kmaq. The government responded by providing only minimal rations from a budget of £100 per year. One settler described in a petition of January 1794 just how desperate the situation was: "A great many Micmac have died for want of victual ... notwithstanding the little they get from the Superintendent ... if they have not some more general relief they and their wives and children must in a few years all perish with cold and hunger *in their own country.*"[11]

George Monk carried out his responsibilities with a great deal of compassion. He, like Joe Howe, lobbied hard on behalf of the Mi'kmaq and used eloquent reports of their sad plight to try to shame the colonial government into rescue action. But the government turned a blind eye.

A paper published by Dr. Virginia Miller in 1982 vividly describes the unspeakable misery the Mi'kmaq were suffering during this period:

> The lack of game animals and trade items also meant that the Micmac had no way of making or otherwise obtaining clothing. This meant that in the middle of a cold Nova Scotia winter, they were at the double disadvantage of having neither food nor clothing, and this took its toll as well. Reports of Indians naked or "miserably clad" in "filthy rags," and whole families owning only one blanket among them "as they lay in sleep in turns" in the middle of winter abounded. As in the case of food, the legislature authorized distribution of small amounts of cloth, a few yards at a time, but this, too, was certainly inadequate to the needs of the Indians. The situation was so desperate that one settler reported that: "*I have seen them in so much distress that those of large families were obliged, while a part of them put on all the clothing they have to beg around the settlement, the rest sat naked in the wigwams.*"

Finally, at the Indian Superintendent's urging, in 1780 the government established a committee to study the situation of the Indians and to make recommendations on dealing with it. The only outcome of this committee was the *establishment of a small sum set aside annually for relief of the Indians. At first 150 pounds, and then gradually increased until it reached 300 pounds in the years just preceding Confederation, the sum was never sufficient to cover the food, clothing, and medical attention that the Micmac people needed.*

The very first year that goods were distributed, the government agent in Antigonish reported that while the Indians in his jurisdiction were certainly in a "miserable condition," some of them "entirely naked," the goods allotted were insufficient to answer the needs of the overwhelming number of Indians who turned up for the distribution. *Essentially, his statement spoke for all the Indians in Nova Scotia since the suffering went on at least until 1867, when the Federal Government assumed responsibility for the Indians.*

Settlers continued to send petitions on behalf of Natives in their neighbourhoods from all around the province; excerpts from these depict a grim scene indeed for the Micmac people. For example, in 1812, a petition on behalf of the natives around Halifax stated that: "game has become so scarce that they cannot live in the woods ... several of them are widows or old and infirm persons, who live chiefly by begging, but have so worn out their benefactor that they are obliged to go every day to town, as they have nothing to eat upon a stormy day if they stay in their wigwams."

By 1827, reports of the Micmac situation drew comment from the Lieutenant Governor who said in a message to the Legislature that "the distresses of these poor people are much greater than is commonly supposed, and there is reason to believe *that unless something is done, they must altogether perish.*" Nothing was done, and petitions continued to come in. An 1831 petition from Rawdon stated that the Indians there were desperate, there being no animals to hunt for food, and only about ten ragged blankets altogether among an encampment of 50 people. An 1834 petition stated that the Micmac camped near Windsor were: "*Unable to maintain themselves through hunting ... many of them are at this instant almost naked and are compelled to sit down in their open and exposed camps without anything to cover or shelter them from the severity of the season,*" and added that if relief did not appear soon, "*they must inevitably perish.*" The Micmac living in Cape Breton weren't any better off at the time; they were receiving rations of meal and flour in an attempt to stave off starvation.

And petitions continued to pour in in ever increasing numbers. To cite just a few more, in 1837 came a petition from Pictou pleading for food and blankets for the Indians in that vicinity. Indian Superintendent Joseph Howe's 1843 report contains accounts of disbursing "miscellaneous charities" to natives all around the province, while *Howe pointed out if the situation continued, "the whole race of Micmac would be extinct in forty years."*

The situation not only continued, but worsened if that is possible, as in 1846 the natives at Digby were reported dying "for want of food and sustenance." In 1851 it was the Micmac in Cape Breton again, this time alleged to be in a state of "famine." In 1855 the Micmac of New Glasgow "were ready to drop from hunger," while in 1856 in nearby Pictou, the Indians were "actually starving, and crying for food." There can be no doubting an Indian Superintendent's 1861 assessment of all the Indians in Nova Scotia and Cape Breton as "destitute and miserable."[12]

Dr. Miller also provides a description of the horrors the Mi'kmaq suffered from disease:

But of course *Micmac people were dying from causes other than simple starvation and exposure during this time. The malnutrition and cold they suffered, the excessive consumption of alcohol by some Micmac, all contributed to lower the Indians' resistance to diseases,* and in the historical records and reports after 1800, we see evidence of much disease among them.

Many diseases they contracted from Europeans. For example, during 1800 and 1801, there seems to have been a widespread epidemic of smallpox, possibly contracted from some recently arrived Scottish immigrants who landed at Pictou. Reports of the epidemic during this time came in from all around the province, including not only nearby Antigonish, but from far away places such as Shelburne, St. Margaret's Bay, and Tatamagouche. Indian families fled from their usual haunts and from settled areas to the woods, hoping to avoid the smallpox, but this movement had two consequences: it spread the disease to other Indians, and it prevented Indians from collecting their relief supplies which were issued in the settlements. Both these factors contributed to additional suffering at the time.

Smallpox was only the first well-documented European disease to affect the Nova Scotia Micmac during the nineteenth century, and recurred several times at least. In 1826, a ship carrying smallpox came to a Cape Breton port; the *smallpox was communicated to people in the area, where, according to one local white resident, "it prevailed for some time, and to a considerable extent, particularly among the Indians, numbers of whom died under the infection."*

Records of smallpox outbreaks are also known from 1838, 1849, 1860, and 1861. As the disease recurred around the province, *Indians came to know and to fear greatly this disease,* in at least one instance refusing blankets which they feared had been in contact with smallpox patients. Since the early years of the century, the government had provided inoculations for immunity against the disease and encouraged the Indians to take them, but the Indians' dislike and avoidance of vaccinations doubtless contributed to the smallpox mortality.

Whooping cough, measles, typhus, typhoid, and numerous outbreaks of unspecified ailments labelled simply as "sickness" all are recorded as causes of death among the Micmac during the first half of the nineteenth century. It appears that outbreaks of diseases occurred locally and when white settlers in the vicinity were made aware of the outbreak, they notified the Indian Superintendent who in turn called a doctor to attend the ailing natives. An example of this procedure is provided by an epidemic of infectious hepatitis which swept through Micmac camps around mainland Nova Scotia in 1846 and 1847. Transmitted by frightened Indians fleeing infected camps, the disease brought considerable suffering and painful deaths to "a number" of Indians before medical doctors were summoned.

Because of the "threatened ... annihilation" from the disease of Micmac people living around Dartmouth, the government built a temporary hospital in order to isolate victims and bring the epidemic under control. But the conditions in which infectious hepatitis flourishes—poor hygiene, inadequate diet, substandard living conditions—testify once again to the mid-nineteenth century living conditions of the majority of Micmac people and thus their vulnerability to all manner of disease.

Infectious diseases as those just cited run their course, for better or worse, in a victim in a relatively short period of time; such diseases dominate the medical records for the Micmac people during the first four decades of the nineteenth century.

Tuberculosis, on the other hand, a lingering, wasting disease also resulting from poor living conditions and exposure to dampness and cold, was not reported until 1841, when a Bear River settler wrote the Lieutenant Governor that "*many have died off with consumption.*" After this year, reports of deaths from consumption, particularly among the elderly natives, came in fairly regularly: in 1847, an Indian Superintendent cited consumption as "frequently induced by intoxication, and exposure to severe cold." Subsequently, in 1853, another Indian Superintendent agreed, saying that "*consumption I regret to state has of late become very prevalent among these poor people ... his I think may be attributed to the privations they have endured.*" And scattered among doctors' bills and reports in the archival records are also mentions of consumption in various stages. In addition to consumption, rheumatism and bronchitis, other consequences of exposure to cold and dampness were regularly treated.

Venereal diseases, scourge of so many North American native groups, were also found among the Nova Scotia Micmac, although not, the records suggest, to the degree they prevailed among some other groups or it would have been so recorded by medical doctors who attended the natives. The earliest possible reference to venereal disease could be Dickson's statement that "outbreaks" occurred among the Cape Breton Micmac, particularly after the arrival of ground troops at Louisbourg in the mid 1750's. Nineteenth century records contain only isolated references to, e.g., a woman with "clap or pox" in 1853, another woman with "uteritis" in 1857, while a Micmac man was reported with inflamed testicles in 1856. One Indian Superintendent, however, claimed that venereal diseases were "by no means rare" and were contracted among the natives by "the visits of the dissolute to the towns." Venereal diseases also took their toll indirectly "while still at the breast," and the venereal diseases may also have been partly responsible for *the infant mortality which was reported to be "very great" in 1847.*

We have seen then, that a great number and variety of diseases were prevalent among the Nova Scotia Micmac people, particularly after 1800 when, because of their impoverished condition, they were forced to come into sus-

tained contact with white settlements to beg for food and as their land base shrank in the face of ever increasing expansion by whites. Indeed, so many of the Micmac people during this half of the nineteenth century required medical attention that several times the province's annual appropriation for the Indians was threatened with being entirely consumed by doctors bills.

The Micmac continued to suffer from diseases and from the threat of starvation after 1850, but as we shall see, their population decline hit its nadir about 1840, and subsequently began to increase. The decline which had begun with initial contact with Europeans sometime before 1500, was a continual one down to 1840, and it was especially intense (or possibly best documented) after 1745. *Judging from the historical records, the principal cause of this decline was disease; as one Indian Superintendent put it, "numbers are swept off annually by complaints unknown to them in their original state." The second most important cause was outright genocide perpetrated by the British, and the third major cause was starvation, once again brought on by the British presence.*[13]

Dr. Miller mentions the fact that a vaccine against smallpox (developed by Dr. Edward Jenner, 1749-1823, and first tested in 1796) was available to the Mi'kmaq in the nineteenth century, but the Mi'kmaq were leery of inoculation. Two factors would explain this attitude. First and foremost, the people offering them a needle to prevent smallpox were the descendants of those who in the not too distant past had been passing out smallpox-infected blankets. Second, the Mi'kmaq lacked the money to pay for vaccination.

The following letter indicates that someone influential must have blown the whistle on the colonial government for its mistreatment and neglect of the Mi'kmaq. In a letter to the colonial Governor dated August 22, 1838, Lord Glenelg asked for an accounting:

Sir:
I have to request, that you will, at your early convenience, furnish me with a report on the state of any of the Aboriginal Inhabitants who may still exist in the Province under your Government, showing their numbers and present condition, increase or decrease, which has, during the last few years, occurred among them, their moral state, and any efforts which have been made for their Civilization.

The proportion settled on the land and cultivating it, and the numbers who still adhere to the habits of Savage life, the amount, if any, of property belonging to them, and the effect of any local Statutes which may have been passed for their Government. I would request you add to this report any other information which you may consider important, and more especially to favour me with any suggestions as to the measures which would be best calculated to ameliorate the condition of these people.

I have the honour to be, Glenelg.[14]

As a result of Lord Glenelg's letter, the Lords of Trade in late 1838 commissioned a study to ascertain the social and economic conditions of the surviving Mi'kmaq. The results were shocking. It reported that they numbered only 1,425, that a large number were living in various stages of starvation, and that their sole means of support was begging and what could be got from harvesting scarce wildlife and some fishing. The size of the original Mi'kmaq population—estimated at about 200,000, or perhaps considerably more, at the onset of European colonization—had been almost wiped out.

These findings did not spur the government to ease the plight of the Mi'kmaq immediately. Perhaps the intention was to wait for another several years in the hope that the "Indian problem" in Nova Scotia would solve itself for all time with the extinction of the People by starvation.

In desperation, Grand Chief Pemmeenauweet wrote to Queen Victoria on January 25, 1841, begging mercy for his people:

Madam,
I am Pausauhmigh Pemmeenauweet, and am called by the White Man Louis Benjamin Porminout. I am the Chief of my people, the Micmac Tribe of Indians in your Province of Nova Scotia, and I was recognized, and declared to be the Chief, by our good friend Sir John Cope Sherbrooke, in the White man's fashion, twenty-five years ago. I have yet the papers which he gave me.

Sorry to hear that the King is dead. Am glad to hear that we have a good Queen, whose Father I saw in this Country. He loved the Indians.

I cannot cross the Great Lake to talk to you, for my Canoe is too small, and I am old and weak. I cannot look upon you, for my eyes do not see so far. You cannot hear my voice across the Great Waters. I therefore send this Waumpum and Paper talk to tell the Queen I am in trouble. My people are in trouble.

I have seen upwards of a thousand Moons. When I was young I had plenty, now I am old, poor and sickly too. My people are poor. No Hunting Grounds, No Beaver, No Otter, No Nothing. Indians poor, poor forever, No Store, No Chest, No Clothes. All these woods once ours. Our Fathers possessed them all. Now we cannot cut a Tree to warm our Wigwam in Winter unless the White Man please.

The Micmacs now receive no presents but one small blanket for a whole family. The Governor is a good man, but he cannot help us now, we look to you the Queen. The White Waumpum tell that we hope in you. Pity your poor Indians in Nova Scotia!

White Man Has taken all that was ours, he has plenty of everything here, but we are told that the White Man has sent to you for more. No wonder I should speak for myself and my people.

The man that takes this talk over the Great Water will tell you what we want to be done for us, let us not perish! Your Indian children love you, and will fight for you against all your enemies.

My head and my heart shall go to the One above for you.
Pausauhmigh Pemmeenauweet, his mark X.[15]

To be forced to endure the horrific spectacle of your people slowly dying from

No wood for the Mi'kmaq

malnutrition and starvation while others feast and thrive must be torture. The Chief, himself in dire straits, had to do just that.

One cannot excuse the government by saying it was poor, because Nova Scotia of the mid-1840s was one of the most prosperous British colonies in the Americas. Not many members of the White population were in great want, except the Acadians, who were kept a little less well off than English-speaking White citizens.

The reason that Mi'kmaq were in such sorry plight during the nineteenth century was the same as always: pure, unadulterated racism. What the White establishment did to the Mi'kmaq during this period is comparable to stripping a person naked in a snowstorm and then leaving him to fend for himself. The English cruelly robbed the Mi'kmaq of any means of support and then left them to fend for themselves without the tools needed for survival, knowing full well they would perish!

It took three and a half years after it had been officially made aware of the dire circumstances of the Mi'kmaq for Her Majesty's colonial government to act. On March 19, 1842, the following Act was passed by the General Assembly of Nova Scotia:

An Act to Provide for the Instruction and Permanent Settlement of the Indians

WHEREAS, it is proper to provide for the Education and Civilization of the Aboriginal Inhabitants of this Province, and for the preservation and productive application for their use of the Lands in different parts of this Province, set aside as Indian Reservations: ...

(I) BE IT ENACTED, by the lieutenant governor, council and assembly, that it shall, and may be lawful for the Governor to appoint ... a fit and proper person to be Commissioner for Indian Affairs, who, upon entering on the Office, shall give security for the faithful performance of its duties, to the satisfaction of the Governor, and Her Majesty's Executive Council.

(II) AND BE IT ENACTED, that it shall be lawful for the Governor, by and with the advice of Her Majesty's Executive Council … to issue instructions to the said Commissioner for his guidance, in performing the duties of his said Office.…

(III) AND BE IT ENACTED, that *it shall be the duty of the said Commissioner for the time being, to take the supervision and management of all Lands that now are, or may hereafter be, set apart as Indian Reservations, or for the use of the Indians*, to ascertain and define their boundaries, to discover and report to the Governor all cases of intrusion, and of the transfer or sale of the said Lands, or of their use or possession by the Indians; and *generally, to protect the said Lands from encroachment and alienation, and preserve them for the use of the Indians.*

(IV) AND BE IT ENACTED, that in cases where there have been, or hereafter may be, erected or made valuable buildings, or improvements on such Lands, it shall be in the power of the Governor, by and with the advice of Her Majesty's Executive Council, to make Agreements with the persons who shall have made the same, or those claiming under them, either by way of satisfaction and compensation for the value of the lands so improved, with so much adjacent Land as may be necessary, or by way of rent or allowance for the use of such Lands, for such term of years, and under such considerations, as may be expressed in the Agreements, and all such Agreements shall insure by way of sale or demise, as may be therein expressed, and shall convey a legal Title to the Parties accordingly; and all monies received in compensation or satisfaction as aforesaid, shall be laid out, either in the purchase of other Lands for the use of the Indians, or in some other manner, for their permanent benefit.…

(V) AND BE IT ENACTED, that in all cases of intrusion, encroachment, or unauthorized settlement, or improvement upon any such Lands as aforesaid, it shall be lawful to proceed by information, in the name of Her Majesty, before Her Majesty's Supreme Court of Halifax, or in the County where the Lands may lie, notwithstanding the legal Title by grant or otherwise, may not be vested in Her Majesty.

(VI) AND BE IT ENACTED, that *it shall be the duty of such Commissioner, under such Instructions, to put himself in communication with the Chiefs of the Different Tribes of the Micmac Race throughout the Province, to explain to them the wishes of the Government, and to invite them to cooperate in the permanent settlement and instruction of their people.*

That it shall be his duty, subject to such instructions aforesaid, to parcel out to each head of family a portion of the Reservations, with such limited power of alienation to Indians only as the said Instructions may, from time to time, authorize; and also, to aid them in the purchase of Implements and Stock. With such moderate assistance from the Fund placed at his disposal, as they may seem … *by their Industry and Sobriety to deserve*, to aid in the erection of *a dwelling for each Chief, a School House and a place of Worship*, and generally, to take such measures as, in his discretion … carry out the Objects of this Act.

(VII) AND BE ENACTED, that such Commissioner shall have power to make arrangements with the Trustees, or Teachers of any Schools, or Academies throughout the Province, for the Board and Tuition of such number of Indian Children as may be desirous of acquiring Education; and ... the expenses shall be paid out of the funds placed at his disposal.

(VIII) AND BE ENACTED, that in order to form a permanent Fund, applicable to the purposes of this Act, the Commissioner shall be authorized to raise subscription, to apply for Contributions from Charitable Institutions, either in this Province, or elsewhere, and to draw from the Treasury, by Warrant from the Governor ... such sum or sums of money, as may, from time to time, be granted by the Legislature for that purpose.

(IX) AND BE IT ENACTED, that the said Commissioner shall, at the close of every year, furnish the Governor, to be laid before the two Branches of the Legislature, a detailed report of his proceedings, and an account of his receipts and expenditures, together with the names of each Chief, for the time being the number of Heads of Families Settled, and Children Educated, and generally, such other information as may enable the Governor and the Legislature to judge of the value and correctness of his proceedings.[16]

Indicative of their "humanity," fully 129 years after they had taken over the province, the British had finally made provision to educate the Mi'kmaq. However, it was done with the intention of speeding up assimilation, not preserving the Nation.

Joseph Howe was appointed Commissioner for Indian Affairs by the Governor under the Act. Except for the intercession of this great statesman, the Mi'kmaq of Nova Scotia would probably have passed into extinction. In his first report, of January 25, 1843, Howe was very condemning, in a compelling diplomatic manner, of the government for permitting the poverty among the Mi'kmaq to exist. He wrote:

My Lord,

In conformity with the 9th Clause of the "Act to provide for the Instruction and Permanent Settlement of the Indians," and in obedience to your Lordship's Instructions, founded upon that Law, it becomes my duty to submit to your Lordship, for the information of the Legislature, a report of my proceedings as Commissioner for Indian Affairs, with an account of the mode in which the grant for that service has been applied.

In accepting the Commission, with which your Lordship was pleased to honour me, I was aware that the task that I was about to assume was one beset with peculiar difficulties. A given amount of money, skilfully and honestly applied, will make a road or a bridge, which every passenger may recognize as a valuable improvement. But the *Civilizing of Barbarous Tribes*, the eradication of habits and prejudices formed with the growth of Centuries, the substitution of one kind of knowledge, absolutely indispensable to success, or even existence, in a new state of Society, for another kind, equally important in the old, is a work of time, that may be entered upon in a season, but which cannot be completed, or yet advanced, even under the most favourable circumstances, but by perseverance in a series of enlightened experiments running over a period of years.

The French and Germans, who inhabit portions of this Province, are still French and Germans in most of the essential characteristics, though surrounded by a British population for nearly a hundred years. Therefore, it was not to be expected that any striking impression could be made among the Micmac in a few months, or that much more could be done than to collect and arrange facts, and lay a foundation for future operations.

Your Lordship, who is quite aware that the energies of the finest minds, aided by the most lavish expenditure, have been employed to little purpose in similar designs, though you may find no inducement in the history of these experiments to shrink from the prosecution of a work of Justice and Philanthropy, will, I am quite assured, be disposed to turn from them with considerate discrimination to the little that may have resulted from my labours.

My first care was to collect and arrange all the information which I could gather from the public Departments, bearing upon the subject embraced by my Commission....

The Indian Statistics collected in 1838 exhibit the number of the Micmac then in the Province as follows:

County of Halifax,	265	Souls.
Island of Cape Breton,	520	
Western District, including Annapolis, Digby, Yarmouth, Shelburne, Queens, and Lunenburg Counties,	415	
Pictou County,	100	
Kings County,	35	
County of Sydney (Afton)	90	
Total	1425	

Assuming this table to have been tolerably accurate in 1838, *the rapidity with which these people had decreased, up to that time, may be judged from the fact that in 1798, forty years before, there were 800 in the County of Pictou alone.* Mr Campbell, in his report to the Government in 1838, says that "two years ago there were 60 or 70 Souls in King's County, but that now there is not more than half that number," while I could not hear of but two or three families there in the Autumn of last year.

It is impossible, however, to estimate the ratio of decrease by the numbers in any particular County or Locality, because almost every family which has not a framed house moves two or three times in a year, and such Counties as King's and Pictou, where the population is rapidly decreasing, the forest disappearing before the axe, and Mills either damming, or in course of erection upon every stream, are very likely to be deserted for others, where, from the indifference of the soil, the march of improvements is not so rapid.

Of the Eastern section of the Province, I cannot speak from actual observation, but think *the decrease in the West must have been equal to 10 percent on the whole number since 1838*. The decrease in the County of Halifax has probably been less, for, although the deaths in proportion to the numbers may have been equal, there is an immigration towards the Capital, particularly in the Summer Season, partly for Religious objects, and partly for the sale of small wares manufactured by the Squaws.

At this rate the whole Race would be extinct in 40 years, *and half a Century hence the very existence of the Tribe would be as a dream and a tradition to our Grandchildren, who would find it difficult to imagine the features or dwelling of a Micmac, as we do to realize those of an Ancient Breton....* Assuming the statistics of 1838 as a basis of a calculation, and deducting 10 percent, *your Lordship will perceive that there must be at least 1,300 Souls still in this Province, appealing to the sympathies of every honourable mind by the contrast of their misfortunes with our prosperity, their fading numbers with our numerical advancement, their ignorance and destitution with the wealth and civilization which surrounds and presses upon them from every side.*

In approaching the Indians, with a sincere desire to faithfully represent in my intercourse with them the benevolent yet judicious intentions of the Government and the Legislature, I found myself in some degree embarrassed by the exaggerated ideas and expectations with which many, from various motives, had thoughtlessly misled the poor people committed to my care.

For many weeks in the Spring my dwelling was besieged, at all hours, by Indians, who had been taught to believe that unbounded wealth was at my disposal, and that they were to be fed and clothed hereafter at the expense of the Government. *Had I yielded to the clamorous demands and even reproaches of these Visitors, the sum voted would barely have sufficed to supply the wants of the Halifax Indians alone for a single month.* But, I resolutely resisted those importunities, and although a great deal of time was necessarily consumed, in explaining the Objects of the Act to numbers, and reasoning with them upon the evil consequences, even to themselves, of indiscriminate habitual relief, still I felt that good humoured perseverance in this course was the only way to disabuse their minds and secure their confidence and cooperation.

The rule I adopted was to give relief only to the old and infirm, the sick and maimed, or to those who had met with some calamity, which, for the time, gave them claim to consideration. A list of trifling sums given to these, appears in the account under the head of "Miscellaneous Charities," and which, including a sum of money paid to redeem a very industrious man's Whaleboat and lines from the hands of the Constable, has been kept within £28....

For many years past, *the Legislature has granted £100 per annum for the use of the Indians*, which has usually been laid out in Great Coats and Blankets, to be distributed in various parts of the Province. I knew that many would calculate on this resource, and that, at least for several years, a portion of the funds would have to be thus applied, until the practical value of assistance in other modes began to be realized, and until they were taught that they must provide clothing for themselves.

As I had anticipated, on the approach of Winter, requisitions came from various parts of the Province, and urgent and hourly applications were made by those families residing near the Capital. To those with whom I had personal communication, I endeavoured to explain that this species of relief, like that given in money throughout the Summer, must be hereafter confined as much as possible to the Indigent and Infirm, to old persons confined to their camps, to widows, orphans, or women at childbirth during the Winter Months. With few exceptions, coats or blankets have only been distributed in Halifax to this class of cases, and gentlemen to whose care small parcels had been sent in Cape Breton, Pictou and Hants, where no other expenditures for the benefit of the Indians have been authorized, have been requested to distribute them with the same care and discrimination. The expenditure under this head has been £46 19s. 2d....

As the Lands reserved for the Indians must form the basis of all the operations of the Government, I endeavoured to ascertain ... their extent, and, by personal inspection of their position, condition and capabilities, *my other avocations afforded me leisure*, to collect information that might eventually lead to their permanent occupation and improvement. The Surveyor General politely furnished me with plans of the Reserves in Nova Scotia.... These consist of:

County of Halifax.	
Western side of Shubenacadie Grand Lake,	1,000 Acres
On Ingrams River, at the Head	
of Margaret's Bay,	300 Acres
County of Hants.	
On two Brooks, falling into the Shubenacadie,	
about five miles from the New Bridge, at	
Parkers's,	1,750 Acres
County of Cumberland.	
On the Chenemecas River,	1,000 Acres
County of Lunenburg.	
On both sides of Gold River,	1,000 Acres
County of Queen's.	
On the Pleasant and Port Medway Rivers,	1,000 Acres
County of Digby.	
At Bear River,	1,000 Acres
County of King's.	
In the rear of the Township of Horton,	1,000 Acres
County of Sydney.	
At Pomket,	1,000 Acres
County of Annapolis.	
Several lots on the Liverpool Road, about	1,000 Acres

In Nova Scotia Proper,	10,050 Acres
In Cape Breton,	12,000 Acres
Total	22,050 Acres

The present condition and capabilities of such of these Lands as I have been enabled to visit may be gathered from the journal which accompanies this report. *It is to be regretted that so little judgement has been exercised in the selection of them; the same quantity, if reserved in spots where the soil was good, on navigable streams, or in places where fish were abundant, and game within reach, would now be a valuable resource. All the land reserved in this County is sterile and comparatively valueless. In Yarmouth, Hants, Colchester, Pictou and Guysborough, there are no Reserves, and in some other places, as at Pomket, and in parts of Cape Breton, it is to be feared that the quantity has been somewhat diminished by the encroachment of the whites. In the neighbourhood of Dartmouth and Halifax,* where the Indians from all parts of the Province resort, at all seasons, particularly in the Summer, *they have no Lands,* and are consequently compelled to build their camps on private property, and are tempted to destroy the wood, and commit depredations which are becoming every year more annoying and vexatious.

Your Lordship will perceive, from my Journal, that directions have been given to the local Surveyors to lay off a few other tracts, in favourable situations, amounting in the whole to perhaps 1,000 to 1,500 Acres. Should your Lordship give an order for the Reservation or Grant of these, it is probable that an equal quantity may, upon further examination, be relinquished as an equivalent.

The present value of the Reserves, which I have visited, may be thus stated:

Reserve at Margaret's Bay,	£ 100
Reserve at Shubenacadie Lake,	150
Reserve in Hants,	452
Reserve at Gold River,	350
Reserve in Queens,	250
Reserve at Bear River,	350
Total	£1,652

The tract of 1,000 Acres in King's County, I did not see, this, with Lands held at Roseway, Tusket, Sabin Lake, May be worth,	£ 348
Making the total value of the Eastern and Halifax Reserves, about,	£ 2,000

Besides the public Lands, a few tracts are held by individuals, either under grant or by possession. Whenever my attention has been called to these, I have endeavoured to ascertain the nature of the Title, and to protect the Indians.

As an illustration of the mode in which the Aboriginal have been deprived of the property, to which were often entitled by Grant, *or by uninterrupted possession*, a case may be mentioned.… A tract at Indian Point, in the Township of Chester, on which there is an excellent limestone quarry, and which is now valued at £500, was purchased 20 years ago, by a person named Cook, who took a Deed from one of three Brothers to whom it was Granted, giving a Note of Hand for £10 in exchange. The Note was deposited in the hands of a third party, claimed by the purchaser after the Indian's death, but there is no satisfactory proof that it was ever discharged. *Meanwhile the white man has almost secured a Title by possession*, and has certainly established a claim to the consideration of the Government by extensive improvements; but the children of the Indians, who are attached to the spot, still mourn over the loss of what they regard as their rightful Inheritance. This dispute I have endeavoured and hope to compromise, by obtaining for the Indians a payment equal to the value of the land in its original state.

The only Reserve, in the management of which any system appears to have been followed, is that at Bear River. Under the direction of the late Judge Wiswell, whose memory is fondly cherished by the Annapolis Indians, a portion of the 1,000 Acres was laid off in 30 Acre lots, and heads of families put in possession of each. If they retained possession and improved, their Title was respected, if they deserted the land for three years, it was given to others of more industrious habits.

The introduction of something like this system being contemplated by the Act of last Session, and by my instructions, I have employed Surveyors to divide the Reserves in those Counties which I have visited, and shall proceed to put well disposed Indians in possession of lots, as soon as the Plans are forwarded, and in sufficient time, I trust, to admit of commencing operations next Spring. These Plans and Surveys will probably cost about £30, although but £9 4s. 9d. has yet been paid under this head of expenditures.

The outlay for "Seed, Implements, Cattle," amounts to £12 8s. 7d. I would have gladly increased this item, but I found it would be of little use to make extensive distributions until … the Government could have some assurance that the bounty granted would be well applied. I could have given away hundreds of bushels of potatoes in the Spring, but they would have been eaten and not planted, I therefore refrained, often under very pressing importunities, and in no instances assisted those who had not some cleared land in occupation, and who showed a disposition to help themselves. The aid given to these, has, I have reason to believe, been seasonable and serviceable, and in most cases has been gratefully acknowledged.

The heaviest item in this portion of the Account has been incurred for the purchase of working Oxen for the Settlement at Bear River, but these were imperatively required, and as they were purchased in a season of depression, and belong to the Government, if not found useful, and well used, may be disposed of without much loss.

Some permanent expenditures, contemplated by the Act, have been authorized at Gold River, the Hants Reserve, and at the Fairy Lake. They will cost about £80, but have not yet been completed.... It seemed to me, that one of the first steps was to lure the Micmac from his Wigwam to a more comfortable habitation, whenever this could be done, and that, to permit the few houses already possessed by those who cultivated the soil, to go to decay, and be abandoned, when a small expenditure in each case might keep them in repair, would be exceedingly bad policy. It also struck me, that, as there was likely to be a large Settlement at the Fairy Lake, the sooner a good example was set, by placing in its midst one family enjoying a degree of comfort, which, by moderate exertion, all might emulate, the more probability was there of advancing Civilization.

As the opening and improvement of cheap roads, in two or three places, is in some degree connected with the ultimate success of these experiments, it will be desirable that a small sum should be placed at the disposal of your Excellency to connect the Reserves with adjoining Settlements.

The Education of the Indians was one of the most important topics to which my attention was called.... With few exceptions, I at first found nearly the whole Tribe strongly prejudiced against learning to read or write any other language than their own. Their books, which contain prayers and portions of their Religious Services, are more numerous than I at first supposed, and if not found in every Wigwam, are carefully preserved and constantly referred to in every encampment.

By visiting the camps, conversing cheerfully with the Indians, giving them familiar illustrations of the rudimental branches, and showing how much they had lost from not knowing how to secure Lands as the Whites had done, or to protect those which they had, an impression was gradually made upon some, while, by explaining the character and utility of different Books in my Library, and reading passages to them, others were interested.

By writing letters about their own business, and receiving answers, I endeavoured to convince them of the superiority of the Post Office over the Courier de Bois.

Having secured the aid of the Rev. Mr. Geary, to whose kind cooperation I am much indebted, a Sunday School was opened for the instruction of the Indians in the Chapel at Dartmouth, and, for several weeks, the attendance was very good, and our pupils of both sexes, and all ages, making fair progress; *but as Mr. Geary was often necessarily absent, visiting different portions of a widely extended Mission, it was found impossible to ensure that certainty and regularity which were essential to the success of the design, and the Sunday School was subsequently abandoned.*

In the Autumn, a Day School was opened at Dartmouth, but as most of the Indians had either moved to the interior, or retired to the woods, to prepare for Winter, the attendance was very slight, and the room was closed at the end of the first quarter.... In the ensuing Spring ... by having a School room, distinct from the Chapel, and open every Sunday, when the Indians have leisure to attend, and usually resort to Dartmouth, I am in hopes that more progress will be made.

Enough has been done, to conquer much prejudice, and to prove the capacity of the Micmac for receiving instruction. Some of the young people at Dartmouth learnt to spell quite as fast as any white children would have done, and required only the steady and assiduous attention of regular teachers to bring them rapidly forward; and one man, with scarcely any instruction, wrote, in a few weeks, a copy book very much better than persons often do who have been twelve months at School.

Whenever I could find Indians near a School House, as at Gold and Bear Rivers, Port Medway, Liverpool, Margaret's, I have endeavoured, by making arrangements for the gratuitous instruction of such children as choose to attend, to pave the way for a more general interest in the cultivation of the intellect. Some of the more intelligent heads of families are fully sensible of the necessity which must soon force upon the rising generation other pursuits than those which have been exclusively followed, and in which new information and ideas are absolutely essential to success.

Meuse, of Bear River, to whom reference is more particularly made in the notes, has had five of his children taught to read and write, two of them now are at School, and one of the copy books of his youngest girl is handed in with this report. The two boys placed in St. Mary's Seminary, after a few first weeks of restless chafing at the restraints necessarily imposed upon them in such an Institution were over, conducted themselves well, and made as much progress as could be expected. The eldest can read some, and writes a fair large hand; the youngest, who was almost too young to derive the full benefit of the instruction imparted, is less advanced, but evinces a lively intelligence, and due appreciation of the advantages which a house has over a camp, and a comfortable bed over a litter of boughs. I should be exceedingly glad to continue these boys at the Seminary until the experiment was fully tried, and they were much further advanced, but as the cost of boarding (education being gratuitous) amounts to £66 per annum for the two, it is for the Government and the Legislature to determine whether they shall be withdrawn, or continued after the close of the current quarter.

The expenses of executing this Commission have amounted to £59 11s. 3d. I would willingly have made them less, but could not, even with the most rigid economy.... *Should the cost of management seem extravagant, I shall not object to being surcharged with any part, or even the whole of the amount, rather than that the expense should be any bar to the carrying on of a work, which, however feebly executed, has been, in the design, but just to the Aborigines and highly honourable to the Country.*

Should the Legislature make a further Grant, and your Excellency honour me by employing me in this work of humanity for another season, I propose to visit Cumberland, and the Eastern Counties, including Cape Breton; and shall endeavour to place within the reach of my successor such information as will enable him to conduct the business chiefly by correspondence, with the aid of an occasional tour of inspection, every third or fourth year.

In concluding this Report, I have again to solicit your Excellency's favourable consideration of the difficulties of the task. *Difficulties scarcely to be overcome in a single year by the sedulous devotion of one person's entire time.*

I have been able to give to such preliminary measures as seemed requisite for their ultimate mastery, only the leisure hours which could be borrowed from other and various duties, both of public and private nature....

I trust, however, that should your Excellency not be satisfied with the results of these first experiments, the blame may be laid upon the Commissioner, rather than be charged upon the capacity, or urged against the claims of a people, for whose many good qualities a more extended intercourse has only increased my respect, and who have, if not by Treaty, at least by all the ties of humanity, a claim upon the Government of the Country, which nothing but their entire extinction, or their elevation to a more permanent, and happy position in the scale of Society, can ever entirely discharge.

I have the honour to be, With high respect, Your Lordship's obedient, Very humble Servant,

Joseph Howe [17]

The number of Mi'kmaq in the province had decreased substantially between the 1838 census and Howe's report in 1842. The statistics Howe gathered put the population at 1,300, a drop of approximately 125. It would be fair to say that the government had not done much to ease starvation within Mi'kmaq communities during that period.

Although legislation had been enacted by the government, it was not overly interested in carrying out the Act's intent. The most telling indicator of the legislature's lack of sincerity is that it set aside only £300 for the project in its first year. Compare this with bounties of £100 per Mi'kmaq scalp paid in 1744, and the government's absence of generosity is starkly illuminated. Another telling indication of the inadequacy of the budget is that Howe said he would pay for some of the expenditures himself if the government declined to do so. Further, in spite of the dire straits of the Mi'kmaq, the Indian Commissioner's work was only a part-time endeavour.

The government's lack of interest in using the Act to effect positive change for the Mi'kmaq was also revealed by its non-enforcement of the land protection section. Because of this inaction the general population continued to encroach with impunity on land reserved for the Mi'kmaq. This is a good example of how positive legislation for the protection of Mi'kmaq land rights was ignored by all, including the enactors. However, because they did create this Act, a large number of modern specific land claims date from that period. And by enacting this section the government was, probably unintentionally, no longer in violation of the provisions of the Royal Proclamation of 1763.

Section VI of the Act indicates that the colonial government recognized the sovereignty of Mi'kmaq communities by accepting that the consent of the Mi'kmaq Chiefs should be sought and received before the plan could proceed. This section also takes the first step towards the creation of divisions within the communities by proposing the building of new homes for the Chiefs. This is a good example of a European-style government attempting to impose its alien values—special perks for leaders—on the Mi'kmaq community. The traditions of the Mi'kmaq Nation provided no such material things for leaders.

The statute requires accountability, which Howe provided in minute detail in his first report. This requirement is important to keep in mind when making comparisons with accountability practices discussed in later chapters.

In his report, Howe emphatically stated that educating the Mi'kmaq was very important to guarantee their survival in the new order. By spelling out the miserly expenditures he made towards this important endeavour, he highlights the feeble interest of the government in the Mi'kmaq cause.

I found it very interesting that a few Mi'kmaq children were brave enough to attend White schools, given the sea of racial intolerance at the time. They must have encountered racial hostility that would have intimidated the bravest soul! During those days several institutions of higher learning in Nova Scotia forbade a Mi'kmaq from even walking through their campuses, let alone receiving an education at them.

Howe's compassionate interest is also highlighted by his correct description of the near worthlessness for agricultural purposes of the lands allocated to Mi'kmaq communities. He also emphasizes in his report, probably unintentionally, how English land ownership laws were applied along racial lines when he states that some of the Whites who had encroached upon Indian Reserve lands may have acquired ownership of the land by twenty years of "uninterrupted possession." This is sickly ironic in view of the fact that the English refused to recognize the close to ten thousand years of uninterrupted possession of Nova Scotia by the Mi'kmaq.

By his eloquence, Howe propelled the reluctant government to do more to assist the Mi'kmaq. However, he was not without his own biases towards the civilization he had been charged to help. His use of the word "barbarous" in describing Mi'kmaq culture leaves the impression that he too harboured views of racial superiority. In spite of that, his influence and labours on behalf of the Mi'kmaq were one of the major factors that allowed the Nation to survive. And his fearlessness in telling bigots within the government that the Mi'kmaq were their intellectual equals was an act of considerable political courage at that time. Howe's humanity immeasurably helped to save the Mi'kmaq race from extinction, and for that he is gratefully remembered!

The Mi'kmaq population is reported by some historians to have stopped declining between 1843 and 1847, when in their estimation the numbers slowly began to increase. They report that at Confederation the population was about 1,600. However, from my research on Mi'kmaq family trees for Indian registration purposes, I can say that this increase was not a result of births. It came mostly from Mi'kmaq moving to Nova Scotia from other jurisdictions—New Brunswick, Prince Edward Island, other parts of Canada and the States. Without this influx the population would have decreased during the period. My view is supported by Commissioner of Indian Affairs Abraham Gesner, a knowledgeable man sympathetic towards the Mi'kmaq, who had gained his expertise from close contact. He made the following comments in 1847:

Unless the progress of their annihilation is soon arrested, the time is close at hand, when … the last of their race, to use their own idea, "will sleep with the bones of their fathers." Unless the vices and diseases of civilization are speedily arrested, the Indians ... will soon be as the Red Men of Newfoundland, or other Tribes of the West, whose existence is forever blotted out from the face of the Earth.[18]

After 1843, continuing their efforts to exterminate by assimilation, governments made several grants by lease of lands to individual Mi'kmaq for their personal use. This questionable generosity was provided in a humiliating way. In one typical example, Samuel Fairbanks reluctantly presented a petition dated November 9, 1866, on behalf of Joseph Paul, my Great-Grandfather, to the Governor for consideration:

Petitions—Joseph Paul—Indian

The petitioner resides at Quoddy—to the Eastward of Halifax. He is represented to be a *sober and industrious Indian* and has built a house on the Island applied for. He asks for a long lease of the Island as well as an addition of one hundred acres.[19]

Fairbanks listed a hundred and one reasons why the land should not be granted, to which the Governor replied, in what must have been one of his better moments, "Let the petitioner have the lease!"[20] The term of the lease is one thousand years!

The fact that my Great-Grandfather had to endure the humilation of being declared a "sober and industrious Indian" before he could acquire a plot of land still riles me. Only those who have experienced this kind of patronizing racist treatment can fully appreciate how degrading the experience is!

Thus ends my account of the Mi'kmaq's horrific experience under colonialism.

12

Confederation and the Indian Act

During the 1860s, politicians from Upper and Lower Canada and the Maritimes began to meet to discuss confederation. In time, Nova Scotia, New Brunswick, Quebec and Ontario worked out a proposal to federate, which was forwarded to Great Britain's Parliament for action. Although it would affect them drastically, because of racist attitudes, First Nations were excluded from participating in the process.

Confederation

In response to the recommendations of the colonial delegates the British Parliament created Canada in 1867 by enacting "The British North America Act." The new country had four provinces with two levels of government, federal and provincial.

The most significant change for the First Nations was that they now had to look to Ottawa instead of provincial and territorial capitals for subsistence allowances. The immediate benefit was that the assistance from Ottawa would be high enough to end starvation. The biggest negative was that communication with the remote Great White Father was very difficult for a largely uneducated population.

Communication was made even harder for Amerindians by the federal government's habit of passing its new responsibilities from department to department. Until Indian affairs were finally anchored with the creation of the Department of Indian Affairs and Northern Development (DIAND) in the 1960s, they were switched at random from one department to another—Secretary of State; Energy, Mines and Resources; Citizenship and Immigration.

In retrospect, placing our People in the hands of Citizenship and Immigration was very offensive. Today it seems like a cruel and tasteless joke that the First Nations peoples, rendered destitute and landless refugees in their own country by the English, were placed under the control of the department responsible for immigrants to Canada. What made it even more atrocious was that Registered Indians were not accorded the same rights and privileges enjoyed by immigrants.

Under the new Constitution both levels of government had their responsibilities and powers clearly defined. Responsibility for the welfare of Treaty Indians and the security of their lands was placed in the hands of the federal government by Section 91(24):

91. It shall be lawful for the Queen, by and with the Advice and Consent of the Senate and House of Commons, to make Laws for the Peace, Order, and good Government of Canada, in relation to all Matters not coming within the Classes of Subjects by this Act assigned exclusively to the Legislatures of the Provinces; and for greater Certainty … (notwithstanding anything in this Act) the exclusive Legislative Authority of the Parliament of Canada extends to all

Matters ... hereinafter enumerated; that is to say,...
  (24) Indians and Lands reserved for Indians.[1]

The new federal government assumed its constitutional trust responsibilities for "Indians" and "Indian lands" with little enthusiasm. What little it did muster had a White supremacist bent, for they adopted the same policy the English had chosen "to solve the Indian problem forever"—extinction by assimilation. The government delayed for more than a year before appointing an Indian agent for Nova Scotia. Then it appointed a man who had already proven to be less than supportive of the Mi'kmaq cause, not by any standard an action demonstrating conscientious care for duty:

> Department of Secretary of State, Ottawa, September 28, 1868
> Mr. Samuel Fairbanks:
>   I have the honour to inform you that, by an Order in Council ... you have been appointed ... Agent for Indian Affairs in the province of Nova Scotia, *with an allowance of ten per cent on all moneys collected by you in that capacity.*... Patents for Lands will be prepared on your transmitting descriptions of the lands sold and paid for; and ... will be forwarded to you for delivery to the purchasers.
>   I have the Honour to be, Sir, Your Obedient Servant,
>   Hector L. Langevin, Secretary of State.[2]

Langevin made it plain in his memo that the government, by agreeing to pay Fairbanks a commission of ten percent on all the revenues he could raise by leasing or selling Indian Reserve lands in Nova Scotia, intended to manage its constitutional responsibility to protect Mi'kmaq lands by alienating them from Mi'kmaq use as fast as possible. This was the beginning of a pattern of dereliction of legal duty by the federal government that still continues to a certain extent today.

Governments continued to get away with such blatant neglect of duty over the ensuing decades because, like the English, they denied to First Nations peoples even the most basic of civil and human rights. We were designated "wards of the Crown" and as such were paternalistically treated as "non-citizens" and forced by the authorities—who shackled us with legislated and unwritten apartheid restrictions—to live in a very confined and regulated "non-person" world. In 2000 this situation still impedes our progress to an unacceptable degree.

Afflicted by a poverty begot by denial of human rights and enforced by exclusions the Mi'kmaq population, which had been approximately 1,400-1,500 at Confederation, remained almost stationary until the late 1940s. The main cause was malnutrition, which kept disease resistance drastically low, causing susceptibility to the ravages of tuberculosis, typhoid etc. The population had increased to only two thousand by 1950.

The Indian Act

If one needs more hard evidence to cement the view that the new country displayed careless indifference towards the management of its Indian and Indian land constitutional trust responsibilities, this fact should provide it: it took the government almost a decade to enact the legislation it needed to manage Indian affairs.

In 1876, Parliament finally devised and legislated the legal code needed to manage its constitutional obligations. However, in direct contradiction of its trust obligations, the government included sections in the Indian Act that were not in the best interests of the people they were constitutionally bound to protect. The following two sections are excellent examples of the federal government's dereliction of duty.

Section 138 made it illegal for an Indian Agent not to make every effort to sell off Indian Reserve lands:

> Every Agent who knowingly and falsely informs, or causes to be informed, any person applying to him to purchase any land within his division and agency, that the same has already been purchased, or who refuses to permit the person so applying to purchase the same according to existing regulations, shall be liable therefore to the person so applying, in the sum of five dollars for each acre of land which the person so applying offered to purchase, recoverable by action of debt in any court of competent jurisdiction.[3]

This section, because it clearly dictates that the sale of Reserve land to interested White parties take precedence over First Nations interests, would have made Indian Affairs a difficult place for a person of conscience to work. Such a person would have recognized that it was not in the best interests of the First Nations to sell off their remaining lands and thus to do so would be unethical. Quit or subvert personal ethics would have been the choice.

Section 86 was the 1876 enfranchisement section:

> Whenever any Indian man, or unmarried woman, of the full age of twenty-one years obtains the consent of the Band of which he or she is a member to become enfranchised, and whenever such Indian has been assigned by the Band a suitable allotment of land for that purpose, the local Agent shall report such action of the Band and the name of the applicant to the Superintendent General.
>
> Whereupon the said Superintendent General, if satisfied that the proposed allotment of land is equitable, shall authorize some competent person to report whether the applicant is an Indian, who from *the degree of civilization to which he or she has attained, and the character for integrity, morality and sobriety which he or she bears,* appears to be qualified to become a proprietor of land in fee simple; and upon the favourable report of such person, the Superintendent General may grant such Indian a location ticket as a *probationary Indian* for the land allotted to him or her by the Band.
>
> (1) *Any Indian who may be admitted to the degree of Doctor of Medicine,*

or to any other degree by any University of Learning, or who may be admitted in any Province of the Dominion to practice law, either as an Advocate or as a Barrister, or Counsellor, or Solicitor, or Attorney, or to be a Notary Public, or who may enter Holy Orders, or who may be licensed by any denomination of Christians as a Minister of the Gospel, shall ipso facto become and be enfranchised under this Act.[4]

These provisions reveal the racist attitudes of the departmental employees who wrote them. Paragraph (1) tells an Indian, "If you dare to aspire to higher education, we shall take away your Indian rights!" For years afterward this provision scared off many Treaty Indians who were interested in educating themselves.

Interestingly, the humiliating assessment criteria that my Grandfather had to contend with—"sober and industrious Indian"— was brought over from colonial times and made part of the Act!

The irony of such sections is that, prior to Confederation, First Nations peoples had suffered unremitting racist persecution mostly of an ad hoc nature; after Confederation, when more enlightened thought was supposed to be afoot, racist persecution was codified in undemocratic federal and provincial laws.

The mentality that produced the Indian Act and its regulations was similar to the mentality of the English in 1725. By negotiating treaties the English recognized the sovereignty of the First Nations, but at the same time they would do practically anything to deny this sovereignty. Canadian governments since Confederation have engaged in the same kind of tug-of-war with the First Nations. The Indian Act itself is a good example of this inconsistency: it recognizes the independence of the Bands and their Councils on one hand, but on the other it makes every effort to render them completely dependent.

The inherent right of Bands to govern themselves is recognized to a certain degree by many parts of the Act. Whether this was intentional or simply accidental is difficult to determine. Some sections of the Act imply inherent rights. Sections 1 and 2:

1. This Act may be cited as the *Indian Act*.

2.   (1)   In this Act, "band" means a body of Indians

(a) for whose use and benefit in common, lands, the legal title to which is vested in Her Majesty, have been set apart before, on or after September 4, 1951, [This statement implies that First Nations' aboriginal interests in their lands are protected by Section 91(24) of the British North America Act.]

(b) for whose use and benefit in common, moneys are held by Her Majesty, or

(c) declared by the Governor in Council to be a band for the purposes of this Act....

"council of the band" means

(a) in the case of a band to which section 74 applies, the council established pursuant to that section [Indian Act election and Band Council procedural sections].

(b) in the case of a band to which section 74 does not apply, *the council chosen according to the custom of the band*, or, where there is no council, *the chief of the band chosen according to the custom of the band.*

This part of Section 2 recognizes that Bands have a *traditional way* of selecting their own form of government, while at same time providing an alternate method if desired by the people. The custom leadership selection methods used by Bands are, in most cases, pre-Columbian. Many of the Bands in Nova Scotia are the same Bands that have existed for hundreds and, in some cases, thousands of years. For example, the Shubenacadie Band has an unbroken history that predates European colonization by inestimable centuries. Up until 1951, the Band selected its government by traditional means, after which, so we are told, it opted for selection under the provisions of the Indian Act. Strangely, born and raised there, I don't recall a plebiscite ever being called to determine if the people wanted to use Indian Act elections; and even stranger, neither does any other Band Member, nor does the Department have any record of it.

Any Band opting for "Indian Act elections" may revert to a traditional form of selecting its government at any time. This provides a good example of government inconsistency. By encoding in law the inherent right of Bands to use traditional means to select their governments, the federal government has, probably unwittingly, made a decision to treat them as self-governing dependent nations. However, although the Indian Act encodes a great deal of other self-governing authorities that First Nations had enjoyed from time immemorial, the federal government has severely restricted these authorities by placing paternalistic provisions in the Act that give it ultimate authority over practically every facet of First Nations life.

Section 2 continues:

Exercise of Powers conferred on Band or Council

2.   (3)   Unless the context otherwise requires or this Act otherwise provides,
   (a) a power conferred on a band shall be deemed not to be exercised unless it is exercised pursuant to the consent of a majority of the electors of a band; and
   (b) a power conferred on the council of a band shall be deemed not to be exercised unless it is exercised pursuant to the consent of a majority of the councillors of the band present at a meeting of the council duly convened.

Section 3 appoints the Minister of Indian Affairs as superintendent general of Indian Affairs and defines how he may delegate authority.

Section 4 defines where, when and how the Act applies to "Registered Indians." Today, the federal government makes every effort to restrict the authority and scope of Band governments to Indian Reserves. This is a deliberate attempt to limit the federal government's responsibility while continuing to divide and conquer. But nowhere does the Royal Proclamation of 1763, the Indian Act or any other law governing First Nations state that legal and aboriginal rights may only be enjoyed when Band members are on Indian Reserves.

Application of the Act

4.   (1)   A reference in this Act to an Indian does not include any person of the race of Aborigines commonly referred to as Inuit.

(2)   The Governor in Council may by proclamation declare that this Act or any portion thereof, except sections 5 to 14.3 or sections 37 to 41, shall not apply to

(a) any Indians or any group or band of Indians, or

(b) any reserve or any surrendered lands or any part thereof, and may by proclamation revoke any such declaration....

(3)   Sections 114 to 122 and, unless the Minister otherwise orders, sections 42 to 52 do not apply to or in respect of any Indian who does not ordinarily reside on a reserve or on lands belonging to Her Majesty in right of Canada or a Province.

The Indian Act as written, with the two exceptions mentioned in Section 4(3), applies equally to all Registered Indians wherever they may reside in Canada. This negates any argument the government may make that they are responsible only for Indians residing on Indian Reserves. By making the Act applicable to all Registered Indians, the government has accepted the fact that Section 91(24) of the British North America Act made the federal government's responsibility for "Indians and Lands reserved for Indians" all inclusive.

Sections 5 to 7 regulate the "Indian Register." Sections 8 to 16 regulate Band membership. Under the old provisions of the Act the Minister had sole responsibility for Indian registration and Band membership. Under the new provisions this has been split in two. The Minister still retains responsibility for Indian registration, but if a Band wants to, it can administer its own membership list. Band membership does not necessarily result in Indian registration. If a Band elects to administer its own list, and if a majority are willing, they can admit non-Natives.

Before 1985 many Band membership provisions in the Act were gender discriminatory and caused a great deal of suffering among Indian women who had married non-Indians. Under these provisions First Nations women who married non-Indians lost their status as Indians, but non-First Nations women who married First Nations men were given Indian status. By enacting these discriminatory provisions the government of Canada assumed the right to assign racial status by deciding who was or was not an Indian.

Native women, supported by many men, fought a prolonged battle to have these sections repealed; they won when Bill C-31, an Act to amend the Indian Act, made retroactive to April 17, 1985, was given Royal Assent in June 1985. This amendment also repealed many other archaic sections of the Act and provided for the reinstatement of those who had been unilaterally removed from Band Lists and the Indian Register. Most of the women and their children who had lost their status under the former discriminatory provisions of the Act have now been reinstated to the Indian Register and, where appropriate, had their names reinstated on Band Lists. Non-Indian women who marry Registered Indians are no longer registered.

The registration of Treaty Indians was started by government to assist itself in the administration of the Act rather than for the benefit of the First Nations peoples. Although many Band members discredit the practice, it has proven to be an extremely helpful tool in court challenges initiated by First Nations Bands.

Personally, I don't have any hang-ups about registration by the federal government. To me it is simply a census method used to keep an accurate count of the populations of First Nations for the purpose of making budget projections etc. In order to maintain their vital statistics, all countries, including Canada, require births, deaths, marriages, divorces and so on to be registered; without the information provided by this registration, governments could not identify their citizens or issue passports, birth certificates, marriage licenses etc. Therefore it is logical that First Nations have a Register for the purpose of issuing aboriginal and treaty rights identification cards, hunting and fishing licenses, and so on; and, most importantly, to ensure that only qualified people benefit from aboriginal rights and claims settlements.

Another good reason to have an Indian Register is that information to legally prove one's ancestry is sometimes very hard to come by. For example, in Nova Scotia, reinstating many of the enfranchised women to the Indian Register was very difficult because proper documentation of their Native origins was often unavailable. These difficulties were encountered primarily because the churches where they or their parents and grandparents had been baptised, married or buried had burnt down in many cases, destroying all records. The fact that members of their immediate families were registered was the only proof of Native ancestry that could be offered.

Thus, if the Indian Register were unilaterally abolished without a viable alternative being put in place, the majority of Registered Indians in Canada would have difficulty proving their ancestry for legal challenges against the Crown. In all major court decisions to date, where the existence of aboriginal and treaty rights has been acknowledged, the litigants were Registered Indians who were members of First Nations.

This was true in the case of *Simon* v. *the Queen*. On November 21, 1985, when recognizing the validity of the Treaty of 1752 under Section 88 of the Indian Act, the Supreme Court of Canada cited the fact that James Simon was a registered member of the Shubenacadie Mi'kmaq Band as proof that he was an "Indian" who qualified for the benefits ensuing from the treaty.

Section 17 covers the creation of new Bands:

17.   (1)   The Minister may, whenever he considers it desirable,
    (a) amalgamate bands that, by a vote of the majority of their electors, request to be amalgamated; and
    (b) constitute new bands and establish band lists with respect thereto from existing band lists, or from the Indian Register, if requested to do so by persons proposing to form the new bands.

The Bands in the Maritimes were organized under these sections during the latter part of the 1950s. And in the 1980s one new Band was created in Nova Scotia by dividing an existing one. (Both events are discussed in Chapter 14.)

Section 18 defines the meaning, use and purpose of Indian Reserves:

18.   (1)   Subject to this Act, reserves are held by Her Majesty for the use and benefit of the respective Bands for which they are set apart, and subject to this Act and to the terms of any treaty or surrender, the Governor in Council may determine whether any purpose for which lands in a reserve are used or are to be used is for the use and benefit of the band....

Under the authority of Section 18, in recent times in Nova Scotia the Minister has authorized one large contested Reserve addition, one large uncontested addition and several minor ones. As the details of the two bigger additions highlight the contradictions of the Department of Indian Affairs in supposedly working for the best interests of First Nations, I'll give a brief description of the bureaucratic shenanigans surrounding both. But first a quick look at the policy the Department has in place for creating new Bands and Reserve additions. This appalling policy assures that new Reserve lands are to be acquired only in the most dire of circumstances.

The following excerpts are taken from the paper that recommended the establishment of the policy:

II.   Background:
(a)   General: In the nineteenth century, *governments saw Reserves as a temporary necessity in the evolution of Indian people towards assimilation* [this was also the view held in the twentieth century]. Reserves were intended to shelter the Indians from White society until they had reached the stage where they were ready to take their place in non-Indian society.

Confining the Indian people to specific tracts of land made it easier for the government to educate Indian people, instruct them in farming and other skills and thus prepare them for assimilation....

Indian people today entirely reject this limited view [they never did accept it] of the purpose of Reserves, as witnessed by their reaction to the "1969 White Paper." To them, Reserves constitute a permanent land base that is crucial to their social, political, and cultural survival and growth.

There seems to be little doubt that the existence of Reserves has been important to the survival of the Indians as a distinct people. However, based on past experience one may ask whether Reserves do or ever will provide a viable social and economic base for most Bands. This in turn raises questions about the extent to which the department should try to achieve Indian socio-economic self-sufficiency by adding land to Reserves.

From a practical standpoint, expanding the Reserve base may not be a viable solution to current social and economic problems because sufficient quantities of suitable land are not available at an affordable price. Trying to solve current socio-economic problems through additions to Reserves would place an enormous burden on the resources of the department, in terms of development costs and ongoing administration.

Furthermore, as long as Reserve Lands are outside provincial and municipal spheres of influence, any large scale additions for these discretionary reasons would be strongly opposed by provinces and municipalities. It may be that, in some cases, forms of land tenure other than Reserve status will prove practical, preferable from a provincial/municipal viewpoint, and acceptable to the Bands. (b) Genesis of present policy: The department's present policy governing additions to Reserves and the creation of new Reserves dates back to 1969. In a brief policy statement approved by the minister, the Honourable Jean Chretien, it was stated that no authorization for additions to Reserves would be given except: (i) To meet an outstanding Treaty obligation; or (ii) In exchange for appropriate Reserve Lands; or (iii) Where overriding economic, social or geographic factors existed *and there were no serious objections from other levels of government.*

The policy statement was rooted in the belief that the Reserve system was not in the long term best interests of the Indian people. Not only did it set them apart from other Canadians, but it was identified by the Senate Committee on Poverty as a major cause of poverty among the Indian population. *Efforts by Bands to increase their Reserve holdings were therefore to be resisted*, except in the circumstances set out in the policy statement.

Many provincial governments shared these concerns, and were further apprehensive about the creation of federally controlled enclaves within their boundaries. At the same time, municipalities were expressing more immediate concerns about the effect of Reserves on their tax base and jurisdictional integrity. As Federal Crown Lands, Indian Reserves are not subject to either municipal taxation or municipal by-laws, although in some provinces non-Indian lessees are taxed by the municipality.

(c) Recent Developments: The views of the provinces and municipalities remain much the same today as they were thirteen years ago. Five major developments in the intervening period have served to heighten provincial/municipal concerns. They are:

(i) The growing social, economic and cultural importance attached by Indian people to the maintenance and expansion of their Reserve land base. This manifests itself in a variety of ways, *including a determination to seek restoration of former Reserve Lands through the land claims process*;

(ii) The fulfilment of outstanding Treaty land entitlements in the Prairie Provinces, and other specific land claims across Canada;

(iii) The desire of resource-rich Bands (especially in Alberta) to use their new-found wealth to purchase land and to have it made Reserve;

(iv) The likelihood of some form of Indian self-government coming into existence which will largely free Bands from government controls over how they use their lands;

(v) The rapid increase in the Indian population, which will put pressure on the existing Reserve land base of many Bands.

In addition, the department is faced with the prospect of widespread demands for more land to accommodate individuals who will become eligible for registration as Indians as a result of changes in the application of the Membership Provisions of the Indian Act.

In a period of growing Indian determination to protect and expand the Reserve land base, and increasing provincial and municipal concern at the tax and jurisdictional implications of this, a review of the current departmental criteria for additions of land to Reserves is required.

The need for a review is all the more important because three of the most common justifications for adding land to Reserves under the present criteria—"social, economic or geographic reasons"—are very broad and have never been clearly defined. Almost every proposal to add land to a Reserve could conceivably be justified on one of these three grounds.

It is important to be more precise as to what constitutes a valid social, economic and geographic need. It may also be useful to try to classify the reasons for adding land to a Reserve in terms of how much discretion the department has when responding to a request from a Band.

III. Reasons for adding land to Reserves:
The reasons for adding to the Reserve land base can be characterized as follows: A. Non-discretionary; B. Partially discretionary; and C. Fully discretionary. In the two former categories, the department has no or only a limited amount of discretion when deciding whether to add land to a Reserve. In the last category there is no obligation to create a Reserve, and the department has much greater freedom to reject the proposal or explore alternatives.[5]

The rest of the policy statement lays out the many possible means for the Department to refuse to grant Reserve status to new lands or to new additions to existing Reserves. An unreflective person sometimes finds it hard to identify systemic racism, but this particular policy is blatantly racist and inconsistent with managing a trust responsibility. This policy statement, like the next that will be cited, has *one priority in mind: the non-Indian establishment's interests.* When reading these statements its almost impossible to believe that they were written and approved by the people who have a trust responsibility to place First Nations' interests above all others.

The Hon. Bill McKnight, Minister of Indian Affairs and Northern Development, released the following directive on December 22, 1987:

Policy for the creation of new Indian Bands, or the establishment, expansion or relocation of Indian Reserve Lands and communities....
9.1 General: the department will consider proposals relative to the creation of Bands, the establishment or expansion of Reserve lands and the establishment or relocation of Reserve communities only under the conditions specified in this program directive.
9.2 New Bands: (a) *The department may recommend for ministerial consideration the creation of a Band when such action will not result in additional funding requirements*, or where any such increase, short and long term, will be

minimal and available within regional budget levels. In this regard, all potential cost areas should be considered, including the cost of acquiring lands, the provision of capital facilities and the cost of on-going program services. Under this provision, the department may recommend for Ministerial consideration a request for new Band status from a group of Indians seeking a split from an existing Band, if an agreement has been reached to divide the existing Band's resource base (land, assets and funding) in a manner which will permit both Bands to provide the normal programs and services, without additional funding requirements. (b) *When a new Band is created as a result of a split from an existing Band, additional Reserve lands will not be provided.* The procedures outlined in Program Circular H-4 "Band Amalgamation or Divisions" are to be followed.

9.3 Relocations due to natural disasters: The department will continue to provide the necessary assistance, including the possible relocation or re-establishment of a Reserve community, when the clear and present threat of a natural disaster endangers the on-going safety of a community's residents or when such a disaster has occurred (for example, the flooding that destroyed the Indian settlement of Winisk in Northern Ontario in 1986). The department is to give priority to work necessary in mitigating the risk of a natural disaster, or when *the most cost-effective* long-term option is to relocate a community, the department will assist the Band in coordinating the re-establishment of the community on an urgent basis.

9.4 Other relocations and establishment of new Reserve Communities: The department may relocate existing communities, or establish new Reserve communities, if: (a) The normal physical development at the existing Reserve location is restricted due to topographic or soil conditions, or due to *other exceptional circumstances* related to health and safety, and (b) The development of the community at the new Reserve site is the most cost-effective alternative. Note: *Relocation proposals which include an immediate or future requirement for financial resources relative to the existing Reserve or community will not be supported.*

9.5 Expansion of existing Reserves: The department will continue to consider requests for expansion of existing Reserves where such requests are consistent with the terms of the current "Addition to Reserves Policy."

9.6 Treaty or land claims settlements and legal commitments: The minister will create a new Band and/or establish a new Reserve community where there is a legal commitment to do so, or when this is in fulfilment of a specific obligation mandated and resourced by the government, on a case by case basis. This would include commitments resulting from Treaty or land claims settlements.

9.7 Deputy Minister Approval: *Departmental managers are not to take any action which could reasonably be perceived as supporting or encouraging an initiative or proposal by a group of Indians, without written concurrence of the Deputy Minister.* This includes the funding of studies, or the commencement or expansion of funding (Capital, or on-going o&m to a new Band, or a new or satellite community.[6]

It is well known that most First Nations in Canada are in dire need of land-base expansion because their existing land base is far too small for realistic and viable economic development and, in general, is not suited for many other uses. However, the federal government has taken a negative position towards expansion and, as the policy attests, has taken several steps to prevent it.

The following are two examples which demonstrate how obstructionist the federal government can be even when a request is an urgent need or a legal duty. The following requests for land additions were submitted by the Acadia and Afton Bands. The properties in question were a plot of land adjacent to Yarmouth Indian Reserve and the Summerside property in Antigonish County.

The Acadia Band request: In 1983, because the Yarmouth Indian Reserve land base of twenty acres was almost completely utilized, the Acadia Band Council decided that it needed to persuade the federal government to find additional land for the Reserve's expansion. By chance, a landowner adjacent to the Reserve was interested in disposing of 46.9 acres. With this in mind, the Band Council submitted a request to the Department for an addition.

When the request came in, I was the Department's Nova Scotia District Superintendent of Lands, Revenues, Trusts and Statutory Requirements. As an ex-employee, I can now admit that I wrote the request for the Band to submit to me. Such assistance, as mentioned in the land addition policy just quoted, was considered a "no-no" by the Department.

Upon receiving the Band's request in January 1984, I accelerated the process of gathering information that would eventually be required by the Minister to make a decision. To comply with the requirement that local authorities must indicate support for any addition, I wrote to both the provincial and municipal governments, laying out in detail the reasons why more land was required by the Band. Within weeks both levels of government gave positive responses to the proposal.

Almost everyone involved with processing the proposal, including the bank holding the mortgage on the property, and the property owners themselves, bent over backwards to accommodate the Band's urgent need for additional lands. There was one notable exception: the Department of Indian Affairs, which turned this well-supported request into a red-tape nightmare. Senior bureaucrats closed rank to mount unbelievable opposition to the proposal, in spite of the fact that the Band was almost out of land for the construction of housing.

I received no cooperation from most of my departmental colleagues in processing the request. As a matter of fact the opposite occurred. One senior bureaucrat suggested to me that I was not acting in the best interests of the Department by promoting the proposal. The more I was opposed, the more determined I became. After I had doggedly pushed the matter for more than four years with the cooperation of two co-workers, by 1987 the proposal needed only an order-in-council to become a reality. During that year, I left the Department and went to work as Executive Director for the Confederacy of Mainland Micmacs. From that position, I continued to lobby for completion. Nit-picking by departmental bureaucrats consumed another three and a half years before an order-in-council was issued on January 31, 1991, setting aside the land as an addition to the Yarmouth Indian Reserve. Seven and a half years had expired since the Band had initiated discussions in 1983, and this had been a matter of considerable urgency!

The Afton Band request: The story of the acquisition of the Summerside property is incredible. From time immemorial the Mi'kmaq have used the lands along the shore of the Northumberland Strait in Antigonish County for camping and fishing. In 1715, French missionaries established a mission for the Mi'kmaq at Summerside and in 1717 they built a church at the site. However, the land was soon to be alienated.

After the American War of Independence, during the late eighteenth and early nineteenth centuries, the colonial government issued land grants to United Empire Loyalists who had left the newly independent United States of America. Two of these land grants, in and around the Heatherton area of Antigonish County, affected the use of the lands at Summerside by the Mi'kmaq. A grant of one thousand acres had been made on February 15, 1818, to a Colonel Colin Campbell of the 72nd British Regiment, and a grant of five hundred acres had been made to the Honourable Henry H. Cogswell of Halifax. These two grants were located along the shore of the Summerside area and included lands traditionally occupied by members of the Afton Band.

During these years, the inclination of the White population was to shaft the Mi'kmaq; therefore, what happened next was a rarity. Three Justices of the Peace by the names of Cunningham, MacDonald and Henry wrote to Sir James Kempt, the Lieutenant-Governor of the colony, on behalf of the Mi'kmaq, recommending, because of the presence of the mission church, burial grounds and camping and fishing sites on land granted to Henry H. Cogswell, that 100-150 acres be set aside for the Mi'kmaq. They must have made a persuasive case, for during 1824 Cogswell set aside one hundred acres of his prime waterfront land for the Band.

From day one, Afton Band members faced opposition to their occupation of these lands. In 1838, although the chapel and burial grounds were located there, a certain John Sutton prevented the People from occupying their property. Somehow, probably with the intervention of the three Justices of the Peace, the issue was resolved favourably on behalf of the Band. On August 4, 1842, Cogswell sold four hundred acres of his lot to Sutton, excluding the one hundred acres he had originally set aside for the Band.

During the transition to Confederation, in an act of incompetence, Samuel Fairbanks, Indian Commissioner for the Colony of Nova Scotia, failed to transfer the hundred acres with the church and burial grounds to the federal government for administration. This omission caused the land to be illegally alienated in the early twentieth century, and today it still remains an outstanding land claim for the Afton Band.

Complicating the issue further, in 1916 the mission church was completely destroyed by fire. The following year, a John A. Chisholm informed the Afton Mi'kmaq that he would buy their property to permit them to rebuild their church on the adjacent vacant land. Largely uninformed as to how property laws were applied, the Afton Band members accepted his offer. They immediately began to occupy the land without objections from anyone. During 1919 the Band rebuilt Saint Anne's Mission Church on the property, again with no outside interference.

I can't help wonder what planet Indian Affairs was on during all this! On

October 1, 1919, Chisholm purchased from the Band seventy acres of their lands from the Cogswell grant for $300, and on the 20th of the same month he purchased another five acres from the Band for $25. He had eighteen Band members, male and female, sign transfer deeds. This was illegal, because at the time only male members were permitted to vote and transfer land title and the transaction did not meet other requirements of the Indian Act.

In 1961, after forty-two years, the Afton Band Council, still using the property for religious purposes, a burial ground and camping and fishing, was advised by the Department that the Summerside property was not theirs but part of the estate of the very late Colin Campbell. The Band members were not pleased.

In 1967, eighty acres of the estate were put up for tax sale by the municipality. Excluded were the twenty acres on which the church and burial grounds were located; these had become church property by "uninterrupted possession" and as such not subject to taxation. (An observation: Although the Mi'kmaq had occupied the land from time immemorial, they weren't allowed to claim "uninterrupted possession.") The Band paid the taxes, preventing the sale from being concluded.

During 1977, under the advice of the Union of Nova Scotia Indians' legal counsellors, John Charles Clifford and Stephen J. Aronson, the Afton Band went to the Supreme Court of Nova Scotia to attempt to acquire title to the Summerside property through use of the Quieting Titles Act. The strange part of this application was that Mordechai Jones, the Supreme Court Justice hearing the case, based on the legal precedent that a Band Council cannot hold land in trust on behalf of its members, had prior to the trial advised the plaintiffs that he would not be able to find on behalf of the Band. In view of this advice, it would have been appropriate to withdraw the action and consider a new approach, but this was not done and the action proceeded to its preordained conclusion.

In dismissing the action on February 22, 1978, Justice Jones stated:

> It is unfortunate that the Band cannot have recourse to the *Quieting Titles Act* simply because the Band is not incorporated or empowered to hold land. The appropriate remedy appears to be a statute of the legislature vesting title in some person or body for the benefit of the Band. I suggested this course to counsel when this action was set down for trial and can only commend it again to all parties concerned, including the appropriate Crown authorities both federal and provincial.[7]

After the action was dismissed, the provincial Minister of Lands and Forests advised the Band and the Department of Indian Affairs that the best approach would be for the Band to acquire the property through a tax sale. In 1979, Indian Affairs appointed an Agent to acquire the Summerside property through this method.

In late 1979 the Agent persuaded Chief Peter Perro to discontinue the Band Council's payment of taxes assessed to the property so it would be put up for tax sale by the municipality. (This course of action had been tried before but hadn't been successful because each time a farmer in the area had intervened and either paid the taxes or, by his presence and threats, forced the Band to pay them.) Because of non-payment of taxes, on February 8, 1983, the property was put up for tax sale by the municipality. On the day of the sale the transaction had to be cancelled because of the interference of the farmer who seemed determined to stop the Band from acquiring clear title to the property.

In early 1984, frustrated with the non-productivity of this process, I decided to get involved and find a solution. My lands officer Donald Julien and I met with the Band's newly elected Council to brief them on the issue. After determining that the resolve of the new Council to acquire the Summerside property as a Reserve was as strong as their predecessors', I told them that somehow I would find a way to get it done. I asked Don to put together a historical sequence of events for the property in preparation for a meeting I planned to arrange with the province. With this information in hand a meeting was set up with the Honourable Edmund Morris, who, in addition to being Nova Scotia's Minister of Social Services, was the chairman of the province's Aboriginal Affairs Committee.

During the meeting we presented Mr. Morris with the history of the property and other information. The meeting ended with the Minister providing assurances that he would give the matter a thorough review and get back to me. After several months, another meeting was arranged, where Morris informed me that he would lend his full support to finding a way to overcome this historical injustice. He was true to his word throughout the negotiations.

We then turned the matter over to the Department of the Attorney General for Nova Scotia and to the federal Department of Justice for legal opinions. They got back to Morris and me with opinions that it would be difficult, if not impossible, to solve the problem.

In late 1985 another meeting was arranged between the parties where a solution to the problem was identified. At this meeting, Morris and I, neither of us members of the legal profession, concluded that, given the resources of both levels of government and their legislative powers, it was inconceivable that clearing the title for one hundred acres of land should pose an insurmountable problem. We thus explored several options and settled upon a simple solution. Lawyers were instructed to work out the terms for a federal-provincial agreement that would have the province expropriate the property and thus clear the title. In early 1986 the Band Council gave their full support for this proposed solution. Lawyers for both levels of government reviewed the proposal, found it workable and began to work out the details. On November 12, 1986, I wrote the following letter to Lands, Revenues and Trusts Regional Director Reg Graves of Indian Affairs:

> Please find appended for your action a letter from the Honourable Ken Streatch, Minister of Lands and Forests, Nova Scotia, offering to expropriate the lands known as the Summerside Property on the Department's behalf by way of a joint agreement for the use and benefit of the Afton Band of Indians.
>
> The Afton Band Council and I have met on two occasions with the Honourable Edmund Morris [other meetings were held between Mr. Morris and me which the Band Council did not attend], Minister of Social Services and Chairperson of the Committee on Aboriginal Affairs, who has been, and is, fully supportive of finding a just and final solution to this particular land problem for the benefit of the members of the Afton Band.

The chief concern of Mr. Morris is that Her Majesty, in the Right of the Province, be held free from litigation in this matter. In particular, any future claim that may possibly ensue from the Heirs, if any, of Mr. Colin Campbell's Estate. As this Estate has lain dormant for a period in excess of one hundred years, with no heirs coming forward, I confidently predict that the possibility of any heirs coming forward at this late date would be, to say the least, very remote.

The Catholic Church and the Municipality of the County of Antigonish have no objections to our acquiring the property on behalf of the Afton Band, with the exception that on acquisition we set aside the Church and Burial Grounds under section 18.2 of the Indian Act for religious purposes; copies of letters from both the Church and the Municipality are also enclosed.

I also attach, as supporting documentation, copies of letters from two former Ministers of the Department supporting acquisition of the Summerside Property for the use and benefit of the Afton Band of Indians, and also a letter from Mr. Cooke, Director General, Atlantic Region, committing up to $10,000 to cover the cost of the acquisition.

Should further information be required, please advise.[8]

By sending this letter, I had called the Department's bluff. Up to then its senior bureaucrats, and politicians, had paid lip service to the idea of clearing title to the property and giving it Reserve status, but now they were suddenly faced with the reality of it. To the uninitiated their response may seem unbelievable. They actually tried to bring the Reserve land addition policy into play in order to stop the deal by claiming there was no justification for giving the land Reserve status! The Department of Justice strongly advised them to forget their policy and get on with the project, which they did with reluctance.

After five years of aggravation for me, and decades of consternation for the Band, an agreement was finally worked out between the two levels of government. On November 1, 1988, after expropriating the land, the province transferred it by order-in-council to the federal government. The federal government then spent another twenty-three months trying to determine whether the same farmer who had in the past blocked the clearance of title by tax sale, purely to attempt to grab the property for himself, had a legal right-of-way over the property. Anyone familiar with the Department's track record for settling similar problems will appreciate that its foot-dragging at the end of this project was par for the course.

Finally, on August 28, 1990, the following order-in-council was issued by the federal government's Privy Council:

WHEREAS Her Majesty in the right of the Province of Nova Scotia, by Nova Scotia Order in Council No. 88-1185 dated November 1, 1988, transferred the administration and control of the land described in the schedule hereto to Her Majesty in right of Canada.

THEREFORE HIS EXCELLENCY, the governor general in council, on the recommendation of the Minister of Indian Affairs and Northern Development, is pleased hereby to accept the transfer from Her Majesty in right of the

Province of Nova Scotia of the administration and control of the land described in the schedule hereto and to set apart the said land for the use and
benefit of the Afton Band of Indians as a reserve to be known as Summerside
Indian Reserve No. 38.[9]

Sadly, before the transaction was finalized, Chief Peter Perro died in office on June
29, 1989, at the age of 73. After spending more than half of his life in pursuit of this
goal, he never saw it reached. Reserve status for the property is a tribute to Peter's
tenacity. Coincidentally, his beloved wife Sofie died on the same day.

Edmund Morris deserves much credit for moving this matter to a satisfactory
conclusion. Without his full cooperation, and the weight of his office behind it, the
project would probably still be in limbo.

Section 19 of the Indian Act authorizes the Minister to conduct surveys, divide
a Reserve into subdivisions, and determine the location and direct the construction
of roads.

Sections 20 to 27 of the Act deal with the possession of Reserve lands by a
Band member. As the title to Reserve land is held by the Crown, a Band member
cannot own individual portions of it. However, these sections give a Band member
the right to have personal use of certain sectors, or lots. Upon recommendation by
the Band Council, the Minister may issue what is called a "Certificate of Possession" to a member. This document gives the holder most of the rights enjoyed by
a private property owner; he or she can even sell it to another Band member;
however, he or she *does not own it*.

Section 28 deals with permits for a non-Band member to occupy or use Reserve lands. The legal wrangling that has ensued because of the illegal use of this
section by the Department to grant permits could fill an encyclopedic number of
volumes. Those yet to come will probably be sufficient enough to fill many more.

28. (1)   Subject to subsection (2), *any deed, lease, contract, instrument, document or agreement of any kind, whether written or oral, by which
a band or a member of a band purports to permit a person other than a member
of that band to occupy or use a reserve or to reside or otherwise exercise any
rights on a reserve is void.*

(2)   The Minister may by permit in writing authorize any person
for a period not exceeding one year, or with the consent of the council of the
band for any longer period, to occupy or use a reserve or to reside or otherwise
exercise rights on a reserve.

Section 29 says "Reserve lands are not subject to seizure under legal process."
The underlying rights to lands in a Reserve belong to all members of a Band
collectively and thus cannot be alienated without their communal consent. This
means Reserve lands cannot be used as collateral by an individual Band member.
However, using enabling provisions under the Act, the Band acting as a unit can
use their lands for that purpose. If all the legalities have been followed, leases and
leasehold improvements can be seized by a lender. A lender who makes a loan
without having proper documentation in place is playing Santa Claus.

Sections 30 and 31 deal with trespass on a Reserve. With the introduction of the Charter of Rights and Freedoms into the Canadian Constitution, and with amendments to the Indian Act covering membership, enforcement of trespass sections are fast becoming very complicated. Strangely, in view of these complications, it is very difficult to convince the Department, even with the backing of the federal Department of Justice, of the need to modernize these sections to protect the future integrity of Reserve lands. With several current intrusions upon Reserve lands in Nova Scotia sitting in limbo, failure to do so will inevitably lead to more costly court cases which, in the end, will benefit the Bands and drain the public purse.

Sections 32 and 33 deal with the sale or barter of produce and, for some strange reason, apply only to the Prairie Provinces. In order for a lay person to appreciate how nuts some parts of the Act are, I'll just give the first part of Section 32. There were penalties for violation of these provisions.

32.   (1)   A transaction of any kind whereby a band or a member thereof purports to sell, barter, exchange, give or otherwise dispose of cattle or other animals, grain or hay, whether wild or cultivated, or root crops or plants or their products from a reserve in Manitoba, Saskatchewan or Alberta, to a person other than a member of that band, is void unless the superintendent approves the transaction in writing.

Section 34 covers the maintenance of "roads and bridges" and is as paternalistic as Sections 32 and 33 are:

34.   (1)   A band shall ensure that the roads, bridges, ditches and fences within the reserve occupied by that band are maintained in accordance with *instructions issued from time to time by the superintendent.*

    (2)   Where, in the opinion of the Minister, a band has not carried out the instructions of the superintendent ... the Minister may cause the instruction to be carried out at the expense of the band or any member thereof.

Section 35 sets out the method by which Reserve lands can be taken for public purposes. This section has been involved in several lawsuits by Bands against the Crown and will continue to be used in future litigation:

Lands Taken for Public Purposes

35.   (1)   Where by an Act of Parliament or a provincial legislature Her Majesty in right of a province, a municipal or local authority or a corporation is empowered to take or to use lands or any interest therein without the consent of the owner, the power may, with the consent of the Governor in Council and subject to any terms that may be prescribed by the Governor in Council, be exercised in relation to lands in a reserve or any interest therein.

    (2)   Unless the Governor in Council otherwise directs, all matters relating to compulsory taking or using of lands in a reserve under subsection

(1) are governed by the statute by which the powers are conferred.

(3)   Whenever the Governor in Council has consented to the exercise by a province, a municipal or local authority or a corporation of the powers referred to in subsection (1), the Governor in Council may, in lieu of the province, authority or corporation taking or using the lands without the consent of the owner, authorize a transfer or grant of the lands to the province, authority or corporation, subject to any terms that may be prescribed by the Governor in Council.

(4)   Any amount that is agreed on or awarded in respect of the compulsory taking or using of land under this section or that is paid for a transfer or grant of land pursuant to this section shall be paid to the Receiver General for the use and benefit of the band or for the use and benefit of any Indian who is entitled to compensation or payment as a result of the exercise of the powers referred to in subsection (1).

Since Confederation, Indian Affairs bureaucrats have carried out their duties under this section in almost total disregard of trust responsibilities to maintain the integrity of Indian lands. They did so by ignoring the law or bending it to fit the needs of their illegal management plans.

Illogically, Section 35 has been used by them to circumvent the surrender provisions of the Act in situations where no expropriation was necessary or called for. In Nova Scotia, to the best of my knowledge, it has never been necessary to expropriate Indian Reserve lands because of urgent public need. If such a need had existed the Mi'kmaq would have cooperated in a responsible way to address it. The use of the expropriation section of the Act has been used in this province only for the sake of expediency.

By far the worst instance of improper use of Section 35 in this province, and perhaps in Canada, is the case of the Nova Scotia government acquiring riparian rights to Boat Harbour from the Pictou Landing Band. In the early 1960s Nova Scotia set out to entice Scott Paper Company to locate a pulp mill in Pictou County. The company agreed and the site selected was Abercrombie. The agreement required the province to assume responsibility for the disposal of industrial and chemical wastes from the mill. For this purpose the province selected Boat Harbour, adjacent to the Pictou Landing Indian Reserve.

Through the offices of the Department of Indian Affairs, the Band was approached with the proposal asking for its approval. To encourage Band members to decide favourably, public meetings were arranged on the Reserve by the bureaucrats to disseminate glowing propaganda. At these meetings members were told that Boat Harbour would not be adversely affected by its use as an industrial waste lagoon. Without conscience these bureaucrats brazenly informed the People that the harbour's water would remain so unpolluted that it would support freshwater fish, and that they would still be able to use it for fishing, swimming and other recreational activities. To prove to them that this would be the case they offered to take the Chief to New Brunswick to see first-hand how well a similar system worked. In reality the only such place in existence at the time in North America was in Minnesota.

Upon arrival in New Brunswick, provincial and federal bureaucrats transported the Chief and Councillor to the disposal unit. While there, a provincial engineer took out a small cup and drank what the Band officials were told was treated industrial waste effluent. Shockingly, in later investigations by the Band's legal counsel, it was discovered that the unit toured was not operational at the time and in fact did not come into operation until two years later. What the bureaucrat drank that day was water coming into the facility from a spring-fed brook.

During this time the Department of Indian Affairs, disregarding its legal duties, made no effort to assist the Band to obtain independent expertise to help them fully appraise the negative effects that Boat Harbour would suffer. In fact, it did just the opposite: it concealed or ignored information which clearly indicated that the Department as trustee should abort the project. In fact both the federal Department of Justice and the Department of Indian Affair's own engineering services had warned the Minister of Indian Affairs not to proceed with the proposed project. Both stated explicitly that it would be detrimental to the best interests of the Band and the Crown itself. However, their advise was ignored and the project proceeded.

The fact that Indian Affairs knew the project was not in the long-range interests of the Band but permitted it to proceed anyway is reprehensible—particularly because it was done in full knowledge that the Pictou Landing Band, like almost all other First Nations Bands in Canada at the time, was almost completely reliant upon the federal government for the protection of their aboriginal rights and lands. As it had done in similar cases with many other Bands, the Crown miserably failed the Pictou Landing Band members at Boat Harbour. Then, when the project went sour and the shit hit the fan, many of the servants of the Crown looked for a means to blame someone else. In attempting to shift responsibility, some federal and provincial bureaucrats even went so far as to state that the Band members themselves were responsible for the befouling of Boat Harbour. Trying to justify this absurd position, they claimed that the Band members had freely given their informed consent without any pressure being applied by outside forces.

A quarter of a century later, in interviews with Elders of the Band, it was discovered that, besides being deliberately misled, the main reason the Band had reluctantly consented to the deal was they had feared reprisals from the Department and society. Just imagine what the public reaction would have been against these already racially oppressed people if they had said no, thus preventing the establishment of an industry which had the potential to employ, either directly or indirectly, thousands of non-Indians. I shudder to think of it!

Those fears were well founded. In 1965, civil and human rights benefits for Registered Indians were virtually non-existent. If there is doubt about the accuracy of this statement, in more modern times, in March 1996, Max Yalden, Chief Commissioner of the Canadian Human Rights Commission, described the position of Canada's Natives to Parliament as "our most serious human rights problem.... They continue to be treated with paternalism, denial and delay."[10]

Adding to the Pictou Landing Band members' fear was the fact that their poverty and unemployment made them almost entirely dependent upon the Department for the necessities of life. They figured that if they didn't cooperate, the Indian Agent might cut off assistance, as had happened many times in the past. For all intents and purposes, in 1965 they were a people with practically no resources or legal recourse. This had created a perfect situation for unscrupulous persons to exploit, and exploit it they did without conscience.

In 1965, with the reluctant acquiesence of the Band, the Department of Indian Affairs illegally used the provisions of Section 35 of the Indian Act to give consent to the use of Boat Harbour as an industrial waste lagoon. An order-in-council which saw the Band receive $60,000 for the loss of its riparian rights was quickly processed. Thus, for this relatively small sum the Band, on the advice and assurances of its trustee, had opened the door to a living hell.

During this time the province, knowing the area around Boat Harbour would become unfit for human habitation, purchased or expropriated all non-Indian lands adjacent to the harbour. In many cases the non-Indians were paid far in excess of $60,000 for their properties. Unbelievably, the province was doing this at the same time Band members were being assured that Boat Harbour would suffer no dramatic environmental changes. Asked about the welfare of the Mi'kmaq who were to be left living next to the polluted mess, an engineer involved in the project replied, "So, they're only Indians."[11]

Shortly after the mill went into production, the Band came face to face with the mess the two senior levels of government had duped them into accepting. Within a short period of time they found themselves living beside a stinking cesspool. Contradictory to the assurances received from provincial officials, it was too toxic for fish to survive, nor could anyone safely swim in the noxious soup or use the Harbour for any other purpose. Later, I was told by some of the Band members, who had been young and had not realized the danger it might present for their health, that they had continued to swim in the harbour for a couple of years afterwards.

The befouling of their formerly pristine natural harbour and the stench, noise and fumes emitted from the pulp mill and the effluent were almost unbearable for most of the Band members. The suicide rate increased dramatically and a good many moved away in despair of their community ever becoming an environmentally safe place to live again. Most, however, stayed and suffered.

Within months after the first effluent began to spill into the harbour, Raymond Francis, outraged by the deceit and resulting mess, began an epic fight to secure justice. For almost fifteen years he, as Chief of the Band, and acting on the advice of the Department of Indian Affairs, the Union of Nova Scotia Indians, and others, pursued a legal route to gain relief from Nova Scotia and Scott Paper Company which led nowhere. Finally, very frustrated with the lack of progress, he visited me in Halifax at the district office in 1981 to talk about the problem. This was shortly after I had been appointed by DIAND as District Superintendent of Lands, Revenues and Trusts for Nova Scotia.

I was appalled by the story he told of the deceit and maliciousness by which the Band had been led down the garden path by the Department. When he left, I got out the files and reviewed the matter, becoming suitably enraged by the treachery. However, knowing the Department's reputation, the racist disregard for the Band's rights that the files revealed shocked but didn't overly surprise me. At our next meeting I advised Raymond that the reason the Band had had no success to date in finding relief was because it was going after the wrong party. My advice to him was that the Band should set aside thoughts of legal action against Nova Scotia and Scott and instead hire an independent attorney to begin proceedings against the federal Crown.

In the meantime, other officials of the Department had convinced the Band Council to join with the Department in a joint legal action against the province. I recognized this ploy as a deliberate attempt to focus the Band Council's attention away from the real culprit, the Department. In playing out what proved to be a charade, with the Band Council's consent, the Department hired a lawyer who supposedly was to report jointly and equally to both. Through all this I continued to caution the Council that they were entering into a no-win situation that would not produce a long-term solution.

Although the Band did not want to break off its "cooperative relationship" with the Department, through my persistence it agreed to seek independent legal counsel. At my recommendation, lawyer E.A. Tony Ross was given access to pertinent documents and asked for his assessment. Ross concurred that the real culprit was the federal Crown and advised the Band Council accordingly. However, even with this legal opinion in hand, the council was still reluctant to break off the "partner relationship" with Indian Affairs.

This changed very quickly in early 1983 when a Department official wrote a memo to "partnership" lawyer Danny Campbell advising him that he should *not* make available to the Band Council all the information connected with the case. With a copy of this memo in hand, I had no further problem persuading the Band Council to go after the federal Crown for redress. The Band employed Ross to litigate the case on their behalf. In 1986, under the guidance of their new Chief, Roderick Francis, the Band filed a notice of action against the Crown at the Federal Court in Halifax.

With the help of many sources, Ross put together a case so strong that before the appointed court date the Department sued for negotiations, which now have been completed. The Band, for its troubles, received a monetary settlement of $35 million. However, Boat Harbour's use as a industrial waste lagoon will continue until 2006, at which time, supposedly, it will be rehabilitated. For the Band, this victory was bittersweet. For many years to come Band members will be concerned about health problems they may suffer from the pollution of Boat Harbour. There is no way to provide Band members with reliable assurances about their health in the future.

While still working for Indian Affairs, I was asked by Tony Ross—as my role in the matter was in direct conflict with the Department's position, which was to minimize damages to the Crown— if I had any feelings of conflict-of-interest in the Boat Harbour case. My sincere answer at that time was no, and in the twenty-first century I can still say the same with a clear conscience. I consider what I did to be a belated effort to attend to the Crown's trust responsibility in the case. After all, the position I held mandated that I look after the Band's best interests first. Therefore, as an ethical person, how could I have done otherwise?

This is my assessment of the Department's role: To fail to fulfil the responsibilities of a trust through incompetence is deplorable, but to fail to meet those responsibilities *with deliberate intent* is unforgivable. All the information the Department had, including that supplied by its own environmental engineer and the federal Department of Justice, had been negative towards the project. This had mandated that in the overall interests of its charges the project should have been stopped. Clearly, in the eyes of key Department employees the political interests of both levels of government and its non-Indian constituency had taken priority over the Band's interests.

People sometimes ask me how Tony Ross, a Black man who had immigrated from the Caribbean, had got involved in Mi'kmaq claims matters and especially how he happened to be appointed legal counsel for the Boat Harbour claim. The answer is reflective of the pre-Marshall racial situation in Nova Scotia. In the late 1970s, land claims activities in the province were at a standstill. Therefore, after settling two small power-utility land claims for two Bands on my own, I decided in the early 1980s to find a way to get a few of the Nova Scotia Bands involved in settling some of their outstanding claims. The main problem was finding a legal advocate who had the capacity to undertake a learning process that would enable her or him to practice "Indian Law," a field almost completely alien to most lawyers in Canada.

Hampering my search was the fact that law and politics were in many respects synonymous with each other at that time. This is exemplified by a situation I knew of in which a White Nova Scotian was having the utmost difficulty in finding a White lawyer to take on his case, despite the fact that he had an almost ironclad legal mismanagement case against another White Nova Scotian. The victim's opponent had something which was and may still be to an unacceptable extent a heavy advantage in this province: he was politically well-connected. When the perpetrator's political connections were discovered by the lawyers he approached, suddenly they had mountains of work that needed to be done yesterday. Eventually he did find an individual to take on his case. I won't reveal his identity because it would identify the people involved.

Given the political affiliations of most Nova Scotian lawyers, and the fact that many of them guarded hopes of judicial or political success, I wondered whom we could retain. The controversial and politically explosive nature of many of the cases the Bands have, which tend to publicly expose the sins of political heavyweights, could possibly end any judicial or political aspirations a lawyer might harbour.

I talked to several lawyers from the White community. Most were uninterested or displayed an unwillingness to learn from a lay person, which was essential because this field of law was not something they had learned about in law school. In more than one instance the prospect told me straight out that, if he got involved, he alone would appraise the possibilities and make the decisions. I walked away from such encounters determined to find someone who would be willing to work with us, not above us.

I concluded that the ideal person to retain would be a Mi'kmaq, because such a person would have a vested interest in seeking equitable settlements. Also, because of racism, he or she would already not have a hope in hell of being elected to anything. This statement is supported by the fact that as of the year 2000 we had never seen one of our brothers or sisters occupy anything more important in Nova Scotia's political set-up than a position such as Native consultant. But, sadly, we didn't have a Mi'kmaq lawyer in 1980.

Therefore, the next choice on my list was a person from the Black community. After all, I reasoned, their situation was almost as bad as ours. Thus, I didn't expect to find too many among them who would be overly concerned about the political consequences of legal actions taken against the Crown, or burdened by a superiority complex. Not knowing much about members of the Bar from that community, I approached a Black friend, the late Dr. Tony Johnstone, who was at the time Coordinator of Ethnic Services with the Nova Scotia Department of Education. Later, from 1985 until his untimely death in 1989, Tony was the Executive Director of the Nova Scotia Human Rights Commission.

Johnstone told me about Tony Ross, an up and coming Black lawyer who, although still in many ways a legal novice, might fit the bill. I set up an appointment with Ross, and at our first meeting he indicated a strong interest. I also discovered that his qualifications were well suited for the job. However, I had one test he needed to pass in order to have the opportunity to take on the challenge. I wanted him to demonstrate how quickly he could acquire knowledge about the Indian Act, Constitution, Royal Proclamation of 1763, etc., so I left on loan a good-sized box full of materials associated with the practice of "Indian Law." Then after two weeks we met again for a discussion on the subject. He passed the test with flying colours, and thus began a working relationship that paid off handsomely for the Pictou Landing Band members.

I will now make a public admission of what DIAND has probably suspected all along. I was the prime mover and shaker in moving the Boat Harbour case forward. From the time Chief Raymond Francis came into my office in 1981, with his tale of woe, until a tentative agreement was reached in 1992, I worked, lobbied and pushed for a deal that would be fair and equitable for the Band members and cost the Crown dearly. Because of this, from 1981 onward, I lived in a pressure cooker while still working for them.

This ended in December 1986 when I became Executive Director with the Confederacy of Mainland Micmacs (CMM). Although no longer in a potential conflict of interest position, as Executive Director the next five years were one mad circus! I was working on the case; setting up and directing CMM; lobbying for funding and fighting budget battles with government departments; starting a newspaper, publishing it and writing much of its copy; opening the Micmac Heritage Gallery in Halifax; helping to negotiate a conservation agreement with the province and doing P.R. work needed to fight the racism that raised its ugly head with the signing of the agreement; lecturing about the history of the Mi'kmaq at schools, universities, service clubs etc.; raising money for a trust fund; sitting on several provincial commissions, including the Human Rights Commission for five years; and involved in many other projects too numerous to mention here except for one other—I was writing the first edition of a book published in 1993 called *We Were Not the Savages*. I was averaging at least 100-110 hours per seven-day work-week.

Tony Ross has said of Boat Harbour:

In the Nova Scotia case of *Jeans* v. *Carl. B. Potter Limited and Lester Archibald Drilling and Blasting Limited*, with respect to exemplary or punitive damages, the topic noted reads as follows: "In addition, the Nova Scotia Court awarded the plaintiff" punitive or exemplary damages arising out of the defendant's "flagrant disregard" and "careless indifference" to the plaintiff's rights.

In preparing the case brought by Chief Roderick Francis and others on behalf of the Pictou Landing Band against Her Majesty the Queen in the Right of Canada, I have reviewed something in excess of four thousand separate documents, and as I recall the facts as they unfolded, *there would be no ten document chronological gap to which the terms "flagrant disregard" and "careless indifference" would not apply.*

This, in my view, was not a mere case of negligence resulting from failure to act, but was gross negligence based upon the facts, which demonstrate, unequivocally, the contemptuous attitude of the Indian and Northern Affairs bureaucracy toward the Pictou Landing Band of Indians. Not only did the Department act in absolute contradiction to the legal advice as given by Hugo Fisher in his capacity as legal adviser from the Department of Justice to the Department of Indian Affairs, but also the advice of Mr. Crapper, the Environmental Engineer with the Department of Indian Affairs, was not merely ignored, but totally disregarded as being an obstruction to the bureaucratic thinking.

Personally, I was appalled to be in attendance in 1986 when Stewart Armstrong, Engineer for the City of Saint John, New Brunswick, took us (Chief Roddie Francis and some members of his Band Council) to the site at Renforth, where Chief Francis and Councillor Sapier had been taken by Dr. Bates and Armand Wigglesworth in 1965, to view and inspect the treated effluent from a "similar facility," only to realize that *the Chief and Councillor were taken to a spot where a fresh water stream merely meandered toward the ocean*, and it was at this point that Armand Wigglesworth was able to secure the signatures of Chief Francis and Councillor Sapier on his pre-drawn handwritten document which led to the illegal use of Boat Harbour as an effluent lagoon.

I became further appalled to learn that legal counsel posed as representing the interests of the Pictou Landing Band until Band Funds had been exhausted and then continued to appear to represent the Band so long as another Indian Organization would continue to pay the fees, and later made its own bid to become an agent of the Federal Government Department of Justice so that, in fact, *it was being paid by Canada* (and frequently so reminded by Canada) *and at the same time supposedly working for the interests of the Band.*

This conflict of interests and bad faith became more so discreditable when legal counsel for the Band (current at that time) informed Canada that the Band had been seeking independent legal advice and Canada, through the Department of Indian Affairs, reconfirmed its authority to the Band's counsel of record of the day to the effect that *although he should continue to work for the Band, he should withhold from the Band any information which would be adverse to the interests of Canada even though beneficial to the Band.*

In my view, these are the two sets of circumstances which are most dishonourable and, but for either one, the Band would not have found itself in the position to have fought an uphill battle against the amassed power of Canada from 1983 when new counsel took over the handling of the file, through 1986, when legal proceedings were commenced, with the severing of liability and damages in 1987 and the continued push for a court date until Canada "blinked" in 1989, and since then Canada has merely adopted the "when a dog barks, you throw him a bone" attitude with respect to settlement *in spite of the written undertaking of Canada and the Band by way of Joint Memoranda that all negotiations would be conducted with the utmost good faith.*

It is not only a sad chapter with respect to morality and man's inhumanity to man, but when so-called reputable legal counsel would prostitute itself and the profession because of its vested interests at the public trough as controlled by the Federal Government accused of shirking a trust responsibility, it is really time for us to take stock of institutions and ask: Who will police the police? Or who will judge the judges? And to reflect on the words of Robert Green Ingersol in his speech to the State Bar association at Albany, N.Y., on January 21, 1880, when he said: "It has been said that the three pests of a community are: A Priest without a charity, a doctor without knowledge, and *a lawyer without a sense of justice.*"[12]

When Wigglesworth was asked under oath at a discovery hearing held March 13, 1987, in Halifax if he knew the system wouldn't function properly, he replied, "As I say, my part was to get the easement rights across the lands and for the use (of Boat Harbour), not to tell them that."[13]

In view of the status of the Reserve lands involved, and the legal mess the government finds itself in because of past mismanagement of Indian assets under Section 35, the involuntary seizure of Reserve lands from Bands by the Crown would today only happen under the most dire and compelling circumstances.

Section 36 of the Indian Act deals with Special Reserves:

> 36.   Where lands have been set apart for the use and benefit of a band and legal title thereto is not vested in Her Majesty, this Act applies as though the lands were a reserve within the meaning of this Act.

This section is open-ended and probably covers lands purchased by Band Development Corporations. It seems to permit a Registered Indian or a Band to reap all the benefits and protection the Indian Act offers within the boundaries of a Reserve on these designated off-Reserve locations. Its exact meaning has not been litigated.

Sections 37 to 41, Surrenders and Designations, provide the legal mechanism for the sale or lease of Indian Reserves. As these sections have embroiled the Department in many lawsuits, they will be fully cited:

> 37.   (1)   Lands in a reserve shall not be sold nor title to them conveyed until they have been absolutely surrendered to Her Majesty pursuant to sub-

section 38(1) by the band for whose use and benefit in common the reserve was set apart.

(2)   Except where this Act otherwise provides, lands in a reserve shall not be leased nor an interest in them granted until they have been surrendered to Her Majesty pursuant to subsection 38(2) by the band for whose use and benefit in common the reserve was set apart.

38.   (1)   A band may absolutely surrender to Her Majesty, conditionally or unconditionally, all of the rights and interests of the band and its members in all or part of a reserve.

(2)   A band may, conditionally or unconditionally, designate, by way of a surrender to Her Majesty that is not absolute, any right or interest of the band and its members in all or part of the reserve, for the purpose of its being leased or a right of interest therein being granted.

39   (1)   An absolute surrender or a designation is void unless
   (a) it is made to Her Majesty;
   (b) it is assented to by a majority of the electors of the band,
        (i) at a general meeting of the band called by the council of the band,
        (ii) at a special meeting of the band called by the Minister for the purpose of considering a proposed absolute surrender or designation, or,
        (iii) by a referendum as provided in the regulations; and
   (c) it is accepted by the Governor in Council.

(2)   Where a majority of the electors of a band did not vote at a meeting or referendum called pursuant to subsection (1), the Minister may, if the proposed absolute surrender or designation was assented to by a majority of the electors who did vote, call another meeting by giving thirty days notice thereof or another referendum as provided in the regulations.

(3)   Where a meeting is called pursuant to subsection (2) and the proposed absolute surrender or designation is assented to at the meeting or referendum by a majority of the electors voting, the surrender or designation shall be deemed, for the purposes of this section, to have been assented to by a majority of the electors of the band.

(4)   The Minister may, at the request of the council of the band or whenever he considers it advisable, order that a vote at any meeting under this section shall be by secret ballot.

(5)   Every meeting under this section shall be held in the presence of the superintendent or some other officer of the Department designated by the Minister.

40.   A proposed absolute surrender or designation that is assented to by the band in accordance with section 39 shall be certified on oath by the superintendent or other officer who attended the meeting and by the chief or a member of the council of the band, and then submitted to the Governor in Council for acceptance or refusal.

41.   An absolute surrender or a designation shall be deemed to confer all rights that are necessary to enable Her Majesty to carry out the terms of the surrender or designation.

The case of *St. Catherine's Milling and Lumber Co.* v. *the Queen* is a good point to start to discuss these sections. In 1888 the Privy Council, the highest court in the land at that time, handed down a decision which recognized that "Indian title" in land was aboriginal in nature and predated Confederation, the Royal Proclamation of 1763 and colonization. In plain English, Indian lands and assets attached to them cannot be sold, leased etc. without the consent of the majority of a Band's members. However, bureaucrats did not take this decision at face value and proceeded to ignore it.

The *Guerin* Decision

The best-known "surrender" mismanagement case to date illustrates how bureaucratic incompetence and condescending paternalism can backfire. The November 1, 1984, Supreme Court of Canada ruling known as the *Guerin* decision concerns a case where the federal government, in a craven attempt to duck responsibility, attempted to have its trust responsibilities to Registered Indians, and for managing their lands, recognized as simply a *"political trust."*

The Indian Reserve land in question, Musqueam Indian Reserve No. 2, is held by the Crown in trust for the Musqueam Band. It is located within the city limits of Vancouver, British Columbia, encompasses 416.53 acres, and is perhaps the most valuable single piece of real estate in the Vancouver area. At the time the lawsuit was launched, the Band had about five hundred members.

In 1956 the Shaughnessy Heights Country Club approached the Musqueam Band Council with a proposal to establish a golf course on 162 acres of its Reserve. At the request of the Band Council, the Department of Indian Affairs became involved in negotiating a land lease with the club. After several months of negotiations a draft lease was worked out and a Band meeting was called to consider the proposal.

The Band members and the Band Council didn't like some of the terms of the proposed lease; therefore, they dictated to Department officials some new terms and conditions they wanted included in the final agreement. The Department ignored these new terms and conditions, which had been approved by the Band's membership at a duly convened surrender meeting, and went ahead with a less favourable leasing agreement. The terms and conditions contained in the new agreement were devised in secrecy by the Department's bureaucrats and were not returned to the Band members for their mandatory approval.

For twelve years after the lease had been entered into by the Crown on their behalf, the Band was unable to obtain a copy of it. It may seem unbelievable—unless one has experience with its contemptuous attitudes towards the people it was mandated to serve and represent—but the Department had a policy which barred it from giving copies of agreements to parties on whose behalf they had executed them. Failing to provide Bands with information vital to their futures was a common practice in the Department up until recent times.

In 1970 the Band finally obtained a copy of the lease and, with this and all other necessary supporting documentation in hand, it took the Crown to court in 1975. The trial judge found that the Crown had breached its "fiduciary trust responsibility" to the Band, and he awarded the Band $10 million.

The judge also found that the Department was guilty of "equitable fraud" because of its failure to return to the Band for approval the final terms and conditions of the lease. However, both this trial judge and, later, the Supreme Court of Canada decided that the fraud was unintentional; in their wisdom, they found that the bureaucrats had made their decisions guided by paternalistic attitudes and not by the intent to cause harm.

This is something I don't buy. To me, if a White supremacist disregards the decisions made by a people of colour for whom he has a trust responsibility because he believes that they can't make intelligent decisions on their own, and then imposes his own decisions without consulting them and causes them harm, his racist deeds make him culpable. If a White did the same to another White, the instigator would be found criminally responsible for equitable fraud and penalized accordingly.

When rendering his decision the trial judge struck down the Crown's attempt to present a defense based on a "political trust." The court instead found that the Department had, upon acceptance of the surrender, a "fiduciary trust" responsibility to carefully manage the Band's beneficial "usufructuary right" in the land, which was inalienable without its consent. By surrendering that right to part of its territory to the Crown over a specified period of time for leasing purposes, the Band could expect and demand from the Crown that their continuing interests would be carefully protected. Therefore, as trustee, it was mandatory for the employees of the Department to follow the directions the beneficiaries had dictated when agreeing to the leasing arrangement.

Canada appealed the decision of the Federal Court Trial Division to the Appeal Division of the same court and won. The Band then appealed to the Supreme Court of Canada, which struck down the decision of the Appeal Division and reinstated the original verdict of the trial judge. The following is part of the Supreme Court of Canada's decision:

Breach of the Fiduciary Obligation

The trial judge found that *the Crown's agents promised the Band to lease the land in question on certain specified terms and then, after surrender, obtained a lease on different terms.* The lease obtained was much less valuable.

As already mentioned, the Surrender Document did not make reference to the *oral terms.* I would not wish to say that those terms had nonetheless somehow been incorporated as conditions into the Surrender. They were not formally assented to by a majority of the electors of the Band, nor were they accepted by the Governor in Council, as required by Section 39 (1) (b) and 39 (1) (c). I agree with Le Dain J. that there is no merit in the appellant's submission that for purposes of Section 39, a Surrender can be considered independently of its terms. This makes no more sense than would a claim that a contract can have an existence which in no way depends on the terms and conditions that comprise it.

Nonetheless, the Crown, in my view, was not empowered by the Surrender Document to ignore the oral terms which the Band understood would be embodied in the lease. The oral representations form the backdrop against which the Crown's conduct in discharging its Fiduciary obligation must be measured. They inform and confine the field of discretion within which the Crown was free to act. After the Crown's agents had induced the Band to surrender its land on the understanding that the land would be leased on certain terms, it would be unconscionable to permit the Crown simply to ignore those terms.

When the promised lease proved impossible to obtain, the Crown, instead of proceeding to lease the land on different, unfavourable terms, should have returned to the Band to explain what had occurred and seek the Band's counsel on how to proceed. The existence of such unconscionability is the key to a conclusion that the Crown breached its Fiduciary Duty. *Equity will not countenance unconscionable behaviour in a Fiduciary, whose duty is that of utmost loyalty to his principal.*

While the existence of the Fiduciary obligation which the Crown owes to the Indians is dependent on the nature of the surrender process, the standard of conduct which the obligation imports is both more general and more exacting than the terms of any particular surrender. In the present case the relevant aspect of the required standard of conduct is defined by a principle analogous to that which underlies the Doctrine of Promissory, or Equitable Estoppel.

The Crown cannot promise the Band that it will obtain a lease of the latter's land on certain stated terms, thereby inducing the Band to alter its legal position by surrendering the land, and then simply ignore that promise to the Band's detriment.

In obtaining without consultation a much less valuable lease than that promised, *the Crown breached the Fiduciary obligation it owed the Band. It must make good the loss suffered in consequence.*[14]

One of the better results of this decision is that the Crown now takes its responsibilities and duties to First Nations much more seriously. Prior to the *Guerin* decision, interests other than those of Band members took precedence in departmental decision-making. But the Department now mostly takes care to ensure in cases with "trust" connotations that the Indian interest predominates.

The past misuses of Sections 37 to 41 by departmental employees have built up a backlog of specific land claims from land sales. When taking surrenders from Band members, the niceties of the law were not considered by many to be important or relevant. The surrender of three Reserves—Sambro, Ingram River and Ship Harbour—by the Halifax County Band in 1919 provides an example of how the misuse of these sections can develop a land claim:

KNOW ALL MEN BY THESE PRESENTS, that we, the undersigned Chief and Principal men of the Micmac Indians residing in the County of Halifax, in the Province of Nova Scotia and Dominion of Canada, for and acting on behalf of the whole people of our said Band in Council assembled, do hereby release, remise, surrender, quit claim and yield up unto our Sovereign Lord the King, His Heirs and successors forever, all and singular, the following Indian Reserve in the County of Halifax, namely: Sambro, situated between Sambro Basin and Long Cove, Sambro Harbour, containing three hundred acres; Ingram River, situated at the mouth of Ingram River, St. Margaret's Bay, containing three hundred and twenty-five acres; and Ship Harbour Lake, situated on the Northeastern shore of Ship Harbour Lake, containing five hundred acres.

TO HAVE AND TO HOLD, the same unto His said Majesty the King, His Heirs and successors forever, in trust to sell the same to such person or persons, and upon such terms as the Government of the Dominion of Canada may deem most conducive to our welfare and that of our people.

AND, upon the further condition that all moneys received from the sale thereof shall be placed to our credit and interest there on paid to us, in the usual way.

AND WE, the said Chief and Principal men of the said Micmac Indians resident in the County of Halifax do on behalf of our people and for ourselves, hereby ratify and confirm, and promise to ratify and confirm, whatever the said Government may do, or cause to be lawfully done, in connection with the sale of the said lands and the disposition of the moneys derived therefrom.

IN WITNESS WHEREOF, we have hereunto set our hands and affixed our seals this 18th day of June in the year of our Lord one thousand nine hundred and nineteen.

Signed, sealed and Delivered in the presence of Robert Taylor.

By: Martin Sack, Principal Man.

Issac Cope, Principal Man.

Louis N. MacDonald, Principal Man and Acting Chief.[15]

A fully researched and documented land claim has been submitted to the federal government in reference to this surrender, because:

1.   The land surrender was taken in the wrong place, namely Truro, Colchester County. It would seem reasonable, because the surrender was taken from the Halifax County Mi'kmaq, to expect it to have occurred in Halifax County where the lands were situated.

2.   *John D. Paul was the recognized Chief of the Halifax County Mi'kmaq. His name was crossed out on the document where he would have signed as Chief* and replaced with the signature of an "Acting Chief," Louis N. MacDonald. However, on an affidavit taken from the Chief and principal men, Martin Sack is listed as the "Acting Chief."

3.   The so-called surrender document is signed by at least two non-Indians and by several Mi'kmaq from places outside of Halifax County, and one from outside Nova Scotia.

4.   The late William G. Paul, whose name appears on the list of electors, whom the acting superintendent Mr. Buoy attests gave their assent to the

surrender, has given an affidavit to the effect that no surrender meeting actually took place. Paul states that rather than holding a surrender meeting, Buoy went from house to house over several days to ascertain if members of the Band wished to dispose of their land.

5. Paul has further stated that he and his father, *John D. Paul, whose name also appears on the surrender, did not consent to the sale of the Reserves.* He further states that to the best of his knowledge *the vast majority of the Mi'kmaq of Halifax County refused to assent to the sale of the land.*

6. Affidavits from several other people support Paul's statements.

7. Buoy attested to the accuracy of the list of electors by stating: "I hereby certify that the above list of thirty-six names constitutes a complete list of the voting members of the Halifax County Band resident in the County or vicinity, that all voted unanimously in favour of the surrender of the Sambro, Ingram River and Ship Harbour Reserves and that they were all present at the meeting called wherein to discuss such surrender." [The list of electors the acting superintendent touted as being complete was actually only a partial list of the Halifax County Band of Mi'kmaq].[16]

The surrender of these Reserves was not undertaken at the instigation of the Mi'kmaq of Halifax County. Virtually all the surrenders that took place in Nova Scotia during this period were initiated by the government. The purpose of these surrenders in many cases was to enhance the bank accounts of close associates of the politicians or bureaucrats involved, and to relieve the government of land management duties. None of these surrenders were helpful to the Mi'kmaq Bands for whom the lands were originally set aside; in fact, they were detrimental.

Another example of irresponsibility, which highlights the desire of the Department's bureaucracy to please their political masters, is the hasty surrender of the one-thousand-acre New Germany Indian Reserve. The Department allowed this Reserve to be surrendered by only two men and to be sold for a pittance!

What is likely to happen with surrender cases such as these is that the Bands pursuing them as land claims will eventually grow impatient with the slow progress being made and pursue a court settlement. Charging the government with equitable fraud should not pose much of a problem in most cases. The Crown will spend many, many moons in court for its careless disregard of trust responsibilities under these sections.

Sections 42 to 52 cover the estates of Registered Indians and the descent of property, and it provides the mechanism for the Minister to manage the affairs of minors and the mentally incompetent. Because these sections are patronizing and paternalistic, they are in need of modernizing. As it now stands, the last will and testament of every Registered Indian is made subject to the approval of the Minister. Believe it or not, the Minister of Indian Affairs may declare an Indian's last will and testament to be void in whole or in part if he or she is satisfied, for instance, that the will imposes a hardship upon persons for whom the testator had a responsibility to provide.

If an Indian wants a court to decide a testamentary matter, the Indian Act provides: "The court that would have jurisdiction if a deceased were not an Indian may, *with the consent of the Minister,* exercise, in accordance with this Act, the jurisdiction and authority ... in ... testamentary matters." This archaic procedure was still in force for the disposal of Indian estates in 2000. I believe that all testamentary matters relating to Indian estates should be referred to a court of competent jurisdiction and should not be left to the whims of laymen.

Under the Act, the Minister has exclusive jurisdiction and authority over the property of mentally incompetent Indians. There may be no appeal of the Minister's exercise of this authority. The Minister also has authority, if he chooses to exercise it, to administer the property of infant children. Among non-Indians the apprehension of incompetents and minors rests exclusively in the hands of the courts, but in all instances non-Indian parents have authority over the affairs of their own children until a court finds sufficient reason to say otherwise. Not so with us.

Sections 53 to 59 deal with the "management of reserves and surrendered and designated lands." Many First Nations people prefer to call it "the *mis*management of reserves and surrendered and designated lands." Under the auspices of these sections, surrendered Indian Reserve lands have been grossly mismanaged, without legitimate reason held in inventory for long periods of time, and often sold to the lowest bidder. Some shining examples: Many Reserves in Nova Scotia, or parts thereof, and no doubt a multitude of others in the rest of Canada, have been surrendered so incompetently for the purpose of selling timber, hay or gravel from them that these *conditional* surrenders have been made *for eternity,* or at least until some legal genius finds a way to unravel the mess. Other Reserves or parts thereof being surrendered *for lease* were also surrendered for eternity. These are just some cases of mismanagement that will provide lucrative lawsuits for First Nations to pursue in the future.

This mismanagement of "Indian lands" was so widespread that several books could be written on the subject. Even the simplest things, e.g., individual land allotments to Band members, have been screwed up so badly that a small army would have to work diligently for years to straighten them out. Add to the mess the multitude of illegal rights-of-way through Reserves which were not properly granted, plus the hundreds of other incompetent administrative errors committed over past decades, and the whole thing becomes unbelievably bizarre. Two extraordinary examples follow.

The first is that the Department has lost or "misplaced" an entire Indian Reserve somewhere in Nova Scotia. The "Port Hood Indian Reserve" was last seen somewhere in the vicinity of the town of Port Hood on the Island of Cape Breton. God only knows where this Reserve went, because the Department certainly doesn't.

The second is the Grand Lake Indian Reserve right-of-way. This Indian Reserve, allotted to the Shubenacadie Band on May 8, 1820, and comprising one thousand acres of prime real estate, is located twenty-five miles from metropolitan Halifax. But, after more than 175 years, it still has no access to a public highway. With no viable right-of-way into the Reserve, the Shubenacadie Band cannot develop this valuable land or use it for much of anything.

If the Department had acted responsibly in the past, obtaining a right-of-way into this Reserve would have presented no problem. The Oblate Fathers, who once owned the property, undoubtedly would have given one if asked. Several others who owned the property before and after the Oblates would also have given legal access. However, in the late 1960s the property needed for access fell into the hands of people who held very racist perceptions of Indians. Not only would they not consider giving a right-of-way to the Band, they would not permit passage over their land for any reason whatsoever. They even refused, on more than one occasion, to permit officials of the Department of Indian Affairs to visit the Reserve to inspect it. I can attest to the accuracy of this statement from personal experience. On three occasions I was, in my capacity as superintendent, refused passage over the land to investigate illegal woodcutting on the reserve.

Because of the lack of foresight, incompetence and negligence of the Department, the Shubenacadie Band has been barred from using its land at Grand Lake for more than a quarter of a century. The Department steadfastly refuses to take the legal steps required to acquire a right-of-way. Eventually, and probably through the courts, the Band will force the Department to acquire one for them. In the process, the Band will probably receive several million dollars for the lost opportunities it suffered.

Donald M. Julien, who served as District Lands Officer during my tenure as District Superintendent, has made the following comments on the competency of the Department of Indian affairs in land management:

I was struck with total amazement when a group of Micmac people, led by Danny Paul, were given an opportunity by the Department of Indian Affairs, Nova Scotia District Office, to execute such an important program as Lands, Revenues and Trusts.

As the person charged with the responsibility of managing the Lands Management Section of the program, my eyes were opened by reviewing the previous work of my predecessors in the field, who were supposedly there to provide competent management of Indian Lands from Confederation onward.

The blatant disregard by these officials of the Indian Act and of the provisions made thereunder, as they pertain to Indian Lands management, was to me, to say the very least, overwhelming. By their actions and attitudes these people demonstrated that they were in total ignorance and apathy toward the Micmac Indians as they existed in their own Country.

Most of the transactions related to lands, permits, leases, surrenders, etc., handled by them were done in isolation of the elected officials of the Bands concerned and in near total incompetence. Their attitudes when processing these transactions were ones of lords and masters, with they of course being the lords and masters and with the Indians of course being the servants.

Unfortunately for the Micmac of Nova Scotia, the Indian agents of the past and others who were involved in the management of Indian Lands and in other aspects of the fiduciary trust responsibilities that they also had to the Indians themselves, were primarily interested in maintaining their employment status with the Department and not in safe-guarding the best interests of the people that they had a legal and moral responsibility to protect.[17]

Section 60 of the Act purports to provide a mechanism for a Band to have control over the management of its lands, but in reality it does not:

> 60.   (1)   The Governor in Council may at the request of a band grant to the band the right to exercise such control and management over lands in the reserve occupied by that band as the Governor in Council considers desirable.
>
>   (2)   The Governor in Council may at any time withdraw from a band a right conferred on the band under subsection (1).

This section is so inconsistent with other sections of the Act that it is rendered ineffectual. All any Band could realistically expect under this section is to be made an administrative assistant to the Department. Section 60 should be rewritten to give it the strength to stand on its own or it should be repealed. As presently written, it raises false expectations among Bands seeking to assume meaningful land management responsibilities.

Sections 61 to 69 prescribe how "Indian moneys" must be managed. These are moneys held in trust by the Department for each Band. These sections require the consent of either a Band or a Band Council to activate. The courts have ruled that a power conferred upon one or the other must be exercised by the body designated. (If you are having trouble understanding the differences between the powers of a Band versus its Band Council, please refer back to Section 2(3).) With its usual incompetence, over the years the Department has permitted Band Councils to exercise powers that fall within the exclusive jurisdiction of Band members. This careless disregard of trust responsibilities will also ultimately increase the bank balances of the Bands.

> 61.   (1)   Indian moneys shall be expended only for the benefit of the Indians or bands for whose use and benefit in common the moneys are received or held, and subject to this Act and to the terms of any treaty or surrender, the Governor in Council may determine whether any purpose for which Indian moneys are used or are to be used is for the use and benefit of the band....
>
> 62.   All Indian moneys derived from the sale of surrendered lands or the sale of capital assets of a band shall be deemed to be capital moneys of the band and all Indian moneys other than capital moneys shall be deemed to revenue moneys of the band.

Sections 63 to 68 prescribe how the Minister with, and in some instances without, the consent of a Band Council may spend either capital or revenue moneys. Moneys can be expended for a multitude of purposes by the Minister, but they must always be for the common good of the Band or, in cases of hardship, a Band member.

Section 69 provides the authority for a Band to administer its revenue moneys:

69.   (1)   The Governor in Council may by order permit a band to control, manage and expend in whole or in part its revenue moneys and may amend or revoke any such order.

(2)   The Governor in Council may make regulations to give effect to subsection (1) and may declare therein the extent to which this Act and the Financial Administration Act shall apply to a band to which an order made under subsection (1) applies.

Under this section, incompetents within the Department have turned over both revenue and capital moneys to Band Councils for administration. In the process, they have neglected to obtain the consent of the Band members before revenue moneys were turned over, and *they forgot that there is no provision under the Act for either a Band or its Council to administer capital moneys.*

To date, very few, if any, of the Bands in Canada have legally taken over administration of trust fund monies pursuant to the provisions of Section 69. The Department, in violation of the law as usual, simply turned administration over to Band Councils, which Section 69 does not provide for. In order for a Band to legally administer its revenue money, a majority of its members must agree to the proposal at a public meeting or through a referendum. The Band members must also agree to the appointment of administrators, which could conceivably exclude the Band Council; also they have to approve how and for what purposes revenues are to be expended.

The capital and revenue trust accounts of most of the Bands in Canada have been illegally depleted through the incompetent actions of bureaucrats playing political games with Band politicians. The Bands have lost most of their moneys without receiving any real benefits. The Department will eventually be held accountable for the gross mismanagement of trust funds and, hopefully, made to restore all moneys illegally taken.

By this time readers might be wondering where Indian Affairs bureaucrats ever got the audacity to be so blatantly racist in the performance of their duties. To add to the wonderment let's take a few moments to discuss a repealed section of the 1927 Indian Act, which further highlights their "believe it or not" conduct. That section placed an impossible burden upon Bands that wished to take legal action against the Crown or file a claim:

Receiving Money for the Prosecution of a Claim

141.   Every person who, *without the consent of the Superintendent General* expressed in writing, receives, obtains, solicits or requests from any Indian any payment or contribution or promise of any payment or contribution for the purpose of raising a fund or providing money for the *prosecution of any claim* which the Tribe or Band of Indians to which such Indian belongs, or of which he is a Member, has or is represented to have for the recovery of any claim or money for the said Tribe or Band, *shall be guilty of an offense* and liable upon summary conviction for each such offence to a penalty not exceeding two hundred dollars and not less than fifty dollars

or to imprisonment for a term not exceeding two months.[18]

This former section essentially said that the Minister must give his or her approval before a lawyer could work for a Band and effectively prevented First Nations from prosecuting claims against the Crown with more vigour. Such racially motivated restrictions rendered Registered Indians almost helpless against governmental assaults upon their rights and property. If it has any ethical and moral values, Canada must now forbid the use of "acquiescence," "laches," "limitations" and so on as a defense against a First Nation's claim. If the government does not voluntarily do so, then judges should make it a policy of the courts.

Back to the modern Indian Act. Section 70 deals with loans to Indians:

> 70.　　(1)　　The Minister of Finance may authorize to the Minister out of the Consolidated Revenue Fund of such sums of money as the Minister may require to enable him
>
> (a) to make loans to bands, groups of Indians or individual Indians for the purchase of farm implements, machinery, livestock, motor vehicles, fishing equipment, seed grain, fencing materials, materials to be used in native handicrafts, any other equipment, and gasoline and other petroleum products, or for the making of repairs or the payment of wages, or for the clearing and breaking of land within reserves;
>
> (b) to expend or to lend money for the carrying out of cooperative projects on behalf of Indians; or
>
> (c) to provide for any other matter prescribed by the Governor in Council.

The rest of this section prescribes how the money will be loaned, granted or otherwise disposed of and accounted for. An economic development program for Bands was established by the Department under this section that proved, after a considerable length of time, to be expensive and useless. This occurred because departmental program administrators used it as an apparatus to score brownie points with Chiefs and leaders of First Nations organizations by granting them, or the Band members they lobbied on behalf of, loans that didn't quite meet the program's lending criteria. The program became a political football. The prime reason that most of these bureaucrats wanted to please a Chief or organization head was that the Department was rapidly expanding, with unlimited opportunities for promotion and lucrative salary increases; and First Nations leaders sat on the selection boards that filled these positions.

Section 71 allows the Minister to operate farms. If this sounds far-fetched, there's more.

> 71　　(1)　　The Minister may operate farms on reserves and may employ such persons as he considers necessary to instruct Indians in farming and may purchase and distribute without charge pure seed to Indian farmers.
>
> (2)　　The Minister may apply any profits that result from the operation of farms pursuant to subsection (1) on reserves to extend farming operations on the reserves or to make loans to Indians to enable them to engage

in farming or other agricultural operations or he may apply those profits in any way that he considers to be desirable to promote the progress and development of the Indians.

Bureaucrats from Confederation onward have firmly believed that First Nations peoples possess an almost supernatural ability to farm. Even knowing that Nova Scotia's Reserves consisted mostly of mountains, clay pits, swamps and other lands unsuited to agriculture, they had a strong faith in the ability of the Mi'kmaq to produce miracles. Almost every year after Confederation they distributed fertilizer and seed potatoes in the expectation that the People would grow abundant crops on non-agricultural lands.

Of course, no significant crops grew. Nonetheless the bureaucrats would continue to be full of expectations for the following year. At one time the Department even decided that *goat farming* was the way to go and set up Band members in Eskasoni and Shubenacadie with herds of the creatures. The Mi'kmaq still remember and talk about how crazy these schemes were.

Section 72 deals with how the Minister pays money due to Bands under treaty obligations, mostly under post-Confederation treaties.

Section 73 provides the mechanism for the Governor in Council to make regulations to govern most of the activities carried on within almost any community. Whenever you hear a Minister of the Crown begging off responsibility because they have no enforcement authority, just recall the following:

73.   (1)   The Governor in Council may make regulations

(a) for the protection and preservation of fur-bearing animals, fish and other game on reserves;

(b) for the destruction of noxious weeds and the prevention of the spreading or prevalence of insects, pests or diseases that may destroy or injure vegetation on Indian reserves;

(c) for the control of the speed, operation and parking of vehicles on roads within reserves;

(d) for the taxation, control and destruction of dogs and for the protection of sheep on reserves;

(e) for the operation, supervision and control of pool rooms, dance halls and other places of amusement on reserves;

(f) to prevent, mitigate and control the spread of diseases on reserves, whether or not the diseases are infectious or communicable;

(g) to provide medical treatment and health services for Indians;

(h) to provide compulsory hospitalization and treatment for infectious diseases among Indians;

(i) to provide for the inspection of premises on reserves and the destruction, alteration or renovation thereof;

(j) to prevent overcrowding of premises on reserves used as dwellings;

(k) to provide for sanitary conditions in private premises on reserves as well as in public places on reserves;

(l) for the construction and maintenance of boundary fences; and

(m) for empowering and authorizing the council of a band to borrow money for band projects or housing purposes and providing for the making of loans out of moneys so borrowed to members of the band for housing purposes.

(2)   The Governor in Council may prescribe the punishment, not exceeding a fine of one hundred dollars or imprisonment for a term not exceeding three months or both, that may be imposed on summary conviction for contravention of a regulation made under subsection (1).

(3)   The Governor in Council may make orders and regulations to carry out the purposes and provisions of this Act.

Both the Prime Minister and the Minister of Indian Affairs appeared on television during the "Oka crisis" and bemoaned their lack of authority to take control of the situation. As anyone who reads can plainly see, under the provisions of the Indian Act discussed so far and yet to come, the Governor in Council and the Minister have the power to take whatever steps needed to bring order to a First Nations community.

Subsection (3) gives the Governor in Council a free hand to make orders and regulations to carry out the provisions of the Act. Regulations have been created for almost every item listed under Section 73, including regulations both complicated and bizarre. One set of regulations worth mentioning, if only to demonstrate incompetence, are the Indian Band Council borrowing regulations:

Regulations Respecting the Borrowing of Money by Councils of Bands and the Disposition of Such Moneys

1.   These regulations may be cited as the Indian Band Council Borrowing Regulations.

2.   The council of a band may borrow money for band projects or housing purposes and may make loans out of moneys so borrowed to members of the band for housing purposes, on such terms and conditions as may be determined by the council.[19]

This regulation is short and useless. Because of the status of Indian Reserve lands and the special status of Band members, regulations for the purpose stated would have to be quite complex to be effective.

Sections 74 to 79 deal with Chief and Band Council elections. Section 74 is quoted below, but Sections 75 to 79, which govern how the process is to be carried out, will receive only general comment:

74.   (1)   Whenever he deems it advisable for the good government of a band, the Minister may declare by order that after a day to be named therein the council of the band, consisting of a chief and councillors, shall be selected by elections to be held in accordance with this Act.

(2)   Unless otherwise ordered by the Minister, the council of a band in respect of which an order has been made under subsection (1) shall

consist of one chief, and one councillor for every one hundred members of the band, but the number of councillors shall not be less than two nor more than twelve and no band shall have more than one chief.

(3)   The Governor in Council may, for the purposes of giving effect to subsection (1), make orders or regulations to provide

(a) that the chief of a band shall be elected by

(i) a majority of the votes of the electors of the band, or

(ii) a majority of the votes of the elected councillors of the band from among themselves, but the chief so elected shall remain a councillor; and

(b) that the councillors of the band shall be elected by

(i) a majority of the votes of the electors of the band,

or

(ii) a majority of the votes of the electors of the band in the electoral section in which the candidate resides and that he proposes to represent on the council of the band.

(4)   A reserve shall for voting purposes consist of one electoral section, except that where the majority of the electors of a band who were present and voted at a referendum or a special meeting held and called for the purpose in accordance with the regulations have decided that the reserve should for voting purposes be divided into electoral sections and the Minister so recommends, the Governor in Council may make orders or regulations to provide for the division of the reserve for voting purposes into not more than six electoral sections containing as nearly as may be an equal number of Indians eligible to vote and to provide for the manner in which electoral sections so established are to be distinguished or identified.

Of the thirteen Bands in Nova Scotia, eleven have opted to elect Councils under the provisions of the Indian Act; two are under custom. The Eskasoni Band is divided into electoral sectors. None of the Bands are satisfied with their present methods of electing Councils, but most would prefer to keep a third-party presence in their elections. The problem with the custom form of election is that in modern society it often produces dictators who, like crazy glue, are hard to get rid of. Indian Act elections are the preferred way to go for the majority of Bands, but not under the present provisions, which are so dated they could have come over on the *Mayflower*.

The portion of Section 77, eligibility of electors, which prevented off-Reserve Band members from voting in Band elections was declared void on May 20, 1999, by the Supreme Court of Canada. The court ruled that it was discriminatory. In rendering the decision, the court stated: "Off-reserve Aboriginal band members can change their status to on-reserve band members only at great cost, if at all.... The reserve, whether they live on or off it, is their and their children's land. The band council represents them as band members to the community at large, in negotiations with the government, and with Aboriginal organizations." As an expert on the Indian Act, I would predict that this ruling will have a very positive effect for Bands with land claims. Whole Reserves and parts of Reserves have been sold, leased or alienated from Bands without the consent of all members. The ones who lived off-Reserve, in some cases the majority, were denied the right to accept or reject the alienation of their lands.

Section 80 deals with regulations governing Band and Band Council meetings:

> 80.   The Governor in Council may make regulations with respect to band meetings and council meetings and, without restricting the generality of the foregoing, may make regulations with respect to
> (a) presiding officers at such meetings,
> (b) notice of such meetings,
> (c) the duties of any representative of the Minister at such meetings; and
> (d) the number of persons required at such meetings to constitute a quorum.

The comments already made about the electoral provisions also apply to Section 80. The procedural regulations made under this section seem to have been, like Band election regulations, passengers on the *Mayflower*.

Sections 81 to 86 deal with the powers of a Band Council. If the federal government had been so inclined, it could have used these to help the First Nations achieve a large measure of self-government years ago:

> 81.   (1)   The council of a band may make by-laws not inconsistent with this Act or with any regulation made by the Governor in Council or the Minister, for any or all of the following purposes, namely,... [The purposes range from public health, traffic control, zoning, land allotments, animal control, observance of law and order, and just about any other purpose needed for self-government. Remedies for by-law violations:]
> (r)   the imposition on summary conviction of a fine not exceeding one thousand dollars or imprisonment for a term not exceeding thirty days, or both, for violation of a by-law made under this section.
> (2)   Where any by-law of a band is contravened and a conviction entered, in addition to any other remedy and to any penalty imposed by the by-law, the court in which the conviction has been entered, and any court of competent jurisdiction thereafter may make an order prohibiting the continuation or repetition of the offence by the person convicted.
> (3)   Where any by-law of a band passed is contravened, in addition to any other remedy and to any penalty imposed by the by-law, such contravention may be restrained by court action at the instance of the band council.

Section 82 is the instrument that permits the Minister to exercise ultimate control over the content and purpose of by-laws.

> 82.   (1)   A copy of every by-law made under section 81 shall be forwarded by mail by the chief or a member of the council of the band to the Minister within four days after it is made.
> (2)   A by-law made under section 81 comes into force forty days after a copy thereof is forwarded to the Minister pursuant to subsection (1),

unless it is disallowed by the Minister within that period, but the Minister may declare the by-law to be in force at any time before the expiration of that period.

Section 83 permits Band Councils to enact by-laws for the purpose of raising money:

> 83.   (1)   Without prejudice to the powers conferred by section 81, the council of a band may, subject to the approval of the Minister, make by-laws for any or all of the following purposes, namely,... [The purposes range from imposing taxation to licenses and other collectable fees and the expenditure of funds so raised. Administrative procedures:]
> (2)   An expenditure made out of moneys raised pursuant to subsection (1) must be so made under the authority of a by-law of the council of the band.
> (3)   A by-law made under paragraph (1)(a) must provide for an appeal procedure in respect of assessments made for the purposes of taxation under that paragraph.
> (4)   The Minister may approve the whole or a part only of a by-law made under subsection (1).
> (5)   The Governor in Council may make regulations respecting the exercise of the by-law making powers of bands under this section.
> (6)   A by-law made under this section remains in force only to the extent that it is consistent with the regulations made under subsection (5).

Subsections 5 and 6 don't make sense. A Band has no by-law making powers, its Council has.

Section 84 provides a collection procedure:

> 84. Where a tax that is imposed on an Indian by or under the authority of a by-law made under section 83 is not paid in accordance with the by-law, the Minister may pay the amount owing together with an amount equal to one-half of one percent thereof out of moneys payable out of the funds of the band to the Indian. [This section means that moneys from a Band member's per capita share of trust funds held by the Minister for the Band can be paid by the Minister to the Band Council to satisfy tax arrears.]

Section 85 was repealed. It was the so-called "advanced Band" section, where the Minister could make a proclamation that in the estimation of him and his bureaucrats, a Band had become "advanced," whatever that was supposed to mean. It was obviously a racist concept.

Section 85.1 provides Band Councils with the power to regulate intoxicants:

> (1)   Subject to subsection (2), the council of the band may make by-laws,
> (a) the sale, barter, supply or manufacture of intoxicants on the reserve of

the band;

(b) prohibiting any person from being intoxicated on the reserve;

(c) prohibiting any person from having intoxicants in his possession on the reserve; and

(d) providing for exceptions to any of the prohibitions established pursuant to paragraph (b) or (c).

(2)   A by-law may not be made under this section unless it is first assented to by a majority of the electors of the band who voted at a special meeting of the band called by the council of the band for the purpose of considering the by-law.

(3)   A copy of every by-law made under this section shall be sent by mail to the Minister by the chief or a member of the council of the band within four days after it is made.

(4)   Every person who contravenes a by-law made under this section is guilty of an offence and liable on summary conviction

(a) in the case of a by-law made under paragraph (1)(a), to a fine of not more than one thousand dollars or to imprisonment for a term not exceeding six months or to both; and

(b) in the case of a by-law made under paragraph (1)(b) or (c), to a fine of not more than one hundred dollars or to imprisonment for a term not exceeding three months or to both.

86.   A copy of a by-law made by the council of a band under this Act, if it is certified to be a true copy by the superintendent, is evidence that the by-law was duly made by the council and approved by the Minister, without proof of the signature or official character of the superintendent, and no such by-law is invalid by reason of any defect in form.

Considering the potential the Band administrative and financial authority sections of the Indian Act have to provide Bands with the wherewithal for a large measure of self-government, this question begs to be addressed: Why, before turning over programs and funds to the Bands to administer, did the Department neglect to require them to enact by-laws to govern the way they were to administer Band affairs and expend public funds? No other governments are permitted to operate without such laws. Why was it thought that a people with no expertise in modern civil administration could govern without legal tools? This practice of the federal government becomes even more suspect when one takes into account that Canada in 1996 would not release monetary aid to the Palestinians until they could assure our government that they had legal procedures in place to properly account for the money granted. Another thing has always disturbed me: The Auditor General of Canada is authorized to trace expenditures of tax dollars by all federally funded entities except Bands and their organizations. Why?

Racism, self-interest, stereotyping, incompetence and careless disregard for trust responsibilities have to be taken into account when trying to fathom the Department's motivations for this stupidity. And no doubt the same attitudes that prompted the Boat Harbour engineer to callously reply, "So, they're only Indians," when asked about the future welfare of the Pictou Landing Band members were involved. Whatever the combination of motivating factors, the harm that the bureaucrats have done by failing to require that tools for good financial management be implemented at the Band Council level is obvious. This has ensured a level of financial incompetence at Band offices that will keep Indian Affairs bureaucrats employed indefinitely.

It's sad to say that at the dawn of the twenty-first century there was still no genuine effort being made by government to fill this void. I can state without reservation that if successive governments had fulfilled their trust responsibilities stipulated under the Act with competence and care, First Nations could have returned to responsible self-government years ago.

The following are two valid but unenforceable by-laws that were validated because the Minister failed to disallow them within the forty days stipulated under Section 82. Laws of this nature should include enforcement provisions and other legal niceties. However, these by-laws, presented exactly as written, do not:

By-Law No. 5—Curfew

All school children under the age of sixteen years of age shall be off the sidewalks, public places such as dance halls, ballfields and so forth during the school days or school nights, nor later than 9:30 p.m. in the winter months and 10:00 p.m. in the summer months.

By-Law No. 6—Vacant Houses

All vacant houses on the Reserve that are fire hazard and health hazard, in the opinion of a Fire Marshall or a Health Inspector shall revert back to the Band to dispose of as they see fit.[20]

These by-laws were passed in 1970 at a duly convened meeting of a Band Council held at an Indian Agency office in the presence of the Indian Agent and his staff. In fact the Indian Agent and his staff wrote them for the Council's approval. Such worthless laws stand as testaments to the incompetence of the Department's bureaucrats.

Sections 87, 88, 89 and 90 deal with Indian taxation, legal rights and personal property. Because it deals with treaties, Section 88 will be discussed after Section 90:

87.   (1)   Notwithstanding any other Act of Parliament or any Act of the legislature of a province, but subject to section 83, the following property is exempt from taxation, namely,

(a) the interests of an Indian or a band *in reserve lands* or surrendered lands; and

(b) the personal property of an Indian or a band situated *on a reserve*.

(2)   No Indian or band is subject to taxation in respect of the ownership, occupation, possession or use of any property mentioned in para-

graph (1)(a) or (b) or is otherwise subject to taxation in respect to any such property.

(3)   No succession duty, inheritance tax or estate duty is payable on the death of any Indian in respect of any property mentioned in paragraphs (1)(a) or (b) or the succession thereto if the property passes to an Indian, nor shall any such property be taken into account in determining the duty payable under the Dominion Succession Duty Act, Chapter 89 of the Revised Statutes of Canada, 1952, or the tax payable under the Estate Tax Act, Chapter E-9 of the Revised Statutes of Canada, 1970, on or in respect of other property passing to an Indian.

89.   (1)   Subject to this Act, the real and personal property of an Indian or a band situated *on a reserve* is not subject to charge, pledge, mortgage, attachment, levy, seizure, distress or execution in favour or at the instance of any person other than an Indian or a band.

(1.1)   Notwithstanding subsection (1), a leasehold interest in designated lands is subject to charge, pledge, mortgage, attachment, levy, seizure, distress and execution.

(2)   A person who sells to a band or a member of a band a chattel under an agreement whereby the right of property or right of possession thereto remains wholly or in part in the seller may exercise his rights under the agreement notwithstanding that the chattel is situated on a reserve.

90.   (1)   For the purposes of sections 87 and 89, personal property that was

(a) purchased by Her Majesty with Indian moneys or moneys appropriated by Parliament for the use and benefit of Indians or bands, or

(b) given to Indians or to a band under a treaty or agreement between a band and Her Majesty, shall be deemed always to be situated on a reserve.

(2)   Every transaction purporting to pass title to any property that is by this section deemed to be situated on a reserve, or any interest in such property, is void unless the transaction is entered into with the consent of the Minister or is entered into between members of a band or between the band and a member thereof.

(3)   Every person who enters into any transaction that is void by virtue of subsection (2) is guilty of an offence, and every person who, without the written consent of the Minister, destroys personal property that is by this section deemed to be situated on a reserve is guilty of an offence.

These sections give Registered Indians *limited* exemptions from taxation. Many a Minister of the Crown, and more than a few senior bureaucrats, have deliberately and maliciously made statements giving the public the impression that status Indians enjoy *full* exemption from taxation in Canada. As is obvious from reading these sections, exemptions are limited to property situated on a Reserve. Any registered Band member who owns personal property or a business off-Reserve is subject to the same taxes as other Canadians. The same applies to any Registered

Indian who works for an employer located off-Reserve.

In any event, to tax First Nations property would not be very lucrative at this time because *poverty* is a very poor asset to tax. To tax the mostly nonproductive leftovers of what were once vast holdings would be contemptible by any standard.

Legal Rights

88.   Subject to the terms of any treaty and any other Act of Parliament, all laws of general application from time to time in force in any province are applicable to and in respect of Indians in the province, except to the extent that those laws are inconsistent with this Act or any order, rule, regulation or by-law made thereunder, and except to the extent that those laws make provision for any matter for which provision is made by or under this Act.

Using this section, the Union of Nova Scotia Indians went to the Supreme Court of Canada to appeal the conviction of a Shubenacadie Band member for hunting out of season. In the *Simon* decision of 1986 the court ruled that the Treaty of 1752 was a valid treaty and that registered Mi'kmaq did not need a provincial license to hunt, fish, and gather. Pertinent sections of the *Simon* decision:

Supreme Court of Canada, decision on appeal from the Court of Appeal for Nova Scotia

Reference: Indians—Treaty Rights—Right to Hunt—Provincial Law Restricting that Right—Whether or not Treaty Rights prevail—Indian Act, Section 88—Lands and Forests Act (Nova Scotia)—Constitution Act, 1982, Section 35.

Appellant, a Registered Micmac Indian, was convicted under Section 150(1) of Nova Scotia's *Lands and Forest Act* for possession of a rifle and shotgun cartridges. Although appellant admitted all essential elements of the charges, *it was argued that the right to hunt set out in the Treaty of 1752, in combination with Section 88 of the* Indian Act, *offered him immunity from prosecution under the Provincial Act.*

Article 4 of that Treaty stated that the Micmac have "free liberty of hunting and fishing as usual" and Section 88 provided that provincial laws of general application applied to Indians, subject to the terms of any Treaty.

The Court of Appeal upheld the trial judge's ruling that the Treaty of 1752 did not exempt appellant from the provisions of the provincial *Lands and Forests Act*. At issue here was whether or not appellant enjoys hunting rights, pursuant to the Treaty of 1752 and Section 88 of the *Indian Act*, which preclude his prosecution for certain offenses under the *Lands and Forests Act*.

Held: The appeal should be allowed.

Both Governor Hopson and the Micmac had the capacity to enter into the

Treaty of 1752 and did so with the intention of creating mutually binding obligations. *The Treaty constitutes a positive source of protection against infringements on hunting rights* and the fact that these rights existed before the Treaty as part of the general Aboriginal Title did not negate or minimize the significance of the rights protected by the Treaty.

Although the right to hunt was not absolute, to be effective, it had to include reasonably incidental activities, such as travelling with the necessary equipment to the hunting grounds and possessing a hunting rifle and ammunition in a safe manner.

The Treaty of 1752 continues to be in force and effect. The principles of international Treaty Law relating to Treaty termination were not determinative because an Indian Treaty is unique and *sui generis*. Furthermore, nothing in the British conduct subsequent to the conclusion of the Treaty, or in the hostilities of 1753, indicated that the Crown considered the terms of the Treaty terminated. Nor was it demonstrated that the hunting rights protected by the Treaty have been extinguished. The court expressed no view whether, as a matter of Law, Treaty rights can be extinguished.

Appellant is an Indian covered by the Treaty. He was a Registered Micmac Indian living in the same area as the original Micmac Indian Tribe which was a party to the Treaty. This was sufficient evidence to prove the appellant's connection to that Tribe. In light of the Micmac tradition of not committing things to writing, to require more, such as proving direct descendance, would be impossible and render nugatory any right to hunt that a present-day Micmac would otherwise have.

The Treaty of 1752 is an enforceable obligation between the Indians and the Crown and is therefore within the meaning of Section 88 of the Indian Act. Section 88 operates to include all agreements concluded by the Crown with the Indians that would be otherwise enforceable Treaties, whether or not land was ceded.

Appellant's possession of a rifle and ammunition in a safe manner was referable to his Treaty right to hunt and was not restricted by Section 150(1) of the *Lands and Forests Act. Section 88 of the* Indian Act, *which applies only to provincial legislation, operates to exempt Indians from legislation restricting or contravening a term of any Treaty and must prevail over Section 150(1) of the* Lands and Forests Act.

It was not necessary to consider Section 35 of the *Constitution Act, 1982* since Section 88 of the *Indian Act* covered the present situation and provided the necessary protection for the appellant.[21]

This case demonstrates how vitally important Indian Registration is when affirming entitlement to aboriginal rights. If Jimmy Simon had not been registered as an Indian, he would not have won his case, because it would have been impossible for him to have proven his ancestry otherwise.

When considering the *Simon* case the Supreme Court of Canada reviewed Judge Patterson's 1929 racist decision in the *Crown* v. *Syliboy* case, which had considered the question of the capacity of the parties to enter into the Treaty of

1752. Patterson's highly reactionary position reflects the biases and prejudices First Nations peoples had to contend with when seeking justice at that time. An excerpt from Patterson's decision:

> Two considerations are involved. First, did the Indians of Nova Scotia have status to enter into a treaty? And second, did Governor Hopson have authority to enter into one with them? Both questions must, I think, be answered in the negative.
>
> (1) "Treaties are unconstrained Acts of independent powers." But the Indians were never regarded as an independent power. *A civilized nation first discovering a country of uncivilized people or savages held such country as its own until such time as by treaty it was transferred to some other civilized nation.*
>
> *The savage's rights of sovereignty, even of ownership, were never recognized. Nova Scotia had passed to Great Britain, not by gift or purchase from or even by conquest of the Indians, but by treaty with France, which had acquired it by priority of discovery and ancient possession; and the Indians passed with it.*
>
> Indeed the very fact that certain Indians sought from the Governor the privilege or right to hunt in Nova Scotia as usual, shows that they did not claim to be an independent nation owning or possessing their lands. If they were, why go to another nation asking this privilege or right and giving promise of good behaviour that they might obtain it?
>
> In my judgement, the Treaty of 1752 is not a treaty at all and is not to be treated as such; it is at best a mere agreement made by the Governor and Council with a handful of Indians, giving them in return for good behaviour, food, presents, and the right to hunt and fish as usual—an agreement that, as we have seen, was very shortly after broken.
>
> (2) Did Governor Hopson have authority to make a treaty? I think not. "Treaties can be made only by the constituted authorities of nations, or by persons specially deputed by them for that purpose." Clearly our treaty was not made with the constituted authorities of Great Britain.
>
> But was Governor Hopson specially deputed by them? Cornwallis's Commission is the manual not only for himself, but for his successors, and you will search it in vain for any power to sign treaties.[22]

Judge Patterson's disparaging comments are extremely offensive to the Mi'kmaq. The fact that he declares the values of his own race to be civilized and those of ours to be uncivilized says it all. Not surprisingly he makes no comment about the civility of Cornwallis's scalping proclamation or the other barbarous actions of colonial officialdom!

In the *Simon* decision, the Supreme Court of Canada, in finding that the Treaty of 1752 was a valid treaty, stated: "With regard to the substance of Judge Patterson's words, leaving aside for the moment the question of whether treaties are international-type documents, his conclusions on capacity are not convincing." The Justices went on to say:

No Court, with the exception of the Nova Scotia Supreme Court, Appeal Division in the present case, has agreed explicitly with the conclusion of Judge Patterson that the Indians and Governor Hopson lacked capacity to enter into an enforceable treaty.

The Treaty of 1752 was implicitly assumed to have been validly created in [the following court cases:] *R. v. Simon* (1958), *R. v. Francis* (1969), *R. v. Paul* (1980), *R. v. Cope, supra*; *R. v. Atwin and Sacobie* (1981), *R. v. Sect. of ex parte Indian association of Alberta and others* (1982), and *The Queen v. Robert J. Paul and Lee J. Polchies* (1984). In *R. v. Issac, supra*, Cooper J.A., after noting Judge Patterson's conclusions on the validity of the Treaty of 1752, expressed doubt as to their correctness, at page 496.

Cooper states: "The Treaty of 1752 was considered in *Rex v. Syliboy*.... It was there held by Patterson, Acting C.C.J., that it did not extend to Cape Breton Indians and further that it was not in reality a treaty. I have doubt as to the second finding and express no opinion on it, but I have no doubt as to the correctness of the first finding."[23]

N.A.M. MacKenzie, in "Indians and Treaties in Law" (1929), also disagreed with Judge Patterson's ruling that the Mi'kmaq did not have the capacity, nor the Governor the authority, to conclude a valid treaty:

As to the capacity of the Indians to contract and the authority of Governor Hopson to enter into such an agreement, with all deference to His Honour, both seem to have been present. Innumerable treaties and agreements of a similar character were made by Great Britain, France, the United States of America and Canada with the Indian tribes inhabiting this continent, and these treaties and agreements have been and still are held to be binding.

Nor would Governor Hopson require special "powers" to enter into such an agreement. Ordinarily "full powers" specially conferred are essential to the proper negotiating of a treaty, but the Indians were not on a par with a sovereign state and fewer formalities were required in their case. Governor Hopson was the representative of His Majesty and as such had sufficient authority to make an agreement with the Indian tribes.[24]

The Supreme Court Justice continued:

The Treaty was entered into for the benefit of both the British Crown and the Micmac People, to maintain peace and order, as well as to recognize and confirm the existing hunting and fishing rights of the Micmac. In my opinion, both the Governor and the Micmac entered into the Treaty with the intention of creating mutually binding obligations which would be solemnly respected.

It also provided a mechanism for dispute resolution. The Micmac Chief, and the three other Micmac signatories, as delegates of the Micmac people, would have possessed full capacity to enter into a binding treaty on behalf of the Micmac. Governor Hopson was the delegate and legal representative of His Majesty the King.

It is fair to assume that the Micmac would have believed that Governor Hopson, acting on behalf of His Majesty the King, had the necessary authority to enter into a valid treaty with them. I would hold that the Treaty of 1752 was validly created by competent Parties.[25]

It is a sad commentary that, even after the findings of the Supreme Court of Canada in the *Simon* case, both the federal and provincial governments have refused to negotiate in good faith the modernization of the Treaty of 1752. To date, the only matters they have shown a willingness to negotiate are those beneficial to their own interests. And, unfortunately, as exemplified in the highly publicized Donald Marshall Jr. wrongful conviction case, the racist attitudes expressed by Judge Patterson in the *Syliboy* case continued to prevail within the Nova Scotia justice system right up to the late 1980s. Section 88 of the Indian Act has been the subject of litigation in many other situations and no doubt will be prominently mentioned in others for years to come.

Sections 91 and 92, trading with Indians, covers the sale and protection of First Nations artifacts and who may trade with Natives.

91.   (1)   No person may, without the written consent of the Minister, acquire title to any of the following property situated on a reserve, namely,

(a)   an Indian grave house;
(b)   a carved grave pole;
(c)   a totem pole;
(d)   a carved house post; or
(e)   a rock embellished with paintings or carvings.

(2)   Subsection (1) does not apply to chattels referred to therein that are manufactured for sale by Indians.

(3)   No person shall remove, take away, mutilate, disfigure, deface or destroy any chattel referred to in subsection (1) without the written consent of the Minister.

(4)   A person who contravenes this section is guilty of an offence and liable on summary conviction to a fine not exceeding two hundred dollars or to imprisonment for a term not exceeding three months.

The most glaring shortcoming of Section 91 is that it only covers artifacts located on Indian Reserves. Most sacred First Nations sites, treasures and artifacts are located off-Reserve and have been left unprotected by the Act. Even skeletal remains of Mi'kmaq have been put on display in Nova Scotia; the most recent were given a decent burial just a few years ago.

Section 92 forbids an officer of the Department, a missionary engaged in mission work, or a teacher who teaches on a Reserve to trade with Registered Indians. A missionary or teacher may obtain a license from the Minister to trade, if they choose, but departmental officials are strictly forbidden to engage in trade. A person found guilty of contravening this section is guilty of an offense and subject to a $500 fine or, if an employee of the Department, dismissal from office. There is no mention of their families engaging in trade.

Section 93 forbids the removal of materials from Reserves without a permit and prescribes the penalties for anyone caught doing so. Any person who illegally removes minerals, stone, sand, gravel, clay or soil, or trees, saplings, shrubs, underbrush, timber, cordwood or hay, or who has any of these from a Reserve in his possession, is guilty of an offense and subject to a fine of not more than $500 or to imprisonment for no more than three months, or both.

Sections 94 to 100 were repealed in 1985. These were the sections that had made it illegal for Registered Indians to enter places that served liquor or sold it, or to be in possession of alcohol, either externally or internally. It was racist based legislation that humiliated the First Nations People of Canada.

Sections 101 to 108 spell out how the Act shall be enforced and how prosecutions shall proceed. They also provide for the appointment of magistrates, justices of the peace and other enforcement officials.

Sections 109 to 113 were the enfranchisement sections. They, like the liquor provisions, were repealed in 1985. These sections were some of the most insidious provisions the government included in the Indian Act. Their enactment was for the express purpose of hastening extinction of Registered Indians by assimilation, which is cultural genocide. The shame for this country is that it had these laws on its books until 1985, another blow to Canada's cultivated image as a gallant warrior in the worldwide crusade for human rights and racial equality. The following are examples of their content and of how they were used by government to try to realize their evil goal.

First, a male Registered Indian, without the consent of his wife and minor children, could alone enfranchise his entire family. The provision stated that any male Registered Indian, with the consent of the Minister or Governor in Council, could enfranchise himself upon application, and his wife and minor children would be automatically enfranchised with him.

Second, under these sections, individuals and entire Bands were enfranchised. To get them to do so, they were hoodwinked into believing that somehow or other, by giving up their rights as Indians, they would reap all the benefits of Canadian citizenship. However, instead of receiving any benefits, most of those who gave up their Indian rights became destitute wanderers who nobody in Canada wanted. Fortunately, despite the best efforts of succeeding governments to entice them, the vast majority of First Nations peoples refused the bait.

In cases where bureaucrats were successful in convincing a person of the "value" of being enfranchised, it is striking how low some of them stooped to succeed. The reason so many were willing to set aside personal ethics was that they were awarded personal achievement points by supervisors for successful enfranchisements on their annual job performance evaluations, which were invaluable when seeking promotion.

Such devious practices were commonplace. The following is a true enfranchisement case from the 1960s, with names and places changed to protect the people involved. The applicant had a wife and six dependent children, was illiterate, had no experience in the profession he wanted to enter and was not gainfully employed. Any one of the last three facts applied alone was enough to prevent an enfranchisement under the Indian Act.

The applicant, Mr. Bear, a member of the Sun Band, residing on-Reserve, wanted to take up farming as a vocation. Because Indian Affairs had a "revolving fund" created specifically to assist Band members in setting up such entrepreneurial ventures, he approached the Department with his proposition. After divulging the nature of his request and his personal facts, believe it or not, Mr. Bear was told by the bureaucrat handling the application that his proposal was a wonderful idea and should be followed up. The bureaucrat made this assessment in full knowledge of Mr. Bear's illiteracy, non-agricultural background and unemployed status. The victim was then told by the bureaucrat that before the proposal could go forward he would have to be enfranchised, and further, that he was required to dispose of his on-Reserve house; for which the Department would pay him compensation. This was an outright lie; there was never any such requirement to receive a loan from the revolving fund.

Mr. Bear and his wife, being uninformed, had no appreciation of the impact that enfranchisement would have on their family's future prospects. Trusting and naive, they went along with the bureaucrat's advice and applied. Bear's initial application for "voluntary" enfranchisement was processed in short order. To "assure" that the application "*met the requirements of the Act*," it was appraised by other bureaucrats and approved even though the applicants did not meet the requirements for voluntary enfranchisement. In fact, the applicants in this case did not even meet the requirements for borrowing money from the revolving fund.

However, in spite of all this, Mr. Bear and his family were enfranchised. Their property on the Reserve was returned to the Band and the family took up life on the farm the government had helped them purchase. Immediately the enterprise was a dismal failure. This result would not have come as a surprise to any knowledgeable person, least of all the individual who processed the Bear application. Mr. Bear and his family were left destitute. Only the employment needs of the uncaring bureaucrat had been met.

This case added a little more to the disgust I feel about the careless indifference Indian Affairs bureaucrats have displayed towards the sufferings of First Nations citizens. In my capacity as Superintendent of Lands, Revenues, and Statutory Requirements with the Department, I took up Bear's case with the Indian Registrar. The response I received in a nutshell was this: "We know Bear has been wronged. However, the place for him to go is the courts." I responded that the family was destitute, and legal aid would not take up a civil case of this nature. The final word was something like "Them's the breaks." The bureaucrat involved in the Bear case went on to occupy a very influential and highly paid office within the Department.

Third, in 1971, after receiving approval of an application for financial assistance from the Department to subsidize the purchase of a home located off-Reserve, and the subsequent purchase of my home, the Regional Director of Indian Affairs, who was a lifelong friend, telephoned me to say, "Dan, there's just one more step you need to take to complete your life and assume full responsibility as a citizen; get enfranchised." I responded without rancour: "Get lost."

Fourth, the bureaucratic drive to enfranchise Registered Indians was so great that some individuals were enfranchised without proper evidence. In Nova Scotia, in many cases after someone simply said a woman had married a non-Indian, she was enfranchised. In one case several women were taken off their Band List by the Department because their Band Council had sent in a resolution alleging they had married non-Indians. This was done despite the fact that the enfranchisement and membership sections of the Act require that proof be provided. After being removed from their Band List on the basis of gossip, these women were told when they protested that they would have to provide official documentation proving that they were not married to non-Indians before they could be reinstated.

In yet another display of treachery, on March 31, 1985, prior to the passage of Bill C-31—which would provide for the reinstatement of those who had been removed from Band Lists under discriminatory provisions of the Indian Act—the government cancelled the Off-Reserve Housing Program. The reason was obvious to all: Bill C-31 was to come into effect on April 17, 1985, and the government did not want to provide off-Reserve housing subsidies to the families of reinstated Indian women.

Finally, some Nova Scotia Mi'kmaq for various reasons (such as having been adopted, or because fires have destroyed church records) cannot furnish proof that they are who they claim to be and are thus denied "Indian" registration. For example, Margaret Paul, an elderly Halifax lady, has no proof of birth but has been known by the People from birth as a Mi'kmaq. The Council of the Band she would be registered under passed a resolution requesting her reinstatement to their Band List, but to no avail; the Department demands written proof of her First Nations ancestry, something impossible to obtain.

Sections 114 to 122 deal with the education of children on a Reserve and provide for the construction, operation and maintenance of on-Reserve schools. Where no on-Reserve schools are available, these sections give the means for contracting out with provinces, territories and municipalities to provide educational services and facilities. Generally the provincial curriculum is taught at a Reserve school. These sections give the Minister the authority to make regulations concerning education for the Bands, mandatory attendance requirements, truancy and related matters.

Three of these sections, which specify who can teach on-Reserve, demonstrate archaic thinking:

118.   Every Indian child who is required to attend school shall attend such school as the Minister may designate, but no child whose parent is Protestant shall be assigned to a school conducted under Roman Catholic auspices and no child whose parent is a Roman Catholic shall be assigned to a school conducted under Protestant auspices, except by written direction of the parent....

120.   (1)   Where the majority of the members of a band belong to one religious denomination, the school established on the reserve that has been set apart for the use and benefit of that band shall be taught by a teacher of that denomination.

(2)   Where the majority of the members of a band are not members of the same religious denomination and the band by a majority vote of

those electors of the band who were present at a meeting called for the purpose requests that day schools on the reserve should be taught by a teacher belonging to a particular religious denomination, the school on that reserve shall be taught by a teacher of that denomination.

121 .   A Protestant or Roman Catholic minority of any band may, with the approval of and under regulations to be made by the Minister, have a separate day school or day school classroom established on the reserve unless, in the opinion of the Governor in Council, the number of children of school age does not so warrant.

The above mentioned is proof that religious discrimination is still enshrined in law in Canada. Muslims, Jews, members of other non-Christian faiths and non-believers can still be legally excluded from teaching First Nations children in Canada in the twenty-first century.

However, these three sections probably had a more insidious purpose than to dictate which foreign religious denomination would teach children of any particular First Nations community. Given the government's assimilation policy, with its goal of extinguishing First Nations culture, one can easily surmise that these sections of the Act were crafted to ensure that the traditional religions of the First Nations were not taught in school.

Was the Indian Act the cause of the First Nations' poverty in Canada? Many would like to say yes, but the answer is no. It was the misuse of the Act by Indian Affairs bureaucrats to oppress First Nations peoples that caused the poverty. If competent and non-biased people had administered it from day one, I firmly believe that the results today would be far different.

The Indian Act was not designed by bureaucrats to preserve First Nations cultures and see them prosper, but to deliver the final blow. Fittingly, as a measure of poetic justice, it has turned out to be a salvation. The men who sought to destroy our cultures, motivated by their racist perceptions of themselves as products of superior civilizations, would roll over in their graves if they knew the actions they had taken to facilitate the demise of First Nations were the very actions that ultimately saved them.

It's not hard to conclude from the careless administration of the Indian Act that those who oversaw it firmly believed that Indians were so mentally deficient that they would never be able to successfully use bureaucratic negligence to win court cases. Any of those types who are still around must be confounded by the intelligent way First Nations are seeking and receiving redress in the courts through landmark decisions. Considering the irresponsible way the Department administered the Indian Act, one can anticipate a bright financial future for the First Nations after these injustices are resolved through litigation.

The federal government would dearly love to repeal the Act in order to get itself off the hook. However, although the reputation of the Indian Act has been tarnished beyond repair by the racist administration of its provisions, it must remain in force until a mutually acceptable replacement is found. The government's will alone must not be allowed to prevail.

This is not to say that the federal government isn't looking for First Nations support to achieve this goal. When I was still the Executive Director of the Confederacy of Mainland Micmacs, on a visit to Ottawa, the Minister tried to convince me to support repeal of the Act by promoting the bureaucratic line that the Act was the cause of our problems. I responded that the blame for our current problems lies with the past racist administration and formulation of the Act and has nothing to do with the Act itself. At that point we agreed to disagree.

A word of caution: A lay person, or a lawyer not conversant in Indian law, who undertakes to use the Indian Act for any legal reason must bear in mind that many sections directly contradict others and, as a result, negate the apparent meanings first read into them. It is a complicated statute. Many sections have been litigated and thereby had their meanings refined. If you have questions about the interpretation of the Act, *consult an expert.*

13

Twentieth-Century Racism
and Centralization

"The twentieth century belongs to Canada," predicted Sir Wilfrid Laurier, Prime Minister of Canada from 1896 to 1911. In many respects this prediction came true. The country became prosperous and developed one of the highest standards of living in the world. However, most citizens of colour did not benefit much from this achievement. They were blatantly victimized by racism and denied economic opportunities. Even in the twenty-first century their exclusion from full participation in economic and social affairs persists to an unacceptable degree in many Canadian jurisdictions.

Twentieth-Century Racism

In the article, "Lessons at the Halfway Point," Michael Levine accurately identifies why intolerance exists: "If you don't personally get to know people from other racial, religious or cultural groups, its very easy to believe ugly things about them and make them frightening in your mind."[1] If Europeans had gotten to know and had accepted Americans and Africans as equals during colonial times, instead of adopting White supremacist racist beliefs, which have ruled supreme in negatively depicting both as savages for the better part of five centuries, these peoples of colour would not have suffered the indescribable hells they have.

In fairness, it must be said that the hells suffered in North America by both groups were not equally severe across the continent. The severity varied from state to state, province to province, and community to community. Because of the way it badly mistreated both the Mi'kmaq and the Africans, Nova Scotia has been deemed by many as among the most racially discriminatory jurisdictions on the continent. In fact, until recent times, some referred to it as "the Mississippi of Canada."

The designation was well deserved. Members of both communities were regularly denied employment, and entrance to most hotels, restaurants and other public places, with impunity (Jews and other minorities also suffered many of these indignities, but not as severely). Even in death intolerance often ruled. Some cemeteries had coloured sections reserved especially for Blacks, indigents and the insane. The Mi'kmaq weren't subjected to this particular indignity because most of our cemeteries are located on-Reserve.

Many other gross indignities were suffered over these years by both peoples. Among the worst of these was that when a crime was committed near one of our communities, we were the first to be accused and were often convicted without due process. The possibility of innocence wasn't much of a consideration. The net result is that the police and the justice system are still generally mistrusted by both Africans and the Mi'kmaq. Since the founding of the Nova Scotia Human Rights

Commission in 1967, blatant racist persecution has abated considerably, but by 2000 there was still a long way to go.

The bulk of the historic racism mentioned was caused by the demonization of both peoples. In the case of First Nations peoples the demonizing began almost with the arrival of Columbus. In more modern times it became so widespread that it was encompassed in almost all aspects of life—movies, radio, television, magazines, newspapers, books, advertisements, religious sermons, textbooks and every other means known. Native Americans were depicted as wanton, cruel, murderous, heartless, lazy and worthless, drunken heathen savages.

The bigots presented this abhorrent propaganda in such a realistic way that a great many First Nations people actually believed it. As a result it wasn't unusual to go to a movie during the 1930s, 1940s or 1950s and find a large group of First Nations children cheering on the good guys, the cowboys, against the bad guys, the Indians. This negative imagery has created a crisis of self-esteem and confidence within our people that is still bearing tragic fruit today.

Fortunately, this negative stereotype in the minds of all members of society is being negated by Native Americans who have learned to research and rediscover the true histories of their civilizations. These researchers are also revealing the true stories of European invasion and subjugation of First Nations peoples. One of the best results of these revelations is that pride is being restored. Our children now go to movies and cheer on the good guys, their own! It was a lack of education that hampered most of our efforts to spread the truth until recently.

Education

Although available on paper, education—a vital tool to provide First Nations citizens with the ability to appreciate and modernize their ancient cultures—was all but denied until recent times. This unwritten requirement of White society—"You may have an education, but only if you agree to assimilate and accept the eventual extinction of your culture"—plus the racism encountered by students attending White schools made an education practically unattainable.

In spite of these impediments, through the efforts of private organizations and churches, by 1867 some Amerindians were able to read and write. However, after Confederation, even in the knowledge that the vast majority of Natives were illiterate, the government made no real effort to provide education until the passage of the Indian Act in 1876. Then it was made unattractive by the provision that automatically enfranchised a Band member who graduated from university. Assimilation was the motivating factor behind these laws.

To hurry assimilation along, during the first six decades of twentieth century, First Nations tongues came under attack across the country. In Nova Scotia, Mi'kmaq children were forbidden to speak their language at schools and discouraged to do so in many other public places. Administrators at the Shubenacadie residential school informed Mi'kmaq and Maliseet children upon enrolment that it was a cardinal offense to speak their own languages. If caught, retribution was swift.

The same rule was followed and strictly enforced by bureaucrats administering schools and other public institutions in First Nations communities across Canada. But nowhere was it pursued with the same dogged determination as on mainland

Nova Scotia. This was not unusual, because from the time the British took over in 1713, the Mi'kmaq of peninsular Nova Scotia had always been singled out for special hatred.

Despite the determined effort made by White society to eradicate the Mi'kmaq language, it is still alive and healthy today throughout most of Cape Breton, New Brunswick and Prince Edward Island; and surprisingly, almost half of the Mi'kmaq on mainland Nova Scotia can still converse in their mother tongue—another example of the Mi'kmaq's dauntless spirit.

The Shubenacadie Indian Residential School

In 1892, trying to come up with a way to educate Maliseet and Mi'kmaq children, the Department toyed with the idea of building a residential school farm in Nova Scotia. However, probably because education was not much of a priority in the Department's estimation, the decision to actually build such a school was not made until 1927. It was opened off-Reserve in the village of Shubenacadie in 1930.

The teaching staff were recruited according to the section of the Indian Act that mandated that teachers be of the same faith as the children they were teaching. As most of the Mi'kmaq and Maliseet were Catholic, the teachers were Roman Catholic nuns and the principal a priest. The curriculum was the same as that prescribed by the Nova Scotia Department of Education for the provincial school system except for the courses in religion and in how to be ashamed of being an Indian. Children were taught about all the advantages of White life and all the evils of First Nations' isolation, language and culture.

Besides delivering second-rate education, these institutions were also used by Indian Affairs for many other purposes—enforcement, punishment and terrorism, to name a few. Because of their "wards of the Crown" status, no possibility for legal redress was available to Registered Indians victimized at these facilities. So, when reading the following material, please bear in mind that the fights waged by parents and other relatives in trying to access and protect their children incarcerated in the Shubenacadie Indian Residential School were taken on without access to the laws that protected White Canadians from being victimized by the heavy hand of the state. Thus many suffered greatly.

I'll start this short overview of the Shubenacadie residential school by relating the less than fond experiences of distinguished former resident Elsie Basque, née Charles. Elsie was born on May 12, 1916, to Margaret Labrador and Joe Charles, at Hectanooga, Digby County, Nova Scotia. She has many fond memories of her early years, but they were not without tears and tragedy. By the end of her third year, Joe was hospitalized with tuberculosis and her mother had left the family permanently. But things got better. In 1922 Joe's TB stabilized and life at home in Hectanooga returned to a peaceful existence.

Elsie remembers "papa"[2] as being her most important childhood influence. His advise that "To be somebody, one needs a good education"[3] is still fondly recalled. In tune with his belief, Joe enroled her in the old one-room school in Hectanooga where she completed grade 7. Then her life was drastically changed by the information contained in an article her father had read in a 1929 edition of the Halifax *Chronicle* which touted the new horizons being opened up for the

Mi'kmaq by the opening of the residential school. Believing the school was a golden opportunity to secure his daughter's education, Joe enroled her.

This is Elsie's assessment of the two years she spent there:

> I've always regarded these years as time wasted.... I was in the 8th grade when I arrived at the school in February 1930 and in the 8th grade when I left in 1932. What had I learned in those 28 months? How to darn a sock, sew a straight seam on the sewing machine, and how to scrub clothes on a washboard. Educationally, how to parse and analyze a sentence.
>
> Volumes have been written about the school. Its total disastrous effect upon the Mi'kmaq/Maliseet Nations will never be known. Generations later, the scars remain. It was not an education institution as we define education. Older children, boys and girls were taken out of the classroom to do chores—milk cows, clean the barn, plant and harvest, etc. The girls were ordered to launder clothes, make uniforms, scrub the floors and so on.[4]

After this disappointment, Elsie, who is fluent in French, returned to Clare and enroled at Meteghan's Sacred Heart Academy, where she graduated with a high school diploma in 1936. She then entered classes at the Provincial Normal College in Truro and was awarded a teacher's certificate in 1937. Thus she became the first licensed Mi'kmaq teacher in Nova Scotia. Notably, she was well treated at the college by peers and administration. The students elected her class president and she describes her time there as a "fun year."[5]

The year was capped by a rare honour. The principal of the college, Dr. Davis, permitted very exceptional students to use his name as a reference. In 1937 only three were permitted to do so, and Elsie was one of them! With teaching license in hand, she applied by mail in mid-1937 to the Inverness County School Inspector for a teaching job at Mabou Ridge. This is how she describes her first face-to-face meeting with the inspector—it was also her first experience with overt racism:

> On our short drive to his home in Port Hastings, he advised that it would be best for me to turn around and go home. He was certain that the good people of Mabou Ridge would never accept a Micmac to teach their children. After much discussion it was agreed that I could at least try. The next day, teaching duties were undertaken without opposition from the community, the year passed without incident. [In the mid-1980s Elsie returned to Mabou Ridge and was given a warm welcome.][6]

If Elsie had applied in person she would not have got the job. Incidents such as this prove that officialdom was at the forefront of racial discrimination in Nova Scotia.

In view of the racism afoot in this province at the time, I had often wondered where Elsie had got the courage to attend a White institution and become a teacher. Then she gave me an explanation that reflected Maritime history. Raised among the Acadian people, Elsie had not experienced the self-confidence-destroying racial discrimination in youth that was suffered by most of Nova Scotia's Mi'kmaq:

I grew up in the area of Nova Scotia known as Clare ... an area where one is accepted for who and what one is, not on ethnic background. The bonds of friendship and understanding that began with Chief Membertou, Champlain, De Monts, Poutrincourt, have never faltered. Their legacy lives on."[7]

In 1992, Marilyn Millward wrote an article about the residential school entitled "Clean Behind the Ears?" These are some shocking excerpts from it:

Many of the students who attended the old Shubenacadie Indian Residential School carry with them the *scars of that experience. But they were not the only ones to suffer. A look at surviving records reveals the anguish many parents endured*, and shows the determination to speak and be heard that was their reaction to the way the educational and governmental bureaucracy dealt with them and their children.

The Indian Residential School at Shubenacadie, Nova Scotia, operated between February 1930 and June 1967. It was intended to accommodate Micmac (and Maliseet) children who were deemed to be "underprivileged," defined by the Federal Department of Indian Affairs as orphaned, neglected, or living too distant to permit attendance at any day school. While children who were orphaned or remote from schools could be easily identified, it was more difficult to interpret the term "neglected." This was a matter to be determined by the local Indian Agent.

Here, the Department intended to "consolidate Indian educational work in the Maritimes" and planned to "*mould the lives of the young Aborigines and aid them in their search towards the goal of complete Canadian Citizenship*." Duncan C. Scott, then Deputy Superintendent General of the Department of Indian Affairs, told the Halifax-Chronicle that their object and desire in establishing the new school was that its graduates should become self-supporting and "*not return to their old environment and habits*."[8]

Millward states that parental permission was necessary for admission. Although she later qualifies this statement, it isn't true. She may not have been aware that, because we were "wards of the Crown," the law as it then stood gave control of such things to Indian Affairs. The parental permission portions of the forms for admission to the school were simply window dressing. The Indian Agents did not legally need our permission to do anything they wanted to do with us, and they used these powers at will.

Ms. Millward substantiates this fact when describing how a Mi'kmaq parent tried to keep a child home:

A mother wanted to keep her children home after their vacation, and believed that only a note to her agent to that effect was necessary. When she learned "*it wasn't her decision to make*," she had a justice of the peace write to the Department on her behalf. His help consisted of a note saying that this mother "says she '*loves*' her children"—the word "loves" was belittled and negated by quotation marks. The agent wrote that she wanted them home only to take care of the house and their younger siblings, and so her request was apparently unsuccessful.[9]

The Department's control over the lives of children and parents was all-encompassing. Ms. Millward reports of vacations:

> Perhaps because of the difficulty in having some of the children returned to the school after summer vacations, *holidays at home were not allowed for any children during Christmas*. Although specific reasons for this policy are not clear from the existing records, they are implied in a 1938 letter from the Department to an agent in the Annapolis Valley: "For many reasons which will no doubt suggest themselves to you, the Department does not allow holidays at Christmas, and I might say further *that no valid reason has yet been given to us why holidays should be allowed at that period of the year*. There is no question that the children attending the Shubenacadie Residential School receive every possible care and attention, and in addition at Christmas time there are always special festivities which the children enjoy."
>
> In 1939, the parents at the Cambridge Reserve in Nova Scotia were determined to have their children home for Christmas, but the agent refused their request and advised them of the Department's rules. Reporting on the matter to the Department, he wrote: "*These people went so far as to have a man go to the school for their children, [but] they did not get the children. The Principal would not let them take them*."
>
> When one of these parents then sent her request to the Department herself, the agent reported: "She thought by writing she would be able to get her children home for Christmas. *These people think that they can have their own way and would like to do so and when they find out they cannot they get mad*."[10]

Indian Agents, other Department and school officials, and other non-Indians have often failed to appreciate that Natives have the same feelings and emotions as people from other races. The reason parents wanted their children home is because *they cherished and loved them*.

Although I never attended the residential school, our family was touched by the cruelty practised there. In the 1930s, because our community lacked educational facilities, my parents registered two of my older brothers. They were kept at the institution until a small day school was located on-Reserve a few years later. During their incarceration they experienced and saw much abuse, which they related to us afterwards. From then on, when we were misbehaving, my mother would say, "If you don't behave, I'll put you in the residential school." That threat was very effective!

Millward reports on the fear of return:

> A former pupil of the school retained a lawyer in an attempt to keep his younger siblings from being returned to the school following their summer vacation in 1936. The lawyer contacted the agent, saying the complainant had related "a very hard story of the treatment young Indian children receive there. It would

appear that his own experience has been so hard that he dreads very much the idea of going back there, and naturally, feels it hard to see his younger brother and sister taken there, where they will receive similar treatment."

The agent did not believe there were grounds for complaint, but forwarded the lawyer's letter to the school principal who, in his written reply to the agent, seemed quite unsettled by it. "To let them get away with their lies doesn't seem the right thing to do—to keep them from spreading falsehoods about those who try to do something for them seems hopeless. And why white people fall for such stories is hard to explain. *For myself I never hope to catch up with him and his lies....* I think the best thing to do is write to the Department and since we have a full school, request a few more beds and insist upon them coming back. *I am getting a bit tired of playing square with the Indian and in turn have him cut my throat.*"

He added that the lawyer didn't understand the regulations, which called for one half day in the classroom and the other half in labour, and recalled that the former pupil who had hired him was merely "a big body with the mind of a ten year old child.... To play a game of baseball was work for him; he would rather sit in the sun and pester a bumble bee or a fly, by pulling off one wing and one leg at a time. *To make an Indian work is the unpardonable sin among them.*"

The principal called the allegations of hard treatment "ridiculous," and could not understand how a lawyer could be "*duped by an Indian.*" *The Department decided not to insist upon the return of the children, but also denied any financial aid that would allow them to pursue an education elsewhere.*[11]

The racist statements of this priest show just what First Nations citizens were up against in trying to acquire civil rights and justice in a prejudiced society. The cutting off of financial aid was a tool the Department used liberally to obtain compliance. As mentioned, this was one of the fears that had compelled the Mi'kmaq at Pictou Landing to give the politicians and bureaucrats what they wanted at Boat Harbour. Millward provides another example:

The same year a fifteen-year-old girl from the nearby Shubenacadie Reserve refused to return to the school and gave the following statement to the agent and the Royal Canadian Mounted Police:

"I have been going to Indian school for the past five years.... Before my holidays this year I was employed in kitchen for eleven weeks.... In the eleven weeks ... I spent a total of two weeks in school. The Sister has beaten me many times over the head and pulled my hair and struck me on the back of neck with a ruler and at times grabbed ahold of me and beat me on the back with her fists.

I have also been ordered *to stand on the outside of the windows with a rope around my waist to clean windows on the fourth floor with a little girl holding the rope.* When I told the Sister I was afraid to go out the window she scolded me and made me clean the window and threatened to beat me if I did not do it. This is being done to other children.

Four stories up and terrified

> After we get a beating we are asked what we got the beating for and if we tell them we do not know we get another beating. The Sisters always tell us not to tell our parents about getting a beating."[12]

The following incident is one of the many my brothers and cousins said happened during their incarcerations that added strength to Mom's threat:

> One student remembers a particularly cruel incident, which took place at meal-time. The top of a salt shaker became loose, and when one boy used it to spice his porridge, the entire contents fell in a pile onto his meal:
> "He started to spoon it back into the salt shaker, at least the dry stuff. The Sister was watching…. She came over to see what was going on. She found the fellow spooning the salt back. She told him to stop that. "Since you like salt on your porridge, you might as well eat what's in your bowl."

Forced feeding of waste

He wouldn't. There was just too much salt in it. Nobody would. So she hit him in the back of the neck. "Eat it!" So he finally took his spoon and took a mouthful of the stuff. It didn't stay down long. It came back up into his bowl. So she whacked him in the back of the head and said, "I told you to eat it!"

So he started to cry, took the spoon and tried to eat some more, and that came back up. About the third time he fainted. Instead of picking him up off the floor to help him up onto the bench, she picked him up by the neck and threw him out to the centre aisle. That Nun was full of that kind of stuff."[13]

Medical experimentation also took place at these institutions. This example, reported in the May 8, 2000, issue of *Maclean's* magazine makes one wonder whether this is modern Canada or a throwback to the Dark Ages:

> *Natives denied dental care*—Federal government doctors withheld specialized dental care, such as professional cleaning and treatment of decay, for aboriginal children living in eight residential schools in the 1940s and 1950s to see what the effect would be on their health. The director of the study, Dr. L.B. Pett, said last week that students' teeth and gums were in terrible condition to begin with, and that delaying treatment did not create more decay, but helped keep the study's results accurate.

Such views about experiments using people deemed "inferior" as guinea pigs were expressed by another majority group, the Nazis. As might be expected from a systemically racist society, to my knowledge not one word of condemnation has been uttered about this revelation from any level of government or human rights commission in Canada.

Isabelle Knockwood, a Mi'kmaq author and former resident of the Shubenacadie residential school, wrote a book entitled *Out of the Depths*, published in 1992, which provides many other vivid accounts of the brutalities suffered by residents.

Many of today's prominent First Nations leaders were once incarcerated and abused in these institutions. Phil Fontaine, former National Chief the Assembly of First Nations, was one of them. He provides this wise advice based on his experience:

The Residential School experience had serious negative consequences for many of our people who have suffered in silence for too long. It is time to take the first step and let others know they are not alone in their suffering. No matter how painful, the stories of our people must be told and heard. Through sharing our past, we can begin to heal ourselves, our communities, and our people as we look to a better tomorrow.[14]

Another negative factor associated with residential schools, though not restricted exclusively to them, was the policy adopted by the Canadian government of permitting the adoption of First Nations children by non-Indians from around the world. Many of these children are re-establishing contact with their racial peers, but many have been lost to their people forever!

In its June 26, 2000, issue *Maclean's* magazine reported that 6,324 former inmates of these institutions have currently filed lawsuits against the federal government and the four Churches it had contracted with to act as administrators— Roman Catholic, Anglican, United and Presbyterian—and predicts that the number of litigants could double. Settlement may run into billions and as a result several of the Churches fear bankruptcy.

Indian Day Schools

I attended the Indian Day School located on Shubenacadie Indian (now Indian Brook) Reserve during my elementary grades. As required by law we were taught by the Roman Catholic Sisters of Charity and had a priest as principal. Here are two of many incidents which have left a lifelong impression on me.

The first was the scene of a Sister dragging one girl, who was very frightened by the prospect of visiting a dentist, down two flights of stairs by the hair of her head to get treatment, then the screams as the dentist and nun forced it upon her. Her parents were not consulted.

The second was when a Sister assigned to the Reserve's convent, because of stereotypical images she held of us as savages, became so frightened upon first contact that she had to be sent back to the Mother House in Halifax for reassignment. She presented a perfect example of how well negative brainwashing works. Although many of the people who stayed were kind and treated the children in the day and residential schools decently, they were just as guilty as the cruel ones because they tolerated the sadism and did nothing to stop it.

During my day school experience I cannot recall any effort being made— except for a brief reference to basket weaving and other traditional crafts—to teach us about our heritage and culture. In fact both schools tried to imprint in our minds a picture of our culture as being inferior to White culture. This effort failed miserably. However, they did succeed in increasing our resentment toward our persecutors, especially the federal government.

One positive thing these institutions did provide was daily doses of vitamins to students. In the long run this proved most beneficial. The incidence of death among young children dropped dramatically and by 1950 the population began slowly to increase. These stats show how the Mi'kmaq population of Nova Scotia fluctuated after Confederation: From Joe Howe's estimate in 1843 of approximately 1,300, the official population climbed to 1,666 in 1871, to 2,076 in 1891, fell to 1,542 in 1901, then rose again to 2,048 in 1921. By 1949 the population reached 2,641 (this included Maliseets and Mi'kmaqs imported from N.B. and P.E.I., the Mi'kmaqs native to Nova Scotia numbered approximately 2,000), grew to 3,561 in 1959, 4,647 in 1970, 5,868 in 1980, and to 11,000 by 1999.[15] The drop of 534 persons between 1891 and 1901 can be explained by a smallpox epidemic and the migration of many families to the States. Infant mortality and death from diseases such as consumption remained high throughout the first sixty years of the twentieth century and slowed population growth. The root cause of the suscepti- bility to these diseases remained the same as it had been in the nineteenth century: substandard living conditions and malnutrition.

The education situation today is much improved. Since the Mi'kmaq began to assume administration of the Department's education programs in the mid-1980s, children are staying in school much longer and enrolment beyond grade school has increased dramatically. But the impact from this will not be felt to any substantial degree in First Nations communities until 2010 or later.

On January 7, 1998, Prime Minister Jean Chretien had Minister of Indian Affairs Jane Stewart issue a half-assed apology for the mistreatment of our children in residential schools. In doing so the government accepted no responsibility for any of what happened. It seems that the apology was given to limit damages to the government and not sincerely to atone for past wrongs.

In contrast, in the case of Japanese Canadians who were detained in camps during the Second World War, the Prime Minister of Canada personally delivered the apology and provided compensation for the wrong committed. In our case we get a junior minister, no real apology and no compensation! This is par for the course when it comes to equal treatment for our peoples.

The One Band Theory

The preposterous "One Nova Scotia Band" concept that the government adopted in the 1920s is tied to its overall incompetence in administering the affairs of the province's Bands. Here is the genesis of this theory:

During the first half of the 1900s, although it paid lip service to the ideal, Indian Affairs made no real effort to assist the Mi'kmaq to overcome the inherited destitution they were living in. In fact the record reveals that during this period, instead of curing poverty, the Indian Affairs Branch's main concerns were whether the Mi'kmaq on the mainland should be forced onto Reserves or off Reserves, or moved to other Reserves.

Indecision about where to move the Mi'kmaq eventually led the bureaucrats to invent a removal program. Although the program was their idea, they deemed that the Mi'kmaq who were to "benefit" from this great idea had to pay for it. To help them pay for something they didn't want, in the early part of the century Indian Affairs engineered the surrender of many Reserves on the mainland. This was the official reason given. However, the main reason I have gleaned from the records, although not mentioned outright, is that members of the White popula- tion in many areas of the province wanted to be rid of the Indians and wanted their land.

To entice Band members to cooperate with the selling off of their lands, the bureaucrats sweetened the proposal by claiming the land sales would also raise money to assist with economic development. The fact that the amounts received for these properties were below market value erodes the economic development contention considerably, but what finishes it off completely is that no economic development ever occurred.

The below-market prices mentioned were so good that they attracted well-connected members of the White population, even Members of Parliament, for example M.B. Daley, MP for Halifax. These deals raise many questions. The most obvious is why the Department didn't demand top dollar for these properties as its trust responsibility required. In seeking answers to such questions I am always forced back to the same conclusions: careless disregard for duty, corruption, incompetence, racism etc.

A fine example of how the bureaucrats used their removal policy is their decision in the early 1900s to move the Mi'kmaq Band of Halifax County to Truro (now Millbrook) Reserve. They financed the move by the sale of the three surrendered Halifax County Reserves: Sambro, Ingram River and Ship Harbour. As an enticement the Department promised that any excess funds from the sale of these properties, after buying more land to add to the existing Reserve at Truro, would be used for economic development.

The irony of this move, touted as a way to improve the Halifax Band's standard of living, was that within twenty years Indian Affairs would be trying to force these same people or their descendants to move again, this time to Indian Brook, also supposedly to improve their standard of living.

The next action is possibly connected to the Department's removal policy, but probably more connected to its incompetence and stupidity. Adding to the mess it was in the middle of creating for itself in Nova Scotia by mismanagement of Indian Reserve land assets, in 1919 the federal government, upon the recommendation of Superintendent Buoy, irresponsibly dumped the accumulated Band trust fund moneys of the Nova Scotia Bands into one pot. It then spent these funds without exercising its responsibility to expend them solely for the benefit of the Band they were raised and held in trust for. In contrast, and in accordance with the law, in New Brunswick trust funds that were transferred to the federal government at Confederation were not consolidated by the Department into one fund.

In the 1930s, probably in realization of the legal blunder it had made in consolidating the trust funds, and in what appears to be a blatant attempt to legitimize its folly, Indian Affairs started pushing the concept of "One Mi'kmaq Band" in Nova Scotia. Such an idea flew in the face of the fact that the Mi'kmaq of Nova Scotia had always been recognized as separate Bands and were members of a structured political system.

In addition, many other facts flatly refute the "One Band" sham. For example, historical documentation shows that the English were at same time at peace with some of the Bands while at war with others. Countless other documents repudiate the concept, such as this report about the Cape Breton Mi'kmaq coming to Halifax in 1864 to protest the use of their "trust fund moneys" to purchase land for the

Pictou Landing Band:

> Your committee had before them Indian delegates, representing the views of
> their tribe, from the Island of Cape Breton, Paul Christmas, Michael Christmas
> and Paul Andrews.... The Cape Breton Indians disapprove of the funds arising
> from the sale of their lands being used for the purchase of lands for the Pictou
> Indians. Your committee would therefore recommend that the purchase of said
> land become a charge upon the Province, and the amount paid out of the Indian
> reserve fund to be again restored as part of said fund.[16]

After rumours of the consolidation began to leak out to the Bands, Indian Affairs
received many inquiries about the location of Band fund monies from Band members, especially members of the Halifax County Band who were concerned about
the whereabouts of the money raised from the sale of their Reserves in the 1920s.
The response to these inquiries was, "No, they are being held separately," an
outright lie.

There is no question in my mind that the preposterous "One Band" notion the
bureaucrats were pushing was intended to cover up their culpability in mismanag-
ing trust moneys. This fact says it all: if the Mi'kmaq truly constituted only one
Band, then the Band funds of the Mi'kmaq of New Brunswick, Prince Edward
Island and Quebec should have also been consolidated in 1919. Cover-up is the
only rational conclusion that can be reached from the information available. The
Mi'kmaq Bands collectively constitute one First Nation, not one Band!

What adds a ton of weight to the conclusion of cover-up is that there was a
strong motive for it. The mishandling of the trust fund monies of the Nova Scotia
Bands could cost the Crown an enormous amount of money if successfully litigated. When one calculates the principal and compound interest on the monies the
Bands had from Confederation to now, the amount owing to them is staggering—
tens of millions of dollars. A successful lawsuit by the Bands based on trust mismanagement could assure their financial security for the foreseeable future.

Centralization

This quote about the near demise of the Wampanoag First Nation from a literary
piece by D.H. Reddall also aptly describes the situation of the Mi'kmaq First
Nation in the twentieth century:

> Today there are only a couple of thousand Wampanoags left in New Eng-
> land. No doubt they would agree with John Steinbeck: "The Indians sur-
> vived our open intentions of wiping them out, and since the tide turned they
> have weathered our good intentions towards them, which can be much more
> deadly."[17]

In late 1935 the Privy Council retained Dr. Thomas Robertson to undertake an
in-depth study of the living conditions of the Indians in the Maritimes. The following is an extract from the report he submitted to the Superintendent General of
Indian Affairs on June 9, 1936:

Housing Conditions

While there are a great many what we might call good houses among the Indians, while conditions vary in different districts, while better conditions exist among the Indians living on Reserves, more particularly those close to an Agent, yet in every district there are unsanitary houses, houses badly in need of repair and, in the great majority of districts, houses that are absolutely unfit for occupation.

Health Conditions

There is a lot of T.B. and venereal diseases. *While there has been considerable improvement in the health of the Indians of late, this condition cannot hope to be continued under the present undernourished conditions*, bad housing and the close contact of children with parents and other members of the family who are suffering from tuberculosis.

From the foregoing it will be seen that conditions among the Indians are very bad and many of them are depending wholly upon what they receive from the Government for their support.

The opinion of the man on the street is that the Indian is lazy, useless and himself responsible for his present conditions. However, a study of the record of each individual shows that the great majority of the Indians are good workers and that *his present condition is due to matters over which he has little or no control.*

For evidence of this we have but to look at conditions as they exist today in the activities by which he formerly obtained his livelihood, i.e., fishing, hunting, trapping, labour, etc. Hunting and trapping is a thing of the past. Very few are engaged in fishing, principally because today fishing is a deep water proposition and the Maritime Indian is not a deep water man. [This incorrect assessment must have been hauled out of the blue.]

No one will employ an Indian today, *he is a "ward" of the Government.*

Farming

While this is not one of the methods by which he formerly obtained his living, it is one on which the Government has expended considerable money in breaking land and supplying him with fertilizer and seed. Before condemning the Indian for not increasing his farming operations, let us look at conditions under which he was asked to do so.

He knew nothing about farming, he needed instruction. *He is a good worker only under supervision.* He was given neither instruction nor supervision. His land was broken, he was given fertilizer and seed and then left to his own devices. If he ate the seed potatoes and sold the fertilizer, as many of them did, he received his full relief allowance, but if he produced a crop his allowance was reduced. *He was penalized for producing and bonused for non-production.*

With the exception of a little labour in the potato fields of Maine, some pulp wood in parts of New Brunswick and Cape Breton and some guiding in Nova Scotia, the only source of revenue the Indian has today is from handles and baskets. Due to factory competition reducing the price, the Indian finds that after paying the costs of marketing his goods there is very little left for himself.

While the fact that the Indian population is increasing demands that he be made self-supporting, and a study of the record of the Indian as a worker shows that this can be done, many years have elapsed under the Government of both political Parties but no plan has been evolved whereby he may be placed in the position where he could be made self-supporting.

The situation today is that the Indian is deteriorating and looking more and more to the Government for his support. *That unless some plan is formulated whereby he may be placed in the position where he will be self-supporting, expenditures for the assistance of the Indian will have to be greatly increased.*

A search for means of increasing the Indian's earnings proves there is nothing to be gained from hunting, fishing or trapping, nor is there much to be hoped for in the realm of labour, but it does show that his revenue from handles, baskets and craft wood could be greatly increased.

With Indian goods superior as they are to the factory product, there can be no doubt a proper organization could secure contracts from consumers of these goods, such as governments, railways, parks, potato companies, etc., and also find new markets among tourists, merchants, etc., in this way saving of time and money now spent by the Indian peddling his goods, as well as increasing his sales.

While increased earnings from handle and craft work would be of great assistance, any plan in which there can be any hope for success in the placing of the Indian in a position where he may be made self-supporting must make agriculture its back-bone *with close and competent supervision its most vital essential.*[18]

Robertson outlined what he viewed to be the major problems facing First Nations in the Maritimes. However, he left out the one problem that is amply demonstrated in the words of his report—racism. Although he discusses it without calling it by name, and describes how it prevents the People from being self-sufficient, he offers no suggestions on how it might be effectively dealt with. Perhaps if he had interviewed my parents about it, he would have understood how terrible it was and made a few additional recommendations.

The following is an account of my parent's shocking experience with racism at the hands of the Saint John, New Brunswick, city council in 1935.

For several years Dad had worked on the Saint John waterfront. In the fall of 1935, due to a work shortage, he was laid off. Having a wife and five children to support and unable to get another job, he was forced to apply to the city for welfare assistance, which he initially received.

Then a bigot complained to the city council about the municipality providing welfare to an Indian. In spite of the fact that he had been a taxpayer prior to his layoff, the city immediately took steps to right what they perceived to be a wrong. In late November, without a home to go to and little more than the clothes on their backs, it sent my parents and their five small children packing on a train to the Indian Brook Reserve near the village of Shubenacadie, Nova Scotia. Making it even more frightening for them was the fact that they had never seen the Reserve before. Up to this time their experience with Reserve living had been very limited. Dad had been born and raised in the Sheet Harbour area of Nova Scotia, and Mom (Sarah, née Noel) had been born and raised near Enfield. The only experience either had had of living on a Reserve was when after getting married and prior to moving to New Brunswick in the 1920s, they had lived on the Millbrook Reserve near Truro for a short while.

However, they were soon to be educated. Upon their arrival at Indian Brook in late November 1935, the Indian Agent provided Dad with a few rolls of tar paper and some nails to build a tar paper shack, in which they spent two years and two cold winters. Then he built a small log cabin in which the family increased by three. I was the last of the three children born in the log cabin. He built a house for us in 1939 with building materials acquired from lumber mills in exchange for labour.

Dad never got over the trauma of being deported with a wife and five small children in late fall, with no home to go to, and ever after would not give a moment's consideration to moving away from the Reserve. The thought of their sad experience of deportation within their own country still leaves a bitter taste.

Robertson states that an "Indian" can work "only under supervision" by a White man. Although he was probably one of the more liberal-minded officials of the day, he was not above making such stereotypical statements. Unfortunately, this stereotype was adopted by the bureaucracy. They would mention their need to provide constant supervision in their reports for decades to come. When he mentions that Whites won't give Band members work because they regard them as lazy, shiftless and entirely responsible for their sad conditions, Robertson identifies a perception that still afflicts the citizens of First Nations in the twenty-first century.

When at Eskasoni gathering research for his report, Robertson met the Grand Chief of the Mi'kmaq and referred to him as the "Chief of Nova Scotia."[19] His ignorance is reminiscent of that of the colonial scribes who failed to identify Chiefs properly. Grand Chief Sylliboy was in fact the spiritual leader of all the Mi'kmaq and not a political leader. Robertson's misleading statement was, of course, based upon erroneous assumptions.

Interestingly, Robertson reported that he asked the Grand Chief if he had anything to suggest for the betterment of his people. The Chief replied, "*Yes, make my people work for everything they get. Make them break more land for cultivation in exchange for relief. You are ruining them.*"[20] If Sylliboy had added, "and help us overcome discrimination, exclusion, and oppression in this country," his statement would have been complete!

Robertson also pointed out in his report, as others had done in the past, that venereal disease was rampant among the Mi'kmaq and other First Nations. The reason why the disease was so prevalent among them is obvious. When a person is starving and society doesn't respond, that person will do almost anything to survive. Some of the women, and no doubt some of the men, turned to prostitution for survival, and by participating in this activity brought home the diseases.

Let's put this prostitution problem into perspective. To be forced to sell oneself for food because no other means is available is not a shame for the individual, it is a shame for society, especially a prosperous one. By its unrelenting bigotry and persecution, society forced the First Nations peoples to do every-thing in their power to survive. Today, with an adequate food supply and no need to buy it with sex, venereal diseases among First Nations citizens have become rare.

Robertson outlined these steps to make the Maritime First Nations self-suffi-cient:

(a)   Placing the Indians on reserves containing good agricultural land where he can be given a decent home. Instructions in farming and *proper supervision*.
(b)   Direct relief to be discontinued and all able to work required to work for anything received.
(c)   The appointment of full time agents whose duty will be not only super-vision, but also to find markets for the Indian's products.
(d)   The teaching of agriculture in the schools by school gardens and talks.
(e)   The giving of short courses in agriculture to a few Indian boys who show interest in agriculture.
(f)   The securing of the cooperation of the Indians by the holding of meetings for the purpose of discussing their problems with them.
(g)   The *full cooperation with the church in everything affecting the Indian*.
(h)   The encouragement of the Indian to produce by sharing with him any reduction in his allowance made possible by his own effort.
(i)   The granting of no assistance to Indians living off their Reserve [to force them back onto the Reserve; the Department did not completely cut off Reg-istered Indians living off Indian Reserves until 1967].

The adoption of this plan or policy would necessitate the securing of more Reserves as *there is not enough good land on the present ones*.[21]

He then provides an explanation for the drastic changes recommended:

The moving of quite a number of Indians. In order to find the Indians' feelings on this subject I spent considerable time discussing it with them in the different parts of the Province. All opposition disappeared when they found it would be to their own benefit.

The building of quite a number of homes. These houses should be built by the Indians themselves and *they should not be finished on the inside for sani-tary reasons*. A house one and a half stories, twenty by thirty, with eight windows and two doors, sufficient for a family of five, built in this way should not cost more than one hundred and seventy-five to two hundred dollars in Nova Scotia (Yarmouth).

The appointment of full-time competent Agents. It is impossible to give the *necessary supervision* with part-time men and that *supervision is absolutely necessary* is amply evidenced by the fact that only at places *where supervision is given* is there any headway being made.

On the appointment of *competent* Agents depends the success or failure of the plan, for we cannot have *proper supervision* without *competent men*. These Agents would not only *supervise* but they would also find markets for the

Indian's products. *In the appointment of these Agents no matter of any kind should be considered except the fitness of the man for the position. It should not be forgotten in the appointment of these men that they are to deal with human beings, whose bodily and spiritual welfare depends to a large extent upon the sympathetic execution of their duty.*

The securing of the Indians' cooperation through meetings. This in my opinion is another vital matter. No organization is ever of any force or effect unless the members feel they are a vital part of it and are consulted re. its affairs. This is true of the White man, and that it is also true of the Red is demonstrated by the fact that at Truro where this system has been adopted this year the Agent is getting full cooperation and is making real headway.

The full cooperation with the Church. This is another vital matter as both are working for the same object, the *welfare* of the Indian, and any friction would injure the cause.

Encouraging the Indian to produce. There is no question of the necessity of this as if there is no incentive there is not much work.

The giving of no assistance to Indians off the Reserve. While this would be the rule, there would be exceptions as there would be a number of cases where Indians had work for the greater part of the year and would require very little assistance to carry them through. In cases of that kind it would be folly to force them to return to the Reserve.[22]

By submitting this report Robertson set the stage for the further humiliation and degradation of the Mi'kmaq and Maliseet. The government used his report to formulate its new policy of "centralization." Under this plan the two peoples were to be relocated to four central locations, two in New Brunswick and two in Nova Scotia. One of the prime factors behind the move was the belief promoted by the bureaucracy that it would be more convenient to deliver services at these central-ized locations instead of the dozens then in existence. In Nova Scotia at that time there were nineteen locations staffed by political appointees. Needless to say, the opinions of the people who were to be affected most by centralization were not asked for or seriously considered.

Before proceeding further with the centralization saga, I want to present a few interesting documents. The following memo reveals one of the many reasons why First Nations peoples were willing to go along with the government's half-assed attempts to make a more prosperous life for them. It went out from the desk of R.A. Hoey, Superintendent of Welfare and Training in Ottawa, to all inspectors and Indian Agents across the country on May 22, 1940, and orders a reduction of the 1940 welfare rates. These indicate the degree of "generosity" the government of the day was dispensing while proceeding towards the implementation of its cen-tralization policy:

Indian Agents throughout the Dominion are instructed to undertake a com-plete revision of their ration lists and relief allowances. It is desirable that this revision should be completed not later than June 15.

It is not expected that *drastic reductions* can be made in the monthly rations authorized at present for the support of aged and physically incapacitated Indians. An attempt should be made, however, to reduce items such as tea or commodities imported from other countries.

The new lists should be submitted in due course for Departmental approval.

Relief allowances in the case of physically fit, able-bodied Indians should be cancelled not later than July 1. It is not the policy of the Department to provide able-bodied Indians with relief. All such Indians must undertake certain tasks either on the reserves or off the reserves. The cultivation of gardens, farm work, clearing land, road construction, drainage projects, wood cutting, etc. in certain districts are all tasks that might be undertaken.

Rations may be supplied to Indians engaged in such work. In no case, however, will it be permissible to supply relief to an Indian who refuses to undertake the task assigned him by the Agent; and the character of the work in which the Indian is engaged must be clearly stated on relief vouchers sent forward to the Department for payment.

We are attaching hereto a ration list to which you must strictly adhere. No payments will be made in future for commodities other than those included in the official list, except in cases of sickness, where special authorization has been secured from the Department.

A number of Indians have enlisted in the Canadian Active Service Force and the wives and dependents of these men are in receipt of government allowances. Care should be exercised by our Agents to prevent overlapping and duplication in Indian welfare effort.

Scale of Monthly Rations for Indian Relief						
No. of Adults	**1**	**2**	**3**	**4**	**5**	**6**
Ration	Lbs.	Lbs.	Lbs.	Lbs.	Lbs.	Lbs.
Flour 2nd grade	24	36	49	61	80	98
Rolled Oats	6	9	12	15	18	18
Baking Powder	1	1 3/4	1 3/4	2	2	2
Tea	1	1 1/2	2	2	2	3
Sugar	2	4	5	7	8	10
Lard	3	5	8	10	10	13
Beans	5	5	7	7	8	8
Rice	2	3	5	5	7	7
Cheese	1	1 1/2	1 1/2	2	2	3
Meat or Fish	$1.00	$1.50	$1.75	$2.00	$2.00	$2.25
Salt	.10 or .15 per month per family					
Matches	.10 to .20 per month per family					

NOTE: Indians under the age of 12 years shall be considered children, and over that age as adults. Issues of rations for each child, of flour, rolled oats, sugar, lard, beans, rice, cheese and meat or fish, shall be one half of the ration for an Adult.

Departmental approval must be secured for special rations recommended by the Medical Health Officer in cases of sickness, and milk that may be necessary in the case of infants.

Storekeepers should be warned that if they vary without authority the items contained in this list they are subject to immediate removal from the list of firms authorized to do Government Business. [These rations were purchase orders made out to specific stores whose owners were affiliated with the political party in power.][23]

Can you imagine this diet month after month, year after year, with very little variation? No milk for your children, no hope for the future except bare survival?

The "generosity" of Indian Affairs displayed in the memo rekindles bitter memories in me. I'll describe just one of them. When I was four or five years old, in 1942 or 1943, Dad had found a job a twenty-mile or so one-way walk away from home and would not get paid until the following week. We ran out of food on Friday and had to go without over the weekend. Early Monday morning Mom and I walked the three miles to the Indian Agency where she asked the well-fed Agent for a special ration.

Before long the Agent had her begging and crying. Then he told her she would have to wait while he thought it over. At about 11:50, ten minutes before his lunchtime, he called us in and gave mother a $2.00 special order, but not before subjecting her to more humiliating verbal abuse. I remember the event so well for two reasons: First, I was so hungry I could have literally eaten a raw porcupine. Second, it was on that day that I made up my mind that when I grew up no one would ever do to me what that bastard had done to my mother, without a fight. To this day no one ever has.

To shed a bit more light on the moronic racist attitudes prevalent in the Department that created such things as centralization, a review of a few more pieces of their sick output is in order. The following letter had been sent out from Ottawa to all Indian Agents by Superintendent General of Indian Affairs Duncan Elliott on December 15, 1921:

Sir:

It is *observed with alarm* that the holding of dances by the Indians on their reserves is in the increase, and that these practices tend to disorganize the efforts which the Department is putting forth to make them self-supporting.

I have, therefore, to direct you to use your utmost endeavours *to dissuade the Indians from excessive indulgence in the practice of dancing.* You should suppress any dances which cause waste of time, interfere with the occupations of the Indians, unsettle them for serious work, injure their health or encourage them in sloth and idleness.

You should also dissuade, and, if possible, *prevent them from leaving their reserves for the purpose of attending fairs, exhibitions, etc.,* when their absence would result in their own farming and other interests being neglected. It is realized that reasonable amusement and recreation should be enjoyed by Indians, but they should *not be allowed* to dissipate their energies and abandon themselves to *demoralizing* amusements. By the use of tact and firmness, you can control and keep it, and this obstacle to continued progress will then disappear.

The rooms, halls or other places in which Indians congregate should be under constant inspection. They should be scrubbed, fumigated, cleansed or disinfected to prevent the dissemination of disease. The Indians should be instructed in regard to the matter of proper ventilation and the avoidance of overcrowded rooms where public assemblies are being held, and proper arrangement should be made for the shelter of their horses and ponies. The Agent will avail himself of the services of the medical attendant of his agency in this connection.[24]

Eliott's memo displays the same White supremacist mentality that guided the authors of Section 140 of the 1927 Indian Act:

Dances and Festivals

140. (1) *Every Indian or other person who engages in, or assists in celebrating or encourages, either directly or indirectly, another to celebrate any Indian Festival, dance, or other ceremony* of which the giving away or paying or giving back of money, goods or articles of any sort forms a part, or is a feature, whether such gift of money, goods or articles takes place before, at, or after the celebration of the same or who engages or assists in any celebration or dance of which *the wounding or mutilation of the dead or living body of any human being* or animal forms a part or is a feature, *is guilty of an offence and is liable on summary conviction to imprisonment for a term not exceeding six months and not less than two months.*

(2) Nothing in this section shall be construed to prevent the holding of any agricultural show or exhibition or the giving away of prizes for exhibits thereat.

(3) Any Indian in the provinces of Manitoba, Saskatchewan, Alberta or British Columbia or in the Territories who participates in *any Indian Dance outside the bounds of his own reserve, or who participates in any show, exhibition, performance, stampede or pageant in aboriginal costume without the consent of the Superintendent General or his authorized agent*, and any person who induces or employs any Indian to take part in such dance, show, exhibition, performance, stampede or pageant, or induces any Indian to leave his reserve or employs any Indian for such a purpose, whether the dance, show, exhibition, stampede or pageant has taken place or nor, *shall on summary conviction be liable to a penalty not exceeding twenty five dollars, or to imprisonment for one month, or to both penalty and imprisonment.*[25]

This section directly attacks the traditions of First Nations. It also denies them an opportunity to earn a living. To demand that permission must be obtained from another racial segment of the population to do something other groups can do without restriction is not paternalism as some would like to believe; it is simply *mindless White supremacist racism.* Never did any Canadian legislation require Scottish Canadians, for instance, to receive government permission to entertain in their traditional costumes for pay.

The prohibition against mutilating the dead in Section 140 is particularly offensive because First Nations peoples of Canada have always held their dead in the highest respect and would never have maliciously mutilated their remains. Some rites performed by certain First Nations over their dead may have caused some people of European Christian extraction some discomfort, but the European practice of performing autopsies and embalming the dead probably caused some First Nations peoples discomfort also.

The following old section of the Indian Act is another delightful example of the "enlightened" European mentality at work:

Poolrooms

140.   (a)   Where it is made to appear in open court that any Indian, summoned before such court, by *inordinate frequenting of a poolroom either on or off a reserve*, misspends or wastes his time or means to the detriment of himself, his family or household, of which he is a member, the police magistrate, stipendiary magistrate, Indian agent, or two justices of the peace holding such court, shall by writing under his or their hand or hands forbid the owner or person in charge of a poolroom which such Indian is in the habit of frequenting to allow such Indian to enter such poolroom for the space of one year from the date of such notice.

Any owner or person in charge of a poolroom who allows an Indian to enter a poolroom in violation of such notice, and *any Indian who enters a poolroom where his admission has been so forbidden, shall be liable on summary conviction to a penalty not exceeding twenty five dollars and costs or to imprisonment for a term not exceeding thirty days.*[26]

I attended business college in Truro during 1960-61 and was not permitted to enter the poolroom because I was a Mi'kmaq. I didn't know then that this had once been mandated by statute. The poolroom operator's attitude was probably a combination of racism and fear of violating a law he may have thought was still in effect.

Another gem set out in the Indian Act of 1930 appears to have been enacted to stifle entrepreneurial initiative:

Prevention of Trade

120.   Every person who buys or otherwise acquires from any Indian, or band or irregular band of Indians, in the province of Manitoba, Saskatchewan, or Alberta, or the Territories, any cattle or other animals or any grain, root crops or other produce or sells to any such Indian any goods or supplies, cattle or other animals contrary to the provisions of this Act, shall on summary conviction, be liable to a penalty not exceeding one hundred dollars, or to imprisonment for a term not exceeding three months, or to both.[27]

The three sections just mentioned remained, in one form or another, part of the Act until 1951.

To get the centralization show on the road, in late 1939 and early 1940, Indian Affairs bureaucrats in Ottawa formulated a plan for the creation of two Indian agencies on the two Reserves in Nova Scotia where the Mi'kmaq were to be relocated—Shubenacadie and Eskasoni. Before implementing the plan, the planners deemed that the land base of the two Reserves was too small for the needs of the envisioned communities and therefore had to be increased substantially. At the same time plans were being prepared to build compounds on the two Reserves to house agency staff and the teachers for the envisioned schools.

During 1941, letters were exchanged between Premier of Nova Scotia A.S. MacMillan and federal Minister of Mines and Resources T.A. Crerar concerning the feasibility of centralizing the province's Mi'kmaq Bands. In his memo to the Premier dated April 24, 1941, the Minister provided an outline of the plan and asked for the Premier's support:

> It is of course not my wish to make any radical changes in the administration of Indian Affairs in your Province without first letting you know what we plan to do. While the *Indians are the "Wards" of the dominion*, their welfare is a matter in which the Provinces are also interested. The co-operation we receive from the Provinces makes our task less difficult or, to put it into other words, the more co-operation we receive from the Provinces the more quickly will it be possible to improve the physical welfare of the Indians.[28]

In the same letter the Minister also informed the Premier that he would be appointing a bureaucrat to come to Nova Scotia to investigate possibilities of acquiring additional lands for the implementation of centralization. He advises that a W.S. Arneil, by reason of experience in land settlement work with the "Soldier Settlement Board," is specially qualified for the task. Mr. Arneil actually knew nothing about First Nations peoples or the laws surrounding the administration of "Indian lands," but in their opinion he was eminently qualified.

The Minister wrote his letter on April 24, 1941, and the Premier gave his full support to the concept, without much review, only five days later:

> Dear Mr. Grerar:
>
> I have your letter with regard to the Indian Reserves in this Province and note carefully all that you have to say. This is entirely a new departure and no doubt will meet with some opposition from the Indians themselves—this, due to the fact that a number of these reservations are located near towns, for instance Shubenacadie, Truro, etc. and being near of course the Indians have the habit of spending their time loafing around the towns. However, I think if an agreement could be reached that the idea is a practical one and there are plenty of vacant lands where they can be placed in this Province.
>
> I shall be glad to meet your representative when he comes, and go into the matter with him and shall also put him in touch with the proper persons in our Lands and Forests Department as well as with our Farm Loan Board which is also an operating body. Possibly when he comes to Halifax he had better see me before discussing this matter with others.
>
> A.S. MacMillan.[29]

It seems that Premier MacMillan may have harboured hopes of putting the Mi'kmaq as far away from White settlements as the boundaries of Nova Scotia might permit. It's a wonder he didn't recommend Sable Island. His quick response to the proposal was truly amazing, in stark contrast to the usual way such matters progressed.

The "qualified" bureaucrat Arneil, with the impressive title of Inspector of Indian Agencies, began his inspections and appraisals of the Reserves and their inhabitants in the Maritime Provinces shortly thereafter. He quickly began to issue short preliminary reports; one of the first was on Eskasoni. His lack of experience regarding Nova Scotia winters is obvious when he states, "*because the houses there are mostly shells, they are very hard to heat, but adequate.*"[30]

As one who has lived in an uninsulated house during a Nova Scotia winter, I can attest to the fact that they are not adequate! I remember waking up after a cold winter's night to find a considerable frost build-up around where my nose was sticking out of the blankets. To avoid freezing to death in cold weather we piled every coat in the house onto our beds.

Mr. Arneil also stated that more than 75 percent of the Mi'kmaq in the province of Nova Scotia were in favour of centralization. As he was in contact with only a few during his travels throughout the Maritimes, this is an outrageous assessment. It would appear that one of the most valued qualities sought in prospective "qualified" employees of the Department was the ability to play fast and loose with the truth when it comes to statistics on Band members.

In 1942, with the Privy Council's endorsement of two agency locations in both Nova Scotia and New Brunswick, the Department hired four full-time Indian Agents and implemented its centralization plan for the Maritimes. Thus a new challenge to the survival of the region's Mi'kmaq and Maliseet cultures was created.

From the onset of the plan's implementation, opposition was very strong among some members of the Bands. As time passed this opposition came to be held by the majority. As a matter of fact the Agent at Eskasoni, J.A. MacLean, in a moment of truth admitted to Hoey in a letter dated May 27, 1944, "*that approximately 75 percent of the Mi'kmaq in Nova Scotia were opposed to centralization.*"[31]

In a response to MacLean's memo, dated June 5, 1944, Hoey said: "The writer is of the opinion that *you should not attach too much importance to this nominal opposition.*"[32] If Mr. Hoey considered 75 percent to be a small opposition, just what would he have considered a large opposition? He went on to say: "It is altogether likely that the delay in moving these bands to Eskasoni has resulted in a certain amount of dissatisfaction."[33]

Among the most ardent and consistent opponents to the centralization plan was a member of the Membertou Band, the late Ben Christmas. Ben was at the time the President of the United General Indian Council of Nova Scotia and, after 1923, Chief of the Membertou Band, a position he held for forty years. Also among the early opponents of the plan was Chief Joseph Julien of Millbrook, Margaret Phillips of Cole Harbour, Noel Marshall of Chapel Island and Joseph Cope of Halifax County.

However, Chief Christmas, a very articulate man, was considered by the Department the most influential among them. He would have been amused by a description of him written by the Eskasoni Indian Agent dated March 1, 1943, concerning his opposition to the Department's centralization plans. MacLean wrote: "It appears that Ben Christmas, an Indian of Membertou Reserve, Sydney, N.S., who is considered to be *somewhat more intelligent than the ordinary Indian....*"[34] MacLean obviously had a low opinion about the intelligence of Native Americans in general and was amazed Mr. Christmas could rise above this standard. He continued: "I have been asked to inform you that no notice should be taken of letters from Mr. Christmas regarding the centralization plan, or from others who may write in this regard, as regardless of whose name may be used as a signature, Mr. Christmas is *the man behind the gun.*"[35]

However, opposition didn't stop the Department from ploughing ahead with implementation. It acquired lands with ease for the expansion of Eskasoni Reserve, but acquiring lands for the expansion of Indian Brook Reserve was a different matter. The Assistant Deputy Minister wrote the following memo dated August 13, 1943, to the Deputy Minister to suggest a way to resolve the matter:

> Further consideration has been given to the situation that has developed in connection with the Shubenacadie Indian Reserve and as a result I have been directed to suggest that *expropriation* be undertaken. If you concur I would ask that you supply me with a plan of survey and description by the surveyor covering the original Reserve and all properties acquired or desired to be acquired for extensions to the same.[36]

Its willingness to expropriate land shows how determined the Department was to erase all obstacles and implement its centralization plan. In contrast, in the late 1970s when I suggested that expropriation be used to acquire a right-of-way into Grand Lake Indian Reserve for the Shubenacadie Band, the Department was horrified and claimed that expropriation could not be used. Given their willingness to use it in the cause of centralization, it may be said without reservation that the only reason there is still no right-of-way into the Grand Lake Indian Reserve is that the Band wants one and the Department does not. If the Department sincerely wants to acquire one for the Band it could simply use its powers of expropriation.

With the centralization plan in motion and budgets in place, work soon commenced on the administrative and residential compounds for the staff. When finished the homes in these compounds housed a group of people who lived like kings and queens in comparison to ourselves. These homes were furnished at government expense with modern conveniences—electric ranges, fridges, freezers etc. They were insulated, had central heating and indoor plumbing, and were finished on the inside—to us a luxury beyond reach.

After these homes were occupied I can remember walking by the convent at meal times in the 1940s and looking through the window into the dining room. There a table would be set with sterling silver and bone china and be loaded down with a wider variety of food than I ever had imagined to exist.

In contrast, this is how we lived in those days: Our homes were uninsulated shells with no services whatsoever. Heat was supplied by cast-iron woodburning kitchen ranges and a tin stove. Water was carried from a hand-dug well and our lights were kerosene lamps. Electricity was brought to the Reserve in 1941 but only to serve the Indian Affairs compound. It was not extended to the entire Reserve until the early 1950s.

The bulk of our furniture was self-produced and generally made of rough lumber. Factory-produced furniture was a luxury mostly beyond our means until Family Allowance was introduced in 1948. Most beds were of the rough-lumber vintage and most mattresses were made out of coarse animal feed bags filled with straw. Our sheets, if any, and much of our underwear were made out of Robin Hood flour bags. Most of our clothing was second-hand. I can remember attending school one year wearing a girl's coat. Most of the men on the Reserve wore used RCMP clothing. I still can see my cousin, who was less than ten years old, wearing huge Mountie boots and coats.

The men invariably carried our rations home on their backs from the village of Shubenacadie, a distance of five miles. At times they made two trips: one to carry home the basic groceries and the second to carry home a ninety-eight-pound bag of flour. Milk was practically an unknown luxury in our household. Instead of drinking milk as a child, more often than not I drank black tea. Expensive cuts of meat, such as steaks and roasts, were also unknown. On more than one occasion a stuffed porcupine took the place of a chicken or turkey at a holiday meal. At one time to find a live porcupine within a five-mile radius of the Shubenacadie Indian Reserve was a rare feat. However, with centralization on the go, our food-shortage problem was coming to an end; the Department had a "plan" to end it.

Around 1946 they implemented their plan to make farmers out of the inexperienced Mi'kmaq. I'll relate my father's experience. He was a man who had no formal education, could neither read nor write, and had worked as a lumberman, rough carpenter, or labourer when work could be found. Now the bureaucrats had developed a strong belief that he, at the age of 46, with no aptitude for it, no experience, and no arable land to use, could become a productive farmer. To help him get the farm up and running the Department provided a loan out of the revolving fund to buy a cow and provided assistance to build a small barn. It also provided seed potatoes and vegetable seed for planting in the sterile clay-and-stone soil. Amazingly, he did manage to grow some crops from this infertile soil, although the fruits of his efforts were only about 25 percent of what could have been grown in good soil. The farming improved our well-being only marginally, if at all.

Perhaps the best way I can attest to the poverty we suffered during these years is by sharing this: I can remember walking down to the village of Shubenacadie on the rare Saturday when we had a few cents to attend a movie, and as I passed the homes and farms of the White people along the way I would dream about someday being as rich as they were. It was not until years later that I realized that most of the people I had envied had in reality been poor themselves. Your poverty must be outstanding if you think the poor of another race are rich.

That centralization and racism were synonymous was amply demonstrated throughout the founding and implementation of the plan. Without a doubt the prime factor in choosing Eskasoni and Shubenacadie was the desire to accommodate the White population's wish to move the "Indian problem" out of sight and out of mind. J. Ralph Kirk, Member of Parliament for Antigonish-Guysborough, affirms this in a memo he wrote on November 15, 1944, to the Director of Indian Affairs, Mr. Hoey:

> Would you be good enough to advise me as to whether or not the Department of Indian Affairs intends to take any move in the near future respecting the transfer of all Indians in Nova Scotia to one or two central places of habitation?
>
> I have had inquires from some of my constituents, *expressing the hope that the Indians living in the neighbourhood of Bayfield, N.S. would be moved away from there soon*, and this leads me to inquire as to the present status of the Department's plans in this connection.
>
> Your early reply re the matter will be much appreciated.
>
> J. Ralph Kirk.[37]

Responding to Mr. Kirk's inquiries, the Acting Director of the Department's welfare program penned the following letter dated January 6, 1945:

> As you are no doubt aware, for many years *the problem of how to administer* the affairs of the small group of Indians in Nova Scotia has been a matter of serious concern and in order to place it on the soundest possible basis a partial consolidation of the Reserves and the gradual *centralization of the Indian population has been decided upon.*
>
> I am sure you will appreciate the difficulties and wasteful expenditure of public moneys that are involved in trying to educate, hospitalize, train and care for the relatively few Indians of your Province when they are scattered in small groups and on widely *separated reserves selected with little regard either to adequacy of area, suitable as to character of the land, or to the amenities of the situation of important white settlements.*
>
> I am sure you will agree that the worst conditions prevail on those reserves that are located on the outskirts of important industrial cities and communities, and in such locations it has been our experience that vice, immorality and poverty exist to a much greater degree than prevails where the Indians live closer to nature and in a less artificial environment.
>
> With the hope of improving conditions, plans were made toward consolidation and centralization of the reserves in the knowledge, may I say, that under such a plan we would be able to offer the Indian better educational and vocational facilities, added attention to his physical, moral and spiritual welfare, and to create a condition more closely approaching a self-sustaining livelihood for him than is possible at present. *It was felt that we would also improve the amenities of the White communities which are not improved by the immediate presence of isolated groups of Indians.*[38]

To assure that Whites could improve the "amenities" of their communities by having Indians removed from close proximity, the government included this section in the Indian Act:

Removal of Indians

46.   (1)   In the case of an Indian reserve which adjoins or is situated wholly or partly within an incorporated town or city having a population of not less than eight thousand … the Governor in Council may, upon the recommendation of the Superintendent General, refer to the judge of the Exchequer Court of Canada for inquiry and report the question as to whether it is expedient, having regard to the *interest of the public* and of the Indians of the band for whose use the reserve is held, that *the Indians should be removed* from the reserve or any part of it.…

If the judge finds that it is expedient that the band of Indians should be removed from the reserve or any part of it, he shall proceed, before making his report, to ascertain the amounts of compensation, if any, which should be paid respectively to individual Indians of the band for the special loss or damages which they will sustain in respect of the buildings or improvements to which they are entitled upon the lands of the reserve for which they are located.….

The judge shall transmit his findings, with the evidence and a report of the proceedings, to the Governor in Council, who shall lay a full report of the proceedings … before Parliament … and upon such findings being approved by resolution of Parliament the Governor in Council may thereupon give effect to the said findings and cause the reserve, or any part thereof from which it is found expedient to remove the Indians, to be sold or leased by public auction after three months advertisement in the public press, upon the best terms which in the opinion of the Governor in Council, may be obtained therefor.

The proceeds of the sale or lease, after deducting the usual percentage for management fund, shall be applied in compensating individual Indians for their buildings or improvements as found by the judge, in purchasing a new reserve for the Indians removed, in transferring the said Indians with their effects thereto, in erecting buildings upon the new reserve, and in providing the Indians with such other assistance as the Superintendent General may consider advisable.…

For the purpose of selecting [a] new reserve to be acquired for the Indians … the Superintendent General shall have all the powers conferred upon the Minister by the Expropriation Act.[39]

Shortly after the turn of the century this provision was used in Nova Scotia. The victims were the Mi'kmaq residing near Kings Road in Sydney (about where the Holiday Inn is now located). Whites residing close to the area went to court and used the provision to force the Band members to move to Membertou Reserve.

No attempt has ever been made by the federal Crown to right this historic wrong. However, on March 21, 1999, at a dinner in Membertou the Mayor of the Cape Breton Regional Municipality, David Muise, officially apologized on behalf of the municipality to the descendants of the Mi'kmaq removed from their Kings Road Reserve starting in 1915. He told the gathering: "There's nothing we can do to undo the move.… What I'm here to do is start the healing process for wrongs of the past."[40] Right on, Mr. Mayor!

Section 46, in addition to being contrary to the laws of a civilized Nation, was contrary to human decency! Until it was repealed in 1951 this obnoxious section gave the bureaucrats an enormous club to wield in their efforts to force the First Nations peoples to do their bidding. The threat of removal caused the Mi'kmaq to think twice before opposing the Department. Adding to the obnoxiousness of the legislation was the fact that the Department could force the People to pay for their own expulsion, as was done in the case of the Sydney Mi'kmaq.

Hoey, in a follow-up memo dated November 16, 1944, to Kirk, assured him: "I can state, however, without hesitation, that there has been no change in the Government policy and that the work of centralization will be expedited by us to the utmost extent possible."[41] To persuade members from other Nova Scotia Bands to move from elsewhere on Cape Breton Island to Eskasoni, or from other locations on the mainland to Shubenacadie, the Department began a propaganda campaign that ran for several years. It painted a rosy future of self-sufficiency in the centralized communities—jobs galore, excellent housing, schools, recreation facilities; most important, food would be plentiful, preventing any more near famines; and accessible medical services would be provided. Clearly the Department deliberately lied to entice the People to move.

As could be expected the promised land never materialized. But in the short term unsustainable economic development was in full swing which helped give credibility to the propaganda. Sawmills were established on both central Reserves and new houses were built with the lumber produced. Tree cutting proceeded as if the wooded areas on both Reserves were inexhaustible, which of course they were not, keeping the sawmills running at full blast. Both mills paid scab wages and were hit by labour unrest around 1946. After the strikes were over, the men were still paid scab wages.

In answer to inquiries from Ottawa regarding the strike the Indian Agent wrote: "There didn't seem to be any communistic connotations to the strike at Eskasoni."[42] It is a testament to the level-headed thinking and intelligence of the First Nations peoples that during all the oppression they endured after Confederation they didn't turn, like other oppressed people in many parts of the world, to extremism to find solutions for their problems.

The Department made many foolish decisions while trying to keep centralization moving along. Perhaps the most incompetent was its decision that all houses were to be built from the *green lumber* produced by the mills. When the lumber dried, the houses twisted and warped beyond repair. In later years when these houses were torn down after being judged unfit for human habitation, cracks of more than one inch were discovered between most of the boards. In addition, the concrete used to lay foundations was of inferior quality and began to crack and crumble almost immediately. Of all the homes constructed during that period, no more than a few still stand.

The Department also used a more forceful approach than propaganda to force people to move to both locations. The residential school at Shubenacadie was put to use in this effort. Many families had their children taken away from them and placed in the school for "protection." The Department's explanation was that their dwellings were unfit for human habitation and therefore the health of their children was at risk. Parents were told their children would be returned to them after they moved to Shubenacadie or Eskasoni.

By 1949, politicians and bureaucrats were becoming increasingly nervous about the health of the centralization policy. In an effort to keep up a semblance of growth in the two centralized communities, Agents were even enticing Mi'kmaq and Maliseet from New Brunswick, Prince Edward Island and Quebec to move to Nova Scotia. At one time the Shubenacadie Indian Reserve was populated by Mi'kmaq from at least two dozen different Bands. But opposition towards further implementation of the policy continued to build among the Bands in the province. By 1949 not one Mi'kmaq community in Nova Scotia was cooperating with the Department. The People were aware that the false promises of economic miracles had not materialized. Those who had moved were still caught in the same poverty cycle, just in a new location.

Thus it became evident that the only means left to achieve centralization was by force. The record indicates that even this option was given some serious consideration by the Department.

Without a doubt the policy of centralization was bankrupt from the day of its conception. It was a blatant attempt to implement cultural genocide! The same horrific practice of herding another race of people to another location in defiance of their wishes was used during the same period by another dictator, Joseph Stalin. During his reign of terror in the USSR, he deported several nationalities to far-flung parts of the former Soviet Union in order to destroy their cultures. However, he failed, just as the Department failed in its attempt to destroy the Mi'kmaq and Maliseet Nations.

During the Department's attempts at centralization in New Brunswick, they even considered moving members of Mi'kmaq and Maliseet First Nations into one community at Kingsclear Indian Reserve. If this move had not been vigorously resisted by both Nations, it would have been a cultural disaster—which, on reflection, had been the government's intent.

Perhaps the best testament to the failure of the centralization policy was contained in a report written by the Agent in charge of the Shubenacadie Indian Agency, H.C. Rice, dated March 23, 1949, to Indian Affairs in Ottawa. Therein he seems to suggest that force should be used to centralize all the Mi'kmaq on the mainland:

It would appear that the time is past due when a *hard and fast policy* should be laid down respecting the position that the Centralized Reserve at Micmac (Shubenacadie), N.S., is to play in respect to the Indians on the Mainland of Nova Scotia.

Here follows a summary of the conditions on the Mainland of Nova Scotia, by Reserves, commencing at the Strait of Canso and proceeding Westward:

Guysborough County: Cook's Cove and Dort's Cove.
22 Indians—7 Families declared destitute by the Medical Officer and now receiving relief in its various forms. [This was one of the communities the Department did manage to wipe out.]

Antigonish County: Heatherton, Afton, Summerside, and South River.
121 Indians—36 Families declared destitute by the Medical Officer and now receiving relief in its various forms. [The Department managed to wipe out the settlements at Heatherton, Summerside, and South River. However, these people regrouped and now mostly reside on the Afton Reserve.]

Pictou County: Pictou Landing Reserve.
74 Indians—36 Families declared destitute by the Medical Officer and now receiving relief in its various forms.

Colchester County: Millbrook Reserve.
124 Indians—24 Families on relief.

Cumberland County: Halfway River and Squatters.
39 Indians—15 Persons on relief. [The settlement at Halfway River was wiped out, but the off-Reserve settlement of Springhill Junction still exists.]

Hants County: Indian Brook Reserve, Micmac, N.S. ... [will be discussed later]

Halifax County: Sheet Harbour and Squatters.
56 Indians—12 Families on relief. [This was a false report; the "squatters" he refers to owned the lots where they resided, but they are all deceased now. There were also two other occupied Reserves in the county that he does not list: Cole Harbour and Beaver Dam. Mrs. Margaret Phillips of Cole Harbour had taken the Department on over the centralization of the residents of Cole Harbour at Shubenacadie and, with the assistance of local politicians, had won the right to remain in Cole Harbour.]

Lunenburg County: Gold River and Squatters.
16 Indians—6 Indians on relief (two wholly maintained). [Mi'kmaq were also living at New Ross Reserve at the time, but he makes no mention of them; probably they were all working.]

Queens County: Wildcat Reserve and Squatters.
45 Indians—19 Families on relief. [Again the "squatters" mostly owned their lots. These people or their descendants still reside in the same area.]

Shelburne County: Squatters.
32 Indians—15 persons on relief. [The Reserve these people had was alienated from them and today is a land claim. As in Queens County, these Mi'kmaq or their descendants still reside in the area.]

Yarmouth County: Yarmouth Reserve and Squatters.
30 Indians—16 Indians on relief.

Digby County: Bear River Reserve.
76 Indians—35 Persons on relief.

Annapolis County: Lequille Reserve and Squatters.
69 Indians—13 Families on relief. [Again the "squatters" mainly owned their
lots.]

Kings County: Cambridge Reserve and Squatters.
112 Indians—37 Families on relief.

It will be noted that outside of Hants County where the Centralized Reserve
is located we have a total of 816 Indians of which 271 Families or part thereof
are on relief.

At Micmac, N.S., we have approximately 700 Indians, we have 88 persons
on relief. Some of these persons have large families and the relief at times is
very high, especially during the Winter months, when there is little or no sale
for Indian Handicraft whereby they could supplement their income.

However, it must be borne in mind that the majority of those on relief here
were destitute in their former abode and it was to supervise their relief as well
as give their families the benefit of education, medical treatment, *spiritual
guidance, etc.*, that they were taken to this Centralized Reserve. *The fact they
are here has been a marvellous benefit to them* and their families *as well as to
the staff here,* whose duty it is to supervise their relief and look after their
welfare.

As the situation now stands, it is costing the Federal Government thousands
of dollars yearly in relief, groceries, milk, fuel and clothing, medical, dental
and hospital services and it is personally felt that in the majority of cases the
desired result is not being obtained.

The shacks, camps, etc., that the Indians off this Reserve are living in are
beyond description. They are not fit in the majority of cases for human habitation, infested with all the various types of parasites, vermin etc., known to
science. Under these circumstances, staple foods, milk and eggs are given
these people [they were lucky; we did not get these groceries on-Reserve] and
they live in filth and exposed to disease in its various forms.

The Medical Services are confined to calls when required and although the
average Physician takes a conscientious view of each case, his work is hampered by the conditions under which these people live. The Indian has lived for
years under these conditions and he now appears to be content with his lot.

However, it must be borne in mind that the Indian is sick, not in the sense
that the term is usually applied, but due to the fact that *he has been undernourished, ill clad and forced to live under conditions only found in the lowest of
slums, until the present generation and possibly a few generations to come, he
will be susceptible to disease*, lacking initiative and in general one that will
take *considerable supervision*, encouragement and understanding if he is to
become a useful citizen of this Country.

The situation as detailed herein is applicable to the Micmacs of Nova Scotia, and it is in their behalf that this letter is being written.

The question now presents itself, what is the best solution to such a case, both from the standpoint of the Federal Government and the Indians as a whole. Bearing in mind that throughout this Province we have, exclusive of Micmac, N.S., 271 Families on relief, the majority of whom are aged, *it would appear that they all should be taken to the Centralized Reserve*, the benefits to them of this transfer is well known and it is not necessary to repeat.

Once we have them here, what then? Should they be given individual houses or should a home for the aged Indians be built? The latter is by far the more economical in the long run, and I personally believe more beneficial to the Indian. In old age, the Indian is no more capable of looking after themselves than any other Race, and living alone (as they prefer to do) is always a worry and expense, as *almost constant supervision must be maintained to get the results desired.*

In a home, which would be *properly supervised* by a Superintendent, they would be kept clean, well fed, warmly clothed, etc., and in general would live the remaining days of their lives in comfort. However, it is realized the Indians desire to be alone, to travel when he or she so wishes, and to be free from anything that pertained to regularity, and he might not be content for some time, but when the benefits of such an institution would become known to him, we might expect their co-operation. This is purely a thought, and may be of some value in arriving at the most logical conclusion to this problem.

The alternative is, as previously stated, to place them in individual welfare houses on this Reserve. The average welfare house costs the Federal Government approximately $1,400.00. I have reference here to the three room bungalow. The larger welfare house costs approximately $1,800.00. The former type is suitable for these aged people, but a quick calculation will show that it is going to cost in the vicinity of $300,000.00 to house these indigents individually. They of course prefer this arrangement, but *is it wise to expend this amount of money, to house them individually, when a much more economical and satisfactory solution would be to house them under one roof.*

It is felt, in view of the fact we are about to enter upon a new year, that this matter be given careful consideration, taking into consideration that the building programme on this Reserve must be governed by your recommendations regarding our indigents. A basic policy should be made regarding these people, if they are to be moved to Micmac, N.S., we can concentrate on houses for them, as distinct from the conventional welfare house for able bodied Indians.

The aged, sick and destitute Indian is of primary concern, and it is felt should receive priority over everything else pertaining to the administration of this Agency. Once we have this problem overcome, we can devote our undivided effort toward establishing industries, encouraging agriculture, advanced education and the various other projects that tend to raise the standard of living of these people.[43]

Rice misstated the population figures. His 1949 report states that 816 Mi'kmaqs resided outside Shubenacadie and that the population at Indian Brook was 700. Adding 816 and 700, plus the 186 he left off his count for the mainland outside of Shubenacadie, gives a total of 1,702 people. But on March 31, 1950, he filed a report showing there were only 1,373 Indians living on mainland Nova Scotia. The difference of 329 gives the impression that someone was padding the figures. Such was often done in order to acquire more money from Ottawa. However—before a false conclusion is reached—it was not done for the benefit of the people. It was done so a good-sized pot could be returned to Ottawa to earn job performance points for good management. After the Indian Register was established in 1951 the practice stopped because figures could then be verified.

On October 16, 1949, Rice wrote to Ottawa once more: "Due to the curtailing of operations at Shubenacadie and the *inability of the Indians to secure employment outside of this Reservation*, I suggest that we allow the cutting of Christmas trees on this Reserve for sale."[44] For all intents and purposes centralization had been abandoned.

By 1950 the people duped into giving up their homes to move to Shubenacadie and Eskasoni found themselves living on meagre rations once more. In reaction many began to leave, some returning to their former homes if they were still standing or building shacks if they were not. (Most of their former homes had been burned down by the Department when they had moved to the centralized reserves.) The majority, however, started an exodus from the province that drew half of the Mi'kmaq from their homeland in search of a better life in the States or Central Canada. Like centralization, this proved a hopeless dream for most.

In search of a better life, I too left Nova Scotia in 1953. I was fifteen years old. Up until that time I had worked full-time for almost a year at the government-owned community store at Indian Brook. I was being paid ten dollars a week for working six and a half days (fifty-two hours) when I resigned.

Boston is where most of us migrated, arriving there over a period of several years with great expectations. However, the reality of how badly Canada had failed us soon became evident. With our lack of education, experience and skills, all that was available to us were the most menial, low-paying jobs. A few prospered, many took to alcohol and died from drinking "Muscatel," and the rest of us reassessed our lives and returned home.

Centralization caused many hardships among the Mi'kmaq. It was a terrible and unwarranted assault upon the village structure of a great civilization. The "Registered Indians," as always, suffered the heaviest consequences of the games the bureaucrats played. The one positive achievement of centralization was that it made our People realize we can fight back and win.

It's probably very difficult for most non-Indians to conceive of having a plan for the life of their race mapped out and implemented by government against their wishes. But this is precisely what was done to the Maliseet and Mi'kmaq in the Maritimes by White supremacists. May the Great Spirit assure that such an un-godly thing never happens to decent people in Canada again!

The Struggle For Freedom

What Then Must We Do?
I sit
on a
man's back
choking him
and making
him carry me
and yet assure myself
and others that I am sorry for him
and wish to lighten his load by
all possible means—except by
getting off his back. (Leo Tolstoy, 1886)

The message delivered in Tolstoy's poem fits the story of the twentieth-century Mi'kmaq to a tee. It eloquently describes how governments and society can oppress a people while pretending to be compassionate.

The following speaks volumes about such pretensions. On April 29, 1948, Frank T. Stanfield, Member of Parliament for Colchester-Hants, and part of one of the country's foremost political families, wrote a letter to the Director of the Indian Affairs Branch about the living conditions of the Mi'kmaq residing at Indian Brook Reserve. It starkly demonstrates the depth of the condescending and paternalistic systemic racism the Mi'kmaq then had to deal with:

Mr. R. A. Hoey, Director
Indian Affairs Branch

When I was home the last time in Truro I was in Shubenacadie. I did not see Mr. Rice but *I saw a number of people around the village and they certainly thought the Indians were very prosperous and should not have much cause for complaint.* Now that the roads are good I will get hold of Mr. Rice and go up and see the Chief on the Reserve and have a good talk with him.

I agree with you it was a good move in getting all the Indians possible gathered together on the Reserve at Shubenacadie on the mainland of Nova Scotia, *as they were causing a lot of trouble scattered around in little groups all over the province.* I also realize it is likely costing your department a lot of money. Something will have to be done *to provide work for the male Indians* and the female too, for that matter, as they will not be able to make a living at farming or cutting the little bit of wood they are allowed to take off the reserve. The trouble is the women go out and get what work they can *but the men are lazy and will do nothing.* Of course there are exceptions. A few of them have done very well for themselves.

Right now, as I see it, it is safe to say that the Indians out there are certainly not suffering from any hardships and are better off than they ever were in their lives before, but *it is the old story that people are never satisfied.* However, as I said above, *something will have to be done to provide work for the Indians at Shubenacadie, sooner or later.*

Frank T. Stanfield, M.P.[1]

What is just as astonishing as the contents of Stanfield's letter is Hoey's response of May 3rd; the one individual who should have had an intimate knowledge of the situation expresses gratitude for being clued in:

Dear Mr. Stanfield:

Please accept my sincere thanks for your letter of April 29th and for the information contained therein. It was to me gratifying to learn that conditions at Shubenacadie *were reasonably satisfactory* and that the Indians were in no sense suffering.

Eking out a living

I should like to discuss with you any time at your convenience ways and means by which we might establish one or two industries on our Indian reserves at Shubenacadie and Eskasoni. I have in mind such industries as glove making, the production of axe handles, or even a small shoe factory. I feel confident that with your experience you would be able to give me valuable advice on the proposals I have in mind.[2]

Stanfield's display of bigotry had to be based upon complete ignorance or cowboy-and-Indian stereotypes. Going to a White village and asking the White population about welfare complaints of Registered Indians, and then accepting their replies without question is ridiculous. It would be akin to a White investigator going into South Africa in the heyday of apartheid and asking Whites about the welfare complaints of its Black population. Most would have said that Black living conditions in that country were very good and echoed Stanfield's "it is the same old story that people are never satisfied."

In contrast to his contention that we were prosperous, I can attest to the truth about our welfare situation in 1948. In comparison with the appalling experiences of our ancestors under English colonial rule, and the hard times they experienced under Canadian rule up to that year, we were far better off than any Mi'kmaq had been in Nova Scotia since France threw our ancestors to the English in 1713. However, not much was needed to make our lives better, just a square meal or two a day.

It was wrong for a wealthy man to accept as truth second-hand information that painted an erroneous picture about the welfare of a poverty-stricken people from another culture, and then with no knowledge of the complexities of the situation, to pass a negative judgment on them and blame them for something they had no control over. If Stanfield's vision had not been so clouded by racial stereotypes, he would have gone into the Mi'kmaq community and found out for himself the true situation of the People and not relied upon two of the most unreliable sources for gathering information about First Nations people—the Department of Indian Affairs and the general public.

The unreliability of these two sources should have been apparent to knowledgable Nova Scotia politicians. Only the most naive among them wouldn't have known that Indian Affairs was an institution that was used by political leaders to do whatever they wanted with Registered Indians: centralization, for example. Also, in view of the fact that these politicians came from the White population they would have known, witnessed by the fact that the vast majority of Mi'kmaq and African Nova Scotians were undereducated and living in abject poverty amidst plenty, that racist beliefs among Whites didn't engender among them much sympathy for the legitimate complaints of either community. George Wallace, the late White supremacist and former Governor of Alabama, was not without peers in this province in the mid-1900s.

Debunking Stanfield's demeaning comments about the work habits of Mi'kmaq males compared to Mi'kmaq females is easy. The two main reasons why women were able to find work more readily than men in those days were that they were viewed by Whites as less threatening than men, and the White establishment badly needed maids, nannies and other domestics.

Because of the degrading way that society depicted the Mi'kmaq male as a mindless savage, when he did find employment off-Reserve it often wasn't a pleasant experience. I know because I've experienced it first-hand. On many occasions I was victimized by the false but widely held negative stereotype of the Native person as an unintelligent buffoon. It is very degrading to have a White person, who in some cases is barely able to tie his own shoelaces, treat you paternalistically as a person with the IQ of an idiot.

In addition to this kind of condescending treatment, during my years of employment in the public and private sectors, I was often referred to, pejoratively, as "Chief." In one incident, among many, a worker at a plant where I worked started screeching out his version of a supposed Indian war whoop in front of me while mimicking a war dance. An extremely thick skin and a cool head was required to hold a job in this kind of environment.

Thankfully, in 1948 the groundwork was laid to eventually outlaw this kind of overt racist conduct. On December 10th of that year the "Universal Declaration of Human Rights" was signed at the United Nations in New York.[3] Although not ratified until 1952, this document slowly but surely compelled Canada and its provinces to repeal their written and unwritten "apartheid laws." Further, it forced the bigots then loose on the Canadian political scene to modify their public postures in relation to discrimination. The age when they were free to make degrading and discriminatory remarks in public about another person's race, creed, colour or religion without paying a price was drawing to a close.

However, because of its own domestic situation, Canada's actions on the global scene at this time reek of hypocrisy. After it signed the U.N. document, although many politicians who had publicly displayed racist tendencies were still in positions of power, Canada did its utmost to promote an image of itself as a champion of the movement for worldwide protection of human and civil rights. At the same time, as far as many Canadian political leaders were concerned, human rights were best protected outside of Canada, because domestically they much preferred the status quo. The continued oppression of Red and Black people attests to this reality.

In 1951, in keeping with the image being built for foreign consumption, the Canadian government overhauled the Indian Act. Some of its most obnoxious provisions were repealed and a few others were added. This was also a year when both the Mi'kmaq and African Nova Scotian communities began to stir and make headway towards organizing an effective attack against racial bigotry in Nova Scotia. These efforts were encouraged by the displays of courage of heroic individuals spearheading the fight against racial segregation in the southern United States. From among them, such men as the Reverend Martin Luther King Jr. provided inspirational role models for the two peoples in organizing their own strategies to achieve racial equality and justice.

However, given the entrenched racist attitudes within the province's White community, the two peoples of colour knew that the battle for racial equality in Nova Scotia and in Canada would not be easily won. This has proven to be true. Racism is a disease that is most easily weeded out generation by generation; some progress can be made with older generations, but it is among the young that real change is possible. Thus, I can foresee a time in the twenty-first century when we can declare that the fight for equality has mostly prevailed!

In 1956, Canada's hypocrisy caught up with it. It was discovered that the country had denied citizenship to many of its First Nations peoples. In response, Canada enacted legislation made retroactive to 1947. I can't help but conclude that this was done to make it appear that all First Nations peoples resident in Canada in 1948 were citizens before Canada signed the "Universal Declaration of Human Rights." To conclude the farce, "An Act to Amend the Canadian Citizenship Act" was enacted by Parliament and given royal assent on June 7, 1956:

> Her Majesty, by and with the advice and consent of the Senate and House of Commons of Canada, enacts as follows: ...
>
> 2. Section 9 of the said Act is amended by adding thereto the following sub-section:
> (4) An Indian as defined in the Indian Act, or a person of the race of aborigines commonly referred to as Eskimos, other than a natural-born Canadian citizen, is a Canadian citizen if that person,
> (a) had a place of domicile in Canada on the 1st day of January, 1947, and
> (b) on the 1st day of January, 1956, had resided in Canada for more than ten years, *and such a person is deemed to have become a Canadian citizen on the 1st day of January, 1947.*[4]

How commendable! After eighty-nine years the citizenship status of all First Nation peoples of Canada had been cleared up on paper. However, what were we before 1947? *Prisoners of war*? Non-persons? Wards of the Crown? Were we still such despite the legislation?

The most honest answer to these questions is that to the majority of Canadians in 1956 the First Nations citizen was *nothing*. For instance, I had known since my early years that I was not considered an equal citizen of Canada with the same basic human rights as Whites. The fact that such things as centralization occurred is ample proof of this statement. Officially, although some now try to pretend we weren't, Treaty Indians were still treated as "wards of the Crown" after 1956.

When or how "wards of the Crown" status was replaced officially with "full citizenship status" I haven't been able to determine. For example, up until the day when Parliament repealed the Indian Act enfranchisement and other sections in 1985, any Registered Indian applying for permission to give up Indian status had to sign a declaration on an application form which stated: *"[I] certify that I am capable of assuming the responsibilities of citizenship."*[5] The disgust I feel over all this would be less if these laws had been enacted to correct a wrong. But knowing that they were passed simply because of politics is irreconcilable with my perception of civilized behaviour.

Did Canada become a better place for the Registered Indian to reside after 1956? Unfortunately not. The injustices and persecution continued as usual, with generally very few restraints placed upon the perpetrators. This is emphasized by the fact that the Canadian government was again making plans that would drastically alter our political system and consequently our way of life without consulting us. Around the end of 1954, in direct opposition to the centralization goals just abandoned and their past efforts to establish that there was only one Band in Nova Scotia, the bureaucrats in Ottawa began to discuss among themselves the reorganization of the Bands in Nova Scotia under the Indian Act. This reorganization would turn out to be easier than they probably supposed because, although centralization had taken its toll on some of the smaller Bands, the Band village system still remained much as it had been from ancient times.

This is how the Mi'kmaq political system was arranged at the time: The Chief of Eskasoni was recognized as the District Chief of the Cape Breton District and the Chief of Shubenacadie was recognized as the District Chief of the Nova Scotia mainland District. Up until the early 1900s, there had been two Districts on the mainland. In 1910 the Chief of Bear River was recognized as the District Chief of Annapolis, Digby, Yarmouth, Shelburne and Queens counties and half of Lunenburg County.[6] Around 1919, the Chief of Shubenacadie became recognized as Chief of the entire mainland.

Under this system all the Mi'kmaq settlements scattered throughout the province had their own Chiefs and Councillors and handled most of their own affairs. It worked quite well. However, probably unaware, or uncaring, that the system they were planning to destroy was the remnant of the ancient Mi'kmaq District system of government, the bureaucrats ploughed ahead with their own idea.

In response to a request from Ottawa, Bart McKinnon, Regional Indian Affairs Supervisor for the Maritimes, submitted a plan to headquarters dated December 4, 1956, to divide the Nova Scotia Mi'kmaq into separate Indian Act Bands. This initiative was tailored to fit the government's national assimilation strategy for permanently solving Canada's "Indian problem." In his proposal McKinnon noted how "integration" and "nature" would solve some of Nova Scotia's Indian problems. No consultations had yet taken place with Mi'kmaq leaders.

Finally, in early January 1957, McKinnon took steps that should have been taken when Indian Affairs first begun to consider the issue in 1954. Two meetings were held with the Mi'kmaq to discuss the proposal: the first with the Cape Breton Mi'kmaq on the 10th, and the second with the mainlanders a few days later. At these meetings both Districts independently agreed to set up their Bands in accordance with the provisions of the Indian Act, and further agreed to distribute their lands as they saw fit. This was logical because both Districts wished to maintain their historic independence from the other. However, in disregard of democratic principles, it wasn't approved by Band members via a referendum.

Although the Department anticipated problems with the distribution of lands, there weren't any. In fact, once the Mi'kmaq became involved the issues were quickly sorted out. The Bands which were eventually organized under the Act were, with one exception, almost identical to what had already existed.

The mainland Bands and their Reserves as organized under the Act in 1958-59 were as follows:

AFTON BAND, Reserves: Afton, Pomquet, Summerside and forty-eight percent of Franklin Manor.

ANNAPOLIS VALLEY BAND, Reserves: Cambridge, Horton, and St. Croix.

BEAR RIVER BAND, Reserves: Bear River, Lequille, and Greywood.

PICTOU LANDING BAND, Reserves: Boat Harbour, Pictou Landing, Merigomish and fifty-two percent of Franklin Manor.

SHUBENACADIE BAND, Reserves: Shubenacadie (Indian Brook), Shubenacadie (Grand Lake), New Ross, and Pennal.

TRURO [now Millbrook] BAND, Reserves: Millbrook, Cole Harbour, Beaver Dam, and two at Sheet Harbour.[7]

The members of the small mainland Bands were put on a general Band List; then in 1967 the Department unilaterally organized them into the Acadia Band. This dictatorial move, made without their consent, has been a bone of contention among the several factions that had previously been treated as separate Bands, and the discontent continues today.

The Department's strong-arm tactics in creating the Annapolis Valley Band came back to haunt them in the 1980s. On June 24, 1984, a large group of the Band's members, who viewed themselves as having been independent prior to 1958, broke away and formed the Horton Band. They felt they were not compatible with the remaining Band members and would be better off doing their own thing. The separation was not without rancour, but it has worked out for the best for both parties. As a result of the organization of the Acadia Band and the breakaway of the Horton Band there are now thirteen Bands in Nova Scotia.

The Cape Breton Island Bands and their Reserves as reorganized were:

CHAPEL ISLAND BAND, Reserves: Chapel Island and twenty percent of Malagwatch.

ESKASONI BAND, Reserves: Eskasoni and twenty percent of Malagwatch.

MIDDLE RIVER [now Wagmatcook] BAND, Reserves: Wagmatcook and twenty percent of Malagwatch.

SYDNEY [now Membertou] BAND, Reserves: Membertou, Caribou Marsh, Lingan and twenty percent of Malagwatch.

WHYCOCOMAGH [now Whycobah] BAND, Reserves: Whycocomagh, Port Hood [the Band that owns the Reserve lost by the Department], Margaree, and twenty percent of Malagwatch.[8]

As this exercise has never been approved by Band members, it's possible that one day it will wind up in court because land transfers, which require Band member consent, were involved.

In line with the new order of Band politics, the 1919 Band fund consolidation was reversed in 1958. The remaining moneys were separated once again into individual Band trust accounts. Distribution was made on a per capita basis.

In 1960, under Prime Minister John Diefenbaker's enlightened thinking, the government made a decision that would prove to be most beneficial in promoting the eventual recognition of the civil and human rights of First Nations citizens. It decided to permit all Registered Indians to vote in federal elections. Registered Indians living on-Reserve had previously been prevented from doing so by this section of the Canada Elections Act:

14.   (2)   The following persons are disqualified from voting in an election and incapable of being registered as electors and shall not vote nor be so registered, that is to say, ...

(e) every Indian, as defined in the Indian Act, ordinarily resident on a reserve, unless

(i) he was a member of His Majesty's Forces during World War I or World War II, or was a member of the Canadian Forces who served on active service subsequent to the 9th day of September, 1950, or

(ii) he executed a waiver, in a form prescribed by the Minister of Citizenship and Immigration, of exemptions under the Indian Act from taxation on and in respect of personal property, and subsequent to the execution of such waiver a writ has issued ordering an election in any electoral district.[9]

An "Act to Amend the Canada Elections Act," repealing the discriminatory parts of Section 14, was given royal assent on March 31, 1960.[10]

By acquiring the right to vote *ninety-three unjustifiable years* after Confederation, the First Nations peoples of Canada had acquired a useful tool in their future struggles for freedom and justice. Politicians now had to address their problems or suffer at the polls. After this, things began to slowly change for the better for First Nations peoples.

Why the change wasn't more rapid is explained by the following example of the racist attitudes that still prevailed among the bureaucrats: When I returned from the States in 1960 with the intention of going back to school, I went to see the Indian Agent with a request for financial assistance to do so. His response was: "Why don't you go get a pick and shovel and go do what you're best qualified for?" With the angry intervention of my Member of Parliament, Mr. Cyril Kennedy, who was a war veteran and a fine gentleman, the Agent changed his attitude and I started business college in September of that year.

Another thing that changed after the vote was granted was that departmental bureaucrats became more adept at concealing their misdeeds and failings from Members of Parliament, who were now answerable to the people making complaints about bureaucratic job performance. The bureaucrats came up with the ideal solution, amazingly never challenged by any politician. To this day they assign themselves to investigate their own misdeeds and failings and, of course, almost always exonerate themselves. The worst result is that First Nations citizens are left with no effective legal recourse for their complaints about the actions of Indian Affairs bureaucrats and Band Councils. As this situation demonstrates, full protection of our People's civil rights is still hard to come by.

In 1962, Premier of Nova Scotia Robert L. Stanfield formed a committee to study the problems faced by minority groups and improve race relations within the province of Nova Scotia. He had the good judgment to appoint Fred MacKinnon as the chairman of the committee. Mr. MacKinnon would prove to be a dedicated advocate for human and civil rights recognition throughout the province and served the People well during his career in several important civil service positions.

Although the Mi'kmaq were excluded, the committee was very helpful to African Nova Scotians, who were in many ways as bad off as we were. Because of discrimination their housing conditions were mostly deplorable, their education had been severely neglected, and other forms of oppression such as exclusion from jobs and the economy were still prevalent.

However, Premier Stanfield's failure to include the province's Mi'kmaq on the committee leaves a mark on his otherwise good record. He tried to justify the exclusion on the basis of federal-provincial jurisdiction at a human rights function in 1991. From my standpoint, as I believe other human rights advocates would agree, had he really believed in equal rights for all people in Nova Scotia he would not have let anything stand in the way of finding equality for all, the Mi'kmaq included.

Perhaps his decision would be more understandable if the Mi'kmaq had not been at the time almost as severely discriminated against as our ancestors were in previous decades. In the 1960s we needed all the help we could muster in our fight for freedom, justice and equality. While making his decision, Stanfield must have been aware that the era when First Nations peoples were pictured as either blood-thirsty barbarians or insensible idiots was still on the go. Cartoons which showed "Indians" with a vocabulary of just one word—"How"—generally accompanied with a grunt—"Ugh"—were still to be seen, and snide racist remarks were still the norm, not the exception!

Unfortunately, the decision made by Stanfield at that time set back the Mi'kmaq's fight for human and civil rights recognition in the province by several years. The establishment of the Nova Scotia Human Rights Commission in 1967 helped the situation somewhat. But it wasn't until 1991, under Premier Donald Cameron's Conservative government, that we were finally provided full protection under Nova Scotia's Human Rights Act.

In spite of Nova Scotia's neglect, things did change for the better for the Mi'kmaq in the 1960s. Indian Affairs abolished the practice of designating on welfare assistance purchase orders which store the People could purchase goods from. A short time later it was decided that welfare payments would be made in cash. Another far-reaching decision made in the early sixties was that the doctors, dentists and so on who served Registered Indians would no longer be appointed based on their political affiliation. In fact, they would no longer be appointed at all!

The end of these practices was received with enthusiasm by First Nations citizens across the country. It's hard to describe how degrading and humiliating it is to be told what doctor, dentist, store etc. you may use and even what you could buy. Especially so, when some of the people you were required to give your business to were among the worst racial bigots in the community. These changes finally gave First Nations citizens some choices, and with choices came better diets and health care.

But even in this more enlightened era—it seems they never learn from experience—governments were not through with trying to make sweeping changes in the lives of First Nations peoples without their consent. After the disaster of centralization, one would have thought that they would have been more sensitive when trying to introduce drastic changes into First Nations communities. But they weren't! In 1969 the government of Canada under the leadership of Pierre Elliott Trudeau had its Minister of Indian Affairs Jean Chretien, later the country's Prime Minister, present to Parliament a draconian policy on Indian Affairs for future implementation. His "White Paper" advocated the complete and immediate integration of First Nations citizens into Canadian society. This would have assured the realization of Britain and Canada's 254-year-old goal of the extinction of First Nations by assimilation.

In line with historic practices, this paper blamed the plight of the Registered Indian on everything and everyone but the biggest culprit of all, Canadian governments. The First Nations peoples were blamed, the provinces were blamed and so on, but Canada walked away almost unscratched.

This definition of the "Indian" used in the White Paper exemplifies the racist mentality still prevalent:

To be an Indian is to be a man [sic], with all a man's needs and abilities. To be an Indian is also to be different. It is to speak different languages, draw different pictures, tell different tales and to rely on a set of values developed in a different world.

Canada is richer for its Indian component, although there have been times when diversity seemed of little value to many Canadians.

But to be a Canadian Indian today is to be someone different in another way. It is to be someone apart—apart in law, apart in the provision of Government Services and, too often, apart in social contacts.

To be an Indian is to lack power—the power to act as owner of your lands, the power to spend your own money and, too often, the power to change your own condition.

Not always, but too often, to be an Indian is to be without—without a job, a good house, or running water; without knowledge, training or technical skill and, above all, without those feelings of dignity and self-confidence that a man must have if he is to walk with his head held high.

All these conditions of the Indians are the product of history and have nothing to do with their abilities and capacities. Indian relations with other Canadians began with *special treatment* by government and society, *and special treatment has been the rule since Europeans first settled in Canada. Special treatment* has made of the Indian a community disadvantaged and apart.

Obviously, the course of history must be changed.

To be an Indian must be to be free—free to develop Indian cultures in an environment of legal, social and economic equality with other Canadians.[11]

Whoever wrote this statement either did not know or chose to ignore Canadian history. It reads like the product of someone's stereotypical imagination. It talks of "special treatment"—does that include the genocide practised in eastern Canada? Does that include the "special treatment" of being denied schooling for 129 years during British colonial times? Does that include the "special treatment" of being denied equal citizenship until Bill C-31 was enacted 118 years or more after Confederation?

The authors discuss the lack of power of First Nations, but they do not explain *why*. They don't mention that White society would not permit First Nations peoples any power. It doesn't mention that the drive to take away the power of the First Nations forever was a fixation with the English and their successors in this country.

Further, the authors don't mention that the drive to strip the First Nations of their dignity, independence and property was exemplified by the 1715 meeting between the Chiefs and the British officers who demanded submission and the extinction of Mi'kmaq culture. The authors of the White Paper would not have displayed such ignorance of Canada's past if schools had taught them the true history of their country. If they had been so taught then they would have been aware that the only "special treatment" First Nations citizens ever received from British society was the "special treatment" of unbridled horrors, and that an almost identical course was adopted by Canada.

Armchair historians such as those who wrote this "statement," which stereotypes First Nations peoples, are one of the enduring obstacles that Canada's First Nations peoples confront in modern times. Native Americans from across the Americas have suffered greatly from the misrepresentation of historical facts by these people. I would suggest that before such people begin to use their pens they should appreciate this: to become a knowledgeable historian of Native American-European relations requires many years of study and research. It is beyond the capacity of any one human being, even over a lifetime, to put a dent in the mountains of material available on the First Nations in this country alone. I can state from experience that the material available on the Mi'kmaq encounter with the Europeans is mountainous and takes years to analyze adequately.

Compounding our problems further, many professional historians write about us with minds clouded by White elitist views. To write objectively about Native American-European relations requires one to have an ability to see Amerindians as dignified human beings in their own social environment. It is incredibly biased to try to judge Native Americans' "degree of civilization" only according to European concepts and standards. I have read many works of individuals who have aspired to write intelligently about the subject, but the stereotypes they hold of *"uncivilized Native American savages"* hamper their efforts greatly.

When trying to appreciate, analyze and understand the First Nations' viewpoints, these writers must put themselves in the shoes of these peoples who suffered continuous oppression under European occupation. They should put themselves in the place of the families and friends of those who were held hostage at British forts; in the place of those who were starving in the midst of plenty in the 1800s; and in the place of peoples who loved their way of life and tried unsuccessfully to fend off the extreme efforts of another civilization over five centuries to bring them to extinction. The non-Native writer must try to understand that, in the midst of the hardship they have been forced to endure because of their race, these people have loved and cared for one another just as non-Natives have loved and cared for family and friends!

The one line of the White Paper that does state the profound truth of *why* is: "All these conditions of the Indians are the product of history and have nothing to do with their abilities and capacities."

The only reason First Nations peoples have been forced to endure their sorry plight for so long is because they wish to maintain their separate identities and cultures. If they had agreed to renounce their civilizations and assimilate, they would not have been subjected to the hideous treatment they have endured. Of course, if they had renounced their civilization, their Nations would no longer exist.

This crucial fact was ignored by the bureaucrats who thought out the White Paper: The First Nations of the Americas are a unique race of people in this world. They cannot be lumped into the same pot with, for instance, the English citizen. Canadians of English heritage have another country called England that they can always refer to as their ancestral homeland, and the same holds true for the French, Italians and so on. The Native Americans have only the Americas to call home. No country beyond the American continents affords them a place under the sun. In this context Canada must give their *inherent right* to revive and enhance their cultures the utmost protection *under law*.

However, the White Paper's summary showed that this was not the thinking in 1969. Like its predecessors in 1715, the government wanted the First Nations to consent to being dumped into the melting pot and swallowed up:

1. BACKGROUND:

The Government has reviewed its programs for Indians and has considered the effects of them on the present situation of Indian People. The review *has drawn on extensive consultations with the Indian People*, and on the knowledge and experience of many people both in and out of Government.

The review was a response to things said by the Indian people at the consultation meetings which began a year ago and culminated in a meeting in Ottawa in April.

This review has shown that this is the right time to change long-standing policies. The Indian people have shown their determination that present conditions shall not persist.

Opportunities are present today in Canadian society and new directions are open. The Government believes that Indian people must not be shut out of Canadian life and must share equally in these opportunities.

The Government could press on with the policy of fostering further education; could go ahead with physical improvement programs now operating in

Reserve communities; could press forward in the direction of recent years, and eventually many of the problems would be solved. But progress would be too slow. The change in Canadian society in recent years has been too great and continues too rapidly for this to be the answer. Something more is needed. We can no longer perpetuate the separation of Canadians. Now is the time to change.

The Government believes in equality. It believes that all men and women have equal rights. It is determined that all shall be treated fairly and that no one shall be shut out of Canadian life, and especially no one shall be shut out because of his race.

This belief is the basis for the Government's determination to open the doors of opportunity to all Canadians, to remove the barriers which impede the development of people, of regions and of the country.

Only a policy based on this belief can enable the Indian people to realize their needs and aspirations.

The Indian people are entitled to such a policy. They are entitled to an equality which preserves and enriches Indian identity and distinction; an equality which stresses Indian participation in its creation and which manifests itself in all aspects of Indian life.

The goals of Indian people cannot be set by others; they must spring from the Indian *itself*—but Government can create a framework within which all persons and groups can seek their own goals.[12]

In my lifetime I've been called many degrading things by bigots, including, in 1993, "you creature you" by a true believer in the saintly nature of the English Governors back in the 1700s. I was called this because I had dared write a newspaper column that identified Cornwallis as a purveyor of genocide. However, until I read the last paragraph of the White Paper above, I had never been called an "it."

The summary states, as is the custom in these kind of policy papers, that "extensive consultations" with the First Nations were carried out prior to the policy being presented to Parliament. As usual, this was an outright manipulation of the truth. The habit of the Department's bureaucrats has been to feed politicians what they want to hear. I would venture to guess in this case that they sought out individuals among the First Nations' leadership whose views matched their own and then "consulted" with them vigorously.

I can attest from first-hand experience that Department "consultations" with the Bands have been one of the biggest jokes within Canadian First Nations communities since 1867. Meaningful consultations have never been carried out by the Canadian government with First Nations. For example, for years the Department put together "management teams" to travel throughout the Atlantic region to negotiate yearly budgets with Band governments. This was always a farce, for the bureaucrats already knew at the outset, right to the cent, exactly what moneys each Band would get for the new fiscal year. They participated in this farce and called it "negotiations." The only, and yet still questionable, value of this "exercise in futility," as the Bands and I put it, was that it gave the Councils an opportunity to meet the enemy *en masse* and appraise them face to face.

The White Paper is accurate when it states that the First Nations have been discriminated against financially and should be accorded the right to participate fully in the financial scheme of Canadian society at large. But then it states that the First Nations citizens' dependence upon government for the necessities of life hampers this aspiration. It does so without addressing the fact that this dependence was created by the Department's paternalism and society's refusal to allow First Nations peoples to participate in the economic life of the country in the first place.

The authors of the third paragraph of the Background blame the past policies of the Department for the plight of the First Nations peoples but do not mention the practices of its employees who perverted the intent of its policies to meet their own needs. The White Paper correctly mentions that our peoples have not enjoyed the fruits of this prosperous nation, but it does not mention that the prime reason is racism. It fails to say that the government of Canada has, by caving into political pressure from anti-Native elements, been used as an instrument to discriminate against First Nations citizens.

The fourth and fifth paragraphs of the Background attempt to blame the results of the racism endured by First Nations on the separate legal status Registered Indians have. They do not acknowledge that the general public is ignorant of the cause and true extent of our separate legal status because school curriculums fail to include these things.

The writers attempt to portray the poverty of First Nations citizens as at the same level as poor Whites. They fail to mention that at least 95 percent or more of Registered Indians are poor, while only about 10 percent of the public at large may be classified as such.

They speak of forming a partnership with the First Nations for the purpose of coming to grips with their social and financial difficulties. Then they mention persuading the peoples to give up their separate status, which will somehow miraculously open up the doors of Canadian society to them. They ask the First Nations to accept the new policy without question because they have declared it to be in their best interests. As always, their concept of partnership with the First Nations is based upon the premise of "We dictate, you accept." The White Paper continues:

2. THE NEW POLICY:
True equality presupposes that the Indian people have the right to full and equal participation in the cultural, social, economic and political life of Canada.
    The Government believes that the framework within which individual Indians and Bands could achieve full participation requires:
1. *that the legislative and constitutional basis for discrimination be removed*;
2. that there be positive recognition by everyone of the unique contribution of Indian culture to Canadian life;
3. *that services come through the same channels and from the same Government agencies for all Canadians*;
4. that those who are farthest behind be helped most;
5. *that lawful obligations be recognized*;
6. that control of Indian lands be transferred to the Indian people.

'The Government would be prepared to take the following steps to create this framework:

1. *Propose to Parliament that the Indian Act be repealed* and take such legislative steps as may be necessary to enable Indians to control Indian lands and to acquire title to them.

2. *Propose to the governments of the provinces that they take over the same responsibility for Indians that they have for other citizens in their provinces.* The take-over would be accompanied by the transfer to the provinces of federal funds normally provided for Indian programs, augmented as may be necessary.

3. Make substantial funds available for Indian economic development as an interim measure.

4. Wind up that part of the Department of Indian Affairs and Northern Development that deals with Indian Affairs. The residual responsibilities of the Federal Government for programs in the field of Indian Affairs would be transferred to other appropriate federal departments.

In addition, the Government will appoint a Commissioner to consult with the Indians and to study and recommend acceptable procedures for the adjudication of claims.

The new policy looks to a better future for all Indian people wherever they may be. The measures for implementation are straightforward. They require discussion, consultation and negotiation with the Indian people—individuals, bands and associations and provincial governments.

Success will depend upon the co-operation and assistance of the Indians and the provinces. The Government seeks this co-operation and will respond when it is offered. [13]

The first numbered point in this part of the White Paper states that the "legislative and *constitutional* basis for discrimination" must be removed. However, there is no basis for discrimination under the Constitution. All the Constitution mentions is that the federal government has absolute responsibility for "Indians and lands reserved for Indians." It took the Department of Indian Affairs to make these few words into a basis for discrimination. Under the same Constitution the provinces are made separate. Nova Scotians are legally separate from Albertans, yet the federal government was making no move to have that changed; and in the case of Quebec, because of language and laws, they have talked about designating that province distinct. Are not the cultures, languages and tenets of First Nations "distinct" also?

The authors of the White Paper should have mentioned that the legislative basis for discrimination was created in 1876, when, instead of confining itself to its trust responsibility to improve the desperate social conditions of First Nations citizens and managing their lands in a competent manner, the government added racist and discriminatory sections to the Indian Act. It's apparent the writers were trying to find a convenient non-human scapegoat for the long mistreatment of Canada's First Nations peoples, but legislation and the Constitution per se did not cause problems for First Nations peoples, *society did*. The policy states that "lawful obligations" must be recognized. Is this finally an admission that the government did not recognize its legal responsibilities before 1969? How else can it be taken?

The policy proposes that "the Indian Act be repealed" and that legislative action should be taken to enable First Nations to own their own lands. This plan to turn over lands to peoples who have had little experience with the complexities of managing real estate, or of the dangers their land would be subjected to as mortgageable property, was not well thought out or was made without conscience. Amidst real estate manipulators and wheeler dealers Band members would have been like lambs among wolves. Under this lands policy First Nations lands would have quickly been mortgaged to the hilt in the peoples' hopes of finding prosperity. If this policy had been accepted in 1969, by now probably more than half of the First Nations land base in this country would have fallen into non–First Nations hands. This must never be allowed to happen. The First Nations' land base in Canada must be expanded, not diminished.

I want to emphasize that I fully agree with the proposition that the land base must someday be turned over to a sovereign people for their management. But the gaps in education and expertise between First Nations citizens and society in general must first be closed. For instance, training in the management of real estate and finances must be provided before the transfer of land takes place. This training must be provided by experts in the field and not—as was the past practice when expert training was identified as a need—supplied by unskilled and unqualified bureaucrats. Then legislative protection must be provided over a considerable transition period to hold the wolves at bay. This will be needed until First Nations peoples acquire the practical experience and skills they'll need to deal with real estate dealers effectively and constructively.

The policy also proposes that all "responsibility for [Registered] Indians" be taken over by the provinces. This is where the real motivation for the policy is revealed: the federal government is making a move to escape the legal obligations it has been saddled with and the escalating costs of administering them.

The new policy was a failure before the ink dried on the paper because it failed to deal with the realities of the situation and tried to propose a cure without honestly diagnosing the problem. The following are the immediate steps the government planned to take towards the implementation of its policy:

3. THE IMMEDIATE STEPS:
Some changes could take place quickly. Others would take longer. It is expected that within five years the Department of Indian Affairs and Northern Development would cease to operate in the field of Indian Affairs; the new laws would be in effect and existing programs would have been devolved. *The Indian lands would require special attention for some time*. The process of transferring control to the Indian people would be under continuous review.

The Government believes this is a policy which is just and necessary. It can only be successful if it has the support of the Indian people, the provinces and all Canadians.

The policy promises all Indian people a new opportunity to expand and develop their identity within the framework of a Canadian society which offers them the rewards and responsibilities of participation, the benefits of involvement and the pride of belonging.[14]

Upon presentation to Parliament by the Minister, the White Paper drew an immediate backlash from First Nations peoples. From Newfoundland to British Columbia they saw the proposed policy for what it was: an open attempt to bring about the final extinction of their civilizations. In the face of the uproar the government backed down, or did they? Let's go abroad to get a likely answer.

When rebellion broke out against British rule in the African colony of Kenya, the Mau Mau fought courageously and tenaciously for their freedom and, after costing the British dearly, eventually won. During that conflict a statement related to the price the British paid was coined that still applies to the destruction that occurs when attempts are made to destroy civilizations: "When you take without consent something of value from another, at some time you must replace it with something of equal value, or somehow, someway, someday, you will pay the consequences." In 1969 the Canadian government was making a blatant attempt to evade payment of consequences for its past actions against First Nations peoples.

This approach is unethical. Because of its racist mismanagement of First Nations affairs, Canada has a legal and moral obligation to help restore the Native American civilizations within its boundaries to their former greatness by providing the financial means needed to do the job. Seeking the extinction of First Nations through assimilation under the guise of new policies such as those prescribed in the White Paper is not the way.

In 1970, to replace the failed system it had set up to manage Indian affairs in the Maritimes in 1942, the federal government decided to reorganize the agency system into two districts, Nova Scotia and New Brunswick. The needs of the Mi'kmaq of Prince Edward Island and Newfoundland were to be serviced through the renamed Atlantic Regional Office situated in Amherst, Nova Scotia. The two district offices were opened in the provincial capitals of Halifax and Fredericton in July 1971. The usual pledges were made to First Nations leaders that this reorganization was to benefit them.

Just before the Halifax district office opened I was offered a position by the Department. They actually contacted me on three separate occasions, appealing to my conscience as a Mi'kmaq by saying that "If I worked for them" I could make a meaningful contribution to changing things for my people. I finally agreed to give up my job as chief bookkeeper with Non Public Funds at the Stadacona Naval Base in Halifax and accepted the employment offer. Thus began the most difficult fifteen and a half years of my life.

Some of the things I saw during that time would have shocked a hardened despot. Many senior bureaucrats gave little thought to principles or ethics. Watching some of these people in action was fascinating, mesmerizing and repelling all at the same time. It could be compared with being spellbound by a poisonous snake about to strike. I will be as objective as possible in relating the facts.

To put these bureaucrats' conduct into perspective, in the early 1960s the government began to establish some new programs and undertake a few new initiatives. As the sixties progressed the Department began to expand and the seeds were planted for new bureaucratic empires. Strangely, this was all powered by the Department's desire to get out of the responsibility of providing direct social services to the First Nations. To facilitate their exit from service delivery, in the latter part of the decade, along with the White Paper policy, the bureaucrats were working on a parallel proposal called "devolution of programs" which was into full implementation by 1971.

First Nations citizens quickly became pawns in the high-stakes job-promotion games that these bureaucrats played. During this period most of the Department's bureaucrats had only one thing in mind: to expand their empires and reap the fruits of the resultant upward reclassification of their positions. The critical act in this circus was to write job descriptions in a way that would indicate that several more employees were required to undertake the task. Then when these new bureaucrats were in place the process was repeated. The campaigns for promotion among bureaucrats during these days made the efforts of professional politicians to get elected look amateurish. These "civil servants" were pros in the true sense; they knew the system and milked it for personal benefit brazenly.

This all illustrates that politicians rarely if ever govern in democracies like Canada. The real governance is done by bureaucrats, who do everything but mouth the words being uttered by politicians. In most cases a politician has no real expertise in the ministerial portfolio he or she occupies and is completely reliant upon the civil servants who come with the turf. Ministers rarely verify facts on their own; all too often they simply accept the words of the bureaucrats. The men and women who have occupied the position of Minister of Indian Affairs have consistently been among the most gullible.

In their empire-building efforts, departmental bureaucrats shamelessly used many First Nations leaders for personal benefit. They arranged a staffing policy that required an official from either a First Nations organization or a Band Council to sit on employee selection boards. The courtship of these Native officials by aspiring bureaucrats was awesome; they would never acknowledge these officials could do wrong nor would they bring them to account if they did. Thus political savvy, not expertise, was a key factor in promotions. As a result, incompetence in the Department's bureaucracy from the top down was widespread by 1971, almost without exception in some programs, and remains widespread today.

During my tenure, this process brought additional racists into the Department. With these added to those already on hand, the Department had quite a number of such employees. This personal experience will illustrate how deeply ingrained racism was: It was a beautiful sunny day in the early spring of 1973. The usual practice of the district staff was to have a communal lunch in the large corner office which housed the construction supervisor and his tools. The walls in the office building we had at the time were only partial and stopped about a foot below the ceiling, so privacy was not entirely possible. Asked by a fellow employee if I would be joining them for lunch, I replied "No." It seemed to be a nice day and I felt it would be great to eat my lunch at the park across the street. However, after stepping outside I quickly changed my mind when I found it too chilly.

Before returning to the office I purchased a newspaper. Then, instead of going into the office where most of the staff were gathered, I went unseen into an office next door to eat and read. For the next quarter hour or so I was inadvertently treated to a discourse on the worthlessness of my people. The comments were about everything from the alleged laziness of a people who supposedly got everything for nothing to the Indian's allegedly irresponsible outlook on life. These "servants" of government, most of whom were engaged in a deliberate rip-off of the system for their own benefit, had the unmitigated cheek to criticize the people they were preying upon in order to maintain their comfortable standards of living.

I was outraged. Here were Indian Affairs bureaucrats, correctly recognized by many Band members as the recipients of the most lucrative welfare assistance in the world, stooping to criticize the very people they had a legal and moral responsibility to protect. This blaming of their victims for the hardship, they themselves had caused for them by incompetence and racism was the epitome of bureaucratic hypocrisy. The Registered Indians in this country never asked anyone to pervert the intention of government-sponsored Indian programs. The corruption of the administration of these programs was instigated by the bureaucrats themselves for their own benefit, not for ours.

During the early 1970s, one of the biggest unexposed scandals that took place was the way the Department handled the "devolution of programs" to Bands. Taxpayers would have been outraged at the time had they known how this was mishandled. Millions upon millions of dollars were distributed by bureaucrats to Band governments without ensuring that they had the wherewithal to manage and account for the funds.

This was wrong and exhibited bureaucratic incompetence at its highest level. And the negative fallout from this incompetence is still felt by Band governments today. Because of it they lack sound financial management procedures and many are debt-ridden. To assure that the newly created Confederacy of Mainland Micmacs wasn't victimized by this, when I was hired as its first Executive Director in 1987, I wrote the operation by-laws in such a way that it requires CMM's manager to operate it in a professional and fully accountable manner. Thus the organization employs only fully qualified people who can do the jobs they've been recruited to do. For this reason the organization has been viewed by a good many Department bureaucrats as a threat to their existence, because if all other Indian organizations followed CMM's lead the Department would soon disappear.

The threat the Confederacy posed to the comfortable situation of the bureaucrats caused them to raise obstructionist obstacles when the organization wanted to assume administrative control of programs. In early 1987, I was instructed by the Chiefs to begin consultations with the Department with the goal of CMM assuming management of the Department's post-secondary education program. The following is an excerpt from the condescending, paternalistic and racist reply of the Department's Regional Director of Education dated January 14, 1987, to our request:

> Subsequent to our discussion in my office on January 13th, I contacted my program people in Ottawa. They advised me that *there are no administration dollars from the education program* and that all your administration would

have to be borne from the funds which you receive through formula funding.

I further checked the Memorandum of Association for the Confederacy and noted that essentially the organization is advisory in nature. I noted, in particular, the resolution of the Millbrook Band which qualified their association on the basis that the Confederacy was to be only advisory in nature and not program delivery. I also noted that Section 2 (h) of the Memorandum of Understanding has provision to administer and operate the program on behalf of a member Band or Bands when specifically requested to do so by the Band in writing.

Given the above, it would seem that Millbrook might withdraw if you began to take control of programs. However, this is a bit presumptuous, although a possibility. *The provision still remains for the Confederacy to deliver programs for its member Bands at their request.*[15]

I still get riled when I read this letter. After all, I had written CMM's constitution, so I didn't need the director's condescending interpretation of it. Despite his opposition, the Tribal Council eventually took over the program on behalf of the Bands and now operates a very productive education program. The program was finally turned over to us with these instructions from the Regional Director General to Robert Pinney: "Turn the program over without any fucking further delay." This was in March 1988.

I'll now give an account of how "well" the Department "insured" that "financial accountability" was in place at the Band level for responsible program management at the start of the devolution process. If you're a hurting taxpayer, this should really blow your mind!

In the summer of 1973, because of my accounting background, I was recruited by the District Manager to go into the field to assist the Bands with setting up reliable bookkeeping systems. This was approximately *four or five years after* the so-called devolution process had gotten under way in this region. Up to this point the Bands had been receiving financial advice from the District Superintendent of Finance and Administration, the office manager and a clerk. Beyond what these bureaucrats knew of departmental financial systems, none of them had any expertise in accounting. This didn't stop them, however. They ploughed ahead, dispensing financial advice as if they were experts, and in the process doing tremendous damage to the prospect of the Bands ever becoming truly efficient and effective managers of their own affairs.

On my first trip to Cape Breton I was shocked to find that the Bands had been operating all that time without any kind of reliable or informative bookkeeping systems. As a example of the lack of expertise among their "teachers," the bureaucrats had advised the Bands that a bank account had to be set up for every program and sub-program taken over from the Department. With no knowledge of accounting practices, they had taken the Department at its word and created multiple bank accounts. The record, if memory serves me correctly, was fifty-five.

I spent the next six months setting up simple bookkeeping systems for these Bands and consolidating bank accounts. However, because accountability had been given such low priority by the Department when devolving programs, the Bands did not appreciate the need for reliable accounting systems, including the need for one of the most essential practices for good business management—budgeting. Further, because supplementary funds to cover overexpenditures were there for the asking, they had no need to be good managers. Thus, during the 1970s and early 1980s, financial bailouts by the Department were many and across the board.

This bailout practice caused no real problems for the Bands at the time. However, as all Canadians are now painfully aware, the governments of the 1970s and early 1980s were spending their tax dollars as if there was no tomorrow. When the financial crunch finally came in the mid-eighties, because of the overexpending habits that were permitted by the Department to develop, the Bands were among the first to feel the effects. There were no more bailouts. As a result, most of the Bands in Nova Scotia today have severe financial difficulties and carry large and costly debts.

If the Department had been staffed by competent and responsible personnel, before turning these programs over to Band Council administration they would have taken the following three steps to insure accountability and good management:

1. Made financial accountability and budgeting mandatory.
2. Required Band Councils to enact effective administrative and financial by-laws under Sections 81 and 83 of the Indian Act to guide their governance of Band affairs. (Because this was not done most Band Councils in Canada today have no legal reference point to guide them in the administration of programs. The by-laws required for Band management are like those any government needs for guidance in the administration of public funds. Most necessary are by-laws which govern the financial management of Band budgets, the activities of staff, and the infrastructure of the community. To assist the Band Councils to enact enforceable by-laws such as these, the Department should have recruited qualified employees, which it appears it still hasn't, because most Bands don't have them.)
3. Recruited fully qualified accountants to act as Band financial advisors.

If the Department had followed these three simple steps during devolution, the vast majority of Bands today would be in sound financial shape. Of course, if this was the case, the bureaucrats would have faded from the scene many moons ago. Instead, as a reward for their incompetence, they are still around and many of the Bands are on the verge of bankruptcy. Perhaps the bureaucrats were not so dumb after all. At an inestimable cost to First Nations, by deceit or ignorance they have protected their own jobs.

In 1978, Indian self-government became the prime topic at Indian Affairs. In 1979 the Department acquired the services of J.W. Beaver to study the issue and make appropriate recommendations. On October 16, 1979, Beaver submitted his report to the President of the National Indian Brotherhood, Noel Starblanket, and the Minister of Indian Affairs and Northern Development, Jack Epp. This report, commonly referred to as the "Beaver Report," made two major policy recommendations:

> 1. That the Indian Bands be given the authority, responsibility, and resources to develop their own policy for the improvement of social and economic conditions in their Communities.
> 2. That the Government of Canada, the Department of Indian Affairs, and the Indian Bands, together with their organizations, accept in principle, and work together to implement:
> (a) Indian self-government, which will give Bands the option to exercise full powers to manage their own affairs; and
> (b) Community-based planning and development, which will set the conditions enabling Indian communities to move in the direction of self-reliance and to root out the devastating effects of dependency.[16]

The following were Beaver's comments on accountability:

> *Strengthened accountability is closely linked to the proposals recommended in this report for Indian Self-Government.* Concurrent with increased powers, responsibilities and the certainty of funding for Band Governments, *is the necessity to improve accountability.* The importance of accountability will be constantly reaffirmed, especially in periods of fiscal restraint.[17]

Beaver proposed that the Bands be given the opportunity to govern themselves by wielding the following powers and controls:

> (a) the governing and administrative structures that should apply to such reserves;
> (b) the necessary legislative, *financial*, and other regulatory controls that they will apply to themselves; and,
> (c) the preparation, education, and training that Indian people will need in order to provide their own effective Government.[18]

With much intelligent thought, Beaver had put together an excellent report. However, to make anything work there must be a will to make it happen. The politicians may have had the will, but the bureaucrats did not. Although community-based planning and self-government received a favourable reception from the bureaucrats, the most important element—accountability—did not. They immediately set out to scuttle the accountability aspect of the process without seeming to do so. Their solution was simple. They came up with financing agreements that would provide for even less accountability from the Band Councils. This enhanced the climate for corruption at the Band level and insured the bureaucrats' jobs—problem solved. If Beaver's blueprint had been followed, *accountable* and *effective* self-government would be well in place in First Nation societies today.

On October 12, 1983, the Canadian House of Commons Sub-Committee on Aboriginal Affairs approved a submission to Parliament called the "Penner Report." This was another excellent report that made recommendations for improving accountability and implementing self-government procedures, but like the Beaver Report, most of its positive recommendations were ignored. Penner subsequently became disenchanted with the games played in politics and went back to a profession he considered more fulfilling and honest: teaching.

The following is a paper I prepared in 1992 concerning moral corruption in the Department and the problems it has bred for our peoples. Unfortunately it is still applicable in the twenty-first century:

Accountability and Responsibility:
Indian Affairs vs. the Bands

I've prepared this overview of the problems that have prevented self-government and prosperity from taking root within our communities in the hope of inspiring a demand for constructive change among Band members. The need for such is starkly illustrated by the fact that after more than a quarter century of managing Indian Affairs programs as their agents, we are no closer to self-government and prosperity than when the process started. It's now evident that if constructive changes are not made, the present state of no progress will go on forever.

To demonstrate that change is possible, using the experience and knowledge garnered from over twenty-two years of employment with both Indian Affairs and the Bands, and that garnered from another twenty or so in private industry, I'll propose solutions. But first let's review how our present stagnated state came about.

Around 1960, the Department of Indian Affairs began to introduce into our communities an uncontrolled socialist system that eventually would have no equal in the world. For instance, the communist socialist political systems which were in place in the former Soviet Union and Eastern Europe up until recent times would in comparison appear to be ultra-conservative.

The imposition of this system was the root of our present problem. It slowly stole our will to excel and our personal responsibility. Under the socialist systems that were imposed upon our people, and the people in the formerly communist-ruled countries of Eastern Europe and the former Soviet Union, a philosophy known as "State Big-Brotherism" replaced individual responsibility.

The concept eventually led to total stagnation in the economies of the communist countries, which in time led to the failure and collapse of their systems. In our case the only thing that keeps our system from failing and collapsing as well is massive funding provided by government. This puts us completely at their mercy. And they keep us this way by forcing us to continue with this totally discredited and non-productive system.

Over the years the only people who really benefitted from this state of affairs were the bureaucrats. It permitted them to build and expand personal empires, which at times in the late 1960s, the entire 1970s, and the early 1980s was taking place at a frenzied rate. New classifications were created on almost a daily basis and the salary levels of Indian Affairs employees became the envy of other departments. In plain English, they created an uncontrollable, self-serving monster that preyed upon our people for sustenance.

In trying to justify their existence these new empires manufactured new programs after new programs which were failures upon failures. Probably the most disastrous program they undertook to implement in Atlantic Canada is the welfare program which burdens us today with its lack of enforceable controls. The rules of the program have been so loosely applied that at times people who were working, drawing unemployment insurance, or contracting were at the same time drawing full welfare.

The Department, through welfare program reviews, has had full knowledge of the improprieties taking place. In a few cases, where the initiative was taken out of their hands, prosecutions took place. However, the real culprits who knew of and authorized the misappropriation by their silence—departmental bureaucrats—walked away unscratched.

To work for a living in this new social environment became a cause for punishment. To be idle was rewarded by having access to every benefit the system could think up: light and heating bills paid in full, special needs for furniture and household accessories were there for the asking, housing repair and maintenance costs paid in full, and so on. If you were crazy enough to work, all the before-mentioned was cut off.

By its very nature the system retarded initiative, it retarded the thirst for education, it retarded the climate for economic development. It sucked away the very will of the people to overcome the poverty that racist persecution had passed to them. This system was and is to this very day a true recipe for long-term stagnation and decay in any society that is unfortunate enough to fall prey to its imposition.

The economic basket case it made of East Germany provides an excellent example of its negative effects. Its damage to that economy is long-term. Because the need to strive for excellence in individual performance was not necessary under the communistic socialist political system that existed in their country for forty-one years, it is estimated that it will take East Germany at least twenty-five years to catch up economically and socially with the western part of the nation. This is so even with the financial backing of billions of dollars from the prosperous western part of the country. Over $100 billion was spent in 1996 alone!

To restore East Germany's economic health the work ethic must be re-instilled in the work force and people must be shown that efficient production of saleable quality merchandise is the key to economic security. The socialist political system in East Germany caused among its population crises of identity, confidence, authority, and security. Before the East can become an equal partner in Germany, it must regain its will to excel.

Imagine, this has occurred in East Germany, a country where the citizens are well educated. With this in mind, can you appreciate the fix First Nations are in? Our people are so poorly educated that the majority would be considered, by any standard, to be functionally illiterate.

Add to this the fact that we have very few independent financial resources to speak of. Our economies are false economies, built upon a base of governmental handouts. We are not at the present time in control of our destinies. We have a confidence crisis caused by centuries of oppression and persecution. There is a lack of authority in our communities and we have absolutely no security.

If this country would undertake today to make an unfettered non-paternalistic effort to help us begin to cure the problems mentioned it would take upwards of a quarter of a century to make any significant impact. Good conscience on the part of the government should dictate that this effort be undertaken without undue delay.

The following lays out what I perceive to be the major failings and problems which have to be addressed before real progress can take place.

Problems

1. Canada/Indian Affairs:
(A) Failure to provide Band members with an independent means of recourse for addressing their complaints and grievances against Band governments and Indian Affairs.
(B) Failure to have in place enforceable contractual arrangements with Band Councils. Present arrangements have been deemed to be unenforceable by the federal government's own Department of Justice.
(C) Failure to proceed with prosecutions when illegal procedures and misappropriation are perpetuated by either federal bureaucrats or Indians.
(D) Failure to follow the dictates of the law (Indian Act) when managing trust responsibilities.
(E) Failure to follow the dictates of the law as stipulated in the Financial Administration Act when contracting with Band governments and Indian organizations.
(F) Failure to follow the intents of Treasury Board regulations and departmental policies and procedures.
(G) Failure to eradicate bureaucratic politicking and corruption.
(H) Failure to ethically address the accountability needs and concerns of Band members when contracting with Band governments.
(I) Failure to require effective accountability from Band governments and Indian organizations.
(J) Failure to legislate a means to overcome a court decision that prevents the Auditor General from doing administrative and financial reviews at the Band level.
(K) Failure to meet the requirements of the federal government's trust responsibilities for Indians and Indian lands by ignoring, when deemed expedient, the dictates of law and the moral connotations of trust responsibility.
(L) Failure to eradicate the practices of negative stereotyping of First Nations peoples and paternalism from the mentality of the Department.
(M) Perhaps most damning of all, failure to work with our people in an atmos-

phere of respect and dignity, failing to accept and treat our people as intellectual equals and continuing to conduct affairs with us with condescending paternalism.

2.   *Bands and First Nations governments:*

(A) Failure to have the fortitude to resist and reject the climate for corruption that was deliberately, or incompetently, created by the Department in its contractual arrangements with Band Councils and Indian organizations.

(B) Failure to recognize the before-mentioned for what it is, namely a devious method to continue to hold our people in human bondage by discouraging us from seeking excellence when administering our affairs and also creating artificial reasons for the continued existence of the Department of Indian Affairs.

(C) Failure to mount a concerted attack upon the racist attitudes which restrict and impede our social and economic development.

(D) Failure to continuously demand respect for our human and civil rights from the public at large.

(E) Failure to find a way to escape from the degrading and economically enslaving social environment which was created for us by the Government of Canada via its bureaucracy.

Solutions

1. First and foremost, the federal government must conduct its financial and other relationships with our people in a professional, accountable, and mutually respectful way.

2. The system that breeds corruption must be discarded and be replaced with a system that will require full accountability from both parties.

3. Legislation giving meaningful legal recourse to Band members must be enacted and proclaimed.

4. The practice of the Department of Indian Affairs investigating itself must be discontinued.

5. Bands must have effective and enforceable constitutions or administrative and financial by-laws in place before funding continues.

6. Discretion in deciding what is a misappropriation of funds, and the prosecution in law of such cases, whether committed by a Band Council, Indian organization, the staff of either one, or a federal bureaucrat, must be removed from the hands of the Indian Affairs bureaucracy and placed in the hands of the legal system where they rightly belong.

7. Where proof is at hand that bureaucrats have ignored the law in their dealings with Bands and their organizations, prosecutions of such bureaucrats must occur where feasible and appropriate job-related disciplinary action must be taken.

8. Cover-ups by the Department of civil or criminal indiscretions committed by its bureaucrats must be discontinued.

9. Fully itemized budgets must be procured from Band Councils and Indian organizations before funding is provided. Funds for the operations of

Band Councils themselves must be a separate budget item and specify a specific dollar value. What is now in place permits a Band Council to set aside whatever funds they want, without any restraints whatsoever, for payment of Council honoraria and travel. Consequently there have been cases where some Chiefs have been paid salaries as high as $85,000 per year. Under the present system the administrative needs of the Band come secondary to Council honoraria and travel. Band members, because of the absence of by-law, have no legal control or recourse whatsoever to put a stop to these kind of practices.

10. A conflict of interest policy must be implemented. To have situations develop where Chiefs and Councillors occupy most Band positions and are their own supervisors is condemnable. The perception of corruption in such instances is inevitable.

11. There is no justification for continuing along the discredited established course, which has produced no appreciable benefits for our people. What is needed for progressive change is a clean sweep, new initiatives based strictly upon the rule of law and personal responsibility![19]

The following is taken from an article written by Steve Maich and published October 31, 1999, in the Halifax *Chronicle-Herald*. The Auditor General's comments about the lack of accountability and corruption tolerated by Indian Affairs are harsh:

Bands spending beyond scrutiny

In the 33rd chapter of the Auditor General of Canada's 1966 report is *a warning about authority being handed over to First Nations without controls on spending and corruption.*

"A serious gap has developed between political agendas and ongoing management needs in both the Department (of Indian Affairs) and First Nations," the report says. "*The Department has been implementing program devolution for many years without obtaining corresponding assurances of appropriate accountability.*"

Since 1991, the auditor general has repeatedly complained about deficiencies in the way the Department of Indian Affairs ensures responsible and accountable government by Canada's First Nations.

But the federal commitment to expanding self-government has created an interesting problem for government's most powerful watchdog.

The mandate of the auditor general limits the office to investigating only Canadian government institutions. That means *the department can be audited and evaluated, but the First Nations funded by about $6 billion in tax revenue can't be*. And that frustrates many native people who say Ottawa has been complicit in the ever-growing problems of financial and political mismanagement among First Nations....

This year's report (1999) by Auditor General Denis Desautels sharply criticized the department's handling of corruption and accountability complaints.

He said *little progress had been made by the department since financial abuses and mismanagement were first raised by his office* more than eight years ago.

He also noted that *until 1998, the department didn't even keep track of allegations, let alone investigate them.*

In the first year the department tracked such allegations, it received more than 300 official complaints relating to 108 of Canada's First Nations, indicating a situation of significant concern, he said.

The Department of Indian Affairs insists it is always working to improve the management of native communities, while respecting aboriginal rights.

"The greatest accountability tool available to aboriginal people is their vote," Larry Pardy, a department spokesman, said recently. "We need to be very careful how far we go telling bands what they can do with their money."

But Mr. Desautels hasn't simply accepted that answer. He says *self-government was never meant to be a simple case of blank cheques and hands-off approach.*

"Ultimately *there is a need for all parties to be accountable to each other and to their respective constituents,*" he wrote in 1996. "We believe that if (these) issues are addressed through consultation, the Department and [First Nations] will be in a better position to meet their needs in the evolving relationship."[20]

The statement made by Larry Pardy is a load of crap. If Canadians were reduced to assuring financial accountability from their governments by only the vote and without laws governing how it's to be done, the country would be a shambles. And, most importantly, the money isn't Band money; it's money from the public purse being administered on behalf of the federal government by Band Councils.

Related to the racism rampant within the Department was a matter which involved the recruitment of Indian employees; it was almost as outrageous as the financial fiasco that the Department was creating for the Bands during these years. It began in 1971. Shortly after the Department's district office opened in Halifax the Regional Director held a meeting with the district staff, which numbered only around twenty-five at the time. He informed us that the Department was planning to Indianize itself and that non-Indian employees could expect to be transferred to other departments in future years. Although more staff were hired in the months following the meeting, despite the Regional Director's instructions, Indian employees were not being recruited.

The oddity of employing *more* staff at this time has always blown my mind. Although programs were being devolved to the Bands along with the work load, amazingly the Department continued to hire *more people* to do *less work.* Obviously this doesn't make logical sense, but when it comes to actions of the Department, often nothing does.

As an excuse for not hiring more Registered Indians, management claimed they were stymied because there were "no qualified Indian people." If true, it would have been another condemnation of the Department; however, the Department deserves to be condemned anyway, because it was not true. The real reason it was having so much trouble recruiting Indian employees was its reputation for mistreating them. This was widely known. Further, the White bureaucrats weren't actually seeking out Indian recruits.

Here is how racism affected Native employees during those years. A Native employee of the Department, especially in the officer category, required an especially thick skin to stay on. On average they lasted only one to two years. Promotions for those who stayed were few and far between. Their job performance had to be twice as good as that of White employees; they were not allowed to make any mistakes. Theirs were exposed and dealt with while those of a White colleague were generally glossed over.

As a result of the Department's ploy of only paying lip service to the ideal of hiring Natives to replace White employees, this racial incident happened to me in the fall of 1975. I was sent to Ottawa on a three-week middle-management course for aspiring departmental employees from across the country. One day after class a group of us decided to go into the dark and dingy lounge of the hotel where the course was being held and have a beer. Because of its lowly lit atmosphere it took several minutes for a person's eyes to adjust. A short time later another group attending the course entered the place and because of the darkness sat down at the next table without recognizing us. A particularly obnoxious ass sat down almost back to back with me.

The conversation at their table turned almost immediately to the rumoured replacement of White employees by Indians. The employee behind me made the following comment, "Just what the fuck do those fucking Indians want now? They get everything for nothing and now the bastards want our jobs!" At our table the silence was deafening. My companions thought I would hit the roof.

However, I had already learned from experience that punching a person such as him in the nose is counterproductive, but words can be devastating. So I used them. I calmly responded by tapping the man on the shoulder. When he turned around he looked like someone who had just come face to face with a monster. He turned pale and for a moment or two could only stutter. I smiled and asked, "What's your job and classification?" He replied, "District Financial Clerk, level 4." I responded, in jest, that he did not have any immediate need to worry about the security of his job because no self-respecting Indian would be interested in taking over his minor position! I then ignored him and went back to the business of enjoying myself.

Another incident that happened during this course involved the stereotypical perception of Indians and alcohol. Two individuals from a Western district office came with the rest of us to a farewell party the night before the course was to end. They kept furtively eyeing me, and after a while it became slightly annoying. I asked a gentleman whom we shall call Jack, although we already had a good idea of what it was, to quietly find out what was bugging them. Jack, using his skills as an interviewer, engaged the two in a conversation and soon had confirmation that the two of them, believing tales they had heard from their peers that an Indian can't drink without going crazy, were nervously waiting for me to go berserk.

As a joke Jack got onto a chair, called for everybody's attention and made the following announcement: "Danny has assured me, and wishes for me to pass the assurance along to all of you, that before he goes bananas from drinking he gets some forewarning. Thus, when he feels that he is about to go over the edge he will let out a whoop. At that point you have no more than two minutes to vacate the premises or he won't be responsible for the consequences."

These are just a few of the disagreeable incidents I personally had to deal with while employed with the Department. Thousands of similar ones happened daily to other Native employees. The following are a few examples: At one time Section 92 of the Indian Act, which forbids a government employee from trading with a Registered Indian, was used by management to try to dismiss a Registered Indian employee. The employee in this case, who doesn't wish to be identified, had purchased a piece of merchandise from a member of one of the Bands with whom he/she worked. Afterwards the Department found out about the deal and decided that the employee should be disciplined and dismissed. They convened a kangaroo court and notified the employee that they would hold a hearing on a date specified. The employee came to me in a highly agitated state with a request for help. Without any arm-twisting I agreed. On the day of the hearing I went with the employee and immediately took the floor. I told the three senior employees that they were victims of mass insanity and that only someone who had taken leave of their senses would even contemplate trying to dismiss a Registered Indian employee for trading with a Band member. They soon saw the error of their ways and hastily retreated.

The Oka crisis of 1990 created a great deal of stress for First Nations employees of the Department and caused some of them to resign from their positions. One news story reported these quotes from various sources:

> "As the Mohawk crisis continues, the tensions it has created are being reflected among native and non-native employees in the Department of Indian and Northern Affairs."
>
> "According to a number of native civil servants and non-native civil servants, the problems for natives working in government, particularly in Indian and Northern Affairs, have been considerable."
>
> "There are tensions—the racist remarks have jumped" said a native civil servant who asked not to be identified.
>
> "Natives have been the object of hostile stares and silences in the office."
>
> "Some natives working for the federal government said they feel that they are no longer trusted by their colleagues or superiors."
>
> "People who did have access to certain things don't have access any more," one at Indian and Northern Affairs said.[21]

The Department's Committee of Native Employment became involved and advised Native employees how to respond. Some quotes from this source:

> "What I've asked the Indian people in the department to do is to record the incidents and snide comments," said a committee member who asked not to be identified.
>
> "We're all offended, but a good many of us have made a conscious decision to hang in there regardless of what they say to us."

"If we all quit, they will simply replace native positions with non-Indians. Then everything we've gained over the last twenty years would be down the tubes."[22]

The non-Native employees in the Department who are racist and make derogatory remarks about us fail to see the irony that they are like parasites living off the misery of a downtrodden people whose misfortunes were planned and engineered by their own European ancestors. If they cannot stand Indians, why do they continue to work for the Department? The answer is simple: *greed*.

Racist thinking was not only confined to the government during these years, but it was prevalent in the legal system also. For example, in 1971 Donald Marshall Jr. was charged, tried and convicted for a murder he didn't commit. Junior was guilty of only one thing—he was a Mi'kmaq. The Marshall Report issued by the *Royal Commission on the Donald Marshall, Jr. Prosecution* in December 1989 castigated the Nova Scotia justice system and society in general for the injustices carried out against an innocent and defenseless Mi'kmaq boy.

However, in the final analysis it wasn't the justice system that failed Junior, it was society. For without the racism that was all too prevalent throughout the province and the country, the justice system would not have dared to do what it did to him in the first place. Hearing his appeal in the 1980s the Nova Scotia Supreme Court Appeal Division's judges felt compelled to blame and humiliate Junior, telling him that he was the author of his own misfortune. This statement provides a measure of how deeply held society's racist views are.

In the 1970s, in what was a long overdue endeavour, the Department finally decided to improve the infrastructure of the Reserves, and thus the lives of the People in the Atlantic Region, by installing central water and sewer systems. The region's Registered Indians were finally going to enjoy some of the amenities of modern civilization: indoor plumbing and heating! The age of the outdoor privy was finally ending on the region's Reserves.

This was followed in the 1980s by another long overdue endeavour: the Department was forced to build decent homes for Reserve communities. Beginning in the early eighties homes had to be built to conform with Canada Mortgage and Housing Corporation (CMHC) standards. New houses were to be decently insulated and provide the same measure of comfort that was the norm for non-Indian society. Actually, the Department was supposed to have been building homes in Reserve communities according to National Housing Act standards from the beginning. However, it had decided to ignore that requirement until circumstances forced its hand. This occurred when most of the homes they had built on the cheap in the 1960s and 1970s were condemned and had to be replaced.

Also, around 1982 the Bands started to use CMHC's housing rehabilitation program to upgrade some of the older homes that were salvageable. After rehabilitation, these homes offered the same level of comfort as those being built under CMHC standards. The First Nations in the Maritime Provinces were at long last being provided with some decent housing, but this was not the norm for First Nations peoples across the country. On some remote Reserves housing conditions are pathetic. On a tour of one Reserve during a state visit South African leader Nelson

Mandela pronounced the living conditions there as *worse* than those found in Soweto.

A prime factor that induced improvement of housing on Indian Reserves in the Maritimes is that most of the region's Reserves are near White communities and have become objects of much closer scrutiny by the world at large. If not for this, much of their housing conditions would probably be identical to the third-world-country housing found on Reserves in many other parts of Canada.

In keeping with the Department's record of inventing new policies that on paper promise the world, on August 8, 1973, Jean Chretien, Minister of Indian Affairs and Northern Development, released a policy statement on assisting First Nations and the Inuit to further land claims. This was a small step in the right direction, but it did not produce many results for First Nations. It did, however, cause the bureaucracy to increase once again. The motherhood statement in the policy was the usual Indian Affairs drivel:

> Many Indian groups in Canada have a relationship with the federal government which is symbolized in treaties entered into by those people with the Crown in historic times. As the government pledged some years ago, lawful obligations must be recognized. This remains the basis of government policy.[23]

The policy proved to be a failure; however, another attempt would be made in 1981 to address the problem. The Department also wanted to enhance its image in the eyes of the Canadian public by self-proclaimed glorifications of its accomplishments. The booklets issued in relation to what was touted to be a new "Aboriginal" claims policy provide two good examples of the Department's preoccupation with its image. These two fairy tales were called "In All Fairness" (1981) and "Outstanding Business" (1982). The hoopla surrounding the release of these documents—supposedly meant to inform the public that Canada was finally going to settle the long outstanding grievances of the country's First Nations peoples—was pure political propaganda.

The Foreword of "In All Fairness," issued in relation to "comprehensive Native land claims" by John Munroe, then Minister of Indian Affairs, is a classic example of how the public was to be suckered into believing that something new and exciting was in the works for First Nations:

> For some years now, the Government of Canada has been engaged in attempting to resolve what have come to be known as Comprehensive Native Land Claims through a negotiation process. There has been moderate success but much more remains to be done. The purpose of this book is to set out for the consideration of *all Canadians* what the Government proposes as the way forward.
>
> I say to all Canadians advisedly: I hope this book will be looked at by Natives and non-Natives, by northerners and southerners, by those among us who seek to conserve and by those among us who seek to develop.
>
> What this statement contains above all, in this time of political uncertainty and general financial restraint, is a formal re-affirmation of a commitment:

that commitment is to bring to a full and satisfactory conclusion the resolution of Native land claims.

All Canadians would agree that claims have been left unresolved for too long. My wish is that this book will give all interested persons an idea of the depth of my personal commitment as well as the Government's to endorsing, developing and implementing the Policy initiated by one of my predecessors, the Honourable Jean Chretien.

Essentially what is *being addressed here are claims based on the concept of "Aboriginal Title"*—their history, current activities surrounding them, and our proposals for dealing with them in the future. While this statement is concerned with claims of this nature it does not preclude Government consideration of claims relating to historic loss of lands by particular Bands or groups of Bands.

Indeed, the government, *in consultation* with Indian organizations across Canada, is currently reviewing its policy with respect to specific claims over a wide spectrum of historic grievances—unfulfilled treaty obligations, administration of Indian assets under the Indian Act and other matters requiring attention. A further statement on government intentions in the area of specific claims will be issued upon completion of that review process.

I ask for the support and understanding of all Canadians: individuals, associations and special interest groups of all kinds. At a time when our country is struggling to redefine itself, to determine what kind of a future we want for everyone in this land, we must in all fairness pay particular attention to the needs and aspirations of Native People without whose good faith and support we cannot fulfil the promise that is Canada.[24]

The Foreword of "Outstanding Business," issued in relation to "specific claims" by Mr. Munroe, added:

The claims referred to in this booklet deal with *specific actions and omissions of government as they relate to obligations undertaken under treaty, requirements spelled out in legislation and responsibilities regarding the management of Indian assets*. They have represented, over a long period of our history, outstanding business between Indians and government which for the sake of justice, equity and prosperity *now must be settled without further delay*.

To date progress in resolving specific claims has been very limited indeed. Claimants have felt hampered by inadequate research capabilities and insufficient funding; government lacked a clear, articulate policy. The result, too often, was frustration and anger. This could not be allowed to continue. The Government of Canada, therefore, undertook a review of the situation including consultation with Indian groups across the country. This booklet represents the outcome of this review.

Together with this effort at meeting the concerns of the Indian People, the Government has approved a substantial increase in the funding made available to claimants for their research and negotiation activities; it has also reinforced the capabilities of the Office of Native Claims. The instruments for greater success are now in place.

The task, however, is enormous, complex and time consuming. Levelheadedness, persistence, mutual respect and cooperation will be required on the parts of government and Indian people alike.

Nevertheless, I think that success is within reach, because success in this endeavour is in the interest of both Indians and government, indeed of all Canadians.[25]

"Comprehensive claims," or "Aboriginal title claims," are claims that relate to the land title of First Nations to Canada as it existed in pre-Columbian days. These are land and legal issues that have long festered and soured the relationship between First Nations and Whites in this country. They will continue to do so until a will is developed by the federal and provincial governments to deal fairly and squarely with the First Nations in settling them.

"In All Fairness" was a statement meant to placate a Canadian public beginning to wake up to national shortcomings in dealing fairly with the First Nations. But the government as usual was double-dealing, telling the Canadian public one thing while doing another. There was to be no honest effort to settle these matters expeditiously. In fact, in many instances, the government actually bent over backwards to find ways to evade their responsibilities for past injustices—Boat Harbour, for instance.

The policy statement made in "Outstanding Business" was supposed to put the settlement of "specific claims" into high gear, but in reality it accomplished virtually nothing. One of the major reasons is that resolutions of specific claims usually expose inadequacies of the bureaucracy. After all, if it weren't for bureaucratic incompetence, the First Nations would have no specific claims to begin with. Many of the people involved in the incompetent mismanagement of Indian assets are still with the Department today, some occupying senior positions. These individuals want to keep a tight lid on the mess for as long as possible.

Although there are several hundred outstanding specific land claims in Nova Scotia, only one major claim has been "successfully" settled since the federal government came out with its first specific claims policy in 1974. This was a claim by the Wagmatcook Band concerning the alienation of about two thousand acres of prime Reserve land in Cape Breton during the late 1880s.

In its statement of claim dated May 30, 1979, the Band originally demanded $10 million as compensation and the return of the land. In a settlement agreement signed in early 1982, it agreed to accept $1,192,000 as compensation. The money only could be used to purchase land for economic development purposes, but, because of the cost of similar land, this was virtually impossible.

The problem in the agreement is found in Section 2(a) of the agreement: "The Minister undertakes to accept the transfer of title of *not less than 2,000 acres of land in Cape Breton* from the Wagmatcook Development Corporation to Her Majesty the Queen in right of Canada to be set aside as an Indian Reserve as defined in the Indian Act."[26] The Minister in fact has no authority to make a commitment to give Reserve status to a parcel of land; this is the prerogative of the Privy Council. This is acknowledged in the next paragraph, 2(b), which for all intents and purposes negates the meaning of the preceding section: "The acceptance of the transfer of lands to Her Majesty in clause 2(a) will be *subject to approval by the Minister and the Governor in Council* and presentation of title to the Crown by the Wagmatcook Development Corporation in form and substance satisfactory to the Minister of Justice."[27] The Minister only has the power to recommend, not approve.

The land lost to the Band in the late 1800s was prime Cape Breton Island real estate. If the Band had taken the entire settlement of $1,192,000 (minus $232,405 for claim preparation expenses, leaving a total of $959,595), and tried to buy two thousand acres with it, they would have only been able to pay about $480 an acre. In 1982 it would have been practically impossible to purchase two thousand acres of prime real estate on the Island at that rate.

This poses a question: Did the Department knowingly mislead the Band in constructing and promoting the agreement? Considering that the government would accept "not less than two thousand acres of land," and then restricted that acceptance to the approval of the Minister and Governor in Council, one might be inclined to think yes. Section 1(d) of the agreement adds weight to such a conclusion: "The Band covenants and agrees that the money paid by the Minister to the Wagmatcook Development Corporation *will be used solely for the purposes of acquiring land and for the economic development of the band....*"[28] If the government *did not* intend to mislead the Band why did it sign an agreement with them that made it all but impossible to replace their lost prime land with the small amount of money available and, if possible, made the acceptance of such land as Reserve land optional? The agreement gives a broad hint that Crown interests were placed first.

Therefore, the government should revisit this claim and determine through an independent tribunal whether justice was really done for the Band and whether its best interests were given top priority. The Supreme Court of Canada spoke loud and clear in handing down the *Guerin* decision. It mandated that in agreements with Bands involving lands the government must act always in the best interests of the Band, even if such action is detrimental to the government itself. In the Wagmatcook case the question is: Was the government acting in the best interests of the Band or in the best interests of the Crown?

The main reason the two new land-claim policies failed to produce effective results was that the government did not insist upon accountability from the Native organizations involved in researching them. The expenditures of funds by these units were governed by unenforceable contracts and the whims of politicians and bureaucrats. Bands and their organizations were not required to be productive, so the process has in too many cases degenerated into no more than a source of employment for Band members.

If the Bands are to be successful in making this process productive, and if the government is truly sincere in its stated desire to settle comprehensive and specific land claims and other legal matters, then the relationship between the parties must be placed within a framework of strict accountability. The settlement of these matters can give the Bands economic independence, but non-settlements and messy settlements will only maintain the status quo of dependency.

During the 1980s things in some ways began to change radically. The Canadian Constitution was repatriated on December 2, 1981. Some recognition was

given to First Nations under Section 35, but this was no revolutionary development. A constitutional conference, mandatory under the provisions of the Constitution, was called to find a method to entrench First Nations self-government. The
conference was held and it flopped. Canada was not yet willing to recognize the
First Nations',—or, as Canada would have it, the *Band's*—inherent right to self-
government, but at least the proposal is still on the table.

I attended the conference as an observer and the thing I recall most vividly was
what a very highly placed provincial official said to an aide in an unguarded
moment as he walked through the foyer of the building where the conference was
being held. Not aware that I was within earshot, he stated, "I don't give a fuck what
those fucking Indians want, they're not getting it."

Inclusion of the word "Aboriginal" under Section 35 of the Canada Act without adequate definition of its meaning is beginning to cause all kinds of problems
for First Nations. People are coming out of the woodwork claiming to be "Aboriginal." And this is how the government receives them: Employment and Immigration
Canada defines an "Aboriginal" as anyone "who perceives himself/herself to be a
... Indian."[29] People who have marginal, if any, First Nations blood in their veins
have availed themselves of this interpretation and are taking advantage of benefits
normally reserved for Registered Indians.

In the 1990s some very important aboriginal rights court cases were litigated
and won. On May 31, 1990, the Supreme Court of Canada handed down a decision,
R. v. Sparrow, which was a major victory for the First Nations. The Court recognized aboriginal rights to hunt and fish:

> We acknowledge the fact that the justificatory standard to be met may place
> a heavy burden on the Crown. However, government policy with respect to
> British Columbia Fishery, regardless of s. 35(1), already dictates that in allo-
> cating the right to take fish, *Indian food fishing is to be given priority over the
> interests of other user groups*. The constitutional entitlement embodied in s.
> 35(1) requires the Crown to ensure that its regulations are in keeping with that
> allocation of priority. *The objective of this requirement is not to undermine
> Parliament's ability and responsibility with respect to creating and adminis-
> tering overall conservation and management plans regarding the salmon fish-
> ery. The objective is rather to guarantee that those plans treat aboriginal
> peoples in a way insuring that their rights are taken seriously.*
>
> We would not wish to set out an exhaustive list of the factors to be considered
> in the assessment of justification. Suffice it to say that *recognition and affir-
> mation requires sensitivity to and respect for the rights of aboriginal peoples*
> on behalf of the government, courts and indeed all Canadians.[30]

Two recent Supreme Court rulings have diminished the impact of *Sparrow*. On
August 21, 1996, the Supreme Court upheld two B.C. Court of Appeal decisions
stating:

> The Native right to catch fish for food does not include the right to sell unless
> the practice existed previously. Chief Justice Antonio Lamer wrote: "Aborigi-

nal rights are not general and universal. Their scope and content must be determined on a case by case basis.[31]

The following day, Justice Lamer handed down a decision rejecting the contention that a Band has a right to operate gaming houses on Indian Reserves:

> Aboriginal rights, including any asserted right to self-government, must be looked at in light of specific circumstances of each case, and in light of the specific history and culture of the aboriginal group claiming the right.... Since gambling wasn't "an integral part of the distinctive cultures" of the bands it can't be considered an issue of self-government.[32]

Two comments by interested parties:

> Hugh Braker, a Native lawyer in Port Alberni, B.C., said "the decisions will result in more court battles.... Bands could argue ... commerce was a tribal responsibility. Aboriginal people are not static ... they are like everyone else. Their culture evolves as time goes by," said Braker, a member of the Tseshahat Band.
>
> Peter Russell, a University of Toronto professor who studies native issues, said the two rulings begin to set boundaries for aboriginal self-government. "They've excluded from the inherent right to self-government modern activities that were not traditionally part of the life of aboriginal communities," said Russell.[33]

The Supreme Court judges are not regarding these activities as practices that existed before European intrusion. In so doing they are failing to consider that the commercial exchanges between Nations in pre-Columbian North America were extensive, and competitions for prizes among North American First Nations have been ongoing since time immemorial. Whether these prizes were accolades from their respective communities, positions of political power, or things such as new canoes or trinkets is of no relevance; they were betting they could best a peer in a competition and devoted a good part of their lives learning or training to do so. Wasn't this a form of gambling?

Judges should remove their blinders and set aside their biases towards the ideals of their own cultures when pondering First Nations matters. They must stop thinking that the citizens of these cultures were static and begin to think of them as intelligent human beings who belonged to well-developed and ancient civilizations that would have, if the European invasion had not occurred, evolved into modern Nations. The pre-Columbian Amerindians were not trapped in a time warp.

Perhaps this item will provide some food for thought for the judges. For centuries it was presumed by White anthropologists that the Natives of California were just gatherers and hunters. These two quotes about their cultivation of vast acorn orchards five thousand years ago proves the assumption false:

As late as 1844, when explorer John C. Fremont led an expedition to the

Sacramento Valley, he described the north state foothills as "smooth and grassy; [the woodlands] had no undergrowth; and in the open valleys of riverlets, or around spring heads, the low groves of oak give the appearance of orchards in an old cultivated country." Similarly, a nineteenth-century visitor to the middle fork of the Tuolumne River near Yosemite Valley found it "like an English park—a lovely valley, wide and grassy, broken with clumps of oak and cedar."[34]

Fires were used to insure good growth and healthy orchards:

> Natives may have been setting fires for 5,000 years speculates Kat Anderson (an ethnobotanist with the Amerindian Studies Centre at UCLA), judging by how long fire-loving giant sequoias have been expanding their range.
> "At first, acorns seem to have been a food of opportunistic significance, not a staple," says anthropologist Helen McCarthy of the University of California at Davis, who has been studying the relationship between California's native people and plants for more than 25 years. "Natives buried them for a long period of time, and ground-water slowly removed the tannin…. Ambitious acorn processing, she says, is associated with stone mortars and pestles … those that have been recovered are 4,000 years old … that leads me to believe acorns became a staple part of their diet around 4,000 years ago."[35]

When the time and trouble is taken by White Canadian society, it may discover, as they did in California, that many of the country's First Nations were cultivating staples while most Europeans were still hanging out in caves.

The biggest problem of federal and provincial governments with decisions such as *Sparrow, Guerin* and *St. Catherine's Milling* is the need to swallow their pride and deal with First Nations citizens as peers and equals. Since these decisions were handed down, governments have continued to react in a negative manner rather than to strive to find settlements that will provide justice and fairness for all.

It is unacceptable that the only way that they will deal fairly with First Nations peoples is under the direction of the Supreme Court of Canada, and even then only reluctantly and obstructively. To begin the honest dialogue needed to resolve contentious issues with First Nations, all Canada needs to do is accept us for what we are, intelligent and sovereign peoples who have been denied for far too long our right to be treated as such. I sincerely believe the world will not come to an end tomorrow if Canada suddenly accepts the fact that we are equals and peers! To continue the exclusion that has been policy since Confederation is to irritate a festering sore. Rather than continuing along that course, let us find a cure!

I want to share an 1990 editorial I wrote for our paper, *Mi'kmaq/Maliseet Nations News*, in relation to the Supreme Court of British Columbia decision in the case of *Delgamuukw (Ken Muldoe)* v. *the Queen*:

White supremacist attitudes prevail at British Columbia land claims trial!

In the decision he handed down after hearing and weighing the evidence in the matter of "Delgamuukw (Ken Muldoe) vs. the Queen," Mr. Chief Justice Allan McEachern of the British Columbia Supreme Court displays all the excesses of a White supremacist.

For instance, when passing judgement, he does not deal in an effective and imaginative manner with the fact that the ancestors of the First Nations people involved in the case elected to live in harmony and in co-existence with the White intruders. This generous approach in dealing with people from an alien culture by Native Americans has never been recognized by Europeans for what it was, a clear and concise testament to the high level of civilized behaviour achieved by its practitioners. Such behaviour deserves to be well considered in forming an opinion of the magnitude attached to the case in hand. Instead, McEachern opts for an immediate assumption that the First Nations' civilization is an inferior civilization, that is to say, when taken into comparison with the British model. This kind of thinking is racist and totally unacceptable in today's jurisprudence.

The Justice infers in the contents of his decision that civilization did not exist in British Columbia prior to White intrusion. He fails to accept the fact that for untold centuries many fully functional sovereign non-White civilizations did in fact exist and prosper in the province prior to White settlement.

The civilization in question, of course, was not identical to the European, Asian, or African models; or for that matter even other Native American models; it was unique unto itself, with its own political and social orders....

Those narrow-minded descendants of European civilizations who refuse to expand their vision enough to accept the fact that different laws and values from other cultures and civilizations have existed, and in many cases are possibly superior to those of their own cultures, are the curse of Native American peoples.

People of this type far too often manage to occupy positions of power, permitting them to sit in judgement upon issues that are of the greatest importance for moving the aspirations of First Nations forward. These individuals do not have the intellectual capacity or sense of fairness to weigh all the factors and evidence that will enable them to produce an enlightened and proactive decision in cases which involve the validity of other cultures and civilizations.

To exclusively apply the tenets of British Common Law as it existed at the time when British intrusion onto the territory of a sovereign First Nation first occurred, without giving any consideration whatsoever to the value system of the society that the British system had intruded upon, is the ultimate of arrogant White supremacist thinking. The laws of the people who were being displaced and dispossessed must receive full consideration and be weighed when sitting in judgement upon the less than honourable methods employed by the invaders in achieving their goal of total possession and unlawful occupation of a sovereign people's lands and assets.

It's hard for an individual to accept the fact that his or her ancestors may have been less than honourable people. However, the fact remains that the White settlers engaged in an activity that had as its final result the total degradation and humiliation of an innocent and almost defenceless people. To continue the charade in modern times of pretending that the theft of another's life is accept-able because the dispossessed people did not meet with your standards is insane and indefensible before humanity.

In the case at hand the Chief Justice even goes to the extreme of attempting to justify the outrage by making the indefensible statement that because the Native Americans only resided upon small parcels of land they would as a consequence have had their aboriginal rights restricted to these small parcels. This outrageous position defies logic and common sense. After all, the English only reside upon small portions of England; does this mean that they only have jurisdiction over the small portions occupied, with the rest of their land up for grabs by anyone? Of course, it doesn't. Without question, the English have jurisdiction over their ancestral territory, just as First Nations peoples had complete jurisdiction over theirs.

In Europe the European peoples had, during the era under consideration, clearly defined territorial boundaries over which they exercised complete and unrestricted jurisdiction and control. Some of these ethnic groups, who had lost jurisdiction and control over their lands—even those that did so several centuries ago—are now regaining sovereignty over them. The same scenario should apply to the First Nations of the Americas—they too should be aided in attempts to regain self-government. To promote otherwise defies the reason and the sense of justice and fairness of "civilized humanity."

The time is long overdue for the majority of society to abandon their attitude of superiority, especially in the justice system, and replace it with a more enlightened, reasonable, and civilized policy which will result in finding eq-uitable solutions for the multitude of long-outstanding disputes between them-selves and First Nations. To continue with the present approach, which at-tempts to deny responsibility for the outrages and excesses of one's ancestors, shows a complete bankruptcy of ethical principles. Since the Americas came under European domination the Native American has been made to suffer every conceivable indignity that can be visited upon man by man. Physical and cultural genocide has been inflicted upon innocent human beings without care or conscience. Without pity or remorse being demonstrated by the invaders, fully functioning and viable First Nations civilizations well advanced in the humanities were maliciously destroyed or marginalized.

How much longer must the Native peoples of the Americas suffer for the sins of the Europeans? Must it be eternal?

Perhaps the Great Spirit in His infinite mercy and wisdom will one day say enough is enough and cause the White man to develop a conscience and began to atone for the sins of his ancestors. The Native Americans have suffered for five hundred years what seems to be a never ending and horrifying nightmare. In the name of all that is holy, it's time for it to stop.[36]

Chief Justice MacEachern hasn't improved his outlook on life. I offer these few quotes from an editorial published in the September 3, 1996, issue of the Halifax *Chronicle-Herald* on the substance of a 1996 speech he gave to delegates at a justice conference in Vancouver:

The ... justice writes that social activist, special interests groups, and agendists "have adopted criticism and litigation as a vehicle for the advancement of their causes." But "uniformed response to judicial decisions," he says, encourages people to look to the courts for cures to society's ills instead of objective law enforcement... His general thesis, then, that judges must "stare down the agendists and the ignoble strife" and remain true to the question of law, is a timely ... reminder of what judicial independence is all about.

But the chief justice takes the argument too far, arguing that legislators should not be influenced either by a public that demands, for example, longer jail terms or quick fixes to youth crime. Impractical as those demands might be, so too is the chief justice's dream of a world in which citizens placidly accept life as it is handed to them.... He writes, "the public and our political masters will eventually understand that popular measures are not necessarily right measures."

For someone so intent on rescuing, or perhaps better defining a separation of powers, this is perilous ground. The chief justice appears to be suggesting that the legislative branch of government should not do what it is supposed to do—make law—because it inconveniences the judicial branch.

The public is not a nuisance that the judiciary must rise above. As the Canadian Bar Association's task force on systems of civil justice noted ... in its final report on proposed reform, the justice system was created for the public's benefit.... It follows, says the report, that the system should only exist "so long as it serves the needs of Canadians and is considered by them to be relevant, accessible and fair."[37]

On December 11, 1997, the Supreme Court of Canada threw out Chief Justice McEachern's decision and sent the matter back for reconsideration. In so doing, the Court strongly suggested that the powers that be in Ottawa and British Columbia should engage in honest negotiations with the Nisga'a First Nation in order to reach an equitable settlement.

As a result, in August 1998 the Nisga'a Nation and the British Columbia and federal governments initialled an agreement which gives the Nation 1,992 square kilometres of land and $130 million cash and other considerations. In November 1998 the Nisga'a approved the treaty by referendum, and the B.C. legislature and Canada's Parliament approved it in 1999. Great things can be accomplished through meaningful negotiations!

On November 3, 1997, less than a month before the Supreme Court of Canada passed down the Nisga'a ruling, Justice John Turnbull of the Court of Queen's Bench in New Brunswick ruled that the province's Mi'kmaq and Maliseet have a right to Crown land. These two decisions and others discussed in this book have passed several aces to Canada's First Nations in their ongoing battles with Canada and the provinces for full recognition of aboriginal rights. However, if both levels of government are not now regrouping in order to find ways to circumvent and nullify them, it would be a first.

After enlightening information about the lifestyles of many Native American Nations, particularly those in North America, had been provided by early European contacts the revelation that fascinated many European intellectuals the most was that the citizens of many of these Nations lived in freedom and equality and enjoyed personal liberty undreamed of in Europe. The absence of dictators and social classes in the vast majority of these civilizations drew special attention. Thus, through the writings of prominent men of the day, Europeans became aware of the possibility of a free society without despotic aristocratic rulers. Sir Thomas More was among the eminent thinkers drawn into this exciting examination of societies where the people ruled.

Unfortunately for humanity European societies developed in an entirely different manner. Throughout much of their histories Europeans have equated civilization with satisfying greed and creating ever more deadly tools of war rather than with human values. Even today, the ability to invent weapons that can more efficiently kill and disable and make a profit for the inventors, producers and users is seen as a mark of civilization. This notion is in dire need of re-examination. Barbarians such as Hitler, Stalin and others too numerous to mention lived and ruled in militaristic countries that claimed to be civilized. Under the leadership of these purveyors of horror were these countries really *civilized*? If honesty is to prevail, the answer must be a resounding no.

These warped perceptions of what constitutes civilization encouraged many European Nations to commit a genocide in the Americas that is unmatched in human history. Which leads to this question: Is this urge among Whites to commit genocide against Amerindians—because they are not descended from civilizations that are mirror images of what Whites believe "civilization" to be—finally dead in this country? A front-page Halifax *Chronicle-Herald* story on April 17, 2000, with the headline "Book blames reserves for natives' plight" proves no. The story revealed that in his book, *First Nations, Second Thoughts*, author Tom Flanagan, a University of Calgary political science professor since 1968, advocates the extinction by assimilation of Canada's First Nations peoples as a means to solve the country's so-called "Indian problem." The news report states:

> Flanagan rejects the idea that native people constituted nations equivalent to those in Europe during the period of North American exploration and discovery [ignoring the fact it had already been discovered and explored]. Rather, natives were "uncivilized" because they lacked intensive agriculture, permanent settlement, writing, advanced technology and organized states.[38]

Because in one form or another First Nations had all of these things, which to me are not measurements of being "civilized" anyway, his suggestions outraged me. Paragraph C of Article Two of the United Nations Convention on the Prevention and Punishment of the Crime of Genocide forbids undertaking what Flanagan suggests: "(C) *Deliberately inflicting on the group conditions of life calculated to bring about its physical destruction in whole or in part.*"[39]

In a chapter entitled "Liberty, Anarchism, and the Noble Savage," Jack Weatherford wrote:

During [the 1700s] the thinkers of Europe forged the ideas that became known as the European Enlightenment, and *much of its light came from the torch of Indian liberty* that still burned brightly in the brief interregnum between [the Indians'] first contact with the Europeans and their decimation by the Europeans.

While a few Europeans chose the path of Violette and left the corrupt world of Europe for America, others began working on ideas and plans to change Europe by incorporating some of the ideas of liberty into their own world. Almost all the plans involved revolutionary changes to overthrow the monarchy, the aristocracy, or the Church, and in some cases even to abolish money and private property.

The greatest political radical to follow the example of the Indians was probably Thomas Paine (1737-1809), the English Quaker and former craftsman who arrived in Philadelphia to visit Benjamin Franklin just in time for Christmas of 1774.

When the American Revolution started, Paine served as Secretary to the Commissioners sent to negotiate with the Iroquois. Through this and subsequent encounters with the Indians, Paine sought to learn their language and throughout the remainder of his political and writing career *he used the Indians as models of how society might be organized.*

In his writings, Paine *castigated Britain for her abusive treatment of the Indians*, and he became the first American to call for the abolition of slavery.[40]

One can cite many words of Europeans praising the enlightened values of democracy and freedom enshrined in early Native American civilizations. Ironically, although appreciated by many renowned European men of the time, the values of these democratic cultures were precisely the reason the ruling class of Europe felt so threatened and reacted so violently in their persecutions of them. Yet the Native Americans by their example sowed the seeds for the long, drawn-out movement towards democracy by the people of Europe, seeds the European aristocracy could not suppress through its attempted extermination of them.

You have now read a history of one of the Native American peoples, a people who gave their all to defend home and country and fought courageously for survival. Based on what you now know, what is your honest judgment about *who the real barbarian savages were* when Europeans and Native Americans collided?

Mi'kmaq civilization was a classic example of a free and independent people forming a society based upon the principle of mutual support and respect. This successful and productive civilization valued individual liberty above all else. For the benefit of humanity, let's ask the Great Spirit to give us the wisdom to reshape our own modern civilizations to include and protect the wonderful values that people such as the Mi'kmaq enjoyed!

Notes

Chapter 1

1. Marion Robertson, *Red Earth: Tales of the Micmac, with an introduction to their customs and beliefs* (Halifax: Nova Scotian Museum, 1965), p. 5.
2. Basil H. Johnston, "The Prophecy," *Canadian Literature* 124-125 (Spring/Summer).
3. Ronald Wright, *Stolen Continents* (Penguin, 1993), p. 231.
4. *Ibid.*, p. 231.
5. Bernard Gilbert Hoffman, "The Historical Ethnography of the Micmac of the Sixteenth and Seventeenth Centuries." Thesis, University of California, 1955, p. 272.
6. Original Minutes of His Majesty's Council at Annapolis Royal, 1710-1739, edited by Archibald M. MacMechan, Public Archives of Nova Scotia (PANS), III, p. 125-28.
7. Hoffman, p. 283.
8. *Ibid.*
9. *Ibid.*, p. 298.
10. *Ibid.*, p. 332.
11. *Ibid.*

Chapter 2

1. Hoffman, p. 190.
2. *Ibid.*
3. Harold F. McGee Jr., Saint Mary's University, "The Case for MicMac Demes," Halifax, 1977.
4. James Wherry, "Eastern Algonquian Relationships to Proto-Algonquian Social Organizations," *Occasional Papers in Anthropology* No. 5, May 1979.
5. Hoffman, p. 146.
6. Dan Conlin, "Year of the Wooden Boat," Halifax *Chronicle-Herald*, April 23, 1996, p. 29.
7. Hoffman, p. 281.
8. Cornelius J. Jaenen, "The French Relationship with the Native Peoples of New France and Acadia" (Ottawa: Canada, Indian Affairs, 1984), p. 60.
9. H.H. Herstein, L.J. Hughes and R.C. Kirbyson, *Challenge & Survival: The History of Canada* (Scarborough, Ont: Prentice-Hall 1970), p. 60
10. Hoffman, p. 274.
11. *Ibid.*
12. *Ibid.*, p. 275.
13. Jaenen, p. 55.
14. *Ibid.*, p. 98.
15. Hoffman, p. 527.
16. *Ibid.*, p. 530.
17. *Ibid.*

18. "Souvenir of the Micmac Tercentenary Celebration, 1610-1910" (Restigouche, N.B.: Frères Mineurs Capuchins, 1910), p. 50-51.
19. *Ibid.*, p. 53.
20. Hoffman, p. 591.
21. *Ibid.*, p. 593.
22. *Ibid.*, p. 595.
23. *Ibid.*, p. 596.
24. *New World Dictionary of the American Language*, second college edition (New York: Simon & Schuster, 1986).
25. Jaenen, p. 109.
26. *Ibid.*, p. 123.

Chapter 3

1. Hoffman, p. 604.
2. *Ibid.*, p. 605.
3. *Ibid.*, p. 38.
4. *Ibid.*, p. 58.
5. *Ibid.*, p. 94.
6. "Chief Seattle Speaks," University of New Brunswick Student Union newspaper, Fall 1990.

Chapter 4

1. Jaenen, p. 12.
2. A Calendar of Two Letter-Books and One Commission-Book in the Possession of the Government of Nova Scotia, 1713-1741, edited by Archibald M. MacMechan, PANS, II, p. 69.
3. Hoffman, p. 97.
4. *Ibid.*, p. 98.
5. *Ibid.*, p. 609.
6. Reuters News Service, March 15, 1996.
7. Treaty of Utrecht, 1713, in Thomas Brodick, *Complete History of the Late War in the Netherlands together with an abstract of the Treaty of Utrecht* (London: Thomas Ward, 1713), PANS.
8. Calendar, p. 5-6. Emphasis added.
9. Jaenen, p. 40.
10. *Ibid.*, p. 19.
11. Wayne E. Daugherty, "Maritime Indian Treaties in Historical Perspective" (Ottawa: Canada, Indian Affairs, Treaties and Historical Research Centre, 1983), p. 19.
12. *Ibid.*, p. 19.
13. John Stewart McLennan, *Louisbourg, from its foundation to its fall, 1713-1758* (Sydney: Fortress Press, 1969), p. 65.
14. *Ibid.*, p. 66.
15. Calendar, p. 72. Emphasis added.
16. Original Minutes, p. 56-57. Emphasis added.

Chapter 5

1. Original Minutes, p. 100-101.
2. *Ibid.*, p. 78-80. Emphasis added.
3. Treaty of 1725, PANS, RG1, Vol. 12. Emphasis added.
4. Treaty No. 239, 1725, PANS, RG1, Vol. 12. Emphasis added.
5. Original Minutes, p. 111.
6. *Ibid.*, p. 114-15.
7. *Ibid.*, p. 115-17.
8. *Ibid.*, p. 117-18.

Chapter 6

1. Original Minutes, p. 106-7.
2. *Ibid.*, p. 107-9.
3. *Ibid.*, p. 113-14. Emphasis added.
4. Calendar, p. 86.
5. *Ibid.*, p. 99-100.
6. *Ibid.*, p. 102. Emphasis added.
7. *Ibid.*, p. 110-11.
8. *Ibid.*, p. 121. Emphasis added.
9. *Ibid.*, p. 128-29.
10. *Ibid.*, p. 124-25.
11. *Ibid.*, p. 125.
12. *Ibid.*, p. 126.
13. *Ibid.*, p. 128.
14. Daugherty, p. 39. Emphasis added.
15. Governor Shirley's declaration of war against the Micmac and scalping proclamation, October 19, 1744, in Charles Henry Lincoln, *Correspondence of Governor Shirley* (New York: MacMillan, 1912). Emphasis added.
16 Collections of the Nova Scotia Historical Society. John Gorham, 1709-1751; Part I: 1744-1749; Part II: 1749-1751, by George T. Bates, p. 30.
17. Daugherty, p. 81.

Chapter 7

1. Virginia P. Miller, "The Decline of the Nova Scotia Micmac Population, 1600-1850," *Culture* 2, No. 3 (1982): 107-20; PANS, VF Vol. 280, No. 7, p. 4.
2. Geoffrey Plank, University of Cincinnati, History Department, paper entitled "The Two Majors Cope: The Boundaries of Nationality in Mid-Eighteenth Century Nova Scotia," August 5, 1995, p. 17.
3. Charles Saunders, February 2, 1994, author's personal papers.
4. "The Convention for the Prevention and Punishment of the Crime of Genocide," adopted by the United Nations on December 9, 1948. Article 2 of the Convention defines genocide.
5. Council Minutes, authorizing scalping proclamation, October 1, PANS, 1747, RG1, Vol. 186, p. 22-23, microfilm 15287. Emphasis added.
6. Scalping Proclamation, Edward Cornwallis, 1749, CO 217/9/118 (F100); mi

crofilm at PANS. Emphasis added.

7. *Culloden*, by John Prebble, (London: Martin Secker & Warburg, 1961, 1981), p. 206-11

8. Collections, p. 69.

9. Daugherty, p. 48. Emphasis added.

10. Herstein, Hughes and Kirbyson, p. 83-84. Emphasis added.

11. *Ibid.*, p. 84. Emphasis added.

12. Daugherty, p. 48. Emphasis added.

13. Jaenen, p. 184.

14. Proclamation of Edward Cornwallis, July 17, 1752, Council minutes, Nova Scotia colonial government, PANS, RG1, Vol. 186-89, p. 185-89. Emphasis added.

15. Halifax Regional Municipality Correspondence, Fitzgerald to Donald Julien, dated February 1, 1999.

16. Plank.

17. Treaty of 1752, CO 217/40/209; microfilm at PANS. Emphasis added.

18. Prevost to Minister, May 12, 1753, Public Archives of Canada (PAC), MG1, C11B, Vol. 33, p. 159.

19. Proclamation of Treaty of 1752, PANS, RG1, Vol. 186.

Chapter 8

1. *Le Canada-Francais—Documents Sur L'Acadie*, PANS, F5400, C16, Vol. 2, No. 3, July 18, 1889, p. 111-12. Emphasis added.

2. *Ibid.* p. 112-13. Emphasis added.

3. *Ibid.* p. 113-26. Emphasis added.

4. Council Minutes—Cape Sables Indians, November 16, 1753, PANS, RG1, Vol. 187.

5. Daugherty, p. 51-52. Emphasis added.

6. *Ibid.*, p. 52-53.

7. Governor Charles Lawrence's response to a Micmac request for land, February 13, 1755, Executive Council Minutes, PANS, RG1, Vol. 187, p. 187-89.

8. Jaenen, p. 182.

9. *Ibid.*, p. 185.

10. Geoffrey Plank, "The Impossibility of Neutrality for Jacques Maurice: The Politics of an Acadian Merchant, 1732-1759," paper, University of Cincinnati, February 1996.

11. Scalping Proclamation, Governor Charles Lawrence, 1756, CO217/16/308; PANS, RG1, Vol. 187, No. 117. Emphasis added.

12. Isaiah W. Wilson, "The Bounty Hunters," in *Geography and History of Digby County*, 1st edition, 1900 (Belleville, Ont.: MIKA, 1972). Emphasis added.

13. Plank, "Two Majors Cope," p. 16-27. Emphasis added.

14. Treaty of Peace, Chief Paul Laurent and Governor Charles Lawrence, March 10, 1760, British Museum, Andrew Brown's Manuscripts, No. 19071, p. 174; microfilm at PANS. Emphasis added.

15. Linwood Rice, letter to the editor, Halifax *Chronicle-Herald*, April 30, 2000.

Chapter 9

1. Burying of the Hatchet Ceremony, Governor's Farm, Halifax, June 25, 1761, PANS, RG1, Vol. 165, p. 162-65. Emphasis added.
2. *Ibid*. Emphasis added.
3. Royal Instructions to Governors, December 9, 1761, PANS, RG1, Vol. 30, No. 58. Emphasis added.
4. Belcher's Proclamation, 1762, CO 217/19/27-28; PANS, RG1, Vol. 11, No. 14. Emphasis added.
5. Letter Book—P.T. Hopson, PANS, RG1, Vol. 38a, p. 1-16. Emphasis added.
6. Royal Proclamation, 1763, *Revised Statutes of Canada*, 1970, Appendices, p. 127-29. Emphasis added.

Chapter 10

1. General Jeffrey Amherst to Colonel Bouquet, July 1763, in Alexander Chisholm, *Church History of Nova Scotia*, PANS, VF Vol. 11, No. 14, p. 68-75.
2. Lawrence Shaw Mayo, "Jeffrey Amherst, A Biography" (New York: Longmans, Green, 1916). Copy can be accessed at National Parks Branch, Fortress Louisbourg Restoration Section, Cape Breton, N.S,. or from the files of the author, p. 234.
3. *Ibid*., p. 234.
4. *Ibid*., p. 234-35.
5. Pontiac, "Chief Detroit," *Dictionary of Canada Biography*, PANS, D.C.B. F009, D55, Vol. 3, 1760-1763, p. 29.
6. Watertown Treaty, July 17, 1776, PANS; CO 217/52/267.
7. Treaty of 1779, September 22, 1779, PANS; CO 217/54/219-22.
8. Licenses of Occupation, Given to the Micmac by the British colonial government, December 17, 1783, PANS, RG1, Vol. 430, p. 23.5 and 27.5.
9. Jaenen, p. 203.
10. *Ibid*.
11. *Ibid*.
12. *Ibid*., p. 203.
13. Treaty of 1794, author's files.
14. Jaenen, p. 203-5. Emphasis added.
15. Jay Treaty, November 19, 1794, in Samuel Flag, *The Jay Treaty: A Study in Commerce and Diplomacy* (New York: Macmillan, 1925). Emphasis added.
16. Executive Council Minutes, PANS, 1819-1825.
17. *Ibid*.

Chapter 11

1. Wright, p. 218.
2. Miller, p. 4.
3. *Ibid*.
4. *Ibid*.
5. *Ibid*., p. 5.
6. *Ibid*., p. 5-6.

7. *Ibid.*, p. 10.
8. *Ibid.*, p. 11.
9. *Ibid.*
10. *Ibid.*
11. *Ibid.*, p. 12. Emphasis added.
12. *Ibid.*, p. 12-15. Emphasis added.
13. *Ibid.*, p. 15-19. Emphasis added.
14. Letter from Lord Glenelg, August 22, 1838, *Journal of Assembly Papers*, 1838, Appendix 80, p. 154.
15. Chief Benjamin Porminout to Queen Victoria, January 25, 1841, CO 217/179/406; microfilm at PANS.
16. An Act to provide for the instruction and permanent settlement of Indians, March 9, 1842, *Statutes of Nova Scotia*. Emphasis added.
17. Indian Commissioner Joseph Howe's Report, *Journal of Assembly Papers*, January 25, 1843, Appendix 1, p. 3; microfilm at PANS. Emphasis added.
18. Report by Commissioner of Indian Affairs Abraham Gesner, 1847, PANS, RG1, Vol. 431 and 432, No. 43, p. 112, 116.
19. Samuel Fairbanks to Governor of Nova Scotia, November 9, 1866, Confederacy of Mainland Micmacs (CMM) files, Truro, N.S. Emphasis added. N.S. Land Registry, Halifax.
20. Fairbanks to Governor (Joseph Paul's grant, registered at provincial Lands Registry Office, Halifax, N.S., 1868).

Chapter 12

1. British North America Act, 1867, 30 & 31 Victoria, Chapter 3, Section 91(24).
2. Hector L. Langevin to Samuel Fairbanks, September 28, 1868 (Ottawa: Canada, Secretary of State, Indian Affairs Archives, 1868). Emphasis added.
3. Indian Act, 1876, *Statutes of Canada*, Chapter 98.
4. Indian Act, 1876. Emphasis added.
5. Canada, Indian Affairs, "Draft Criteria Governing Additions to Indian Reserves" (Ottawa, 1982) and author's files. Emphasis added.
6. Canada, Indian Affairs, Communiqué, Minister McKnight announces policy on new Indian Bands, Reserves, and Communities, December 22, 1987 (Ottawa). Emphasis added.
7. *Afton Band of Indians* v. *the Queen* (Nova Scotia), 1978, Dominion Law Reports 3rd, Vol. 85, p. 454.
8. Daniel N. Paul to Reg Graves, November 12, 1986, DIAND files, Amherst and Ottawa; and author's files.
9. Canada, Privy Council, Order-in-Council No. P.C. 1990–1904, "Afton Band of Indians, New Reserve, Summerside Indian Reserve No. 38," August 28, 1990.
10. Canadian Human Rights Commission's annual report (1996) to the Canadian House of Commons by Chief Commissioner Max Yalden, Ottawa.
11. Boat Harbour documents, Indian Affairs, Ottawa and Amherst; Ross and author's files, 1965-96.

12. E.A. "Tony" Ross, "Boat Harbour: One Lawyer's Perspective," written state-ment to author, April 17, 1992. Emphasis added.
13. Federal Court of Canada, Trial Division: Between the Pictou Landing Indian Band and Her Majesty the Queen (Boat Harbour discovery transcript). This is the evidence taken by the discovery, with the consent of all parties, held at Halifax, Province of Nova Scotia, on March 13, 1987, of Mr. A.F. Wigglesworth. Counsel for the Plaintiffs: Mr. E.A. Ross. For the Defendants: Mr. R. Anderson and Ms. S. Shea.
14. *Guerin* v. *the Queen*, Supreme Court Reports, 1984, Vol. 2, p. 335. Emphasis added.
15. Surrender documents for the surrender of Sambro, Ingram River, and Ship Harbour Indian Reserves, 1919 (Ottawa: Canada, Indian Affairs, Lands Divi-sion, 1919), and author's files.
16. *Ibid*. Emphasis added.
17. Donald M. Julien, written statement to author, February 22, 1992.
18. Indian Act, 1927, Section 141, Receiving money for the prosecution of a claim.
19. Indian Band Council Borrowing Regulations, C.R.C. 1978, Chapter 949.
20. Canada, Indian Affairs Band By-Law Registry, 1970, Ottawa.
21. *Simon* v. *the Queen*, Dominion Law Reports, 4th, 1986, Vol. 24, p. 390, and author's files. Emphasis added.
22. *Ibid*. Emphasis added.
23. *Ibid*.
24. *Ibid*.
25. *Ibid*.

Chapter 13

1. Michael Levine, "Lessons at the Halfway Point," *Readers' Digest*, November 1996, p. 48-49.
2. Author's personal correspondence, and author's column "Elsie Basque: Micmac pioneer," Halifax *Chronicle-Herald,* October 6, 1995.
3. *Ibid*.
4. *Ibid*.
5. *Ibid*.
6. *Ibid*.
7. *Ibid*.
8. Marilyn Millward, "Clean Behind the Ears? Micmac Parents, Micmac Chil-dren, and the Shubenacadie Residential School," *New Maritimes* (March/April 1992). Emphasis added.
9. *Ibid*. Emphasis added.
10. *Ibid*. Emphasis added.
11. *Ibid*. Emphasis added.
12. *Ibid*. Emphasis added.
13. *Ibid*.
14. Isabelle Knockwood, "Out of the Depths" (Lockeport, N.S.: Roseway, 1992),

quote from Phil Fontaine on back cover.

15. The Canada Census is the source for population figures of 1871-1921; the figures after 1921 are derived from Indian Affairs Band Lists, Indian Registrar, Indian Affairs, Ottawa.
16. The Cape Breton Mi'kmaq meet with colonial authorities about their Band fund moneys being used to buy land for the Pictou Mi'kmaq, Nova Scotia Assembly *Journals*, February 1, 1864, Appendix 37, Indian Affairs, p. 1-7.
17. D.H. Reddall, "Foursome," *Alfred Hitchcock Mystery Magazine*, 1996.
18. Canada, Indian Affairs, Eskasoni and Shubenacadie Indian Agencies, Centralization correspondence, 1938-1952; also in CMM and author's files.
19. *Ibid.*
20. *Ibid.* Emphasis added.
21. *Ibid.* Emphasis added.
22. *Ibid.* Emphasis added.
23. Canada, Department of Energy Mines and Resources or the Department of Indian Affairs and Northern Development, Ottawa: Eskasoni and Shubenacadie Indian Agencies, Centralization correspondence, 1938-1952; also can be found in CMM or author's files. Emphasis added.
24. Canada, Indian Affairs, Circular Letter by the Superintendent General of Indian Affairs, Duncan Elliott (forbidding dancing), December 15, 1921, Ottawa. Emphasis added.
25. Indian Act, Section 140, Dances and Festivals, 1927, Chapter 98. Emphasis added.
26. Indian Act, Section 140A, Poolrooms, 1930, Chapter 98. Emphasis added.
27. Indian Act, Section 120, Prevention of Trade, 1930, Chapter 98.
28. Centralization correspondence. Emphasis added.
29. *Ibid.*
30. *Ibid.* Emphasis added.
31. *Ibid.* Emphasis added.
32. *Ibid.* Emphasis added.
33. *Ibid.*
34. *Ibid.* Emphasis added.
35. *Ibid.* Emphasis added.
36. *Ibid.* Emphasis added.
37. *Ibid.* Emphasis added.
38. *Ibid.* Emphasis added.
39. Indian Act, Section 46, 1911, Inquiry and Report by Exchequer Court as to Removal of Indians, Chapter 14. Emphasis added.
40. Halifax *Chronicle-Herald*, March 21, 1999.
41. Centralization correspondence.
42. *Ibid.*
43. *Ibid.* Emphasis added.
44. *Ibid.* Emphasis added.

Chapter 14

1. Centralization correspondence, Atlantic Region. Emphasis added.
2. *Ibid*. Emphasis added.
3. United Nations, December 10, 1948, New York.
4. An Act to amend the Canadian Citizenship Act, June 7, 1956, *Statutes of Canada*, 1956, Chapter 6. Emphasis added.
5. Canada, Indian Affairs, Ottawa, Band Membership Division, Enfranchisement Form. Emphasis added.
6. Canada, Indian Affairs, Land Division, "Division of Indian Bands and Assets, Province of Nova Scotia," December 4, 1956, to 1959, Ottawa.
7. *Ibid*.
8. *Ibid*.
9. Canada Elections Act Amendments, 1960.
10. An Act to amend the Canada Elections Act, March 31, 1960, 8-9 Elizabeth II, Chapter 7.
11. Canada, Indian Affairs, "Indian Policy, 1969" (White Paper), Hansard, House of Commons, Ottawa, Queen's Printer Cat. No. R32-2469. Emphasis added.
12. *Ibid*. Emphasis added.
13. *Ibid*. Emphasis added.
14. *Ibid*. Emphasis added.
15. Robert Pinney to Daniel Paul, January 14, 1987, DIAND, Amherst, N.S., CMM and author's files. Emphasis added.
16. J.W. Beaver, "To Have What Is One's Own" (Beaver Report), submitted to the House of Commons and the National Indian Brotherhood, October 16, 1979 (Ottawa: National Indian Socio-Economic Development Committee, 1979), Hansard and author's files.
17. *Ibid*. Emphasis added.
18. *Ibid*. Emphasis added.
19. Daniel N. Paul, "Accountability and Responsibility: Indian Affairs vs. the Bands." *Micmac/Maliseet Nations News*, February 20, 1992, CMM and author's files.
20. Steve Maich, "Bands spending beyond scrutiny." Halifax *Chronicle-Herald*, October 31, 1999. Emphasis added.
21. *Globe and Mail*, September 10, 1990.
22. *Ibid*.
23. Canada, Indian Affairs, Policy statement on claims of Indians and Inuit peoples by Minister Jean Chretien, August 8, 1973, Ottawa.
24. Canada, Indian Affairs, 1981, "In All Fairness: A Native Claims Policy, Comprehensive Claims Division," Ottawa.
25. Canada, Indian Affairs, 1982, "Outstanding Business: A Native Claim Policy, Specific Claims," Ottawa.
26. Canada, Indian Affairs, Land claim settlement, Wagmatcook Band (Ottawa: Lands Registry Office, 1982). Emphasis added.
27. *Ibid*. Emphasis added.
28. *Ibid*. Emphasis added.

29. Canada, Employment and Immigration Canada, Ottawa, Employment Manual, 1993, definitions.

30. *R.* v. *Sparrow*, [1990] Vol. 1, S.C.R. 1075. Emphasis added.

31. Canada, *Supreme Court Reports*, August 21, 1996.

32. Canada, *Supreme Court Reports*, August 22, 1996.

33. Halifax *Chronicle-Herald*, August 23, 1996.

34. Glen Martin, "Keepers of the Oaks," *Discover: The World of Science*, August 1996, p. 46-47.

35. *Ibid*.

36. Author's files.

37. Halifax *Chronicle-Herald*, editorial, September 3, 1996, p. B1.

38. "Book blames reserves for natives' plight," Halifax *Chronicle-Herald*, April 17, 2000.

39. *Ibid*. Emphasis added.

40. Jack Weatherford, *Indian Givers* (New York: Crown, 1988). Emphasis added.

Select Bibliography

Primary Sources

Public Archives (historical order)

Le Canada-Francais—Documents Sur L'Acadie. Public Archives of Nova Scotia (PANS), F5400, C16, Vol. 2, No. 3, July 18, 1889.

Governors of the Province of Nova Scotia, 1710-1925. Public Archives of Canada (PAC), MG2, 1961, 64-65.

Treaty of Utrecht, 1713. In Thomas Brodrick, *Complete History of the Late War in the Netherlands together with an abstract of the Treaty of Utrecht*. London: Thomas Ward, 1713. PANS, D238.5 B78 C73.

A Calendar of Two Letter-Books and One Commission-Book in the Possession of the Government of Nova Scotia, 1713-1741. Edited by Archibald M. MacMechan. PANS, Nova Scotia Archives II, 1900.

Original Minutes of His Majesty's Council at Annapolis Royal, 1720-1739. Edited by Archibald M. MacMechan. PANS, Nova Scotia Archives III, 1908.

Treaty of 1725. PANS, RG1, Vol. 12.

Treaty No. 239, 1725. PANS, RG1, Vol. 12.

Governor Shirley's declaration of war against the Micmac and scalping proclamation, October 19, 1744. In Charles Henry Lincoln, *Correspondence of Governor Shirley*. New York: MacMillan, 1912. Massachusetts State Archives, Boston.

Collections of the Nova Scotia Historical Society. John Gorham, 1709-1751; Part I: 1744-1749; Part II: 1749-1751; by George T. Bates, p. 27-77.

Council Minutes, authorizing scalping proclamation, October 1, 1747. PANS, RG1, Vol. 186, p. 22—3, microfilm 15287.

Scalping Proclamation, Governor Edward Cornwallis, 1749. CO 217/9/118 (F100). Microfilm at PANS.

Treaty of 1752. CO 217/40/209. Microfilm at PANS.

Proclamation of Treaty of 1752. PANS, RG1, Vol. 186.

Proclamation of Governor Cornwallis, July 17, 1752, Council minutes, Nova Scotia colonial government. PANS, RG1, Vol. 186-89, p. 185-89.

Letter to the Lords of Trade, October 1752. Letter Book—P.T. Hopson. PANS, RG1, Vol. 38a, p. 1-16.

Prevost to Minister, May 12, 1753. PAC and Louisbourg Archives, MG1, C11B, Vol. 33, p. 159.

Council Minutes—Cape Sables Indians, November 16, 1753. PANS, RG1, Vol. 187.

Governor Charles Lawrence's response to a Micmac request for land, February 13, 1755. Executive Council Minutes. PANS, RG1, Vol. 187, p. 187-89.

Scalping proclamation, Governor Charles Lawrence, 1756. CO 217/16/308; PANS, RG1, Vol. 187, No. 117.

Treaty of Peace, Chief Paul Laurent and Governor Charles Lawrence, 1760, British Museum, Andrew Brown's Manuscripts, No. 19071, p. 174; PANS, RG1, Vol. 36, No. 2.

Burying of the Hatchet Ceremony, Governor's Farm, Halifax, June 25, 1761. PANS, RG1, Vol. 165, p. 162-65.

Treaty of Merimichi, Jediach, Pogmouch and Cape Breton, June 25, 1761. CO 217/8/276-284. Microfilm at PANS.

Royal Instructions to Governors, December 9, 1761. PANS, RG1, Vol. 30, No. 58.

Belcher's Proclamation, 1762. CO 217/19/27-28; PANS, RG1, Vol. 11, No. 14.

Royal Proclamation, 1763. Revised Statutes of Canada, 1970. Appendices, p. 127-29.

General Amherst to Colonel Bouquet, July 1763. In Alexander Chisholm, *Church History of Nova Scotia*. PANS, VF Vol. 11, No. 14, p. 68-75.

Watertown Treaty, July 17, 1776. CO 217/52/267. Microfilm at PANS.

Treaty of 1779, September 22, 1779. CO 217/54/219-222. Microfilm at PANS.

Licenses of Occupation given to the Micmac by the British colonial government, December 17, 1783. PANS, RG1, Vol. 430, p. 23.5 and 27.5.

Jay Treaty, November 19, 1794. In Samuel Flag, *The Jay Treaty: A Study in Commerce and Diplomacy*. New York: Macmillan, 1925, PANS.

Indian Reserves, March 1801. PANS, RG1, Vol. 430, p. 54.

Official Allotment, Indian Reserves, May 8, 1820. Executive Council Minutes, 1819-1825. PANS, RG1, Vol. 214.5A, p. 136-43.

Chief Benjamin Porminout, Letter to the Queen, January 25, 1841. CO 217/179/406. Microfilm at PANS.

Report by [Nova Scotia] Commissioner of Indian Affairs Abraham Gesner, 1847. PANS, RG1, Vol. 431 and 432, No. 43.

Public Documents

Boat Harbour documents, 1965 to 1996, Indian Affairs, Ottawa and Amherst; Ross and author's files.

Canada, House of Commons. 1979. Beaver, J.W. "To Have What Is Ones's Own" (Beaver Report). Submitted to the House of Commons and the National Indian Brotherhood, October 16, 1979. Ottawa: National Indian Socio-Economic Development Committee, 1979.

____. 1983. *Indian Self-Government in Canada: Report of the Special Committee* (Penner Report). Issue No. 40. Ottawa.

____. 1990. Standing Committee on Aboriginal Affairs. Fifth Report (re. Kanesatake and Kahnawake [Oka]), October 22, 1990. Ottawa.

Canada, Indian Affairs. No date. Reserve General Registry. Reserve Register sheet for Port Hood Indian Reserve (Whycocomagh Band). W10773/02/3. Ottawa.

____. 1715-1983. Lands Registry. Summerside property, Antigonish County, N.S., 1715-1983. Ottawa.

____. 1919. Lands Division. Surrender documents for surrender of Sambro, Ingram River, and Ship Harbour Indian Reserves, 1919. Ottawa.

____. 1921. Circular letter (forbidding dancing). December 15, 1921. Ottawa.

____. 1940. Welfare Rates List, May 22, 1940. Ottawa.

____. 1956. Lands Division. "Division of Indian Bands and Assets, Province of Nova Scotia." December 4, 1956. Ottawa.

____. 1965-1992. Correspondence and other documents, Boat Harbour law suit, Pictou Landing Band. Ottawa.

____. 1969. "Indian Policy, 1969" (White Paper). Ottawa.

____. 1970. Band by-laws, 1970. By-law registry. Ottawa.

____. 1972. "Chiefs Past and Present." August 9, 1972. Ottawa.

____. 1973. Policy statement on claims of Indian and Inuit peoples by Minister Jean Chrétien, August 8, 1973. Ottawa.

____. 1978. Treaties and Historical Research Centre. "The Historical Development of the Indian Act." Ottawa, August 1978.

____. 1981. "In All Fairness: A Native Claims Policy, Comprehensive Claims." Ottawa.

____. 1981-1986. Lands Registry. Correspondence re. Summerside property, 1981-1986. Ottawa.

____. 1982. "Criteria Governing Additions to Indian Reserves." Ottawa.

____. 1982. Lands Registry Office. Land Claim Settlement, Wagmatcook Band. Ottawa.

____. 1982. "Outstanding Business: A Native Claims Policy, Specific Claims." Ottawa.

____. c. 1985. Atlantic Region. "Land Acquisition-Reserve Status." Regional Directive issued by W.R. Cooke, Director General. No. 5005-5. Ottawa, no date.

____. 1987. Communiqué, December 22, 1987. Minister McKnight announces policy on new Indian Bands, Reserves, and communities. Ottawa.

Canada, Privy Council. 1990. Order-in-Council No.P.C. 1990-1904. "Afton Band of Indians, New Reserve, Summerside Indian Reserve No. 38." August 28, 1990.

____. 1991. Order-in-Council No.P.C. 1991-185. "Acadia Band of Indians, Land Addition, Yarmouth Indian Reserve No. 33, in the Province of Nova Scotia." January 31, 1991.

Canada. Secretary of State. 1868, Hector L. Langevin to Samuel Fairbanks, September 28, 1868. Appointment of first federal Indian Commissioner for Nova Scotia. Ottawa, 1868.

Canadian Human Rights Commission. 1996. Annual report (1996) to the Canadian House of Commons by Chief Commissioner Max Yalden. Ottawa and the Commission.

Nova Scotia. 1838. Letter from Lord Glenelg, August 22, 1838. Journal of Assembly Papers, Appendix 80, p. 154.

____. 1843. Indian Commissioner Joseph Howe's Report. Journal of Assembly Papers, January 25, 1843. Appendix 1, p. 3. Halifax. Microfilm at PANS.

____. 1864. Cape Breton and Pictou Micmacs, Land for Pictou. Nova Scotia Assembly Journals, February 1, 1864. Appendix 37-Indian Affairs, p. 1-7. Halifax. Microfilm at PANS.

___. 1989. *Royal Commission on the Donald Marshall, Jr., Prosecution: Digest of Findings and Recommendations.* December 1989. Halifax.

United Nations, 1948. "The Convention for the Prevention and Punishment of the Crime of Genocide," December 9, 1948. New York.

United States of America. 1988. *Congressional Record.* October 3, 1988. Washington, D.C. Acknowledgement of the contribution of Native Americans to the U.S. Constitution and Bill of Rights.

Confederacy of Mainland Micmacs (CMM) and Author's Files

Canada, Indian Affairs. 1866. Samuel Fairbanks to Lieutenant-Governor of Nova Scotia, November 9, 1866. "Petitions—Joseph Paul—Indian" [land lease]. Ottawa, CMM files, Truro, N.S. Also available at the Nova Scotia Land Registry; lease was granted in 1868.

___. 1936-1952. Atlantic Region. Centralization and other correspondence, 1936-52. CMM files, Truro N.S. Also at PAC and author's files.

___. 1938-1952. Eskasoni Indian Agency. Centralization correspondence, 1938-52. CMM files, Truro, N.S. Also at PAC and author's files.

___. 1938-1952. Shubenacadie Indian Agency. Centralization correspondence, 1938-52. CMM files, Truro, N.S. Also at PAC and author's files

___. 1948. Frank T. Stanfield to R.A. Hoey, April 29, 1948. Centralization correspondence, 1938-52. CMM files, Truro, N.S and Author's files.

___. Donald M. Julien, 1974. "Sequence of Historical Events: Afton and Pomquet Indian Reserve No. 23." DIAND, Amherst, and CMM files, Truro, N.S.

___. 1987. Robert Pinney to Daniel Paul, January 14, 1987, re. education takeover. DIAND, Amherst, and CMM and author's files.

___. Donald M. Julien, written statement to author, February 22, 1992.

Lazier, Christina. 1988. "Contesting the Rules of the Game: The Significance of *Simon* v. *the Queen* for Micmac Hunting Rights and Game Management in Nova Scotia." Paper for P. Saunders, Dalhousie University, May 1988. CMM files, Truro, N.S.

Paul, Daniel N. 1986. Letter to Reg Graves, Regional Director of Lands, Revenues, and Trusts, Indian Affairs, Atlantic Region, November 12, 1986. Author's files and Departments.

___. 1988. Presentation to the House of Commons Committee for Indian Affairs, April 1988. CMM files, Truro, N.S.

___. 1990. Letter to Minister of Indian Affairs, September 13, 1990, concerning racism in the Department during the "Oka crisis." Attached news clippings from *Globe and Mail*, September 10, 1990. CMM files, Truro, N.S.

___. 1992. "Accountability and Responsibility: Indian Affairs vs. the Bands." Paper submitted to the House of Commons Committee on Aboriginal Affairs, February 20, 1992. CMM files, Truro, N.S.

Ross, E.A. "Tony." 1992. "Boat Harbour: One Lawyer's Perspective." Written statement to author, April 17, 1992.

Saunders, Charles. 1994. Personal correspondence with author, February 2, 1994.

Treaty of 1794. Author's files.

Statutes (historical order)

An Act to Provide for the Instruction and Permanent Settlement of the Indians. March 19, 1842. *Statutes of Nova Scotia.*

British North America Act, 1867. 30 & 31 Victoria, Chapter 3.

Indian Act, 1876-1992. *Statues of Canada.*

Indian Act Amendments, 1876-1996. *Statutes of Canada*, Chapter 98.

An Act to amend the Canadian Citizenship Act, June 7, 1956. *Statutes of Canada, 1956*, Chapter 6. "Registered Indians are made citizens of Canada."

An Act to amend the Canada Election Act. *Statutes of Canada*, March 31, 1960, 8-9 Elizabeth II, Chapter 7. Registered "Indians" are given the right to vote.

Indian Band Council Borrowing Regulations. 1978, Chapter 949. Regulations made pursuant to the provisions of Section 73 of the Indian Act.

Indian Reserve Traffic Regulations. 1978, Chapter 959. Regulations made pursuant to the provisions of Section 73 of the Indian Act.

Constitution Act, 1982. *Revised Statutes of Canada*, 1985, Appendix II, No. 44.

Court Cases

Afton Band of Indians v. *the Queen (Nova Scotia)* (1978), 85 D.L.R. (3rd), p. 454. *Guerin* [Musqueam Band] v. *the Queen*. 1984, Vol. 2 S.C.R. 335.

Pictou Landing Indian Band v. *the Queen* (Boat Harbour discovery transcript): Federal Court of Canada, Trial Division: This is the evidence, taken by way of the discovery, with the consent of all parties, held at Halifax, Nova Scotia, on March 13, 1987, of Mr. A.F. Wigglesworth. Counsel for the Plaintiffs, Mr. E.A. Ross; for the Defendants, Mr. R. Anderson and Ms. S. Shea. Court and author's files.

R. v. *Sparrow*, 1990, 1 S.C.R. 1075; [1990] 3 C.N.L.R. 160; 70 D.L.R. (4th) 385.

R. v. *Syliboy* (1928), 50 C.C.C. 389; [1929] 1 D.L.R. 307.

St. Catherine's Milling and Lumber Co. v. *the Queen* (1888), 14 App. Cas. 46 (Prov. Ct.).

Simon v. *the Queen,* 1986, 24 D.L.R. (4th) 390.

Secondary Sources

"1492-1992: 500 Years of Resistance." 1992. Pamphlet. Halifax: OXFAM-Canada/ Deveric.

Allen, C.R. 1879. *Illustrated Historical Atlas of Pictou County, Nova Scotia.* Philadelphia: J.H. Meacham.

Bartlett, Richard H. 1986. Indian Reserves in the Atlantic Provinces of Canada. *Studies in Aboriginal Rights* No. 9. Saskatoon: University of Saskatchewan Native Law Centre.

"Chief Seattle Speaks." 1990. University of New Brunswick student union newspaper, Fall 1990.

Christmas, Peter. 1977. *Wejkwapniaq.* Sydney, N.S.: Micmac Association of Cultural Studies.

Confederacy of Mainland Micmacs Newsletter (today the *Micmac/Maliseet Nations News*). 1988-. Truro, N.S.

Conlin, Dan. "Year of the Wooden Boat." Halifax *Chronicle-Herald*, April 23, 1996.

Daugherty, Wayne E. 1983. "Maritime Indian Treaties in Historical Perspective." 2nd ed. Ottawa: Canada, Indian Affairs, Treaties and Historical Research Centre.

Hoffman, Bernard Gilbert. 1955. "The Historical Ethnography of the Micmac of the Sixteenth and Seventeenth Centuries." Thesis, University of California.

Herstein, H.H., L.J. Hughes and R.C. Kirbyson. 1970. *Challenge & Survival: The History of Canada*. Scarborough, Ont.: Prentice-Hall.

"The Indian Residential School." 1990. *Micmac News*, Sydney, N.S., September 1990.

Jaenen, Cornelius J. 1984. "The French Relationship with the Native People of New France and Acadia." Ottawa: Canada, Indian Affairs.

Johnston, Basil H. 1990. "The Prophecy." *Canadian Literature* 124-125 (Spring/Summer 1990).

Knockwood, Isabelle. 1992. "Out of the Depths." Lockeport, N.S.: Roseway.

Levine, Michael. 1996. "Lessons at the Halfway Point." *Reader's Digest* (November).

Maich, Steve. 1999. "Bands spending beyond scrutiny," Halifax *Chronicle-Herald*, October 31.

Mander, Jerry. 1991. "What You Don't Know About Indians." *Utne Reader* (November/December 1991).

Martin, Glen. 1996. "Keepers of the Oaks." *Discover* (August).

Mayo, Lawrence Shaw. 1916. "Jeffrey Amherst, A Biography." New York: Longmans, Green. National Parks Branch, Fortress Louisbourg Restoration Section, Cape Breton, N.S., and the author's archives.

McBride, Bunny, and Harald Prins. 1982. *Micmac Redbook: Resources Manual for the Micmac Recognition Effort*.

McGee, Harold F., Jr. 1997. "The Case for MicMac Demes." Paper, Saint Mary's University, Halifax.

McLennan, John Stewart. 1969. "Louisbourg, from its foundation to its fall, 1713-1758." Sydney, N.S.: Fortress Press.

Miller, Virginia P. 1982. "The Decline of the Nova Scotia Micmac Population, 1600-1850." *Culture* 2, No. 3 (1982): 107-20. PANS, VF Vol. 280, No. 7.

Millwood, Marilyn. 1992. "Clean Behind the Ears? Micmac Parents, Micmac Children, and the Shubenacadie Residential School." *New Maritimes*, March/April 1992.

Morrison, Kenneth M. 1975. "People of the Dawn: Abnaki and Their Relations with New England and France, 1600–1727." Thesis, University of Maine, Orono, August 1975.

"Nova Scotia Micmac Aboriginal Rights Position Paper." 1976. Presented to the Government of Canada by the Union of Nova Scotia Indians. *Micmac News*, Sydney, N.S., December 1976.

Paul, Daniel N. 1990. *Confrontation: Micmac and European Civilizations*. Truro, N.S.: Confederacy of Mainland Micmacs.

___. 1995. "Elsie Basque: Mi'kmaq Pioneer." Halifax *Chronicle-Herald*, October 6, 1995.

Plank, Geoffrey. 1995. "The Two Majors Cope: The Boundaries of Nationality in Mid-Eighteenth Century Nova Scotia." Paper, University of Cincinnati.

___. 1996. "The Impossibility of Neutrality for Jacques Maurice: The Politics of an Acadian Merchant, 1732-1759." Paper, University of Cincinnati.

Prebble, John. 1961, 1981. *Culloden*. London: Martin Secker & Warburg.

Preliminary draft manuscript, Maine, April 1982. Boston: Association of Aroostock Indians.

Rand, Silas T. 1894. *Legends of the Micmacs*. New York: Longmans, Green.

Reddall, D.H. 1996. "Foursome," *Alfred Hitchcock Mystery Magazine*.

Robertson, Marion Robertson. 1965. *Red Earth: Tales of the Micmac, with an introduction to their customs and beliefs*. Halifax: Nova Scotia Museum.

"Souvenir of the Micmac Tercentenary Celebration, 1618-1910." 1910. Restigouche, N.B.: Frères Mineurs Capuchins.

Upton, L.F.S. 1979. *Micmacs and the Colonists, 1713-1867*. Vancouver: University of British Columbia Press.

Weatherford, Jack. 1988. *Indian Givers*. New York: Crown.

Wherry, James. 1979. "Eastern Algonquian Relationships to Proto-Algonquian Social Organizations." *Occasional Papers in Anthropology*, No. 5 (May).

Wilson, Isaiah W. 1900. "The Bounty Hunters." In *Geography and History of Digby County*. 1st edition. Belleville, Ont.: MIKA, 1972.

World Council of Indigenous Peoples Newsletter. 1989. Ottawa, October 1989.

Wright, Ronald. 1993. "Stolen Continents." Toronto: Penguin.

Copies, in full or in part, of all the documents in this bibliography are also located in the Confederacy of Mainland Micmacs files in Truro, N.S., or in the author's personal files.

Index

About the Cover

The picture of Joe Paul, a Wagmatcook man believed to be over a century old, was taken from a postcard printed in the early 1900s. The condition of Paul's attire, and the publicizing of his apparent poverty stricken existence on a postcard, leaves one wondering if having the Mi'kmaq reduced to such a pathetic state was something that Nova Scotians of that era took pride in.

About the Author

Daniel N. Paul was born in 1938 on the Indian Brook Reserve, Hants County, Nova Scotia. Paul lives with his wife Patricia in Halifax. They have two daughters, Lenore and Cerena.

An ardent spokesperson and activist for human rights Paul is also a freelance lecturer, runs a small advisory business, is a bi-weekly columnist for the op-ed page of the Halifax *Chronicle-Herald* and is a Justice of the Peace for the Province of Nova Scotia. He has served on many provincial commissions—including the Province's Human Rights Commission and was a member of the Nova Scotia Department of Justice's Court Restructuring Task Force. He holds an honourary degree in letters from Universite Saint-Anne, Church Point, Nova Scotia. Among many other awards—on January 14, 2000, Paul was honoured by the City of Halifax with a millenium award for contributing in a special way towards making the community a better place to live.

From 1971 to 1986 Paul was employed by the Department of Indian Affairs—the last five of which was as District Superintendent of Lands, Revenues, Trusts, and Statutory Requirements for the Nova Scotia District. In 1986 he accepted employment as the founding executive director of what would be the new Confederacy of Mainland Micmacs. After building the Tribal Council into what became one of the best operated in the country he retired from the position in 1994.